The Great Uprising

Between 1963 and 1972 America experienced over 750 urban revolts. Considered collectively, they comprise what Peter B. Levy terms a "Great Uprising." Levy examines these uprisings over the arc of the entire decade, in various cities across America. He challenges both conservative and liberal interpretations, emphasizing that these riots must be placed within historical context to be properly understood. By focusing on three specific cities as case studies – Cambridge and Baltimore, Maryland, and York, Pennsylvania – Levy demonstrates the impact that these uprisings had on millions of ordinary Americans. He shows how conservatives profited politically by constructing a misleading narrative of their causes, and also suggests that the riots did not represent a sharp break or rupture from the civil rights movement. Finally, Levy presents a cautionary tale by challenging us to consider if the conditions that produced this "Great Uprising" are still predominant in American culture today.

Peter B. Levy is a professor of history at York College, Pennsylvania, where he teaches US history classes. His books include *Civil War on Race Street: The Civil Rights Movement in Cambridge, Maryland* (2003).

The Great Uprising

Race Riots in Urban America during the 1960s

PETER B. LEVY

York College, Pennsylvania

CAMBRIDGE
UNIVERSITY PRESS

CAMBRIDGE
UNIVERSITY PRESS

University Printing House, Cambridge CB2 8BS, United Kingdom

One Liberty Plaza, 20th Floor, New York, NY 10006, USA

477 Williamstown Road, Port Melbourne, VIC 3207, Australia

314–321, 3rd Floor, Plot 3, Splendor Forum, Jasola District Centre, New Delhi 110025, India

79 Anson Road, #06–04/06, Singapore 079906

Cambridge University Press is part of the University of Cambridge.

It furthers the University's mission by disseminating knowledge in the pursuit of education, learning, and research at the highest international levels of excellence.

www.cambridge.org
Information on this title: www.cambridge.org/9781108422406
DOI: 10.1017/9781108381659

First published 2018

Printed in the United States of America by Sheridan Books, Inc.

A catalogue record for this publication is available from the British Library

ISBN 978-1-108-42240-6 Hardback
ISBN 978-1-108-43403-4 Paperback

Contents

Figures and Tables

Figures

Tables

Acknowledgments

Looking back I can see that the seeds of this study were planted decades ago in a graduate seminar on recent American history at Columbia University taught by William Leuchtenburg. Fortuitously, I was assigned to lead our seminar's discussion of William Chafe's *Civilities and Civil Rights*. Ever since, Chafe's insights into the progressive mystique and the limits of liberalism as well as Chafe's method of uncovering the past, namely via a case study, has stuck with me. Hence I would like to thank Chafe and Luechtenburg for setting me on the long path that resulted in this book.

Several years after I completed this graduate seminar, thanks to Jan Lewis, Clem Price, and the New Jersey Council for the Humanities, I had the opportunity to teach a course and convene a speaker's series on the civil rights movement at Rutgers University, Newark. This allowed me to interact with Clayborn Carson, David Garrow, and J. Mills Thornton, three pioneers in the scholarship of the black freedom struggle. Though I didn't know it at the time, Thornton's examination of the protests in Montgomery, Birmingham, and Selma, provided a model for my own comparative consideration of the race revolts of the 1960s. In addition, I owe special thanks to one of my guest speakers, Ken Gibson, Newark's first black mayor, and, even more importantly, to one of my nontraditional students, Mary – whose last name I have unfortunately forgotten. Their personal recollections of Newark's 1967 rebellion prodded me to challenge orthodox interpretations of the "riots" as unconstructive and apolitical acts.

While teaching this course, I determined to write a community study of the civil rights movement in Cambridge, a decision cemented by my move from New York to Maryland in 1989. How I happened on Cambridge, a city that I knew virtually nothing about when I began my research, I do not know. I do know that a panoply of men and women convinced me that its story was worth telling and helped me tell it in a more effective and meaningful manner. At the top of this list was Gloria Richardson, arguably the most important but least known leader of the modern civil rights movement. From early interviews to more recent interactions, she has been and remains an inspiration. Her argument, which she made in 1963, that human rights are human rights, not white rights that can be given or taken away, made an indelible impression on me in terms of understanding both Cambridge and the broader black freedom struggle.

In 2003, I participated in a conference focused on black women and the movement at Sarah Lawrence College, which in turn begat a long-term relationship with two scholars who have had a profound influence on my thinking and on this work, Komozi Woodard and Jeanne Theoharis. Two years later, Komozi and Jeanne included a piece of my research in their path-breaking collection, *Groundwork*, and over a decade later invited me to participate in their NEH (National Endowment for the Humanities) seminar on Jim Crow North and West held at Sarah Lawrence College and the Schomburg Center in New York City. More so than anything else, this NEH seminar, particularly its participants' careful reading of a draft of one of the chapters of this work, encouraged me to complete this book and made it a better study, and I would like to personally thank all of them for offering their constructive feedback: Laura Hill, Kris Burrell, Crystal Moten, Say Burgin, Mary Barr, Shannon King, Ayesha Hardison, Balthazar Becker, Verdis Robinson, John Portlock, Tahir Butt, Aliyah Dunn-Salahuddin, Natanya Duncan, Hassan Jeffries, Lynnell Thomas, Ujju Aggrarwal, and Stephan Bradley. Out of this seminar, five of the group – Hill, Burrell, Moten, Burgin, and myself – formed the North East Freedom North Studies Writing Group and during our quarterly gatherings at Laura's home in Binghamton and via our virtual meetings I garnered from them nonpareil feedback and, just as importantly, incomparable collegial support. I also owe special thanks to Brian Purnell. In the fall of 2016, Brian sponsored a follow-up session to the NEH at Bowdoin College, where I had another opportunity to gather feedback from my colleagues. Brian also read my entire manuscript, offering invaluable and insightful ways to frame my questions and to structure my book.

A cluster of scholars and public historians read or commented on my research on Cambridge, as published here or in much earlier forms, and/or provided me with public forums to present my findings, which in turn allowed me to garner additional insights, including Randall Miller, Stanley Harold, Josh Wright, Doug Rossinow, John McMillian, Paul Buhle, Patricia Anderson, and Joe Fitzgerald. From the time we first met as copanelists at Sarah Lawrence College in 2003 to the present, I have enjoyed an exceptional relationship with Fitzgerald. We have shared sources, exchanged and commented on each other's works, and endeavored to expand the public's knowledge about Gloria Richardson, and I look forward to the publication of his definitive study of her life.

Serendipitously, my work on Cambridge garnered me an invitation to participate in the University of Baltimore's "Baltimore '68: Riots and Rebirth" project. First as a consultant and then as a semester-long-scholar in residence, I worked with its codirectors, Jessica Elfenbein, Thomas Hollowak, and Elizabeth Nix, to undertake a study of Baltimore's 1968 riots and to share our findings with the public via a website, a public conference, and a collection of essays. They won many well-deserved public history awards for their efforts; I benefited from their collegiality, lunchtime discussions, and dedication to recovering this and by inference many of the national uprisings that took place in the wake of Martin Luther King Jr.'s assassination from virtual oblivion. While at the University of Baltimore, I also had the luck to bounce my ideas off a separate set of researchers, including Clay Risen, John Breihan, Howell Baum, Deborah Weiner, and John Schwallenberg. They helped me refine my understanding of Baltimore's revolts and provided me with key leads and resources. I also need to give special thanks to Kathryn Kulbicki, who helped create a set of GIS maps on Baltimore's revolts.

I arrived at York College in the fall of 1989, knowing little about the place and nothing about York's 1969 revolt. Over twenty years later, my then Dean, Dominic Delli Carpini, gently prodded me to make a presentation on York's revolts at the Crispus Attucks Center as part of its Black History Month lectures. Fortunately, I was able to build on a set of senior theses about the riot or related events, including Karen Rice's 1992 oral history with members of the Newberry Street Boys, Jeff Warner and Jacob Whiteford's studies of the near riot of 1968, Olysa Townsley's consideration of other movements in York, Mike Mountz's examination of the region's rightward political shift in the late 1960s and early 1970s, and Greg Bivona's analysis of York's recent financial crisis. I also benefited from the research of Deb Noel, another one of my former students, whose thirtieth anniversary stories on York's riots which appeared in the local newspaper had a transformative impact on the course of York's history. Subsequently, several of my other students, most importantly Brandon

MacDonald and Caitlyn McEachern, aided me by creating GIS maps and transcribing oral histories, respectively. Jim McClure, of the *York Daily Record*, deserves special thanks as well.

My understanding of York's revolts and my understanding of the black freedom struggle was deepened even further by my participation in a separate NEH seminar, directed by Patricia Sullivan and Waldo Martin, held at Harvard University's W. E. B. DuBois Center during one of the hottest summers on record. This seminar provided me with the opportunity to interact with an exceptional array of scholars, including Peniel Joseph, Steven Hahn, Ray Gavins, Gerald Early, and Blair Kelly, all of whom indirectly shaped this book. While all of my classmates at the Harvard Seminar sharpened my thinking, several have read and/or commented on my manuscript since, including Jeff Littlejohn, Reggie Ellis, Joshua Wright, and Erik Gellman. Gellman's reading of my entire manuscript proved especially important.

Over the past twenty-five years I have also benefited from the suggestions of numerous copanelists and commentators, too numerous to name (or remember). But I would be remiss if I did not acknowledge at least some of those who posed challenging questions and made important suggestions. In no particular order, let me thank Avital Bloch, Martin Klimke, Charles Ford, Lester Spence, Roger Simon, Barbara Tischler, James Banner, Roger Horowitz, and Alan Draper. Similarly, I have benefited from numerous opportunities to present my findings at public forums and to "classes" of my colleagues. So let me thank Niklas Robinson for his multiple invitations to address his students at Delaware State University; Josh Wright, for chances to interact with his classes at the University of Maryland, Eastern Shore; Terry Taylor, for repeated opportunities to share my research with Baltimore City teachers at the Reginald Lewis Museum of African American History & Culture; Jacquie Martino, Cindy Leiphart, and Frank Countell; and Gordon Freireich and Gary Lauer for invitations to address the York community at the Crispus Attucks Center and Rotary Club of York, respectively. I also wish to give a booming shout out to Dion Banks and Kisha Petticolas and the Eastern Shore Network for Change for allowing me to present my research during the fiftieth anniversary "Reflections on Pine Street" in Cambridge, Maryland, this past July.

While I have done my best to document all of the books, articles, and manuscript collections I have used, I have done a poor job of recording the names of all of the librarians and archivists who have provided priceless aid in locating these sources. So let me thank a few by name, and many others anonymously, without whose support I could not have completed this book. To Sue McMillan and Karen Rice, of York College's Schmidt Library, I owe nearly three decades of thanks. To the librarians at the Enoch Pratt Free Library in Baltimore, particularly those who staff the desks at the Maryland and African American rooms, and the Schomburg Center in New York City, likewise. The librarians at the Dorchester County Public Library and the Martin Memorial Library in York similarly helped me locate crucial material. To the librarians and archivists of the Manuscript Room at the Library of Congress; the Maryland State Archives in Annapolis; the National Archives in College Park; the Baltimore City Archives; the Kennedy, Johnson, and Nixon Presidential Libraries and Archives; the National Archives in Philadelphia, Pennsylvania, and Suitland, Maryland; the Pennsylvania State Archives in Harrisburg; the Stuart A. Rose Manuscript, Archives and Rare Book Library at Emory University in Atlanta, Georgia; the Archives and Manuscript Department at the University of Maryland, College Park; the State Historical Society of Wisconsin, in Madison, Wisconsin; the Martin Luther King Jr. Center for Nonviolent Social Change in Atlanta, Georgia; and the Hoover Institution's Library and Archives at Stanford University – thank you as well. And let me give a special shout out to Lila Fourhman-Shaull of the York Historical Society for her years of lending a helping hand. Along the same lines, I owe special thanks to my editors at Cambridge University Press, especially Deborah Gershenowitz, who supported my work on this project from the first time we met to its completion, and Alta Bridges, whose very careful copy-editing made this a much better work.

In addition, I would like to thank my colleagues at York College, from my chairs, Phil Avillo, John Altman, and Mel Kulbicki, a coterie of fellow department members, especially Paul Doutrich and Corey Brooks, a succession of deans, most importantly Tom Bogart and Dominic Delli Carpini, and the members of the Faculty Development Committee. Without their support and encouragement this book would not have been completed. Finally, I must thank my family, which in my case goes well beyond the love and support they have provided. When I first conceived of studying Cambridge, Maryland, my daughter, Jessica, was still a toddler and my son, Brian, an infant. As I worked my way through completing a book on Cambridge's civil rights movement, researching and writing about Baltimore's revolt and then York's riot, and then bringing the three projects together, not only did my children mature into adults but my daughter grew into a scholar of the black freedom struggle and my son became a defender of the indigent in Baltimore and its environs. Put somewhat differently, they literally contributed their knowledge and expertise to my work. Meanwhile, my wife, Diane, has listened to my conversations about the struggles for racial equality for decades, while helping me put food on the table, a roof over our heads, and a little spark in our lives. Even when we have traveled to faraway places, I have brought my work with me, such that she has had to listen to me make comparisons between Jim Crow in the United States and apartheid and the post-apartheid system in South Africa, the caste and post-caste system in India, and the racial and class hierarchies in Brazil, Peru, and Chile. I thank her for her patience and I pledge to pay a bit more attention to some other subject matters at the dinner table in our future journeys together.

Introduction

One Day, to everyone's astonishment, someone drops a match in the powder keg and everything blows up. Before the dust has settled or the blood
congealed, editorials, speeches, and civil rights commissions are loud in
the land, demanding to know what happened. What happened is that the
Negroes wanted to be treated like [humans].

James Baldwin, 1960

Between 1963 and 1972 America experienced over 750 urban revolts.
Upwards of 525 cities were affected, including nearly every one with a
black population over 50,000. The two largest waves of uprisings came
during the summer of 1967 and during Holy Week in 1968 following
the assassination of Martin Luther King Jr. In these two years alone,
125 people were killed, nearly 7,000 were injured, approximately 45,000
arrests were made, and property damage topped $127 million or approx-
imately $900 million in 2017 dollars. And this does not take into account
a large wave of prison revolts and racially oriented unrest at the nation's
high schools. Considered collectively and with the advantage of hindsight,
these revolts constituted a "Great Uprising," a term neither contemporary
pundits and social scientists nor historians have employed. Like the Great
War and the Great Depression, the Great Uprising was one of the central
developments of modern American history.[1]

---

[1] Legally, "riots" were defined in many states as involving at least thirty participants and
personal injury and/or property damage. Data comes from: Gregg Lee Carter, "In the Narrows of the 1960s U.S. Black Rioting," *Journal of Conflict Resolution*, 30 (March 1986):
115–127; Gregg Lee Carter, "Explaining the Severity of the 1960s Black Rioting," PhD
dissertation, Columbia University, 1983; Lemberg Center for the Study of Violence, *Riot*

While estimates of the number of people who were impacted by the
revolts vary widely, in the least the Great Uprising affected millions of
Americans, from those who took to the streets and whose businesses were
looted or burned to the ground, to those who responded to the unrest,
either directly or indirectly. As contemporaries, from Martin Luther King
Jr. to H. Rap Brown, observed, and as most historians have agreed, the
Great Uprising demonstrated the inadequacies or shortcomings of the
civil rights movement, waking up the nation to the fact that the enactment of the Civil Rights Act of 1964 and the Voting Rights Act of 1965
did not signify the fulfillment of the black freedom struggle. In recognition of these shortcomings, King, SNCC (Student Nonviolent Coordinating Committee), and others reoriented their efforts in an attempt to speak
to and for those who had participated in the revolts. The Great Uprising
challenged the primacy of nonviolence as a means to overcoming racial
inequality and boosted the fortunes of both the Black Power movement
and the New Right. Moreover, the revolts provided cover or additional
justification for a variety of repressive measures, from the expansion of
COINTELPRO (Counter Intelligence Program) to the enactment of gun
control, all of which helped lay the groundwork for the war on crime and
the rise of the carceral state. Just as significantly, the uprisings demonstrated, for those who continued to believe otherwise, that race was not
a Southern problem but rather one that knew no regional bounds.

Given the abundance of scholarship on the civil rights movement one
would think that the urban revolts of the 1960s would have attracted
considerable attention. After all, historians of the civil rights years have
pushed the boundaries of the movement back in time, expanded the field
of subjects well beyond national figures and organizations, incorporated
women into their narratives, produced a startling array of community
studies, explored the intersection of the black freedom struggle and the
Cold War, and grappled with the role of armed self-defense in the nonviolent movement. Nonetheless, the Great Uprising has achieved far less

Data Review (Waltham, MA: Brandeis University, 1968); Jane Baskin, Ralph G. Lewis,
Joyce Hartweg Mannis, and Lester W. McCullough Jr., *The Long Hot Summer? An Analysis of Summer Disorders, 1967–71* (Waltham, MA: Brandeis University, Lemberg Center
for the Study of Violence, 1972); House Select Committee on Crime, *Report: Reform
of Our Correctional Systems, June 26, 1973* (Washington, DC: GPO, 1973); Charles E.
Billings, "Black Activists and the Schools," *The High School Journal*, 54:2 (November
1970): 96–107; Gael Graham, *Young Activists: American High School Students in the
Age Protest* (DeKalb: Northern Illinois Press, 2006). Walter Rucker and James Nathaniel
Upton, eds., *Encyclopedia of American Race Riots*, 2 vols. (Westport, CT: Greenwood
Press, 2006).

attention than the "heroic stage" of the civil rights movement and/or the student/youth rebellions of the latter half of the 1960s. Illustratively, Taylor Branch's exhaustive three volume work on the civil rights years ends with Martin Luther King Jr.'s death, thus providing only minimal discussion of the major wave of rebellions that followed. And narratives of the 1960s continue to privilege protests at Columbia and Chicago in 1968 over those catalyzed by King's assassination.[2]

This is not to argue that historians have ignored the urban revolts of the 1960s; rather it is to suggest that they deserve still more attention. Numerous fine studies of individual revolts exist, including examinations of those in Watts, Newark, and Detroit.[3] Scholars have written a handful of insightful comparative works and more specialized studies that focus on a broad range of questions from whether riots caused "white flight" to how they impacted local politics.[4] Recently, books have been published on the riots of the long hot summer of 1967 and the wave of unrest that took place following Martin Luther King Jr.'s assassination in the spring of 1968.[5] They have also probed the uniqueness of revolts in the Midwest and considered the role played by black anti-rioters.[6] Central to

[2] Taylor Branch, *At Canaan's Edge: America in the King Years, 1965–68* (New York: Simon & Schuster, 2006). For examples of the Chicago protests, see Terry Anderson, *The Sixties*, 3rd edn. (New York: Pearson, 2007); Todd Gitlin, *The Sixties: Years of Hope and Days of Rage*, rev. edn. (New York: Bantam, 1993).

[3] Thomas Sugrue, *The Origins of the Urban Crisis: Race and Inequality in Postwar Detroit* (Princeton, NJ: Princeton University Press, 2005); Kevin Mumford, *Newark: A History of Race, Rights, and Riots in America* (New York: New York University Press, 2007); Sidney Fine, *Violence in the Model City: The Cavanaugh Administration, Race Relations, and the Detroit Riot of 1967* (Ann Arbor: University of Michigan Press, 1989); Gerald Horne, *Fire This Time: The Watts Uprising and the 1960s* (New York: DeCapo Press, 1995).

[4] Max Herman, *Fighting in the Streets: Ethnic Succession and Urban Unrest in Twentieth-Century America* (New York: Peter Lang, 2005); Janet L. Abu-Lughod, *Race, Space, and Riots in Chicago, New York, and Los Angeles* (New York: Oxford University Press, 2007); William Frey, "Central City White Flight: Racial and Nonracial Causes," *American Sociological Review*, 44:3 (June 1979): 425–448; Leah Platt Boustan, "Was Postwar Suburbanization 'White Flight'? Evidence from the Black Migration," *Quarterly Journal of Economics*, 125 (February 2010): 417–443; Kyle Crowder and Scott J. South, "Spatial Dynamics of White Flight: The Effects of Local and Extra-Local Racial Conditions on Neighborhood Out-Migration," *American Sociological Review*, 73 (October 2008): 792–795. Alyssa Ribeiro, "'A Period of Turmoil': Pittsburgh's April 1968 Riots and Their Aftermath," *Journal of Urban History*, 39 (April 2012): 147–171.

[5] Clay Risen, *A Nation on Fire: America in the Wake of the King Assassination* (Hoboken, NJ: John Wiley & Sons, 2009); Malcolm McLaughlin, *The Long, Hot Summer of 1967: Urban Rebellion in America* (New York: Palgrave Macmillan, 2014).

[6] Ashley Howard, "Prairie Fires: Urban Rebellions as Black Working Class Politics in Three Midwestern Cities," unpublished dissertation, University of Illinois, 2012; Amanda I.

many of these works has been a set of straightforward questions – essentially the same as those posed by President Johnson when he established the National Commission on Civil Disorders (Kerner Commission) in the immediate aftermath of the long hot summer of 1967: What happened? Why did it happen? And what could have been done to prevent them from happening? Or, from a historical perspective, what was or was not done?[7]

From the start, analysts fell into roughly two schools of thought. On one side stood those who argued that the disturbances were caused by "riot makers" or "agitators" (generally outside agitators) and that most of the rioters were composed of the "riff raff" of society who were "seeking the thrill and excitement occasioned by looting and burning." Rioters, in other words, were opportunists who looted and burned for "profit and fun."[8] On the other side were those like the Kerner Commission, which argued that the "disorders" grew out of conditions of life faced by blacks who lived in America's ghettos and that "white institutions [which had] created…maintain[ed]…and condone[d]" the ghettos in the first place. Unlike the first school of thought, the second one did not find that rioting was limited to the riffraff or evidence that the unrest was caused or planned by outside agitators. On the contrary, most revolts, this school asserted, were sparked by a single incident (real or rumored) involving the police.[9] While the bulk of scholarly works subsequently written by

Seligman, "'But Burn – No': The Rest of the Crowd in Three Civil Disorders in 1960s Chicago," *Journal of Urban History* 37 (March 2001): 230–255.

[7] National Advisory Commission on Civil Disorders, *Report of the National Advisory Commission on Civil Disorders, New York Times edition* (New York: Alfred P. Knopf, 1968), p. 536 (henceforth cited as Kerner Commission, *Report.*)

[8] California Governor's Commission on the Los Angeles Riot (McCone Commission), *Violence in the City – An End or a Beginning?* (Los Angeles: Governor's Commission on the Los Angeles Riot, 1965); Edward Banfield, *The UnHeavenly City: The Nature and Future of Our Urban Crisis* (Boston: Little, Brown, 1970); Edward Banfield, "Rioting Mainly for Fun and Profit," in *The Metropolitan Enigma*, ed. by James Q. Wilson (Cambridge: MA: Harvard University Press, 1968); Eugene Methvin, *The Riot Makers: The Technology of Social Demolition* (New York: Arlington House, 1970). For a good early review of this debate, see Abraham Miller, Louis Bolce, and Mark Halligan, "The New Urban Blacks" *Ethnicity*, 3 (1976): 338–367. For a more recent overview, see Heather Ann Thompson, "Urban Uprisings: Riots or Rebellions," in *The Columbia Guide to the 1960s*, ed. by David Farber and Beth Bailey (New York: Columbia University Press, 2001).

[9] Kerner Commission, *Report*; National Advisory Commission on Civil Disorders, *Supplemental Studies, July 1968* (Washington, DC: GPO, 1968); David Sears, *The Politics of Violence* (Boston: Houghton Mifflin, 1973); Benjamin Singer, *Black Rioters* (Lexington, MA: Heath, Lexington Books, 1970); Joseph Boskin, "The Revolt of the Urban Ghettos, 1964–67," *Annals of the American Academy of Political Science*, 382 (1969): 1–14.

social scientists supported the latter interpretation, no consensus emerged regarding why some cities experienced revolts while others did not and why some revolts were more severe than others.[10] Nor did a consensus emerge regarding the impact or legacy of the revolts. Some claimed that "disorders" resulted in the collapse of the New Deal or liberal coalition; others argued that the liberal coalition had been weak all along, especially when it came to racial matters; and still others contended that cities that experienced the revolts enjoyed a surge of black power, including the election of blacks to leadership positions.[11] A third variant or school of

[10] A good summary of the sociological literature can be found in: Rob Gillezeau, "Johnson's War on Poverty and the 1960s Riots: An Investigation into the Relationship between Community Action Agencies and the Riots," March 3, 2009, http://paa2009.princeton .edu/papers/91756 [accessed July 24, 2017]. Seymour Spilerman, "The Causes and Consequences of Racial Disturbances: A Comparison of Alternative Explanations," *American Sociological Review*, 35:4 (August 1970): 627–649; Seymour Spilerman, "Structural Characteristics of Cities and the Severity of Racial Disorders," *American Sociological Review* 41:5 (October 1976): 771–793. Ted R. Gurr, *Why Men Rebel* (Princeton, NJ: Princeton University Press, 1970); Ted R. Gurr, "A Comparative Study of Civil Strife," in *Violence in America: Historical and Comparative Perspectives*, ed. by H. D. Davis and T. R. Gurr, vol. II (Washington, DC: GPO, 1969); Leonard Berkowitz, "The Study of Urban Violence: Some Implications of Laboratory Studies of Frustration and Aggression," *American Behavioral Scientist*, 2 (1968): 14–17; Jerome L. McElroy and Larry D. Singell, "Riot and Nonriot Cities: An Examination of Structural Contours," *Urban Affairs Quarterly*, 8 (March 1973): 281–302; R. C. Porter and J. H. Nagel, *Declining Inequality and Rising Expectations: Relative Deprivation and the Black Urban Riots* (Philadelphia: University of Pennsylvania Press, 1976); Susan Olzak, *The Dynamics of Ethnic Competition* (Stanford, CA: Stanford University Press, 1992); Donald J. Myers, "Racial Rioting in the 1960s: An Event Analysis of Local Conditions," *American Sociological Review*, 62 (February 1997): 94–112. Kenneth Kumer, ed., *The Ghetto Crisis of the 1960s: Causes and Consequences*, vol. 7 (New York: Garland Press, 1991).

[11] On liberalism's collapse, see Allen Matusow, *The Unraveling of America: Jim Sleeper, Closest of Strangers: Liberalism and the Politics of Race in New York* (New York: W. W. Norton, 1991); Jonathan Rieder, *Canarsie: The Jews and Italians of Brooklyn Against Liberalism* (Cambridge: Harvard University Press, 1987); Michael Flamm, *Law and Order: Street Crime, Civil Unrest, and the Crisis of Liberalism in the 1960s* (New York: Columbia University Press, 2005); Thomas Edsall and Mary D. Edsall, *Chain Reaction: The Impact of Race, Rights, and Taxes on American Politics* (New York: W. W. Norton, 1992); Peter Kraska, "Militarizing Criminal Justice: Exploring the Possibilities," *Journal of Politics and Military Strategy*, 27 (Winter 1999): 205; Dennis Loo and Ruth-Ellen Grimes, "Polls, Politics, and Crime: The Law and Order Issue of the 1960s," *Western Criminology Review*, 5 (2004): 50–67. For those who question the strength of the liberal coalition prior to the revolts, see Thomas Sugrue, "Crabgrass-Roots Politics: Race, Rights, and the Reaction Against Liberalism in the Urban North, 1940–1964," *Journal of American History*, 82:2 (September, 1995): 551–578; Arnold Hirsch, *Making of the Second Ghetto: Race and Housing in Chicago, 1940–1960* (Chicago: University of Chicago Press, 1998); Thomas Sugrue, *The Origins of the Urban Crisis; Matthew Lassiter,*

thought cast the urban revolts as rational political developments, aimed at fostering deep structural and political change. This argument often built upon historical and theoretical studies of collective action, such as the works of Charles Tilly and George Rudy, and at times paralleled contemporary arguments made by black radicals, who celebrated the revolts, and by a cluster of social scientists and historians, some of whom briefly worked for the Kerner Commission and crafted an unpublished study entitled "The Harvest of American Racism."[12]

To an extent, both the Kerner Commission's findings and this third variant echoed James Baldwin's prescient observation that black Americans simply wanted to be "treated like men" and that the nation should not act befuddled when "everything blows up." "Northerners," Baldwin cautioned in 1960, should not "indulge" in the false belief "that because they fought on the right side during the Civil War, and won, they have earned the right merely to deplore what is going on in the South…and…ignore what is happening in Northern cities." Jim Crow resided on both sides of the Mason–Dixon line, Baldwin emphasized, and suggesting that prejudice and racial discrimination might be worse in the South than the North did not justify the perpetuation of inhuman

The Silent Majority: Suburban Politics in the Sunbelt South (Princeton, NJ: Princeton University Press, 2007); Kevin Kruse, *White Flight: Atlanta and the Making of Modern Conservatism* (Princeton, NJ: Princeton University Press, 2007); Robert O. Self, *American Babylon: Race and the Struggle for Postwar Oakland* (Princeton, NJ: Princeton University Press, 2005). On the Black Power surge, see Robert C. Smith, "The Changing Shape of Urban Black Politics, 1960–1970," *Annals of the American Academy of Political and Social Sciences*, 439 (1978): 16–28, reprinted in Kenneth Kusmer, ed., *The Ghetto Crisis*; Komozi Woodard, "Message from the Grassroots: The Black Power Experiment in Newark, New Jersey," in *Groundwork: Local Black Freedom Movements in America*, ed. by Jeanne Theoharis and Komozi Woodard (New York: New York University Press, 2005), p. 93; Komozi Woodard, *A Nation within a Nation: Amiri Baraka (LeRoi Jones) and Black Power Politics* (Chapel Hill: The University of North Carolina Press, 1999); Heather Ann Thompson, *Whose Detroit? Politics, Labor, and Race in a Modern American City* (Ithaca, NY: Cornell University Press, 2004). For a less sanguine view of the political impact of the revolts, see Ribeiro, "'A Period of Turmoil.'"
[12] Eric Hobsbawm and George Rude, *Captain Swing* (New York: W. W. Norton, 1975); Charles Tilly, "Speaking Your Mind Without Elections, Surveys, or Social Movements," *Public Opinion Quarterly*, 47 (1983): 461–478; Charles Tilly, *The Politics of Collective Violence* (Cambridge University Press 2003). A good discussion of "The Harvest of Racism" can be found in McLaughlin, *The Long Hot Summer of 1967*. For this alternative view, see also David Boesel and Peter Rossi, eds., *Cities Under Siege: An Anatomy of the Ghetto Riots, 1964–1968* (New York: Basic Books, 1971); Manning Marable, *Race, Reform, and Rebellion: The Second Reconstruction and Beyond in Black America, 1946–2006*, 3rd edn. (Jackson: University of Mississippi Press, 2007).

conditions that so many of America's ghetto residents were compelled to endure. Nor, Baldwin warned, would the fact that things might be worse in the Deep South than in the North inure it from the risk of a great uprising. Indeed, in the spring of 1963, in the immediate aftermath of a riot in Birmingham, Alabama, Attorney General Robert F. Kennedy (RFK) got Baldwin to organize a special meeting at the Kennedy family's apartment at the Plaza Hotel. Presumably, RFK wanted to meet with Baldwin and other blacks outside the moderate mainstream so that he could better understand this violent turn of events. At the meeting, Kennedy sought to dismiss warnings that the Negro masses were on the verge of "kissing nonviolence goodbye." But as urban uprisings spread across the nation in the mid-1960s, Robert Kennedy came to recognize the truthfulness of Baldwin's warnings and the urgency of addressing their root cause.[13]

The different terms contemporaries and scholars used to describe the "collective violence" of the 1960s and early 1970s illustrated these different interpretations. Writes Thomas Sugrue: those who employed the term "'civil disorder'" or "disturbance" sought to occupy an "ostensibly neutral" stance and suggest that the nation had experienced only a temporary disruption of an otherwise tranquil state of affairs. "Riot," in contrast, emphasized the irrationality of the mobs' actions. "'Uprisings' was the least used but perhaps most accurate expression of discontent," adds Sugrue, "something with political content, but short of a full-fledged revolutionary act," while "'rebellion described a deliberate insurgency against an illegitimate regime, an act of political resistance with the intent of destabilizing or overturning the status quo." Indeed, Sugrue has probably done a better job of incorporating these various studies and views into a single synthetic than anyone else. In *Sweet Land of Liberty* he argued that the uprisings generally began with a police incident, targeted property, not people, though rarely if ever "white dominated institutions," such as schools, government buildings, churches, factories, or sports stadiums, and did not spread into white neighborhoods, white fears notwithstanding. Finally, Sugrue explains, officials failed to uncover persuasive evidence that radicals had organized the riots,

---

[13] James Baldwin, "Fifth Avenue, Uptown: A Letter From Harlem," in *Nobody Knows My Name: More Notes of a Native Son* (New York: Dial Press, 1961), p. 63, originally published in *Esquire* (July 1960); Taylor Branch, *Parting the Waters: America in the King Years, 1954–63* (New York: Simon & Schuster, 1989), pp. 809–813.

proclamations by politicians and pundits and widely held public sentiments notwithstanding.[14]

While this work will build on the insights of Sugrue and others, it adopts a
different methodological approach and suggests several revisions to both
the conventional and revisionist canons. Rather than focus on a single city
or conduct statistical analysis on hundreds of riots, it examines revolts in
three places: Cambridge and Baltimore in Maryland and York in Pennsylvania. These three cities were selected due to personal circumstances
and because collectively and individually they offer keen insights into the
Great Uprising. Although I was raised in California and went to graduate
school in New York City, over twenty years ago I conducted and completed a history of the long civil rights movement in Cambridge, Maryland. Based upon this research, I was invited to participate in a remarkable
collaborative investigation and commemoration of the fortieth anniversary of Baltimore's 1968 revolt sponsored by the University of Baltimore
(UB). Meanwhile as part of my duties as a professor, both before and after
my participation in the UB project, I oversaw several student research
papers on York's revolt, the city where I teach, and subsequently conducted my own independent research on the same. Put somewhat differently, it made sense for me to build on my research strengths on the three
cities that I knew best.[15]

   At the same time, as I discovered while doing my research, especially
when it comes to considering the geography, chronology, and typology of
the Great Uprising, these three cities offered several overlapping advantages. As noted above, uprisings took place in over five hundred communities. Some of these places were big, like Baltimore, some small, like
Cambridge, and many more in between, like York. Yet, too much of our
understanding of the race revolts of the 1960s has been shaped by studies of Watts, Newark, and Detroit. In fact, the majority of revolts took
place in cities with populations between 25,000 and 100,000 residents,
not large cities. One of the dangers of skewing the geography of the urban
race revolts of the 1960s is that it misleads us into believing that we
only need to think about race as a problem associated with the nation's

---

[14] Thomas Sugrue, *Sweet Land of Liberty: The Forgotten Struggles for Civil Rights in the
   North* (New York: Random House, 2008), pp. 325–327, 334.
[15] Peter B. Levy, *Civil War on Race Street: The Civil Rights Movement in Cambridge, Maryland* (Gainesville: University of Florida Press, 2003); Baltimore '68: Riots and Rebirth,
   "Overview," http://archives.ubalt.edu/bsr/ [accessed October 7, 2016].

TABLE I.I *Number of disorders by year, 1964–1971*[16]

Year	1964	1965	1966	1967	1968	1969	1970	1971
Number	8	5	21	233	360	131	67	46

inner cities, those with large ghettos, often large enough to have their own name, like Watts and Harlem. Put somewhat differently, for years Americans mistakenly conceived of race as a "Southern problem" and believed that Jim Crow only resided south of the Mason–Dixon Line. The uprisings of the 1960s rudely awakened the nation to the speciousness of this belief. Yet, ironically, we have tended to replace this false paradigm with a new one, namely one that considers race primarily as a "problem" of our large cities and their inner city ghettos, when, in fact, racism is a national problem that transcends simple geographic categories. In other words, by examining Cambridge, Baltimore, and York, three cities that are regionally proximate yet demographically different, both in terms of their absolute size and the relative and absolute size of their black populations, we can transcend the narrow geographic confines of much of the existent scholarship.[17]

In addition, these three cases allow us to reconsider the chronology of the Great Uprising. Too often, historians cast Watts (1965) as the beginning of the "urban rebellions" and Newark and Detroit (1967) as its apex, with the post-King riots as an afterthought. This temporal narrowing of the Great Uprising is particularly apparent in secondary works which often ignore and/or downplay the uprisings that took place prior to 1965 or after Martin Luther King Jr. was assassinated. As Table I.I suggests, the uprisings peaked in 1968 and continued at a steady pace through the early 1970s; and this chart does not even include data on prison and high school revolts, both of which grew in number and frequency after 1967. Nor does this chart include data on revolts prior to 1964 because no reliable data on such risings exists. Yet, as we shall see, Cambridge experienced revolts as early as 1963 – so too did Birmingham, Alabama.

---

[16] Sources: Kerner Commission, Report; US Senate, Permanent Subcommittee on Investigations of the Committee on Government Operations, *Hearings: Riots, Civil and Criminal Disorders*, (Washington, DC: GPO, 1968); Riot Data Review, 2 (August 1968); Jane Baskin et al., *The Long Hot Summer?*

[17] One of the few works to look at rioting in a small or midsize community is Andrew Goodman and Thomas Sugrue, "Plainfield Burnings: Black Rebellion in the Suburban North," *Journal of Urban History*, 33 (May 2007): 568–601.

Beyond simply getting the years of the Great Uprising wrong, this truncation of the chronology of the Great Uprising may lead to another problematic assumption. Most simply, by placing the race revolts, chronologically speaking, after the "heroic stage" of the civil rights movement (roughly 1954 to 1965), contemporaries and many historians reinforced the notion that the struggle for racial equality can and should be broken into two distinct phases: a nonviolent, southern, and constructive phase, followed by a violent, northern, and destructive one. Recent works on the existence of armed self-defense alongside "nonviolent" movements in the south during the earlier phase of the movement, along with an increasing number of studies on battles against Jim Crow in the north, raise questions about this temporal configuration. Along the same lines, by ending their discussions of the civil rights years with King's assassination, too many studies reinforce the belief that the movement collapsed with an orgy of violence following King's death, which, as we shall see, was not the case.[18]

In addition, these three case studies allow us to refine our understanding of what took place and why. Regarding the former, Cambridge and York suggest that the Kerner Commission and many others have mischaracterized the wave of urban revolts of the 1960s as "commodity riots," ignoring the numerous instances of "community (interpersonal) riots." As most explicitly spelled out by Morris Janowitz, "commodity riots" involved attacks on property but not persons – looting and arson – while "communal riots" were characterized by interpersonal and interracial violence.[19] Cambridge's initial revolts, in 1963 and 1964, were clearly communal. Its better known "Brown riot," of 1967, consisted primarily of a large fire and hence appears to fit the definition of a commodity riot; yet, as we shall see it too was interpersonal in character. While Baltimore experienced a "typical" commodity riot, one with much looting and arson but few if any direct clashes between white and black residents, York experienced virtually no looting, a smattering of fires (arson), and a bevy of gunfire and assaults, including shots exchanged between black and white citizens and repeated incidences of attacks on persons and property,

---

[18] Charles Cobb, *This Nonviolent Stuff'll Get You Killed: How Guns Made the Civil Rights Movement Possible* (New York: Basic Books, 2014); Akinyele Omowale Umoja, *We Will Shoot Back: Armed Resistance in the Mississippi Freedom Movement*, repr. edn. (New York: New York University Press, 2014).

[19] Paul A. Gilje, *Rioting in America* (Bloomington: Indiana University Press, 1996); Morris Janowitz, *Social Control of Escalated Riots* (Chicago: University of Chicago Center for Policy Studies, 1968).

leading one commentator to contend that York did not experience a riot but rather a "war."[20]

All three studies demonstrate that the revolts were not caused by radicals or riot makers; instead, they lend weight to the Kerner Commission's interpretation that social and economic conditions underlay them. Yet, at the same time, by placing each community within historical context, by chronicling the long course of their struggles for racial equality and white resistance to altering the racial status quo, these three studies suggest a richer framework for understanding the causes of the Great Uprising. Put somewhat differently, this book will demonstrate that the Great Uprising was a product of the long civil rights movement, the Great Migration, and the political economy of the postwar era, which raised but left unfulfilled the expectations of black migrants, who expected that by changing their geographic place (i.e., moving from the rural south to the north), they would change places socially and economically. This view contrasts with the classic presentation of the urban race revolts of the 1960s as spontaneous explosions of anger which, even if understandable, failed to present constructive solutions and, to make matters worse, unleashed white backlash. This interpretive framework, Jeanne Theoharis has insightfully observed, allowed white people at the time and since to "demonize" black men and women "for the outpouring of anger during the uprising." It simultaneously made it easier for society to "avoid responsibility" for the perpetuation of racial injustices and inequalities which black people outside of Dixie had protested against for years.[21]

Of course, one of the reasons why the riots of the 1960s were perceived as spontaneous and/or unexpected, and one of the reasons why the public has seen them either as unrelated to the civil rights movement or as a betrayal of the goals of the movement, is, as suggested above, because of our temporal configuration of the movement. Orthodox histories of the movement, such as *Eyes on the Prize*, which rightfully received much acclaim when it premiered in 1987, began their discussions of the civil rights movement in the mid-1950s and ended them with the triumphant march from Selma to Montgomery, Alabama, in the spring of 1965. They essentially treated the riots of the 1960s as epilogues of the movement.

---

[20] Mary Conway Stewart, *No Peace, No Justice* (Xlibris, 2006).

[21] Jeanne Theoharis, "'Alabama on Avalon': Rethinking the Watts Uprising and the Character of Black Protest in Lost Angeles," in *The Black Power Movement: Rethinking the Civil Rights–Black Power Era*, ed. by Peniel E. Joseph (New York: Routledge, 2006), pp. 27–54.

For instance, only in the last few shots of this six part series did the producers of *Eyes on the Prize* present a brief montage of images of the Watts riot accompanied by a statement that this revolt startled the nation out of its complacency. In other words, *Eyes*, like many other standard works, treated the riots as representing a rupture from the past, marking a sharp break from a movement that was conceived as confined to the South, aimed at integrating American institutions and winning basic civil rights, such as the vote, and doing so through nonviolent protest. Yet, to a large extent the producers of *Eyes* should not be faulted because they built on standard journalistic treatments of the civil rights movement, stretching back to Anthony Lewis's *Portrait of a Decade*, which omitted or minimized descriptions of racial protests in the North, exaggerated the predominance of nonviolence, and overlooked the call for jobs, housing, and other basic human rights. Furthermore, not until fairly recently have historians begun to produce an alternative telling of the black freedom struggle and it remains unclear if their revisionist works have had much of an impact on the public's memory of the civil rights years.[22]

Somewhat paradoxically, Cambridge, Baltimore, and York afford another advantage, namely the opportunity to see how this faulty interpretation of the race revolts took hold. The notion that radicals and culturally permissive liberals caused the riots and that the rioters were apolitical riffraff who, as Edward Banfield put it, had no connection whatsoever to the civil rights movement, did not evolve naturally. Rather, it was constructed by public figures: politicians, pundits, and scholars. A number of the most important figures who constructed this framework drew heavily on Cambridge's "Brown riot" of 1967 to make the case that radicals caused the revolts and on Baltimore to finger cultural liberalism as an underlying cause. Spiro Agnew's rapid rise from obscurity to the vice presidency, as we shall see, grew out of response to these two uprisings. Fortuitously, Cambridge and Baltimore provide us with the opportunity to explore how conservatives, often with the complicit support of

---

[22] Brian Purnell, *Fighting Jim Crow in the County of Kings: The Congress of Racial Equality in Brooklyn* (Lexington: University of Kentucky Press, 2013); Clarence Taylor, *Civil Rights in New York City: From World War II to the Giuliana Era* (New York: Fordham University Press, 2013); Matthew J. Countryman, *Up South: Civil Rights and Black Power in Philadelphia* (Philadelphia: University of Pennsylvania Press, 2007); Martha Biondi, *To Stand and Fight: The Struggle for Civil Rights in Postwar New York City* (Cambridge, MA: Harvard University Press, 2006); Jeanne Theoharis and Komozi Woodard, eds. *Freedom North: Black Freedom Struggles Outside of the South, 1940–1980* (New York: Palgrave Macmillan, 2003).

liberals, deflected responsibility away from themselves, while simultaneously ignoring and/or repressing alternative understandings of the causes of the revolts and attendant recommendations for radically restructuring the racial status quo. Finally, this study affords us the opportunity to consider the impact of the Great Uprising on the lives of ordinary men and women more fully than most existent works. It does so because exceptionally rich sources for studying them exist, in the form of nearly one hundred transcribed oral histories in the case of Baltimore and thousands of pages of riot-related trial transcripts in the case of York.

A note about the structure of and terms used in this work. The book is broken into three parts, one each on Cambridge, Baltimore, and York, and a conclusion which returns to the original questions posed in the introduction and offers some summative findings. Each part begins with a discussion of the history of the long black freedom struggle, then turns to the revolts themselves and concludes with an examination of their impact both locally and, in the case of Cambridge and Baltimore, nationally. This approach was adopted to counter the tendency to see riots as spontaneous and apolitical explosions of violence disconnected from long-standing locally based efforts to alter the racial status quo.

This study will use the terms *revolt*, *uprising*, and *riot* interchangeably, although, as I hope will become apparent, I consider the terms *revolt* and *uprising* a more accurate description of the events being described. Nonetheless, since so much of the public, at the time and since, used the term *riot*, I chose not to eliminate it from this work.

PART I

CAMBRIDGE, MARYLAND

I

The Making of the "Negro Revolt"

> There is no peace in Cambridge, nor can there be real peace until there is
> justice. This white man's peace is for our people a slave's peace. We have
> nothing to gain from a peace with a system that makes us less than men.
>
> Gloria Richardson, 1963

During the summer of 1967, the United States experienced its largest wave
of race revolts in history (only to be surpassed by those that followed
King's assassination the following spring). On June 11, looting broke out
in Tampa, Florida, after a police officer shot and killed an alleged robbery
suspect in the back. The following day, a much larger revolt erupted in
Cincinnati, Ohio, similarly provoked by a confrontation with the police.
Less than a week later, Atlanta, the so-called "city too busy to hate," experienced its own uprising. By the end of the summer, upwards of 170 cities
had experienced riots leaving tens dead and millions of dollars in property
damage. Though tiny in comparison to all of these cities, approximately
thirty times smaller than Newark and 125 times smaller than Detroit,
the sites of the two largest revolts, Cambridge, Maryland, shared headlines alongside these major cities because it figured prominently in the
contemporary quest to understand why riots were taking place. As the
Washington Post's July 26th headline implied, many believed that radical advocates of black power were to blame. For instance, the *Washington Post*'s headline read: "Detroit Smolders...Guard Patrols Riot-Torn
Cambridge...Agnew Blames [H. Rap] Brown."[1]

---

[1] Kerner Commission, *Report*, pp. 47–108; "Detroit Smolders...Riot-Torn Cambridge...Agnew Blames Brown," *Washington Post*, July 26, 1967, p. 1; Baskin et al., *The
Long Hot Summer?*

Numerous scholars cemented Cambridge's place in the history books by retelling the story of H. Rap Brown's fiery address and the riot that followed. For instance, in *The Troubled Feast* William Leuchtenburg explained that after Brown, "urged a black audience in Cambridge, Maryland, to 'get your guns' and 'burn this town down,' [a] fire consumed a large section of the community." In his popular textbook, *The Sixties*, Terry Anderson similarly related that "Brown exclaimed to a stunned group of reporters, 'Violence is as American as cherry pie.' He told a Black crowd in Cambridge, Maryland, to 'get some guns,'" and that "for the third time in three years, riots erupted." Likewise, in his study of the civil rights movement, Harvard Sitkoff recounted that not long after Brown declared: "'It's time for Cambridge to explode'" a riot consumed the community. Even James Michener, in his best-selling novel, *Chesapeake*, blamed Cambridge's riot on the SNCC's leader. According to Michener, LeRoy, the novel's black protagonist, delivered a fiery address in Cambridge, after which "the gang" immediately marched on an old elementary school, which LeRoy had singled out, and proceeded to set in on fire. "The effect was intoxicating . . . Many blacks rushed blazing fagots to ignite other buildings," until fire fighters, who were, according to Michener, blocked from putting out the fire, decided they had to "let the whole damned place go up."[2]

Paradoxically, the very reason why Cambridge captured the public's gaze and found a place in the history books proved riddled with false assumptions. Not only did Brown not incite a riot, he was the victim of white violence and long-term state efforts to repress him and other advocates of black power under false pretenses. But this does not mean that we should relegate Cambridge to a historical footnote. On the contrary, as suggested in the introduction, Cambridge deserves our attention because it allows us to rethink the geography, chronology, and typology of the uprisings. Moreover, rather than ignore the ways that many contemporaries misconstrued Brown's actions, we should examine how and why they did so, in order to gain a better sense of the nation's understanding of the causes of the Great Uprising and its response. Finally, Cambridge's story affords us the opportunity to see the relationship between the civil rights movement and the revolts, more specifically the ways they were

---

[2] William E. Leuchtenburg, *A Troubled Feast: American Society Since 1945*, rev. edn. (Boston: Little Brown, 1979), p. 163; Robert Weisbrot, *Freedom Bound* (New York: W. W. Norton, 1989), pp. 264–265; Anderson, The Sixties, pp. 84–85; Harvard Sitkoff, *The Struggle for Black Equality, 1954–1992*, rev. edn. (New York: Hill & Wang, 1993), pp. 203–204; James Michener, *Chesapeake* (New York: Random House, 1978), pp. 792–793.

intertwined rather than disconnected. As H. Rap Brown adeptly observed, attempts to suggest otherwise were made in order to shift "the burden of responsibility for the upheavals from the oppressors to the oppressed."[3]

"The Only Time Whites ever Visited a Jail in Connection with a Colored Prisoner Was to Lynch Him"

Our discussion of Cambridge begins with a very brief overview of its history. This history makes clear that the racial revolts of the 1960s did not erupt spontaneously, sparked by outside agitators and local malcontents, widely held sentiments notwithstanding. Rather they grew out of centuries of racial discrimination and long-standing white resistance to altering the racial status quo. From Cambridge's founding in 1684 as the capital of Dorchester County on the eastern shore of the Chesapeake Bay, racial caste structured the life of its residents and those in its immediate environs. As a port city, its economy revolved around the trade of products produced by slaves and the trade of slaves themselves. Even after the Civil War, caste privileges enjoyed by white people, including poor ones, did not disappear. Black people gained virtually no political power and they remained subservient economically, relegated to the least skilled jobs and provided with few, if any, avenues of social mobility. Nor did the end of slavery produce a color blind system of justice. On the contrary, writes C. Christopher Brown, the justice system, "operated by white, male judges, lawyers, and jurors – set the parameters of permissible behavior ... and provided white society's ultimate sanction: imposition of the death penalty on those who failed to conform." And when, Brown adds, "the judicial process could not be counted upon for suppression, mob violence or 'Judge Lynch' swiftly appeared without fear of the court system."[4] As the nineteenth century drew to a close, Cambridge began to

---

3 Gloria Richardson, "Cambridge, Maryland," *Freedomways* (Winter 1964), 28; H. Rap Brown, "Dear [SNCC] Friends," n.d., Ella Baker Papers, Box 6, Folder: H. Rap Brown, Schomburg Center, New York Public Library, New York. For examples of contemporary analysists who juxtaposed the civil rights movement to the revolts, see Howard Hubbard, "Five Long Hot Summers and How They Grew," *Public Interest* (Summer 1968): 3–24; and Lewis Killan, *The Impossible Revolution: Black Power and the American Dream* (New York: Random House, 1968).
4 Elias Jones, *New Revised History of Dorchester County, Maryland* (Cambridge: Tidewater Press, 1960); Kay Najiyah McElvay, "Early Black Dorchester, 1776–1870," EdD dissertation, University of Maryland, 1991; Charles B. Clark, *The Eastern Shore of Maryland and Virginia*, 3 vols. (New York: Lewis Historical, 1950); Robert J. Brugger, *Maryland: A Middle Temperament, 1634–1980* (Baltimore: Johns Hopkins University Press,

experience a socioeconomic revolution, turning into a center for the processing and manufacturing of food goods, first from the Chesapeake Bay and then from the surrounding farmlands. The Phillips Packing Company emerged as Cambridge's dominant force, employing thousands of workers in its packing and tin can production plants, and as the city's dominant political player. For Cambridge's black population, Phillips's rise proved a mixed blessing with many finding employment in its factories. Yet, Phillips largely relegated black workers to the least skilled, worst-paying, and most unstable occupations. In other words, Phillips's rise did not make caste obsolete; rather it constructed class barriers on top of caste ones.[5]

Outside of the workplace, for instance, racial caste lines persisted in the area of housing. As Phillips grew so too did Cambridge. Between 1910 and 1960 the city's overall population nearly doubled, from 6407 to 12,239, with the number of black residents rising even faster than the number of white residents, from 2,000 to 4,284, or from 31 percent to 35 percent of the total population. Yet, with almost no exceptions, black men and women resided in only one of Cambridge's five wards, the Second Ward, literally divided from the rest of the city by "Race Street." While no "sunset laws" officially barred black people from moving into the other wards of the city, acts of legal commission and omission guaranteed residential segregation in Cambridge. Landlords refused to rent units to blacks outside the Second Ward and federal housing policies, aimed at expanding home ownership, discriminated against black people by disqualifying them from these programs. Notorious lynchings on Maryland's Eastern Shore, most notably those of Matthew Williams and George Armwood in Salisbury and Princess Anne, in 1931 and 1933, respectively, reinforced the racial order in Cambridge by suppressing black attempts to challenge it.[6]

This said, partly because black politicians cooperated with the Phillips Packing Company, they were never disenfranchised, as were their

1988); C. Christopher Brown, *The Road to Jim Crow: The African American Struggle on Maryland's Eastern Shore, 1860–1915* (Baltimore: Maryland Historical Society, 2016), p. 150.

[5] Phillips Packing Company, vertical file, Enoch Pratt Free Library, Baltimore, Maryland; Phillips Packing Company, "Annual Reports," 1939–1956; US Department of Commerce, Bureau of Census, *County and City Data Book* (Washington, DC: GPO, 1952); *FTA (Food and Tobacco Workers) News*, January 5, 1947.

[6] Sherrilyn A. Ifill, *On the Courthouse Lawn: Confronting the Legacy of Lynching in the Twenty-First Century* (Boston: Beacon Press, 2007), especially chapter 2.

counterparts in the Deep South, and they enjoyed continuous representation on the town council. H. Maynadier St. Clair represented the Second Ward for much of the first half of the twentieth century. Essentially following the gradualist philosophy of Booker T. Washington, he rarely, if ever, criticized the packing company, believing it would help uplift the black community. At the same time, St. Clair identified himself as a "race man" and promoted the notion that better-off black people had the responsibility to serve their race, a lesson his granddaughter, Gloria Richardson, imbibed. (In the 1950s, Charles Cornish succeeded St. Clair as the Second Ward's representative on the town council. Throughout the 1950s and early 1960s Cornish maintained the same gradualist approach.)[7]

For a brief moment during the mid-1930s, black and white workers united to challenge the Phillips Packing Company by going on strike and attempting to form a union. Part of the wave of labor organizing that swept across the nation in 1937, this unprecedented effort nearly overcame historic caste barriers. Beginning with a spontaneous walkout of skilled white tin can makers, the strike quickly spread to involve over 2,000 workers, a majority of whom were unskilled black operatives. On one occasion, upwards of 1,000 black and white workers marched downtown to demand the release of James McKnight, a black striker, who had been arrested following a confrontation with truck drivers who had tried to cross the picket line. Writing for the *Afro-American*, William Jones poignantly captured the significance of this biracial march. "Down here on the Shore," Jones wrote, "the only time whites ever visited a jail in connection with a colored prisoner was to lynch him." Yet on this occasion, Jones continued, "a group of white strikers went to the jail and made police turn a colored striker loose." On separate occasions, the strikers forced city policemen to seek cover inside one of the plants and compelled the local sheriff to disarm company guards.[8]

---

[7] George Kent, "The Negro in Politics in Dorchester County," MA thesis, University of Maryland, 1961; Enez Grubb, *In Spite Of* (Cambridge, MD, 1999); Interview with Gloria Richardson, by author, May 13, 2000 (in author's possession); *Joseph W. Williams et al. v. Rescue and Fire Company*, 242 F. Supp, 556 (1966); *Joseph W. Williams et al. v. United States District Court*, District of Maryland, Civil Action 16658, Case file, Record Group 21, National Archives, Mid-Atlantic Regions, Philadelphia, PA.

[8] "Strikers Chase Three Officers," *The Plain Speaker* (Hazelton, PA), June 23, 1967, p. 1; "One Man Hurt in Cambridge Strike Clash," The Morning Herald (Hagerstown, MD), June 25, 1937; "New Violence Marks Strike at Cambridge," *The Morning Herald*, July 2, 1937, p. 1; "Lull Marking Strike Moves at Cambridge," Evening Times (Cumberland, MD), July 8, 1937; "Whites Join Protest Which Frees Worker," *Afro-American*, July 3, 1967, p. 16; William Jones, "Day by Day: Revolution on the Eastern Shore,"

Yet, by using legal and extra legal means, the company quickly crushed this cross-caste alliance. At one point, city officials, allied with Phillips, dug up an old reconstruction law to charge three strikers with "inciting a riot." At another point, a white truck driver ran over and killed, Joseph Cephas, a black worker, yet wasn't charged with a crime. On still another occasion, an armed security guard shot and injured a black striker with impunity. As the conflict between striking workers and the Phillips Packing Company intensified, thousands of white farmers from the region, many whom were contractually obligated to sell their products to Phillips, formed vigilante groups that sought to compel the workers to return to their jobs. At no point did the company disavow these actions and it may have incited them. Simultaneously, the city deputized over fifty additional officers (all white) to protect private property and black workers found themselves facing eviction notices from their homes, many of which were owned by the Phillips Packing Company or its associates. Ultimately, Phillips recognized the Dorchester County Workers Association or DORCO, a company union headed by the corporation's supervisors. It immediately announced that it had won a ten cents per hour raise. Accustomed to accommodating the Phillips wishes, St. Clair encouraged black workers to accept the offer, which most of them did. In spite of complaints of unfair labor practices and a series of favorable National Labor Relations Board judgments, neither AFL (American Federation of Labor) nor CIO (Congress of Industrial Organizations) unions were able to dislodge the company union. Phillips easily defeated a post-World War II effort by the left-leaning Food and Tobacco Workers to organize a union as well.[9]

Afro-American, July 3, 1937, p. 4. See also, Daniel Hardin, "1937 Phillips Packinghouse Strike – Promise & Defeat," https://washingtonspark.wordpress.com/2014/09/18/1937-phillips-packinghouse-strike-promise-defeat/ [accessed May 5, 2016].

[9] "Canning Firm Striker Held on Riot Charge," *Evening Times*, July 29, 1937, p. 2; "Organizer is Threatened by Drivers," *The Daily Mail*, June 26, 1937, p. 1; "Truck Coming From Cannery Kills Picket," *The Daily Mail*, June 25, 1937, p. 1; National Labor Relations Board (NLRB), Phillips Packing Company, case file, RG 625, entry 155, box 1608; NLRB, Decisions and Orders of the National Labor Relations *Board*, 5: 272–287; United Canner, Agricultural, Packing and Allied Workers of America, Official Proceedings, First National Convention, Denver Colorado, July 9–12, 1937; "Canner Striker Wounded As Peace Offer is Rejected," *Baltimore Sun*, July 2, 1937, p. 1; "Farmers Facing Loss By Strike are Saved," *New York Times* (henceforth *NYT*), June 28, 1937, p. 3; "Halt Armed Farmers on Way to Picket Line," *NYT*, June 26, 1937, p. 2; "Maryland Canners Jeer Farmers Plea," *NYT*, June 27, 1937, p. 5; "Worker Tells Board He Joined 3 Unions," *Afro-American*, August 28, 1937, p. 2;. "Phillips Packing Company Pays Colored Group Million a Year," *Afro-American*, August 28, 1937, p. 2.

While the Phillips Packing Company successfully turned back the labor movement, it proved unable to overcome profound shifts in the food processing industry. Once the third largest producer of canned goods in the nation, Phillips saw its stock price plummet from $3.64 a share in 1947 to $.0.02 a share in 1956. As a result, in the late 1950s the city fell into a deep economic depression. This collapse hit Cambridge's black residents particularly hard because they depended disproportionately on work inside the Phillips plants. While the nation prospered, Cambridge's unemployment rate skyrocketed to near-Great Depression rates – in 1963 the unemployment rate for Cambridge's black men and women stood at over 29 percent. All of these developments prefigured the wave of deindustrialization that was beginning to hit many northern cities, evidenced in many cases by the movement of jobs to the south and finally abroad. The collapse of Phillips Packing Company also destabilized the community's political economy, which according to some scholars served as one of the preconditions of the rise of protest movements. White workers, for instance, long locked out of power became increasingly assertive, seeking to elect representatives who were not beholden to the Phillips machine. Simultaneously, Charles Cornish, who succeeded St. Clair, faced opposition from members of the St. Clair family and others who sought a less gradualist approach.[10]

Nonetheless, Cambridge did not join the great wave of massive resistance that arose elsewhere following the *Brown* decision. The school board officially adopted a plan to gradually desegregate local schools; no attempt was made to disenfranchise black voters, and citizens' councils and Ku Klux Klan chapters did not arise as they did in the Deep South. In 1960, Calvin Mowbray, a political moderate easily won the mayoral race. In turn, he greeted John F. Kennedy during a campaign stop and helped honor Roosevelt Burlington, the first secretary of the Liberian embassy, at the annual Harriet Tubman Day commemoration. (Tubman was born in Dorchester County and her memory was regularly celebrated by local blacks.) Two of the nation's most famous newscasters, Chet Huntley and David Brinkley, even touted Cambridge as a "model city" in terms of race relations. Building on this reputation, business leaders emphasized that Cambridge enjoyed racial and labor peace in their pitches to prospective

---

[10] J. Mills Thornton, "Municipal Politics and the Course of the Civil Rights Movement," in *New Directions in Civil Rights Studies*, ed. by Armstead Robinson and Patricia Sullivan (Charlottesville: University of Virginia Press, 1991), pp. 38–64; Boesel and Rossi, *Cities Under Siege*, "Introduction."

employers. But, as we shall see, the bubble of racial peace, or what Gloria Richardson termed a "slave's peace," was about to burst.[11]

"Please Fight for Freedom and Let Us Know That We are Not Going Away in Vain"

In early 1962, in spite of its boast that it was a "place making progress," Cambridge found itself in the crosshairs of the civil rights movement. While many locals insisted that outside agitators and local malcontents caused its racial troubles, more accurately, the persistence of white privileges in education, housing, employment, recreation, government, and the criminal justice system, underlay this rising.[12] In February 1962, after staging a series of "freedom rides" along Route 40, which ran through Maryland and Delaware, on the western shore of the Chesapeake Bay – essentially parallel to today's Interstate 95 – a coalition of civil rights activists from Baltimore and other Mid-Atlantic cities decided to extend their protests to Maryland's Eastern Shore.[13] Following demonstrations in Maryland Governor Millard Tawes's hometown of Crisfield, Reginald Robinson and William Hansen, two SNCC activists, took up residence with Herbert St. Clair, Maynadier St. Clair's son, who in turn arranged for them to meet with representatives of the city's Equal Opportunity Commission (EOC) and members of the town council. These officials, including Charles Cornish, informed the SNCC activists that protests were unwarranted because they alleged that Cambridge enjoyed good race relations, as proven by the fact that blacks enjoyed the franchise, were represented on the town council and had voluntarily agreed to gradually desegregate its schools. Armed with information provided to them by the St. Clairs, Hansen and Robinson retorted that as of 1962 not a

---

[11] Levy, *Civil War on Race Street*, pp. 35–36; "Harriet Tubman Day Observed," Democrat and News (Easton, MD), November 9, 1961.

[12] Numan V. Bartley, *The Rise of Massive Resistance: Race and Politics in the South during the 1950s* (Baton Rouge: Louisiana State University Press, 1969); Neil McMillen, *The Citizens Council: Organized Resistance to the Second Reconstruction, 1954–64* (Champaign: University of Illinois Press, 1994); Clive Webb, *Massive Resistance: Southern Opposition to the Second Reconstruction* (New York: Oxford University Press, 2005).

[13] Renee Romano, "Diplomatic Immunity: African Diplomats, the State Department, and Civil Rights, 1961–1964," *Journal of American History* 87 (September 2000): 546–579; Robert Palumbos, "Student Involvement in the Baltimore Civil Rights Movement, 1953–1963," *Maryland Historical Magazine* 94 (Winter 1999): 449–492; Clarence Logan Notes and Clipping File (partial copy in author's possession).

single black person had attended any white schools and that the EOC was a farce. They added that black policeman were restricted to arresting black men and women and that the majority of local restaurants did not serve non-whites, EOC claims notwithstanding. They could have added that Dorchester County's state senator Frederick Malkus fiercely opposed integration.[14]

At this point an interesting dynamic set in, namely a split between upper class and traditional black leaders and more militant working-class-oriented black activists. After the initial meetings with Robinson and Hansen, representatives of Cambridge's black elite, including several ministers and a doctor, revived a moribund branch of the NAACP (National Association for the Advancement of Colored People). While they did not contend, as did Cornish and Helen Waters, that all was fine, they maintained a very gradualist approach. (Waters was the single black representative on the school board.) For instance, in a letter to the EOC, the NAACP's William Hemphill went out of his way *not* to offend the city's leaders. Unlike SNCC, he did not threaten the city with any actions, from legal suits to sit-ins, if its "requests" went unfulfilled. In contrast, when the city refused to meet Robinson's and Hansen's demands, they helped organize a series of demonstrations that ebbed and flowed for over two years.[15]

Beginning on January 13, 1962, approximately one hundred activists participated in Cambridge's first "freedom rides." Many of the protesters came from regional colleges, most notably Howard University, Morgan State, Johns Hopkins University, and Swarthmore College. Some belonged to SNCC, others to Congress of Racial Equality (CORE) or the lesser-known Civil Interest Group or CIG, a Baltimore-based organization. They were joined by men and women of all ages from Cambridge, especially many young people, who, like their counterparts in other parts of the nation, had grown tired with the slow pace of change. Rather than negotiate, local elites responded by belittling the budding movement. Police Chief Brice Kinnamon, for instance, proclaimed that SNCC was using "youngsters...to picket beer joints," and the Cambridge *Daily Banner*

---

[14] Levy, *Civil War on Race Street*, pp. 37–40; "Cambridge Report," 1962, CORE Papers [microfilm edition] (Sanford, NC: Microfilming Corporation of America, 1980), reel 40.

[15] Dorchester County Branch of NAACP to William Hemphill, February 1, 1962, August Meier Papers, Schomburg Center for Research in Black Culture, New York Public Library, New York, Box 67, Folder, Civil Rights Movement, Cambridge. Boesel and Rossi, *Cities Under Siege*, "Introduction."

warned that the demonstrations jeopardized "four decades of biracial progress."[16]

By the summer of 1962, the freedom movement in Cambridge had distinguished itself from those budding up across the country in several ways. First, it was led by Gloria Richardson, a remarkable black middle-aged single mother of two, a graduate of Howard University (in the 1940s) and the granddaughter of Maynadier St. Clair. While Richardson did not initiate the movement in Cambridge – by her own admission she was drawn into it by her daughters who participated in some of the early sit-ins – she came to symbolize its militancy. She faced threats to her life, went to jail – as did her mother and daughter – and endured the sexist barbs of some civil rights leaders who were unaccustomed to playing second fiddle to women, in general, not to mention women in the civil rights movement. Roy Innes of CORE, for example, described her as a "castrator."[17] Though often forgotten today, Richardson was prominent enough at the time to be one of a handful of women to be formally recognized at the March on Washington, alongside Rosa Parks. Many SNCC activists later recalled Richardson as a seminal person in their development (for an iconic image of Richardson, see Figure 1.1). For instance, SNCC veterans Judy Richardson and Jean Riley described Richardson as simply "phenomenal." "I know what always stood out for me," Judy Richardson (no relation) recollected, "Gloria was strong! . . . She was just unbending." Similarly, Wiley remembered how Richardson "ignited the energy in the Black community" and how much the people "adored Gloria . . . She was phenomenal."[18]

Second, under Richardson's leadership, the Cambridge Nonviolent Action Committee (CNAC), the local affiliate of SNCC, dedicated itself to building a movement from the grassroots up, one which catered, as Richardson put it, to the churched and the unchurched and which focused on the primary concerns of poor and working-class blacks, namely jobs, housing, and better recreation. Finally, Richardson and the local

---

[16] Levy, *Civil War on Race Street*, pp. 36–49. "Cambridge CORE," n.d., August Meier Papers, Box 67, Folder: Civil Rights Movement, Cambridge.

[17] Anon., "Cambridge, April–May, 1963," August Meier Papers, Box 67, Cambridge, MD; Joe Fitzgerald, "The Struggle Is Eternal" (unpublished manuscript in author's possession).

[18] To determine the needs of the community, CNAC conducted a door-to-door canvass of the residents of the Second Ward. See CNAC, "Study," Cambridge Nonviolent Action Committee Papers, State Historical Society of Wisconsin, Madison. Interview with Judy Richardson, by Jean Wiley, February, 2007, www.crmvet.org/nars/judyrich.htm [accessed January 19, 2016].

FIGURE 1.1 Gloria Richardson pushes aside a National Guardsman's bayonet during civil rights protest in Cambridge, Maryland, July 21, 1963. By permission of AP Photo.

movement quickly gained a reputation for their fearlessness and unwill-ingness to accommodate white moderates, including a readiness to defend themselves with guns if necessary. Or as Victoria Jackson-Stanley recalled, her father kept a "pistol in his boot, a knife in his pocket, a shotgun in the trunk, a rifle under the front seat, and a handgun in his pocket" to protect his family and himself because, at the time, "you just weren't sure who would approach you to hurt you." This does not mean that Richardson promoted violence. On the contrary, she helped orchestrate some of the finest examples of nonviolent direct action protest in the history of the civil rights movement. But she did not believe that this committed black people to jettisoning their right to protect themselves, their families, and the community; a view, which historians have recently revealed prevailed, even if not always openly, through much of the movement.[19]

[19] Levy, *Civil War on Race Street*; Stanley-Jackson quoted in: Southern Food Alliance, "Counter Histories: Cambridge, Maryland," www.southernfoodways.org/project/counter-histories/ [accessed May 6, 2016]; Jenny Walker, "The 'Gun-Toting' Gloria Richardson: Black Violence in Cambridge, Maryland," in *Gender in the Civil Rights*

From the start, activists encountered a system bent upon denying justice to black citizens who demanded equal treatment while simultaneously refusing to punish business owners and/or policemen who infringed upon their rights. For instance, soon after he arrived in Cambridge, Brooklyn CORE stalwart Arnold Goldwag sought to swear out a warrant against a police officer for physically and illegally removing him from the White Owl Inn where he had gone to "confer with the owner" about the possibility of employing a black worker. Instead of listening to his complaint, local authorities threw him in jail. Further attempts to get the state police or the state's attorney to investigate resulted in the arrest of additional CNAC members. To make matters worse, local authorities routinely allowed white mobs to attack nonviolent protesters, such as William Hansen, who was thrown through a plate glass window, with impunity.[20]

In late spring 1963, CNAC staged protests at Dorset Theater, the offices of the Maryland State Employment Service, Airpax Electronics Corporation, and the Rescue and Fire Company's (RFC) arena – this mix of public accommodations and employment agencies and workplaces reflected CNAC's foci. At the RFC's arena, the fire chief – and the city's future mayor – got the police chief (who himself was a former fire chief), to forcibly remove Richardson and her fellow activists. As the *Baltimore Sun* reported, Police Chief Brice Kinnamon "seized her (Richardson) by the left arm and jerked her down the steps" and charged her with "disorderly conduct, tending to incite a riot and refusal to obey a police officer." Meanwhile, a feisty crowd of whites "shoved the marchers and threw pennies and pebbles at them." Subsequently, at a mass meeting at one of the local black churches, Richardson announced a "boycott of the downtown area" as the "only way...to break Cambridge."[21]

The initial phase of the protests in Cambridge came to a climax in early May 1963 at the so-called "penny trials," when Judge W. Laird Henry Jr. found forty-seven defendants, black and white, guilty of one count of disorderly conduct for their sit-ins at local establishments. After dismissing all of the remaining charges, Henry sentenced each defendant "one

Movement, ed. by Peter J. Ling and Sharon Montieth (New York: Garland Publishing, 1999), pp. 169–185; Cobb, *This Nonviolent Stuff'll Get You Killed*.

[20] Arnold Goldwag, "Cambridge, Maryland: Brief History with Background Information," Arnold Goldwag Papers, Box 3, Folder: Cambridge, Maryland, Brooklyn Historical Society, Brooklyn, NY.

[21] "17 Arrested in Protests in Cambridge," *Baltimore Sun*, March 31, 1963, p. 36; "17 Students Jailed in Cambridge Protest," *Afro-American*, April 6, 1963, p. 14; Fitzgerald, "The Struggle Is Eternal," pp. 4–7.

penny" and then turned his attention to Richardson. Calling her a disgrace to her family's good name, Henry insisted that Cambridge was trying hard "to do what is good for you and your people." "Do you know of any other community in this area making greater strides in integration than Cambridge?" Henry probably hoped that Richardson would respond to this paternalistic rebuke much in the same way her grandfather had, by accommodating herself to the demands of the white elite. Instead she retorted: "You are not going to like this but I think far greater progress is being made in Salisbury," a city, which both Henry and Richardson knew had long been associated with one of the most brutal lynchings in modern American history. As SNCC activist Courtland Cox later observed, if Richardson, a solid member of the black middle class was no longer willing to follow the lead of the white elite, than the elite had to wonder what protection it had from the unruly working- and lower-class blacks. For years, it had depended on the black middle class to act as a bulwark against rash actions. By refusing to play this role, Richardson put the city on notice that she and CNAC intended to challenge the racial caste system in an uncompromising fashion.[22]

Tensions in Cambridge reached new heights not long after the penny trials when authorities arrested two black youths, Dwight Cromwell and Dinez White. Even though their actual offense was praying outside a segregated bowling alley, which its owner admitted was done in an orderly manner, the two were charged with disorderly conduct and thrown in jail without bail and subsequently sentenced to indefinite terms in the state institution for juvenile delinquents. In response, White crafted a "Letter from a Jail Cell," which she modeled after King's recently published "Letter from a Birmingham Jail." "They think they have you scared because they are sending us away," White declared. "Please fight for freedom and let us know that we are not going away in vain." Following her advice, CNAC organized a series of mass meetings and demonstrations and Richardson sharpened her rhetorical criticism of the white community. For instance, Richardson "wonder[ed] if black folk were dealing with Christian people or heathen," and warned that it was "becoming more and more difficult to contain violence in the Second Ward among those

---

[22] Dorchester County Circuit Court, Criminal Papers, Case File 1415–1417 (April 1963), Maryland State Archives, Annapolis, Maryland (henceforth MSA); "54 Demonstrators Found Guilty, Fined 1 Cent," *Democrat and News*, May 9, 1963; Fitzgerald, "The Struggle Is Eternal"; Interview with Courtland Cox, by author, Washington, DC, March 24, 2000. Ifill, *On the Courthouse Lawn.*

not committed and not believing in the effectiveness of the non-violent approach."[23]

On the evening of June 11, CNAC staged a downtown march, where it decried White's and Cromwell's imprisonment. There, black protesters encountered crowds of roughly 150 to 200 whites, and some skirmishes broke out. The following day, Clemon Cephas, who had been struck in the head by a rock thrown by one of the white counterdemonstrators, led more than one hundred black and white protesters on another downtown march. Waving flags and singing freedom songs, they had to be separated from equally large crowds of whites by hard-helmeted police and state troopers. At the time, in spite of the escalating tensions, Herbert St. Clair, Richardson's uncle, made clear that CNAC had no intention of backing down. "We are not going to initiate violence," he declared, "but if we are attacked, we are not going to turn the other cheek." CNAC, as suggested above, had already endorsed the right of black citizens to carry weapons in defense of themselves and their property.[24]

Indeed, not long after Judge Duer, a jurist who already had a poor reputation in the black community, officially sentenced White and Cromwell, Richardson's warning proved prescient. When authorities arrested local black residents for protesting against this decision – nonviolently – some began to destroy the toilet and wash facilities of their cells inside the jail while others smashed windows and threatened white motorists outside. Several days of even fiercer confrontations followed, including the shooting of two white people, the throwing of bricks and Molotov cocktails through storefront windows on Race Street and of Helen Waters's home, and a near clash between black and white demonstrators at the courthouse. After this near clash, at a mass meeting at the Bethel Church, Richardson warned Cambridge's black community not to allow white people to goad them into a race "war." The situation, which the *Afro-American* described as "guerilla warfare," was exacerbated by the disbandment of a special committee created by Judge Henry, which he had

[23] MICPRR, "Report on Racial Situation in Cambridge," Governor J. Millard Tawes Papers, MSA; "Pickets at Prayer Are Arrested in Cambridge," *Cambridge Daily Banner* (henceforth *CDB*), May 31, 1963, p. 1. White's letter quoted in: Howard Schneider, "Summer of Fire," *Washington Post Magazine*, June 26, 1992, p. 14; Burke Marshall, "'Memorandum,' June 17, 1963, Burke Marshall Papers," in Civil Rights During the Kennedy Administration, 1961–1963 [microform], ed. by Carl M. Brauer (Frederick, MD: University Publications of America, 1986), reel 28; Fitzgerald, "The Struggle Is Eternal," pp. 19–20.
[24] Levy, *Civil War on Race Street*, pp. 79–82.

created to find some middle ground, and the decision of the Maryland Commission on Interracial Problems and Relations to leave town. Both made these moves because of the intransigence of white political and business leaders. One day later, a large mob of whites called for lynching Richardson – a threat made more poignant by the assassination of Mississippi's Medgar Evers the night before. Faced with the prospect of civil war, Mayor Mowbray requested that Governor Tawes declare martial law and send in the National Guard, which he did on June 14, 1963.[25]

With armed troops encamped on Race Street, local authorities engaged in negotiations with CNAC. In these negotiations, CNAC called for the town council to enact a public accommodations ordinance, which would make segregated establishments illegal. Rather than accede to this demand, the council passed a public accommodations amendment to the city's charter. CNAC correctly predicted that this amendment could and would be placed to a vote in a citywide referendum and repealed by the white majority. CNAC also objected to the amendment because it did not explicitly cover several key establishments, including the RFC's facilities and the Dorsett Theater, both sites of protest. Nonetheless, judging the amendment as a sign of good faith, Governor Tawes announced that he would withdraw the National Guard at noon on Monday, July 8. Ironically, Richardson lamented this decision, in part because the Guard had provided more protection to black protesters than had the state or local police. In contrast, many white people, including William Yates, a local attorney who would play a key role in the subsequent prosecution of H. Rap Brown, welcomed the removal of what he termed an "army of occupation."[26]

"Where Once Slaves Were Sold"

No sooner had the Guard left than CNAC resumed demonstrations. Among the first and most famous of these took place at Dizzyland, a local

[25] Fitzgerald, "The Struggle Is Eternal," pp. 22–27; Levy, *Civil War on Race Street*, pp. 83–84; "Riot Averted as Whites March in Cambridge, MD," *NYT*, June 14, 1963, p. 14; "White Mob Forms in Cambridge; Negro Hiring Accord Seen Here," *Baltimore Sun*, June 14, 1963, p. 44; "Mob Rule Feared in Cambridge," *Baltimore News-Post* (evening), June 14, 1963, p. 1; "Cambridge Still Tension-Ridden," *Washington Post*, June 13, 1963, p. A8; "3 Fires Set in Cambridge," *Baltimore Sun*, June 13, 1963, p. 54; "Negroes Parade in Cambridge, MD," *NYT*, June 13, 1963, p. 17; "Mood Is One of Bitterness," *Afro-American*, June 22, 1963, p. 1; "Racial Violence Hits Cambridge Last Night," *CDB*, June 22, 1963, p. 1.

[26] Levy, *Civil War on Race Street*, pp. 83–84.

FIGURE 1.2 Dizzyland's owner, Robert Fehsenfeld, cracks egg over Edward Dickerson's head during sit-ins at his restaurant, July 8, 1963. By permission of AP Photo.

white hangout. This protest made national headlines when news photographers captured the restaurant's owner, Robert Fehsenfeld, cracking an egg over the head of Edward Dickerson (see Figure 1.2). Overnight, Dickerson, a native of Cambridge, became the subject of a number of national stories. The *New York Post*'s James Wechsler, for one, wrote: "There was little in Edward Dickerson's history to project him as a recruit in this...army of equality. He grew up in Cambridge, Maryland, one of a large family...By his own account, the only matters that interested him...were the pursuit of girls, learning to drink, and, most of all, 'using my fists.' As for his destiny, he assumed that he was to be a 'little white Southern bricklayer.'" By his own admission, when the freedom riders first appeared on the eastern shore, Dickerson viewed them as outsiders who sought to upset Cambridge's "southern way of life," and he put on his "kicking boots and brass knuckles" and went with his brother to beat them up. But once Dickerson joined the civil rights protests, virtually the entire white community viewed and treated him as a race traitor, including his family.[27]

---

[27] For the photo of Dickerson being cracked with a raw egg, see *NYT*, July 9, 1963 p. 1; "Photo: Trade Blows," *New York Journal-American*, July 18, 1963; "Photo: Hands Off,"

After Fehsenfeld cracked the egg on Dickerson's head, a larger melee broke out inside the restaurant, abetted by local authorities who refused to protect the protesters from white attackers. Subsequently, separate and simultaneous marches by blacks and whites to the courthouse took place. Later that same night, carloads of whites drove through the Second Ward and exchanged gunfire with black residents. George Collins, a reporter for the *Afro-American* vividly described the scene. "For what seemed like an eternity the Second Ward" became "a replica of the Old West as men and boys of all ages roamed the streets, stood in the shadows, and leaned out of windows with their weapons in full view." By dawn more than twelve people had been shot and several white-owned stores in the Second Ward had been set afire. It was only an "act of God," Collins added, that no one was killed.[28] The *Chicago Defender* similarly described "a night of shotgun and rifle blasts, fires, Molotov cocktails, flying bricks." "Racial hate," the paper added, "left five men injured, three stores damaged by flames and fears of renewed violence." The violence began, the *Chicago Defender* explained, after "chanting, singing and praying Negroes" about "200 strong, snaked their way through a white residential section and surrounded the Dorchester County jail where 20 Negroes arrested in demonstrations the night before were being held." They were met by a "large crowd of whites," who responded with heckles, rocks, and "a rain of firecrackers" and by white "night riders." At one point during these confrontations, several white people were arrested for assaulting civil rights activists. In response to this arrest, crowds of white people chanted: "Let him go" and "Arrest the niggers."[29]

National newspapers confirmed the direness of the situation. The *Washington Post* stated that "guerilla warfare, open and bloody" had "broken out." Police Major George Davidson described "shooting all over the city – almost on the scale of warfare." Maceo Hubbard, the highest ranking black official in the Department of Justice, characterized the situation in Cambridge as dangerous as "a stick of dynamite."[30] Faced

---

Newsday, July 18, 1963, p. 3; James Wechsler, "The Recruit," *New York Post*, December 3, 1962; Jhan and June Robbins, "Why Didn't They Hit Back?" *The Reporter*, n.d.; Arnold Goldwag, "Cambridge, Maryland: Brief Recent History [handwritten notes]," Arnold Goldwag Papers, Box 3.

[28] Levy, *Civil War on Race Street*, pp. 84–86.

[29] "5 Hurt, Stores Burned As Riot Flares in Md," *Chicago Defender*, June 13,1963, p. 6; George Collins, "Cambridge," *Afro-American*, July 13, 1963, p. 1; "Roving Gunman Wounded 6 Whites, Troops Ordered to Cambridge," *The Bridgeport Post*, July 12, 1963, p. 1.

[30] "Md Racial Strife Called "Dynamite," *New York Journal-American*, July 11, 1963, p. 4.

with such reports, Governor Tawes declared martial law and announced that since the city could not "peacefully resolve the differences that exist," he had no other choice but to redeploy the National Guard. They would remain in Cambridge for nearly a year, one of the longest peace-time occupations of a city by the military in history.[31]

The insurgency in Cambridge also attracted the attention of President Kennedy and his brother, Robert. Upon returning from his triumphant tour of Europe, where he had delivered his famous *Ich bin ein Berliner* speech, JFK took a pause from his otherwise buoyant press conference to single out the freedom movement in Cambridge for criticism. "In Cambridge, Maryland…you have an increasingly dangerous situation." Activists there have "almost lost sight of what the demonstration is about" and "I am concerned…because they go beyond information, they go beyond protest, and they get into a very bad situation where you get violence, and I think the cause of advancing equal opportunities only loses…so I have warned against demonstrations which could lead to *riots* [emphasis added], demonstrations which could lead to bloodshed, and I warn now against it." President Kennedy also explicitly compared what was happening in Cambridge to the "responsible" demonstrations being planned for Washington, DC, which he described as being part of a "great tradition." Ironically, up to this point in time, JFK had opposed the planned March on Washington, arguing, in part, that they might lead to riots and undermine his civil rights bill.[32]

By asserting that blacks had gone "beyond protest," the president, like much of the national press, blamed the violence on Cambridge's black community. *The Washington Post*, for instance, asserted that "Negro leaders" in Cambridge had displayed a "lack of judgment" by "failing to discipline their troops." This view echoed those of Cambridge's local elites, such as the editors of *Daily Banner*, who asserted that "twice within the past month the Negro civil rights movement in Cambridge has gotten out of control and produced civil disorder and bloodshed."[33]

A cluster of other sources, nearly all of them published by blacks, presented a significantly different interpretation of events in Cambridge. Black leaders had not lost control, rather white authorities had initiated the violence, declared the *Cambridge Free Press*, CNAC's

---

[31] "A Failure of Judgment," *Washington Post*, July 13, 1963, p. A6; "Five Whites Shot in Cambridge, Md; Guard in Control," *NYT*, July 12, 1963, p. 1.

[32] John F. Kennedy, "The President's News Conference," 17 July 1963, www.presidency .ucsb.edu/ws/index.php?pid=9348 [accessed October 31, 2014].

[33] "A Failure of Judgment," *Washington Post*, July 13, 1963, p. A6.

intermittently published newspaper. "YOUR children," who were demon-strating nonviolently at Dizzyland and the all-white Rescue and Fire Company's Recreation Center," were "slapped in the face" and "threat-ened with high power fire hoses." When CNAC staged a mass nighttime demonstration outside the city jail, the *Free Press* continued, authorities used "Birmingham tactics" against them.[34] Similarly, *Muhammad Speaks*, the mouthpiece of the Nation of Islam, observed that Cambridge's 4,000 black residents were "sick of endless negotiations and empty promises." For several years, peaceful protesters had been "met with beatings, whole-sale jailings [and] police brutality." But ultimately, "Negro fighters for equal justice" decided to "defend themselves," to meet "fire with fire," and "exchange[d] bullet for bullet ... until the white power structure ... fearful of an all-out war ... sent out their frantic call for the National Guard."[35]

Along the same lines, George Collins, who in an earlier piece had described Cambridge as a "smoldering volcano" which could "erupt at any minute," did not hold blacks and whites equally culpable. On the contrary, he located the cause of the revolt in the desire of Cambridge's "4,000 black citizens" for "complete freedom ... now!" and the "city's white guardians of segregation" determination not to allow "them to have it – now, or ever." Likewise, in an editorial entitled "Sun Tan for President Kennedy," the *Afro-American* suggested that President Kennedy should spend some time in Cambridge "living as a black person. If he took this step he could better understand black people's social and economic con-ditions and he would probably not think of criticizing them from demon-strating against their oppressors."[36]

Ironically, even though his brother cast the actions of Cambridge's free-dom movement as counterproductive, Robert Kennedy, in his capacity as attorney general, suggested otherwise by reaching out to Richardson to negotiate an unprecedented deal. In its first couple of years in office, the Kennedy Administration had evaded involving itself directly in the affairs of local communities beset by racial conflicts. In response to the freedom rides, RFK had negotiated a deal with Mississippi's white lead-ers which guaranteed black safety but then allowed for the arrest and imprisonment of the riders. A year later, the administration refused to

[34] *Cambridge Free Press*, May 16, 1963, in August Meier Papers, Box 67.
[35] "Cambridge: A Negro Revolt: Where Once Slaves Were Sold," *Muhammad Speaks*, August 2, 1963; "The Bitter Battle of Cambridge," *Muhammed Speaks*, July 5, 1963; "The Awesome Fortitude of 4,000," *Muhammed Speaks*, August 2, 1963.
[36] George Collins, "Mood Is One of Bitterness," *Afro-American*, June 22, 1963, p. 1; "Sun Tan for the President," quoted in Joe Fitzgerald, "The Struggle Is Eternal," p. 47.

intervene in Albany, Georgia, and reacted tepidly to the crisis at the University of Mississippi. It took on a more interventionist approach in the spring of 1963, but nowhere, even in Birmingham, did it become as deeply involved in local affairs as it did in Cambridge. Ignoring criticisms that such intervention rewarded violence, RFK conducted lengthy talks with Gloria Richardson. In addition to producing an agreement to desegregate public facilities, build public housing, and foster jobs, Richardson's grueling negotiations with RFK, according to multiple sources, indelibly impacted him. Previously, RFK saw integration and the franchise as the main goals of the movement; afterwards, to a large degree due to the presentation that Richardson made, he realized that something much larger was at stake, particularly the need for jobs and housing, a view he would build on in the latter half of the 1960s.[37]

Cambridge also stood out because it was not alone; it was not the only place where black people decided to defend themselves during this time period. Put somewhat differently, in several other communities black activists employed both the tactics of nonviolence and armed self-resistance to achieve equality. Nearly two months before Tawes redeployed the National Guard in Cambridge, Birmingham, Alabama, often portrayed as the embodiment of the nonviolent movement, had a riot. Sparked by the bombings of the house where Martin Luther King Jr. had been residing and the Gaston Motel, black residents looted and torched buildings and attacked white authorities. This revolt, not the earlier nonviolent demonstrations, asserted Malcolm X, convinced the president to finally intervene.[38] Revolts also erupted in Savannah in Georgia, Lexington in North Carolina, Chicago, and Philadelphia. And in numerous other cities, from Gadsen in Alabama to Jackson in Mississippi, the threat of

---

[37] John Lewis, *Walking With the Wind: A Memoir of the Movement* (New York: Simon & Schuster, 1998), pp. 212–213; Interview with Gloria Richardson, by Author, May 13, 2000.

[38] Malcolm X, "Message to the Grassroots," in Nicholas Andrew Bryant, *The Bystander: John F. Kennedy And the Struggle for Black Equality* (New York: Basic Books, 2006), p. 338; On Birmingham's riot, see Diane McWhorter, *Carry Me Home: Birmingham, Alabama: The Climatic Battle of the Civil Rights Revolution* (New York: Simon & Schuster, 2001), pp. 430–431; Glenn T. Eskew, *But for Birmingham: The Local and National Movements in the Civil Rights Struggle* (Chapel Hill: University of North Carolina Press, 1997), pp. 300–301; Rampaging Mobs in Pre-Dawn Riots," *Civil Rights Movement Scrapbook, Alabama Events*, Volume 5, Birmingham Public Library Digital Collections, http://bplonline.cdmhost.com/cdm/compoundobject/collection/BPLSB02/id/658/rec/16 [accessed November 11, 2014]; Taylor Branch, *Parting the Waters*, pp. 793–802; John F. Kennedy, "Radio and Television Remarks Following Renewal of Racial Strife in Birmingham," 12 May, 1963, www.presidency.ucsb.edu/

black violence, attracted national attention and may have helped avert larger confrontations.³⁹

Unfortunately, the tendency to foreground nonviolence and downplay armed self-defense detoured scholars away from recognizing the role that these revolts played in fomenting change.⁴⁰ In a series of very influential articles, the sociologist Seymour Spilerman chose to exclude "collective acts of violence" which grew directly out of civil rights struggles from his databases and thus his analysis of racial rioting. Greg Carter, one of Spilerman's mentees, who developed an extensive data set on the revolts, which both he and tens of other social scientists depended on to explain the causes and consequences of the riots, did the same. So too did various government bodies.⁴¹ As a result, it is difficult to know if Cambridge or, for that matter, any revolts prior to 1964 were the exceptions that proved the rule. But it is reasonable to believe that if we alter our definition of *riots*

ws/index.php?pid=9206&st=&st1= [accessed November 4, 2014]; M S. Handler, "Malcolm X Scores Kennedy on Racial Policy: Says He Is 'Wrong Because His Motivation Is Wrong': Head of Black Muslim Group Cites Birmingham Crisis," *NYT*, May 17, 1963.

³⁹ "Seven Negroes Jailed in Aftermath of Riot," *The Corpus-Christi Caller-Times*, June 7, 1963; "Man Killed in Riot," *The Monroe News-Star*," June 7, 1963, p. 1; "Four Men Hurt in Negro Riot in Georgia," *The Emporia Gazette*, June 20, 1963, p. 10; Southern Regional Conference, "The Civil Rights Crisis: A Synopsis of Recent Developments, April 1963–June 24, 1963," in *Let Freedom Ring: A Documentary History of the Modern Civil Rights Movement*, ed. by Peter B. Levy (Westport, CT: Greenwood Press, 1992), pp. 117–119.

⁴⁰ Among those who have challenged the traditional framing of the 1960s are: Jenny Walker, "A Media-Made Movement? Black Violence and Nonviolence in the Historiography of the Civil Rights Movement," in *Media, Culture, and the Modern African American Freedom Struggle*, ed. by Brian Ward (Gainesville: University Press of Florida, 2001); Cobb, *This Nonviolent Stuff'll Get You Killed*; Christopher Strain, *Pure Fire: Self Defense as Activism in the Civil Rights Era* (Athens: University of Georgia Press, 2005); Simon Wendt, *The Spirit and the Shotgun: Armed Resistance and the Struggle for Civil Rights* (Gainesville: University Press of Florida, 2007).

⁴¹ Spilerman, "The Causes and Consequences of Racial Disturbances"; Spilerman, "Structural Characteristics of Cities and the Severity of Racial Disorders." Carter, "In the Narrows of the 1960s U.S. Black Rioting," Carter, "Explaining the Severity of the 1960s Black Rioting." Among those to rely on Spilerman's and Carter's data sets were: William Frey, "Central City White Flight: Racial and Nonracial Causes," Susan Olzak and Suzanne Shanahan, "Deprivation and Race Riots: An Extension of Spilerman's Analysis," *Social Forces*, 74:3 (March 1996): 931–961; Myers, "Racial Rioting in the 1960s"; William J. Collins and Robert Margo, "The Economic Aftermath of the 1960s Riots in American Cities," *Journal of Economic History* 67:4 (December 2007): 841–883.

Jane Baskin et al., *The Long Hot Summer?*; Lemberg Center for the Study of Violence, *April Aftermath of the King Assassination* (Waltham: MA: Brandeis University, 1968); US Senate, Committee on Government Operations, *Hearings Before the Permanent Subcommittee on Investigations of the Committee on Government Operations, September 5, October 10 and 11, 1968*, (Washington, DC: GPO, 1968), pp. 2752–2777.

to include rather than exclude those which grew directly out of civil rights protest and which involved clashes between blacks and whites, we will have to expand our timeline of the Great Uprising, amend our mental map of where they took place, reconsider the predominance of commodity as opposed to communal riots, and rethink the relationship between the so-called heroic nonviolent, integrationist, and black power stages of the movement.

"The Choice: Progress or Anarchy"

Even after the Kennedy Administration helped negotiate the "Agreement," the situation in Cambridge remained extremely tense. In the fall of 1963, local white supremacists, working through the newly formed Dorchester Business and Citizens Association (DBCA), which was loosely modeled after the white citizens councils in the Deep South, challenged the charter amendment, as CNAC predicted it would. After easily gathering 1,000 signatures, well over the requisite number to hold a special referendum, Cambridge was forced to vote on whether to allow for segregated establishments or not. To the surprise of many, Richardson and CNAC called upon voters to boycott this special election on the grounds that "Human rights are human rights, not white rights" and that "whites have no power to give or take away" such inalienable rights. Or, put somewhat differently, natural rights should not be left up to the whim of the white majority. On October 2nd, 1963, Cambridge's residents went to the polls in record numbers and the amendment was repealed.[42]

Even before the votes were tallied, white and black moderates in Cambridge and nationwide sought to blame Richardson for the results. Yet, it was not Richardson's advocacy of the boycott that produced the final outcome. Rather it was the fact that white voters vastly outnumbered black voters. By voting in record numbers, white people determined that Cambridge would remain segregated. Eighty-five percent of white people voted; turnout was especially high in the working-class wards, which voted in favor of segregation by very large margins. Just under 80 percent of the largely Fourth Ward, comprised primarily white blue-collar workers, supported the DBCA sponsored measure. Even the upper class white First Ward, which had supported the moderate Calvin Mowbray for mayor in the 1960s, voted against banning segregated establishments.

---

[42] CNAC, "Statement" and Gloria Richardson, "Press Release," Burke Marshall Papers, reel 26.

This vote prefigured similar pro-segregation votes in various open housing referendums, including Proposition 14 in California, which nullified the Rumford Fair Housing Act, and which, according to some historians, helped provoke Watts's rebellion the following year.[43]

Emboldened by their victory, the DBCA decided to sponsor a major address by Alabama Governor George Wallace, the national symbol of white supremacy. The previous fall Wallace had participated in a debate at Goucher College in Baltimore with Cambridge's state senator Frederick Malkus, where the two had critiqued the Kennedy Administration's civil rights' proposal. Building on these connections, Wallace launched the Maryland leg of his presidential campaign at the RFC's arena in Cambridge.[44] Following a rousing introduction by the DBCA's president, William Wise, Wallace delivered an emotional oration to an overflow crowd of upwards of 2,500. Rather than using blatant racist language, Wallace deployed various coded terms or phrases which the audience clearly understood as a defense of white supremacy. "I have spoken all the way from New Hampshire to Alabama ... [and] I believe there are in this country thousands of people who say stand firm and keep working." Pending civil rights legislation, Wallace forewarned, endangered long-held American beliefs, most prominently the right of association. Americans had to protect their individual liberties from the encroachment of the federal government; local communities had to fight to protect their autonomy before the federal government's power grew too great." To sharpen his case, he decried the federal government's ban on school prayer and condemned the pending civil rights bill's provision that stripped defendants

---

43 CNAC "Statement," and Gloria Richardson, "Press Release," both in Burke Marshall Papers; *Afro-American*, September 28,1963; *Afro-American*, October 5, 1963; Interview with Philip Savage by John Britton, September 20, 1967, Civil Rights Documentation Project, Howard University, Washington, DC; Interview with Gloria Richardson; Murray Kempton, "Gloria, Gloria," *New Republic*, November 11, 1963, pp. 15–17; Robert Liston, "Who Can We Surrender To?" *Saturday Evening Post*, October 5, 1963, pp. 78–80; Belinda Robnet, *How Long? How Long? African-American Women in the Struggle for Civil Rights* (New York: Oxford University Press, 1998); Jeanne Theoharis, "'Alabama on Avalon.'" On Philip Savage's and the NAACP's criticism of Richardson, see Philip Savage to All Concerned, October 14, 1963; "NAACP's Statement Regarding Defeat of Charter Amendment, October 1, 1963, Cambridge, Maryland"; William S. White (Untitled and undated column); and "We Appeal to You!," n.d., all in Philip H. Savage, Field Secretary Files, Papers of the NAACP, Part 25, Branch Department Files, Series D, General Department Files, 1956–65, Library of Congress, also available via ProQuest Historical Vault.

44 William G. Jones, *The Wallace Story* (Northport, AL: American Southern Publishing, 1968), pp. 276–280; "Governor Wallace Gets Punched on Chin," *Afro-American*, September 21, 1963, p. 1.

FIGURE 1.3 Demonstrations in Cambridge against the appearance of Alabama Governor George Wallace result in confrontation between National Guard and civil rights protesters, May 11, 1964. © Danny Lyon/Magnum Photos.

of their right to a jury of their peers. The Associate Press reported that the audience "interrupted his speech 48 times with applause and hollered "We'll Win, We'll Win."[45]

While Wallace spoke, CNAC, joined by civil rights activists from across the eastern seaboard, protested outside. After listening to speakers, including one by SNCC chairman, John Lewis, who called for "a great revolt for freedom," Richardson led approximately 400 demonstrators toward the RFC arena. But before they arrived, they encountered National Guards' forces, temporarily under the command of Colonel Tawes, the governor's nephew, bayonets drawn (see Figure 1.3). When Tawes ordered the demonstrators to disperse, about half did so, but the other half, including Richardson, stood fast. SNCC's Cleveland Sellers recalled, "It was a crucial moment, the kind that can make or break a movement...If she had told us to return to the [Elks] lodge, we would have done so." In a similar situation, in Selma in 1965, King would turn protesters around. Instead, Richardson declared: "I'm going through." No sooner had she stepped forward than the National Guard placed her under arrest and whisked

[45] "Wallace to Speak in City Tonight," *CDB*, May 11, 1964; "DBCA Addressed by Gov. Wallace," *Democrat and News*, May 12, 1964; "7 Hurt in Cambridge Violence," *The Salisbury Times*, May 12, 1964; Jones, *The Wallace Story*, pp. 276–280.

her away. When other demonstrators went limp in the street, Colonel Tawes commanded his troops to don their gas masks and to spray the crowd indiscriminately with tear gas. Among those seriously injured in the melee was SNCC stalwart Stokely Carmichael, who apparently was knocked unconscious by a tear gas canister. Later that night, when a black child died, some of Cambridge's blacks accused the government of intentionally gassing them to death. While Carmichael did not go so far, he did contend that the use of force was not an accident but rather took place because of the "awful specter of an armed black community determined to defend itself against white attack."[46]

Put somewhat differently, virtually a year after the Kennedy Administration had brokered an agreement aimed at restoring order in Cambridge and a year after the National Guard had first arrived, the community remained on the verge of a civil war. "Every male in this town – black and white – is armed," General Gelston informed a reporter for the *Afro-American*. "Our job is to keep them apart. If they ever get together, it will be h__l." When asked who represented the greater problem, black activists or working-class white people, Gelston responded the latter, which, in his words, was "just waiting for a chance to start an all-out war" and an "excuse to wipe the colored persons out." Postmaster J. Edward Walter termed the situation "a powder keg" and predicted "10 or 15 years of trouble." Cambridge's *Daily Banner* editor, Maurice Rimpo declared: "We're at the point of no return – no we've just passed it." Likewise, Maryland Governor J. Millard Tawes stated he was strongly considering asking the federal government to send in troops, even though it had denied a similar request the previous summer. In this case the black press concurred, with the *Chicago Defender* asserting that Cambridge was "a prelude to more massive manifestations of discontent that will occur this summer."[47]

---

[46] Cleveland Sellers, *The River of No Return: The Autobiography of a Black Militant* (New York: William Morrow, 1973), p. 71; "Cambridge, Md., Negroes Routed by Tear Gas after Wallace Talk," *NYT*, May 12, 1964, p. 1; Interview with Courtland Cox, by author, March 24, 2000, Washington, DC; Peniel Joseph, *Stokely: A Life* (New York: Basic Books, 2014), pp. 53–54, 118; Stokely Carmichael with Michael Thelwell, *Ready for the Revolution: The Life and Struggles of Stokely Carmichael* (New York: Scribner, 2003), pp. 340–347; "Cambridge: Pressure Mounts in Dying City," *The Movement*, May 19, 1964, p. 1; "Cambridge, Md.: Wallace Visit Unleashes Race Riots in Cambridge," *Chicago Defender*, May 13, 1964, p. 1.

[47] "Decade of Trouble Seen for Cambridge," *Washington Post*, May 31, 1964, p. A1; "Harris to Cambridge," *Afro-American*, May 30, 1964, p. 11; Guardsmen Head Says Leaders Lost Control," *Atlanta Daily World*, May 27, 1964, p. 1; "Cambridge Explodes," *Chicago Defender*, May 23, 1964, p. 8.

Rather than accede to calls for a cooling off period, Gloria Richardson and CNAC decided to continue to challenge the system. More specifically, CNAC invited Dick Gregory, the militant-comedian, to speak. When General Gelston refused to ban his "show," local white people exploded. Police Chief Brice Kinnamon decried Gelston for his "even handedness" and the DBCA's William Wise warned of white violence if Gelston did not demonstrate firmer control of the situation, including what one of his fellows termed "Queen Gloria." Along the same lines, the *Salisbury Times* upbraided Gregory for threatening to shut down white venues if Gregory was not allowed to perform.[48]

White people in Cambridge also displayed their commitment to maintaining white supremacy at the polling booth. In the Democratic Party's presidential primary, voters could choose between Senator Daniel Brewster, President Johnson's stand-in, or George Wallace. While the state voted for Brewster, barely, citizens of Dorchester County supported Wallace by a nearly five to one margin. Likewise, in July 1964, Cambridge elected Osvrey Pritchett as its mayor. Four years earlier, Pritchett, the chief of the RFC and an advocate of the anti-desegregation referendum, had lost by a wide margin to Calvin Mowbray. But in 1964, campaigning on a platform of "law and order" and white supremacy, he easily defeated the moderate incumbent, winning 71 percent of the white vote, 30 percent more than he had won in 1960. Ninety percent of the white blue-collar Fourth Ward voted for him; in contrast, he won less than 4 percent of the votes of the residents of the all-black Second Ward.[49]

Reflecting on the state of race relations, Gloria Richardson warned that the nation faced a choice. It could choose either progress or anarchy. Even though Cambridge was a small town, she explained, it offered a unique lens on the broader "Negro Revolt," because it displayed "all that is wrong with America today." The initial protests in the community, she observed, signaled the arrival of a new determination among Cambridge's blacks, especially the young, to win "full equality." Lest the "white power structure," which had received assurances from

---

[48] "Tensions in Cambridge Lessened by Gregory," *Washington Post*, June 1, 1964, p. A6; "Decade of Trouble Seen for Cambridge," *Washington Post*, May 31, 1964, p. A1; "Tension in Cambridge Lessened by Gregory," *Baltimore Sun*, June 1, 1964, p. A6; "Gelston Meets Gregory's Plane; Cancels Show," *Washington Post*, May 28, 1964, p. A1; "Show Slated by Gregory," *Baltimore Sun*, May 30, 1964, p. 17; "What's Happening?" *The Salisbury Times*, June 3, 1964, p. 6.

[49] "Racial Views Seen as an Issue in Forthcoming July City Election: Pritchett Top Vote Getter," *CDB*, June 8, 1964; "Pritchett Elected Mayor," *CDB*, July 15, 1964.

"well-thinking Negro moderates" believe that enough progress had already been made, she assured them it had not. On the contrary, Richardson warned that the broader civil rights movement was "ready to go into a new phase." The failure of the federal government "to act with vigor," to stand by as those who simply sought to exercise their rights as citizens were brutality violated, was sowing the seeds of violence within the black community. Richardson made clear that neither she nor the black masses wanted "violence or bloodshed." But if Cambridge and America did not deliver on extending full rights to black men and women, if instead white people "remain[ed] indifferent and insensitive to change, then all of us, in Cambridge and throughout America will have to sacrifice and risk our personal lives and future in a nonviolent battle that could turn into a civil war." At the time, few paid much heed to Richardson's words. But when a series of revolts erupted in Harlem, Rochester, and Philadelphia in the summer of 1964 and an even larger one in Watts, the following year, she proved remarkably prescient. Ironically, as we shall see, by then she had moved to New York City to live with her new husband, Frank Dandridge, leaving many in Cambridge concluding that she, in tandem with radical outside agitators, not the persistence of caste and the white community's refusal to alter the racial status quo, had been the cause of their city's turmoil all along.[50]

[50] Gloria Richardson, "Cambridge, Maryland," *Freedomways*, 4:1 (1964), pp. 28–36.

2

The Fire This Time

You are so right when you say that Cambridge is no longer a sleepy fishing
village. The black people has woke up and we intend to stay awoke [*sic*].
Black Action Federation, "Letter to the Editor," July 26, 1967

In the wake of Gloria Richardson's departure, Cambridge's elite reaffirmed their belief that Cambridge was a progressive community whose
racial peace temporarily had been upset by outside agitators and local
malcontents. Buoyed by reports issued by outside agencies, most notably
the "Miles Committee," which recommended the removal of the National
Guard – a recommendation the governor followed – local white leaders
insisted that the turmoil of the previous few years would not return as long
as Richardson and the agitators stayed away. Along the same lines, the
editors of the *Daily Banner* congratulated the city for implementing the
rest of the "Agreement," which led to the building of some public housing
units and the hiring of some blacks in the federally funded employment
office. Newspaper editorials also juxtaposed the history of black representation on Cambridge's town council to developments in the Deep South,
where white southern diehards viciously attacked civil rights marchers
merely for trying to register to vote. Cambridge's gradual economic recovery allowed many white people to add that the unique conditions that
had given rise to black discontent, specifically the collapse of the Phillips
Packing Company, had been overcome and that better days, for all, lay
ahead.[1]

---

[1] "Services Held in Cambridge for Rev. Reeb," *CDB*, March 15, 1965; "The Right to
Vote," *CDB*, March 19, 1965; "Report of the Miles Committee," Governor Tawes Papers,

Even some local civil rights activist shared this optimistic assessment. Commenting on the changing situation, Stanley Wise, SNCC's field worker in Cambridge, wrote: "If developments in Cambridge follow their present course, perhaps we can go back [to college] soon." Steve Fraser, a participant in Mississippi Summer, showed up in Cambridge in 1965 expecting a hotbed of radicalism but instead found CNAC and remaining SNCC field representatives preoccupied with applying for federal grants and other bureaucratic tasks. Two years later, multiple news sources reported a similar scene. "Ask about racial demonstrations in Cambridge these days," began an Associated Press story, "and you're likely to hear, instead, about the gleaming new housing development." "Progress," not strife, "is a favorite word." The Maryland Interracial Relations Commission offered a similar assessment, asserting that the city had made progress in five crucial areas, including jobs and housing. Even former CNAC member, Frederick Jackson, declared, "If you look at the entire county today, it doesn't even seem like the same place as 1963."[2]

But appearances could prove very deceiving. In the immediate aftermath of Watt's revolt, California Governor Pat Brown declared "nobody told me there was an explosive situation in Los Angeles."[3] In fact, he had plenty of reason to know that black discontent had been on the rise for some time. Likewise, more discerning observers easily could have noted that fundamentally little if anything had changed and that Cambridge's black community demonstrated its dissatisfaction with the racial status quo via legal suits, labor organizing drives, the formation of new militant organizations and the rejuvenation of older more moderate ones. But by remaining "indifferent and insensitive" to black demands for an end

S1041–1557; "Last Troops Quit Cambridge, Maryland," *NYT*, July 12, 1964, p. 54; "Negro Elected to Head Cambridge, MD, Council," *NYT*, July 21, 1964, p. 20. Interview with Steve Fraser, by author, Chicago, Illinois, March 30, 1996; "Progress in Cambridge during Last Four Years Cited by Associated Press, *CDB*, April 5, 1967; "Report Praises Cambridge," *CDB*, April 13, 1967. Office of Assistant Deputy Director for Research" Staff, "Paper No. 4: 'Analysis of Cambridge, Maryland Disturbance (Draft),'" October 29, 1967" (henceforth, "Analysis of Cambridge"), in *Records of the National Advisory Commission on Civil Disorders* (henceforth: *Kerner Commission Records*), *Civil Rights During the Johnson Administration, 1963–1969*: Part 5 [microfilm], ed. by Stephen F. Lawson (Lanham, MD: University Publications of America, 1984).
2 "Report of the Miles Committee," Governor Tawes Papers, S1041–1557; "Last Troops Quit Cambridge, Maryland," *NYT*, July 12, 1964, p. 54; "Negro Elected to Head Cambridge, MD, Council," *NYT*, July 21, 1964, p. 20. Interview with Steve Fraser; "Progress in Cambridge During Last Four Years Cited by Associated Press, *CDB*, April 5, 1967; "Report Praises Cambridge," *CDB*, April 13, 1967.
3 Brown quoted in Theoharis, "'Alabama on Avalon.'"

to residential segregation, job discrimination, unequal education, and a broken criminal justice system, Cambridge's whites chose to risk another round of revolts. Ironically, when this round occurred, whites did their best to divert attention away from themselves, insisting even more vociferously than they had in the past that a radical outsider, in the person of H. Rap Brown, had caused the turmoil. Faced with the largest wave of revolts in American history, much of the nation proved willing to believe them.

"[The RFC] Should Open [the Pool] or Burn it Down"

Throughout the 1960s the Rescue and Fire Company stood as a symbol of the racism of the white power structure in Cambridge and served as a target of black protesters. CNAC had protested against its segregated facilities prior to Richardson's departure and continued to clash with the company and its leaders, particularly Police Chief Kinnamon and the town's new mayor, Osvrey Pritchett, afterwards. As an investigator for the Kerner Commission later reported, the RFC operated like Tamney Hall. Mayor Pritchett was a former chief of the RFC; Kinnamon had been its leader for years. Frederick Malkus used the RFC as a political base, as did the DBCA, which had sponsored George Wallace's speech at the RFC's arena.[4]

When the Civil Rights Act of 1964 was enacted, the RFC insisted it did not have to comply with the law because its pool was a private rather than a public facility. An interracial cluster of activists disagreed and decided to seek entry to the pool on July 4, 1965. One of them, Reverend Joseph Williams, later stated that he targeted the RFC because he sought to provide black youths with a constructive alternative to recreating in the Second Ward's pool halls and bars. Regardless, the choice of July 4th as the date to test the facility was ripe with symbolism. After an RFC cashier handed one of the "testers" a ticket to enter the pool, a separate attendant quickly took it away on the grounds that he did not belong to the RFC's Arena and Pool club. When Thomas Holt, a Howard University student, attempted to apply for membership, he was informed that the pool was private property. Emphasizing that Police Chief Kinnamon was on the grounds, the attendant threatened the activists with arrest if they did not

---

[4] "Reconnaissance Survey: Field Research Report" Inter-Office Memorandum – Draft, n.d. and "Analysis of Cambridge," *Kerner Commission Records*, reels 19 and 23; Interview with Enez Grubb, by author, Cambridge, Maryland, February 11, 2000 (in author's possession); Interview with Frederick Malkus, by author, Annapolis, Maryland, February 2, 1993 (in author's possession).

depart immediately. The testers retreated temporarily, only to return a couple of hours later when they were placed under arrest, charged with trespassing, and sent to jail without bail.[5]

In response, Reverend Williams and several other arrestees filed suit in federal court arguing that the RFC, the mayor, and the City of Cambridge had violated the Civil Rights Act of 1964. At the heart of their case, detailed by Baltimore-based civil rights attorneys Marvin Braiterman and Elsbeth Levy Bothe and supported by an amicus curiae brief submitted by the United States Justice Department, was the claim the pool club was a public facility not a private establishment. Through documents obtained through discovery, the plaintiff's lawyers demonstrated that government funding had made construction of the pool possible and allowed the RFC to remain fiscally sound. In addition, the government had paid for the preparation of the pool site and provided the fire company with facilities free of charge, as well as defraying much of its annual operating expense. Moreover, the plaintiffs showed that the RFC's recently established club status was an intentional subterfuge, aimed at subverting the law. When Kinnamon testified that no "Negroes" were members of the club because none had ever applied, the plaintiffs proved that black residents who had sought to join the RFC as volunteer fireman, which guaranteed membership in the pool, had been informed that there were no openings. Yet, at the same time, openings had been found for white applicants.[6]

Judge Northrup rejected every one of the defendant's claims, ruling in clear and unambiguous language that the RFC had violated the Civil Rights Act of 1964. Besides losing the case, the trial confirmed what some have termed the "hidden in plain sight" nature of Jim Crow in the North. Unlike in the Deep South, where state laws demanded the segregation of public facilities, in the North segregation was maintained in less obvious but just as invidious manners. Though not officially state sanctioned, the RFC case demonstrated that the state was not impartial. The all-white RFC received public funding and it did so under the guise of private ownership. In addition, its monopoly status, as the town's only fire-fighting force, fostered the myth that the fire company served the entire public,

---

[5] *Joseph W. Williams et al. v. Rescue and Fire Company*, 242 F. Supp (1966); *Joseph W. Williams et al. v. United States District of Maryland, Civil Action 16658*, Case File; "RFC Pool Is Declared a Private Club," *CDB*, July 7, 1965; "Court Hears Case Today," *CDB*, November 23, 1965; "Mayor Testifies in Arena Case," *CDB*, November 24, 1965; Dorchester County Circuit Court, Criminal Docket, Thomas Holt, 1892–93, October 8, 1965, MSA.

[6] *Joseph W. Williams et al. v. Rescue and Fire Company*, 242 F. Supp (1966); *Joseph W. Williams et al., United States District of Maryland, Civil Action 16658*, Case File.

when in fact it played a crucial role in perpetuating white power and privilege.[7]

Rather than comply with the court's decision, the RFC voted to shut down and sell their facilities. When asked what he thought about the RFC's decision, Robert Perry, a middle-aged black resident of the Second Ward, expressed his discontent, arguing that the company should "let the people go to it like the court said." Minnie Dockins, a black youth agreed, stating the RFC "should open it" for all youths, or "burn it down." Many white residents of Cambridge, in contrast, seemed far less indignant. Clifford Collins, an elderly white male, supported the RFC's decision to sell its facilities, in spite of the fact that when the pool had opened in 1958 it had been heralded as a symbol of Cambridge's prowess. Sharon Hynson, a young white woman who lived on Race Street, opposed selling the property but not the RFC's decision to close the pool. Instead, she and several other whites suggested that the RFC's facilities should be retrofitted into an expanded firehouse.[8]

Ironically, though he opposed desegregating the pool, Kinnamon got the fire company to sell the facility to none other than himself for $100,000, well below its appraised value. He then leased it back to the city. As the weather heated up in the summer of 1967, the city scrambled to secure federal funds to allow summer school students to swim there. To insure that black and white adults did not join together in such intimate quarters, however, the school superintendent, James Busick, a longtime ally of the RFC, limited the swim program to school children who were participating in special summer school classes, all of whom were black. The pool waters may have proved cooling, but the entire process left the black community inflamed.[9]

Moreover, the court's decision did not affect the RFC's commitment to remain an all-white fire-fighting force directed by members who assumed white superiority, clothed in rhetoric of community service. In the wake

---

[7] "Mayor Testifies in Arena Case," *CDB*, November 24, 1965; *Joseph W. Williams et al. v. Rescue and Fire Company*, 242 F. Supp (1966); *Joseph W. Williams et al., United States District of Maryland, Civil Action 16658*, Case File.

[8] "The Inquiring Photographer," *CDB*, October 10, 1966; *Joseph W. Williams et al. v. Rescue and Fire Company*, 242 F. Supp (1966); *Joseph W. Williams et al. v. United States District of Maryland, Civil Action 16658*, Case File.

[9] *Joseph W. Williams et al. v. Rescue and Fire Company*, 242 F. Supp (1966); *Joseph W. Williams et al., United States District of Maryland, Civil Action 16658*, Case File.; "RFC Votes To Sell Arena," *CDB*, October 7, 1966; "R.F.C. Arena Sold to Police Chief," *CDB*, February 17, 1967; "NAACP is Reactivated in Cambridge," *Baltimore Sun*, June 21, 1967, p. A8.

of the so-called "Brown riot," novelist John Barth, a native of Cambridge, would criticize the RFC (for the actual accusations see Chapter 3). Kinnamon and other town leaders responded by defending the RFC in the strongest of language. Describing the RFC as "one of the few self-sacrificing, dedicated bodies in our county," he wished there were "more such dedicated citizens to help foster and preserve our city, county, state and nation, especially now, when so many citizens care only for self-interest and greed and are trying to grab everything for themselves and contribute nothing." Likewise, the *Daily Banner*, which at times broached the idea of establishing a paid fire force, expressed its admiration for the "esprit de corps" of the RFC. "The members are bound together with a kind of fellowship that no other local organization enjoys...City Council members sometimes shake their heads in amazement when a question concerning the fire company comes to the surface."[10]

Yet Kinnamon's and the *Daily Banner*'s analysis of the RFC obscured one central fact. It was all white and there could be little doubt that race impacted its response to the fire that swept across the Second Ward following Brown's speech in the summer of 1967. In the least, a desegregated force would have responded more promptly if for filial attachments alone. Most likely a desegregated force would have become less of an adversary of the civil rights movement all along. Even years later, when the RFC finally desegregated, Enez Grubb, who along with her cousin Gregory Meekins became RFC's first black members, insisted it still operated as a bastion of white supremacy. "Many evil things had taken place there," she recalled in a 2000 interview and its ultimate integration in the 1980s did not necessarily signal a change in its member's mindset.[11]

"Deep-Seated Racial Prejudice Overwhelms Every Positive Feature...Expected to Bring Improvements"

Based on its extensive door-to-door survey of the Second Ward, which CNAC conducted in the summer of 1963, CNAC concluded that the local movement had already gone through two phases and was entering a third.

[10] Cecil K. Applegarth, "Letter to the Editor," *CDB*, 12 September 1967; "A Paid Fire Company," *CDB*, 12 September 1967; "Remarkable Records," *CDB*, December 22, 1967. "RFC Officers Are Elected," *CDB*, October 24, 1967. John McGreevy, *Parish Boundaries: The Catholic Encounter with Race in the Twentieth Century Urban North* (Chicago: University of Chicago Press, 1996) examines a similar sense of ethnic pride among white people in the North.

[11] Interview with Enez Grubb.

In the first, it asserted, the movement had focused on the outward "indignities" of the segregationist system, such as restaurants which refused to serve black people. In the second, it had broadened its demands to include "equal police protection, and integrated schools." In the third phase, black citizens would focus on winning "better housing, full employment, better working conditions, [and] better education." Whether people in power would, of "their own free will and accord," rearrange or reform the "structures of racism" that maintained these inequities, to borrow Richardson's words, remained to be seen. But Richardson, among others, had her doubts that they would.[12]

Central to the structure of racism in Cambridge and in virtually every city that experienced riots during the 1960s were the structures where blacks resided. As we will see, hyper-segregation characterized Baltimore's housing market; a disproportionate number of York's black residents lived in a small area characterized by substandard housing, and virtually all of Cambridge's blacks lived in the all-black Second Ward. Moreover, in spite of the construction of approximately 150 public housing units, part of the 1963 "Agreement," blacks continued to face deplorable housing conditions. SNCC field worker John Batiste, who took over for Robinson and Hansen, described many of the homes in the Second Ward as "nothing more than converted horse barns, corn cribs, and company shacks which lacked hot running water, flush toilets, and electricity." To make matters worse, Batiste observed that "political and business 'power structure'" was deeply invested, literally, in maintaining these rental properties in their current status.[13] Separate and independent investigations by federal officials confirmed Batiste's claims. "We were shown block after block of tottering, single-family frame structures, often lined along dirt roads and generally with little or no set-back, crowded almost against each other, and on small lots sometimes of no more than fifty or sixty foot depth," reported one HUD (US Department of Housing and Urban Development) official. "These dwellings are obviously obsolete and in disrepair, with tumbling porches and steps. Many were without inside toilets...and in several instances the outside privy served more than one

[12] CNAC, "The Negro Ward in Cambridge, Maryland: A Study In Social Change," CNAC Papers, September, 1963. Richardson quoted in "Reflections on 1967...1992 and into the Future" *CDB*, July 24, 1992, pp. 1, 16.
[13] John Batiste, "Cambridge, Maryland," n.d. Student Nonviolent Coordinating Committee (SNCC) Papers, Martin Luther King Jr. Center for Nonviolent Change, Atlanta, GA, Box 52; A copy of this memo can also be found in the Ella Baker Papers, Box 8, folder 5.

family...Hot water is rarely available...and several are without inside water...Overcrowding is clearly a common pattern." "Two old frame structures," the report continued, had "originally been a stable for horses and the other a chicken coop."[14]

By restricting where they could live, residential segregation also compelled black residents to pay proportionately far more of their income for housing – 56 percent more than whites according to one analysis of Cambridge. In addition, knowing that their renters had fewer choices, landlords had less of an incentive to maintain and/or upgrade their properties. In contrast, white renters and homebuyers, who could take advantage of federal subsidies, such as loan guarantees, could demand more, both in terms of amenities and price. Statistics on home ownership further revealed the impact of the split housing market. A majority of whites in Cambridge owned their homes, while only 25 percent of non-whites did and black-owned homes were nearly five times as likely to be overcrowded and four times as likely to lack plumbing facilities as white ones. In turn, this helped create a virtuous cycle for whites and vicious one for blacks, as the former accumulated wealth while black citizens did not.[15]

Efforts to overcome these conditions encountered several overlapping roadblocks. Black residents faced powerful white landlords who evaded complying with housing codes and opposed constructing additional public housing units because they did not want to provide their renters with alternatives to residing in substandard homes. Cambridge's black renters and homeowners also faced the complicity of the much larger white community that refused to countenance building additional public housing or renting units outside of the Second Ward to black persons. This in turn exacerbated overcrowding and housing inequities. Just as important, whites turned a blind eye to the forces that produced residential segregation. They "naturalized" the racial discrepancies in the housing

---

[14] George Nesbitt to Dan Hummell, August 31, 1967, Box 342, Folder HAA Low Rent Public Housing, 1968, Md-Mn, Department of Housing and Urban Development Papers, Record Group 207, National Archives, College Park, MD.

[15] For a trenchant study of the development of a racially segregated housing market in a single community and its disparate impact on blacks and whites, see Nathan Connolly, *A World More Concrete: Real Estate and the Remaking of Jim Crow South Florida* (Chicago: University of Chicago Press, 2014); Douglass S. Massey and Nancy Denton, *American Apartheid: Segregation and the Making of the Underclass* (Cambridge, MA: Harvard University Press, 1993); see also Dalton Conley, *Being Black, Living in the Red: Race Wealth and Social Policy in America*, 10th Anniversary edition (Berkeley: University of California Press, 2009).

market by contending that blacks were free to move out of the Second Ward and/or by claiming that market forces accounted for these differences. At the same time, they overlooked federal housing policies which made it easier for whites to obtain home loans, such as the redlining of black communities by the Federal Housing Authority. Robert Brooks, a black World War II veteran, for instance, recalled that he had difficulty getting GI loans to purchase a home in Cambridge, when "I knew white vets were building homes with nothing down" – he knew this, he added, because he helped build their homes. Paradoxically, conservatives, such as Mayor Osvrey Pritchett, opposed public housing on the grounds that the federal government should not interfere in the housing market. Instead, Pritchett and the DBCA proposed a plan that would allow blacks to earn sweat equity in their homes, which, it went without saying, were to be built in the Second Ward. At the same time, neither Pritchett nor the DBCA saw anything wrong or inconsistent with federal programs that guaranteed the loans of white home owners or that paid for expanded sewers and roads to white neighborhoods, not to mention the tax benefits from which whites disproportionally benefited.[16]

This form of affirmative action for whites, to borrow Ira Katznelson's terminology, similarly played itself out in the realm of public education. Following the "Brown riot," Police Chief Kinnamon would testify that Cambridge had the best schools in the state. Yet Kinnamon's braggadocio ignored long-standing racial disparities in education in Cambridge, not to mention persistent demands by local civil rights forces, including the moderate NAACP, for Dorchester County to jettison its "freedom of choice" plan in favor of one that would achieve the rapid and full integration of the system. Such a plan would entail drawing school district lines based on geography, not race, and would compel white students to attend historically black schools, rather than simply allowing black

---

[16] George Nesbitt to Stanly Newman, "Cambridge Maryland Complaints – Review of Regional Office Findings – Final Report," September 7, 1967, HUD Papers, Box 342. For a listing of some of the largest landlords, see Cambridge Black Action Federation to City Engineer, n.d. For an analysis of racial housing discrepancies in Cambridge, see "Social-Economic Profile of Cambridge, Maryland," October 19, 1967, in *Kerner Commission Records*, reel 27; Interview with S. Edward Smith and Albert Atkinson (Executive and Program Directors of Maryland Office of Economic Opportunity) by Katherine Shannon, 8 September 1967, Civil Rights Documentation Center, Howard University, Washington, DC; Dan Rummell to Spiro T. Agnew, 31 October, 1967, Governor Spiro T. Agnew Papers, MSA, Annapolis, Maryland, Box 14. "Reflections on 1967 ... 1992 ... and into the Future," *CDB*, July 24, 1992, pp. 1, 16.

students to apply for admittance to historically white ones. Full integration, moreover, would entail employing more black teachers in "white" schools, including in supervisorial positions. Finally, full and real integration would demand a cultural shift in the mindset of white teachers and administrators, who routinely mistreated and/or denigrated black students.[17]

Outside evaluators affirmed that segregated education meant unequal education. Black schools, in particular, were overcrowded, with "over 90 children in some classrooms," according to one federal report. Likewise, teacher turnover was exceptionally high and only a small percentage of black graduates qualified for college or for "responsible jobs in industry." In contrast, the report continued, white schools sent a large percentage of their graduates to institutions of higher education. A separate investigation affirmed that black teachers feared "speaking out" because of threats made to them by Superintendent James Busick.[18]

In spite of, or perhaps because of, these inequities, Busick adamantly defended the "freedom of choice" plan that Dorchester County had implemented in the wake of *Brown v. Board of Education*. In 1964, he testified that "not a single [black] parent had expressed any disapproval of the County's plan." In response to a 1965 US Commission on Civil Rights study, which found "only marginal progress had been made to desegregate" the county's schools, Busick insisted that he "would go to court before [he] would be compelled to assign students to a particular school by geographic zoning." Two years later, Busick again rejected a county planning commission's recommendation "to create new school districts or to utilize busing to enhance desegregation." Busick also denied charges that more black families did not apply to attend white schools because they feared economic reprisals for doing so.[19]

Throughout, Busick not only enjoyed the strong support of working-class and poor white people, he garnered the backing of Cambridge's self-professed moderate white elites who claimed they favored school

---

[17] On the beating of Fletcher, see John Batiste, "Cambridge, Maryland," SNCC Papers, Box 52.

[18] "Reconnaissance Survey"; US Commission on Civil Rights, "School Desegregation in Dorchester County, Maryland: A Staff Report," September 1977; John Batiste, "Cambridge, Maryland," n.d., SNCC Papers, Box 52.

[19] US Commission on Civil Rights, "School Desegregation in Dorchester County"; "Freedom of Choice School Plan Hit," *CDB*, February 21, 1966. Matthew Delmont, *Why Busing Failed: Race, Media, and the National Resistance to School Desegregation* (Berkeley: University of California Press, 2015).

desegregation. In the fall of 1966, the *Daily Banner* emphasized that "desegregation is proceeding at a steady pace." Perhaps the pace wasn't "swift enough to satisfy metropolitan newspaper editors," the *Banner's* editors declared but the community was moving fast enough to win the approval of the US Office of Education. As the 1966–1967 school year came to an end, the paper reiterated that federal officials were "pleased" with the progress of the state's school system. In making this claim, the paper downplayed the federal government's citation of nearby Somerset County's for refusing to budge from its freedom of choice plan and its praise of neighboring Talbot County's for its decision to jettison its own.[20] By reporting on the school situation in this way, the editors of the newspaper along with political leaders who allied with Busick, including Malkus, Pritchett, and the county commissioners, demonstrated that in education as with housing they were complicit in a system that perpetuated white privilege. Merely by using the phrase, freedom of choice, the newspaper clothed the county's policy in language that made it seem that the whites supported freedom, while averting claims that the system perpetuated inequality. Cambridge's whites received additional cover from Helen Waters, the lone black representative on the school board, who openly and adamantly supported the freedom of choice plan.[21]

Unequal education overlapped with and reinforced a third pillar of the system of racial inequality, a racially based labor market. Put somewhat simply, whites got better paying, more secure, and safer jobs because of a variety of factors, ranging from outright discrimination to the more subtle segmentation of the labor market along racial and gender lines. For instance, 80 percent of all workers at Coastal Foods, where work was seasonal and poorly paid, were black. In contrast, 99 percent of all employees at Air Pax Electronics and Cambridge Wire and Cloth, both of which offered better paying and steadier jobs, were white. Poor employment opportunities, in turn, produced vast income disparities. In 1960, median family income for black men and women in Cambridge stood at

[20] "Church Creek Has Only One Room School In Dorchester County," *CDB*, September 1, 1966. "Report from the Schools," *CDB*, September 10, 1966; "Dorchester County to Maintain Freedom of Choice Plan" *CDB*, March 16, 1967; "Editorials: Freedom of Choice," *CDB*, April 1, 1967; "Officials Pleased with State's School Desegregation Progress," *CDB*, April 15, 1967, p. 1. For an example of black efforts to desegregate schools, see CNAC, "Field Report," April 26, 1965, SNCC Papers, Box 52.
[21] Research to Stephen Kurzman, October 30, 1967 and Research to Stephen Kurzman, November 2, 1967, Patricia Bennett, Memo, November 29, 1967, all in *Kerner Commission Records*, reel 12; Levy, *Civil War on Race Street*, pp. 126–132. "Employment in the Cambridge, Maryland Area," June 18, 1963, Burke Marshall Papers, reel 26.

$2,450, less than one-half of white median income. Ten years later, this gap had not closed.[22]

One way black workers sought to overcome these inequities was by organizing unions. Yet here too they faced major obstacles to obtaining equal economic opportunities. Beginning in late 1962, the United Packinghouse Workers of America (UPWA), one of the most racially progressive unions in the nation, initiated a formal organizing drive in Cambridge. To enhance its appeal, it openly identified with the civil rights movement, something many unions did not do – for instance, the AFL-CIO refused to endorse the March on Washington. UPWA organizers spoke at CNAC's mass meetings, members of both organizations joined hands at the March on Washington in August 1963, and the union honored Richardson at its twentieth anniversary convention in New York City. While this strategy paid off with a series of victories at Coastal Foods, Maryland Tuna (Bumble Bee), and Chung King, it could not overcome the segmentation of the labor market along racial lines. These plants employed few whites and white business leaders were able to make the case to their white workers in their places of employment that unionization would jeopardize the city's economic recovery. In turn, white workers at Airpax and Cambridge Wire and Cloth voted against recognizing the United Automobile Workers and Steelworkers Unions, respectively. In other words, the cross-caste alliance, which briefly appeared during the strike against the Phillips Packing Company in 1937, did not re-emerge in the 1960s.[23]

Moreover, at the one worksite where white workers were unionized, the docks, the union conspired with their employers to keep out black workers. A bit more specifically, Cambridge's shipping companies negotiated a deal with the segregated and all-white local Longshoremen's Union that granted the union control over hiring. In turn, the Longshoremen

[22] Research to Stephen Kurzman, October 30, 1967 and Research to Stephen Kurzman, November 2, 1967, Patricia Bennett, Memo, November 29, 1967, all in *Kerner Commission Records*, reel 12; "Employment in the Cambridge, Maryland Area," June 18, 1963, Burke Marshall Papers, reel 26.

[23] Levy, *Civil War on Race Street*, pp. 127–130; "Coastal Foods Co. Campaign," n.d. folder 2, box 178, United Packinghouse Workers of America (UPWA) Papers, Wisconsin Historical Society, Madison, WI; "How the Union Came to Town in Troubled Cambridge, Maryland," *Packinghouse Worker*, May 1964; "District 6 Cheers 20th Birthday," *Packinghouse Worker*, April 1964; "The View from the Eastern Shore," *Packinghouse Worker*, June 1963; "Choice is Made, Wire Cloth Rejects Union," and "Airpax Votes Against Union," *CDB*, November 27, 1967; "UAW is Rejected Again at Airpax," *Baltimore Sun*, July 26, 1968, p. C8.

restricted work to union members, who, not so coincidentally, were all white. For civil rights activists, this deal proved that white employers and white employees colluded to limit the opportunities available to black workers, a point they made in a complaint filed with the National Labor Relations Board (NLRB). After a series of hearings, the NLRB ruled in favor of the plaintiffs. But the process of having to win access to union jobs, like the process of winning access to the RFC's pool, confirmed the white community's commitment to maintaining the racial status quo. Or as one federal investigator put it: "unadulterated, widespread, and deep-seated racial prejudice overwhelms every positive feature that might have been expected to bring improvements."[24]

"What Kind of ... [System] ... Have We Got – an Equal Right and Just One, or Just [a] White One?"

During this same time period, white authorities also sought to prevent the civil rights movement from enjoying a resurgence by punishing and/or coopting civil rights activists. For instance, local authorities threatened to stop the distribution of surplus food to many of Dorchester County's rural poor who were disproportionately black, if CNAC did not stop agitating on welfare issues. As SNCC field worker, John Batiste, explained, poor rural blacks, many of whom did not own cars, had to travel "up to 35 miles one way ... on a particular day of the week" simply to certify their eligibility for surplus food programs. "The cost of traveling this distance," Batiste added, "often exceeds the worth of commodities." Local authorities refused to alter this process not to save money or because they ideologically opposed distributing surplus food but rather as a backhanded way of punishing the CNAC.[25] Simultaneously, local authorities sought to detour activists away from direct action protests toward more mundane and bureaucratic tasks. As noted above, Steve Fraser arrived in Cambridge in 1965 expecting a hotbed of radicalism but instead found CNAC and SNCC field representatives preoccupied with the bureaucratic work of

---

[24] Research to Stephen Kurzman, October 30, 1967 and Research to Stephen Kurzman, November 2, 1967, both in *Kerner Commission Records*, reel 16; Levy, *Civil War on Race Street*, pp. 130–133; "Cargo Handlers, Inc. and Ronald Sampson, " in *NLRB Decisions and Orders*, vol. 159.

[25] John Batiste, "Cambridge, Maryland," n.d.; Mary Potorti, "'What We Eat Is Politics': SNCC, Hunger, and Voting Rights in Mississippi" (unpublished manuscript in author's possession).

applying for federal grants. Successful applications allowed for the establishment of a Head Start and jobs training programs which benefited a sizable number of black youths – the former, for instance, enrolled 218 children, 204 of whom were black, in its first year (1965–1966). Yet uncertainty over continual funding, exacerbated by the competing demands of the Vietnam War, as well as white control over the purse strings of these programs, fueled growing demands for greater black political power, locally and nationally.[26]

As suggested above, from the arrival of the first freedom riders, whites contended that electoral politics demonstrated Cambridge's progressive racial record. For instance, they touted Charles Cornish's position on the city council as proof that black citizens in Cambridge were treated equally. Yet, white support for George Wallace and Osvrey Pritchett and subsequently George Mahoney, whose 1966 gubernatorial campaign centered around a blatant defense of residential segregation – revealed a pattern of governance which placed white racial identity above all other concerns. So too did Dorchester County's repeated support of Frederick Malkus. Initially elected in 1950 as an upstart or insurgent against the powerful Winterbottom machine, which was aligned with the Phillips Packing Company, Malkus quickly became one of the most vociferous opponents of racial desegregation in the state, blocking efforts to desegregate schools, public accommodations, and housing, and forging, instead, ties with George Wallace, the national symbol of white supremacy. While race was not Malkus's only issue – in an era when rural counties were losing political power he fought hard to preserve it – it was central to his appeal and voters demonstrated their support for his racial views by re-electing him to office time and time again. (Malkus represented the citizens of Dorchester County in the state legislature for 48 years. Today, the bridge on the main highway which leads into Cambridge bears Malkus's name.)[27]

---

[26] Interview with Steve Fraser; Interview with Albert B. Atkinson.
[27] Democratic Gubernatorial Results," *CDB*, September 15, 1966; "Republican Agnew Defeats Mahoney; Countians Give Democrats Majority," *CDB*, November 9, 1966; "Mahoney Gets Friendly Welcome on Shore," *CDB*, October 25, 1966; "Sen. Malkus Continues Battle Against Racial Legislation," *CDB*, March 2, 1967. Interview with Frederick Malkus; *CDB*, January 24, and February 1 and 2, 1961; "Gov. Wallace Gets Punched Flush on Chin," *Afro-American* (Baltimore, MD), September 21, 1963, p. 1; "Malkus Accepts N.A.A.C.P. Attack," *Baltimore Sun*, July 22, 1963; "Malkus Assails Racial Probers," *Baltimore Sun*, February 25, 1966; "Unofficial Dorchester Vote," *CDB*, November 9, 1966. "Frederick Malkus Jr., 86, Legislator Who Served in Assembly for 48 Years," *Baltimore Sun*, November 11, 1999.

Whites also demonstrated that race came first when it came to casting their votes by refusing to support black candidates. In 1966, for instance, Josiah Cephas, who had helped organize an interracial union of food processing workers, ran in the Republican primary for a seat on the Dorchester County Commission. In a field of six, he came in dead last, with only 14 percent of the vote, even though he won the overwhelming majority of the vote of Cambridge's Second Ward. Nor did even the most enlightened whites broach the inequity of the ward system in Cambridge which trapped black citizens in a permanently inferior position. Though black residents comprised about one-third of the population, since virtually all blacks lived in one ward, the best they could count on was to win one-fifth of the town council's seats. Rather than recognize the racist bias of this system of representation (recall that this was an era in which the courts were demanding redistricting of state legislatures based upon population rather than geography), most whites touted Cambridge's progressive record of having a black town council member at a time when black people were denied the right to vote through much of the nation.[28]

Looking at over twenty-five years of voting records in the region, Maryland Attorney General Stephan Sachs would conclude in a 1985 report that "white voters of Dorchester County [had] consistently not voted for black candidates, though black voters [had] demonstrated their willingness to support white candidates in black–white contests." In turn, this had an impact on who got appointed to government positions, on the ability of the RFC to persist as an all-white and all-volunteer force, and on the services that the black community received.[29]

It is important to note that Cambridge's black people shared much in common with their counterparts in places across the nation, from New York City and Chicago, home to two of the largest black populations in the nation. In New York and Chicago, as in Cambridge, black men and women voted and enjoyed representation in city councils. Yet, this did not translate into equal representation or political power. For example, in Chicago, as a number of scholars have shown, the Daley machine, with the support of key black patrons, continued to privilege white constituents in terms of city services, jobs, and housing. Put somewhat differently, for many at the time, securing voting rights represented the finish line of the

[28] Interview with Gloria Richardson, by author.
[29] Stephan A. Sachs, "At Large Election of County Commission: An Audit Conducted by the Office of the Attorney General," July 18, 1985 (Baltimore, MD: Office of the Attorney General, 1985).

movement. Upon signing the bill, President Johnson declared "we strike away the last major shackle" and the *Washington Post* termed the securing of the vote "the capstone" of the movement. Subsequent elections which saw black voter participation skyrocket and the election of literally thousands of blacks top public office, ranging from congressional seats in the states of the old confederacy to mayoral posts in major American cities, tended to reaffirm this view. Yet, Cambridge's history provided a cautionary tale in these regards. It was not by accident that Richardson called for black citizens to boycott the special referendum vote on the local public accommodations measure in 1963. As she observed, Cambridge's blacks had enjoyed the franchise for nearly a century. Yet, history had shown that they had proven unable to use their vote to attain racial equality.[30]

Finally, persistent disparities in the criminal justice system, which whites displayed little if any interest in changing, undermined claims that Cambridge was making progress. "In so far as the Negro Second Ward is concerned," one Kerner Commission investigator subsequently reported, "the sole objective of police activity is to hunt, detain, and assist in the prosecution of persons in criminal pursuits." The Police Department conducted no forms of community outreach, such as police athletic leagues. Many Second Ward residents viewed the town's black policemen as corrupt and most of the white policemen were poorly trained and uneducated. Furthermore, the state's attorney, William Yates, who was swept into office in 1964 as part of the DBCA slate, "behaved repeatedly in ways inimical to the ... interests of the Negro community," rather than as an impartial arbitrator of justice.[31] A case in point was the disparate treatment Yates meted out to black and white defendants during the spring of 1967. In one instance, two black youths, who were arrested for "sneering at a police officer," were fined between $50 and $100 and sentenced to sixty to hundred days in prison. In a separate case, two white youths, who were charged with siccing their dog on a black youth, received only a 30 day suspended sentence. Judge Robert Farnell, who presided over both cases, justified the first sentence on the grounds that, "As long as I

---

[30] President Lyndon B. Johnson, "Remarks in the Capitol Rotunda at the Signing of the Voting Rights Act, August 6, 1965," Public Papers of the Presidents, www.presidency.ucsb .edu/ws/index.php?pid=27140&st=&st1= [accessed June 3, 2015]. "The Capstone," *Washington Post*, August 6, 1965, p. A16; Gloria Richardson, "Press Release," n.d. in The Papers of Burke Marshall, reel 26; "Reflections on 1967 ... 1992 and into the Future" *CDB*, July 24, 1992, pp. 1, 16; Lani Guinier, *Tyranny of the Majority: Fundamental Fairness in Representative Democracy* (New York: Free Press, 1994).

[31] "Reconnaissance Survey."

am magistrate there is going to be respect for the law and order," even if
he had to fill up the jails. In contrast, he explained his light sentence for
Nicky Parks, the white youth convicted of assault, on the grounds that
Parks's decision to bring the dog was "highly understandable," a position
he did not feel a need to elaborate on since he assumed that others agreed
with the assumption that black males were innately dangerous and whites
had the right to defend themselves from them with deadly force.[32]

The criminal justice system's treatment of Dwight Cromwell, another
black resident, further angered the black community. In 1963, Cromwell
had been sentenced to a juvenile facility for an indefinite term for protesting nonviolently outside a segregated establishment. Four years later, following the outbreak of a series of small fires at white establishments in
the Second Ward and at the Pine Street Elementary School, all deemed
arson by the state Fire Marshall, Cromwell was arrested again, this time
on charges of turning in a false fire alarm. From the moment that police
placed him into custody to his sentencing by Judge Burnam Mace, authorities made clear that they sought to make an example of him so as to suppress the re-energized civil rights movement, of which Cromwell played
a leading part. Whereas Parks's bond on assault charge had been set at
$100, the court set Cromwell's bail at $5,000. When Juanita Mitchell
of Baltimore's NAACP tried to intervene, imploring Yates to release
Cromwell on his own recognizance, Yates replied that he would display
no leniency to those associated with the recent spate of fires. In reaction,
George Jones, father of Nicky Jones, the black youth mauled by Parks's
dog, wondered: "What kind of public defender [state's attorney] have
we got – an equal right and just one, or just [a] white one?" Much of
the black community felt exactly the same.[33] At the trial, the state's witnesses, all city employees, argued that the police had spotted Cromwell at
a telephone booth, where, according to the town's dispatcher, calls reporting the outbreak of a fire had originated. Cromwell's counsel countered

[32] "Teens Sentenced, Fined," CDB, April 4, 1967; Youth Found Guilty, CDB, June 23, 1967;
Mr. and Mrs. George Jones, "Letter to the Editor," CDB, June 6, 1967; Muriel Twilley,
"Letter to the Editor," CDB, June 19, 1967. For a discussion of the ways blacks had
been criminalized in the white mind, see Khalil Gibran Muhammad, *The Condemnation
of Blackness: Race, Crime, and the Making of Modern America* (Cambridge: Harvard
University Press, 2010).

[33] "Youth Found Guilty," CDB, June 23, 1967; Letters to the Editor, CDB, July 3 and July
26 1967; "Analysis of Cambridge"; "Fire Marshall Investigating Fires Here," CDB, June
27, 1968; "Arson Cause of Fire," June 28, 1969, CDB, "Arrested For Turning In False
Alarm," CDB, June 29, 1968; "$500 Offered For Arson Clues," *Baltimore Sun*, July 6,
1967, p. C6.

that there was no direct evidence that Cromwell had placed a call. He also summoned a set of witnesses, including Betty Jews, a member of CNAC, who testified that Cromwell was with her at the time of the alleged calls. The jury found Yates's witnesses and argument more convincing and Judge Burnham subsequently fined Cromwell $250 and sentenced him to one year in prison.[34]

One reason both the Parks/Jones and Cromwell cases inflamed the African American community was because they were seen as part of a long history of a dual or unfair system of justice. Arguably, the most egregious instances of this dual system involved sexual abuse or alleged sexual abuse. Historically, authorities had provided little if any protection to black women from the advances of white men. At the same time, black men were routinely lynched and/or sentenced to death for allegedly raping white women, even when the evidence against them was flimsy a best. In a comprehensive study of the imposition of the death penalty from 1945 to 1965, Marvin Wolfgang and Marc Riedel found that out of a total of 3,000 rape convictions in eleven states not a single death penalty was issued for the rape of a black woman by a white man and that black men were much, much more likely to be sentenced to death for the rape of white women than if a white man committed the same crime. Dorchester County's arrest records fit this pattern. Most infamously, in the fall of 1963 Arthur Moore, a white man accused of molesting an eight-year-old black girl in the Second Ward, was deemed not guilty by the courts. During the trial, the girl testified that Moore gave her some pennies and then "ran his hand across the front of her blouse and inside." Louis Gilbert, a black resident of the Second Ward, corroborated the young girl's story, declaring he witnessed Moore "molesting the child." Nonetheless, the all-white jury believed Moore's claim that he had done nothing wrong. In response to this verdict, an incensed Gloria Richardson lambasted the jury for ignoring eyewitness testimony. She also called for a total economic boycott of white merchants on the grounds that the "bigotry of the white citizens of Cambridge has now infected our judicial system" as well as the executive and legislative branch of the city. Illustrative of the white community's double standard, the *Daily Banner* gave just as much coverage to William Hansen's marriage to a black woman in Pine Bluff, Arkansas, as it did to Moore's acquittal. Hansen, the paper reminded its readers, had instigated the freedom rides in January 1962 and his marriage to a black woman

---

34 *State of Maryland v. Dwight Cromwell*, Case File 2145, Dorchester County Circuit Court, MSA.

violated Arkansas' anti-miscegenation laws. A less biased report would have emphasized the unjustness of Arkansas' laws and jury's verdict in the Moore case.[35]

At the time, Richardson did not contrast the justice system's treatment of Moore to that of similarly accused black men but she easily could have. At high noon on June 27, 1947, William Cooper, a twenty-year-old black World War II veteran, was hung for the rape of a young nurse at the Easton Hospital, in nearby Talbot County. Two years later, James Williams, a black man escaped a similar fate only by pleading guilty in the midst of his trial for allegedly raping a white woman, in spite of the fact that he had denied the charges from the get go. He did so, his attorney Calvin Harrington suggested, so as to avoid the death penalty and a white mob which has threatened to lynch him upon his arrest in Cambridge. (Williams unsuccessfully appealed his conviction for over fifteen years.) Numerous other black men were arrested and convicted of raping white women on the Eastern Shore over the next fifteen years, though no white men were convicted of committing sexual crimes against any black women. In one of the more noteworthy cases, in 1966, Winfield Scott Waters, an eighty-one-year-old black man, was arrested for trying to rape a fifty-six-year-old white woman during an alleged burglary of her home in nearby Somerset County. Even though he insisted that he had never seen his accuser or been to her home, and presented an alibi witness, he was convicted by Judge William Travers (he waved his right to a jury trial) who termed Waters "little better than an animal." Only because the state's attorney recommended a life sentence, did the judge

[35] "CNAC Chief Calls for Boycott: Integrationist Is Unhappy with Jury Decision," *CDB*, November 8, 1963, p. 1; "White SNCC Leader Weds Negro Girl," *CDB*, November 11, 1963, p. 1; "Cambridge Police Probe Rape Charge," *The Daily Times* (Salisbury, MD), December 27, 1956, p. 2; "Fish Peddler Held for Rape of Colored Girl," *New Journal and Guide*, August 6, 1949, p. A2; "Shore Trial Is Assailed," *Baltimore Sun*, November 8, 1963, p. 11; "Man Acquitted on Assault on Negro Girl," *Washington Post*, November 8, 1963, p. A3; Marvin E. Wolfgang and Marc Riedel, "Judicial Discretion and the Death Penalty," *The Annals of the American Academy of Political and Social Science*, 407 (May, 1973): 119–133; Barrett Foerster and Michael Meltsner, *Race, Rape and Injustice* (Knoxville: University of Tennessee Press, 2012); Daniel McGuire, *At the Dark End of the Street: Black Women, Rape, and Resistance – A New History of the Civil Rights Movement from Rosa Parks to the Rise of Black Power* (New York: Alfred Knopf, 2010); Dorchester County, Circuit Court, Criminal Docket Index, 1949–1993, MSA, http://guide.msa.maryland.gov/pages/series.aspx?id=CE206 [accessed February 16, 2017]; Dorchester County Circuit Court, Criminal Docket, 1949–2000, MSA, digital copy at http://guide.msa.maryland.gov/pages/item.aspx?ID=CE201-3 [accessed February 28, 2017]; *State of Maryland v. Jerry Moore*, Dorchester County Circuit Court, Case File 1643, MSA.

not hand down a death sentence. When Waters's attorney's appeal to the Maryland Court of Appeal failed, Waters, with the help of the American Civil Liberties Union's (ACLU) William Zinman, filed a writ of habeas corpus petition in federal court and won a reversal of the original conviction. In issuing the federal court's ruling, Judge Alexander Harvey II ruled that there was "no evidence that the gaunt, stoop-shouldered defendant *could have* [emphasis added] attempted sexual assault." This said, Judge Harvey did not go so far as to echo Zinman's claim that the "bigotry and prejudice of the courts" accounted for Waters's conviction in the first place nor his declaration that "on the Eastern Shore... there are two standards of justice," one "for whites... and the rich" and the other for "blacks and the poor."[36]

"Gloria Richardson is Back and She is Going to Tear This Town Down!"

Yates's determination to make an example out of Cromwell suggested that Cambridge's white elites feared a renewed uprising, public proclamations that the city was making racial progress notwithstanding. While Cromwell had not set any fires, others had, and these fires, coupled with the revolts that had erupted across the nation, heightened white anxieties. Among the buildings set afire prior to Cromwell's arrest was the Pine Street Elementary School. The building was an old wood-framed structure and thus "very vulnerable, a tinder box," explained the school superintendent, James Busick. Ironically, this was exactly the point black activists had been making for years while pushing unsuccessfully for its replacement and/or a jettisoning of the freedom of choice plan. One of the other buildings that was intentionally torched was the While Owl Inn, one of the initial sites of sit-ins staged by CNAC. Still another was the headquarters of County Commissioner E. Roscoe Wiley's trucking firm, long-rumored to be one of the owners of many of the most decrepit homes in the Second Ward. In addition to these fires, Cambridge's officials were

---

[36] "Man Hanged for Rape on Md. Eastern Shore," *Washington Post*, June 28, 1947, p. B2; "Angry Crowd Causes Shift of Prisoner," *Philadelphia Tribune*, November 18, 1952, p. 1; "Shore Man Held on Rape Charge," *Baltimore Sun*, July 16, 1951, p. 26; "Fowler Gets Venue Shift," *Baltimore Sun*, August 18, 1967, p. C6; "Change of Venue Asked in Slaying," *The Daily Times*, September 11, 1964, p. 1; "Judge Frees Man Too Old For Sex Crime," *Afro-American*, April 17, 1971, p. 1; "Man Freed in Rape After 4 Years," *Washington Post*, April 8, 1971, p. A3; "Federal Court Voice Octogenarian's Life Sentence in Shore Rape Case," *Baltimore Sun*, January 23, 1971, p. A11.

alarmed by Gloria Richardson's announcement that she intended to pay Cambridge an extended visit because "the white power structure" had failed to help Cambridge's black community since 1963. Upon hearing of her decision, Dwight Cromwell exclaimed, "Gloria Richardson is back and she is going to tear this town down!" Indeed, Cromwell had spent some time with Richardson on the night of the alleged false alarms and she had gone down to the police station to protest his arrest on that same night.[37]

Concomitantly, Juanita Jackson Mitchell helped reactivate the local branch of the NAACP. Among those to join the chapter were Dr. J. Edwin Fassett, long a supporter of CNAC, and Rosalie Fletcher, a recent graduate of Morgan State University, whose family had also been involved in the movement throughout the decade.[38] Of even greater concern to Cambridge's white elites was the formation of a new organization, the Black Action Federation (BAF). Headed by Lemuel Chester and Elaine Adams and heavily influenced by the Black Power movement, the BAF got Richardson to agree to bring a leading black militant, such as Stokely Carmichael or H. Rap Brown, to speak in Cambridge, to help them expand their organization. In the weeks leading up to this event, BAF members kept abreast of developments at the second annual Black Power conference in Newark, New Jersey. Held in the immediate wake of Newark's revolt, this gathering caused great consternation among many whites (and black moderates) across the nation. But for many black people, including members of BAF, its discussion of black self-governance, economic empowerment, armed self-defense, and black pride, proved invigorating. Partly inspired by this meeting and by the rebellions, nationwide, BAF activist Kenneth Brown (no relation to H. Rap Brown) warned that blacks in Cambridge were "fired up" and that black youths in Cambridge, in particular, "would rather die here in Cambridge fighting for their human dignity and their human rights than go to the rice paddies of

[37] "Quiet Settle On Tense City of Cambridge," *Washington Post*, June 30, 1967, p. B2; "Cambridge Police Patrol Negro Area," *Washington Post*, June 29, 1967, p. B1; "Reward Set for Arsonist in Cambridge," *Washington Post*, July 6, 1967, p. B7; "Explosives Sets Cambridge Fire," *Baltimore Sun*, July 5, 1967, p. C7; "Two Blazes in Cambridge Called Arson," *Baltimore Sun*, July 24, 1967, p. C18; "Arson Termed Cause of Fire At School," *CDB*, July 24, 1967, p. 1; *State of Maryland v. Dwight Cromwell*.

[38] "Cambridge Police Patrol Negro Area," *Washington Post*, June 29, 1967, p. B1; "N.A.A.C.P. Is Reactivated in Cambridge," *Washington Post*, June 21, 1967, p. A8; Interview with Gloria Richardson by John Britton; Wayne Page, "H. Rap Brown and the Cambridge Incident: A Cast Study," MA Thesis, University of Maryland, College Park, 1970.

Vietnam" to fight for freedom half way across the world. BAF leaders also endorsed a resolution issued by the first national Black Power conference that black citizens had "the right to revolt when they deem it necessary."[39]

Simultaneously, a segment of the white population demonstrated that it had no intention of meeting the re-energized local movement's demands. On the contrary, hoping to capitalize on growing white fears, the National States Rights Party (NSP), which the FBI acknowledged had a "long record of hatemongering" and ties to the Ku Klux Klan (KKK) and American Nazi Party, announced it would hold a white power rally in Cambridge on the night of July 16, 1967. At the rally, the NSP's leader, Joe Carroll, who had gained national fame a year earlier when he orchestrated a white power rally in Baltimore, delivered a virulent address. While no transcript of this specific speech exists, there is good reason to believe it closely resembled the one that Carroll had delivered in nearby Princess Anne, Maryland, the previous summer where he had called for whites "to oppose black terror, the Communist conspiracy in the United States, unconstitutional injunctions against good white people, [and the] mongrelization of the races." Carroll added that whites had "taken enough of the 'niggers' and enough of 'Martin Lucifer Coon'" and he "urged white people to get their gun[s]" and to defend their communities, with force if necessary.[40]

In spite of a steady rain, approximately 150 whites gathered to hear Carroll's July 16 speech. Nearby, members of the BAF held a counter-rally. Before the two groups could square off, however, Cambridge's chief of police, Brice Kinnamon, escorted Carroll away. While Kinnamon informed reporters that he had arrested Carroll for "attempting

---

[39] "Letters to the Editor," *CDB*, June 26, 1967; "Tensions Remain in Cambridge," *Baltimore Sun*, July 26, 1992, p. 1C; Interview of Lemuel Chester, Cambridge, Maryland, by Sandra Harney, August 27, 1997 (in author's possession); Kenneth Brown quoted in Page, "H. Rap Brown," *Time*, August 4, 1967, p. 10; Peniel E. Joseph, *Waiting 'Til the Midnight Hour: A Narrative History of Black Power in America* (New York: Owl Books, 2006), pp. 186–187.

[40] Federal Bureau of Investigation, "White Extremist Organizations: Part II: National States Rights Party," May 1970, in FBI's "The Vault," https://vault.fbi.gov/National%20States%20Rights%20Party/National%20States%20Rights%20Party%20Part%201%20of%201%20/view [accessed November 2, 2015]. For a sense of the NSP's views, see *Carroll v. President and Commissioners of Princess Anne*, 247 Md 126 (1967) 230 A.2d 452 www.leagle.com/decision/1967373247Md126_1357/CARROLL%20v.%20PRESIDENT%20AND%20COMMISSIONERS%20OF%20PRINCESS%20ANNE [accessed November 2, 2015]; See also SAC, Baltimore to FBI, Director, Possible Racial Violence in Major Urban Areas, June 20, 1967.

to incite a riot," in fact, Carroll emerged from police headquarters fifteen minutes later. As one *Baltimore Sun* reporter observed, a "smiling" Carroll declared "They didn't arrest me: I was taken into protective custody." State Attorney William Yates confirmed that Carroll had been ushered away for his "own protection." As we shall see, local authorities responded quite differently to Brown's appearance just over a week later.[41]

At the same time, national events intertwined with local ones to heighten white anxieties. By mid-July, long past Richardson's announcement that she intended to return to Cambridge, at least a half-dozen other cities had experienced revolts, including Newark and Detroit. Headlines in local papers reflected the confluence of national and local developments. On July 14, for instance, the *Salisbury Daily Times* highlighted "Race Riots" "searing Newark," and Maryland Attorney General Francis Burch's determination to keep "watch" over a rally and possible counter-rally planned by the National States Rights Party and the Black Action Federation in Cambridge. Ten days later, the Cambridge *Daily Banner* coupled banner headlines on Detroit's "Race Riot" with a front page story on the most recent incident of arson at the Pine Street Elementary School. Unbeknownst to most of the *Banner*'s readers, the BAF had also sent a letter to the editor of the local newspaper warning that Cambridge had reached the point of ignition. "You are so right when you say that Cambridge is no longer a sleepy fishing village," the letter warned. "The black people has woke up and we intend to stay awoke [*sic*]."[42]

"Don't Tear up Your Brother's Stuff, Hear?"

H. Rap Brown arrived in Cambridge about 8:45 p.m. on July 24, over an hour late, having missed his bus connection in Washington, DC. Although

[41] On the National States' Right Rally, see Spiro Agnew to William Yates, July 12, 1967, Governor Agnew Papers, S1041–1713, Box 14; Kenneth Brown quoted in Page, "H. Rap Brown," *Time*, August 4, 1967, p. 10; "Rights Rally Is Broken Up," *CDB*, July 17, 1967; "Loud Speaking Equipment Is Denied Segregationist," *CDB*, July 25, 1967; "Racist Silenced to Avoid Trouble," *Baltimore Sun*, July 16, 1967, p. 24. Patrick C. Kennicott and Wayne E. Page, "H. Rap Brown: The Cambridge Incident," *Quarterly Journal of Speech*, 57:3 (October 1971), pp. 325–334.
[42] For the dates and "casualties" of these revolts, see US Senate, Committee on Government Operations, *Hearings: Riots, Civil and Criminal Disorders*, pp. 2762–2777; "7,000 Guardsmen Quell Race Riot in Detroit," *CDB*, July 24, 1967, p. 1; "Arson Termed Cause of Fire at School," *CDB*, July 24, 1967, p. 1; "Letter to the Editor," *CDB*, July 26, 1967; "Race Riots Sear Newark, N.J.," *The Daily Times*, July 14, 1967, p. 1.

Brown was not a native of Cambridge, he was no stranger to this small city or its struggles for racial equality. Born in Louisiana as Hubert Geroid Brown and introduced into SNCC by his older brother Ed, he had been one of many activists to have participated in demonstrations in Cambridge during the early 1960s. As he recalled in his autobiography, *Die Nigger Die!*, he journeyed to Cambridge in the summer of 1963 along with his SNCC colleagues, Courtland Cox and Cleveland Sellers. Though he and Cox planned to go for only a day, they ended up staying for a week. Brown remembered being impressed by the willingness of local blacks to defend themselves with guns and by Richardson's forthrightness, a view shared by a number of other SNCC activists.[43]

Not long after his initial journey to Cambridge, Brown began to rise in the ranks of SNCC. Time spent in Mississippi as a participant in Freedom Summers and then as a field worker in rural Alabama, allowed him to develop and display his skills as an organizer. Even before joining SNCC, Brown had earned the nicknamed "Rap" because of his knack for speaking quickly and spontaneously. Or as one reporter put it, "Twenty years before rap became a musical phenomenon, Brown was creating and reciting his own raps in a game called the Dozens," a game where, as Brown put it, "'you try to totally destroy somebody else with words.'" While many hoped that Brown would concentrate on "organizing," a goal he endorsed in his first public statements after taking over the leadership of SNCC, it quickly became clear that he would forcefully advocate for "Black Power," which Stokely Carmichael had popularized in 1966. Like Carmichael, Brown believed that the cry for black power better articulated the goals and demands of the black freedom struggle than did the slogan "Freedom Now." For instance, he considered the advocacy of armed self-defense to be intertwined with the goal of attaining self-respect and empowerment.[44]

From atop the hood of a 1955 Buick, located adjacent to the recently burned Pine Street Elementary School and black Elks Lodge, Brown spoke

43 H. Rap Brown, *Die, Nigger, Die* (New York: Dial Press, 1969); Page, "H. Rap Brown"; Sellers, *The River of No Return*, p. 68. Another SNCC activist who was influenced by developments in Cambridge was Stokely Carmichael. See Joseph, *Stokely: A Life*, pp. 53–54, 118.
44 Brown, *Die Nigger Die!*; Clayborne Carson, *In Struggle: SNCC and the Black Awakening* (Cambridge, MA: Harvard University Press, 1981), pp. 252–255; "H. Rap 'The Lamb' Turns Erring Lion," *Afro-American* (Baltimore, MD), 19 August, 1967; John Lewis, "Private Revolution," *Baltimore City Paper*, January 24, 1992, pp. 7–14; Strain, *Pure Fire*, ch. 7.

to a crowd of roughly 350–400, mostly young blacks between the ages of 15 and 30. Brown set the tenor of his address with his opening lines. Echoing the immortal words of the black poet Langston Hughes, he inquired: "What happens to a dream deferred? Does it dry up like a raisin in the sun? ... Or does it explode? Detroit exploded, Newark exploded," Brown exclaimed, in reference to the urban rebellions that had recently taken place in two of the nation's largest cities. "It's time for Cambridge to explode."[45] For nearly an hour Brown lambasted "white honkies," promoted "black power," and admonished "Uncle Toms," such as Cambridge's black policemen who stood on the edge of the crowd. Peppered with calls for blacks to "get some guns" and to control their own communities, Brown's words alternatively aroused the emotions of listeners and mentored them on subjects ranging from the bias of the national media to Vietnam. Regarding the former, Brown derided the media for characterizing the revolts in Newark, Detroit, and elsewhere as riots. "This ain't no riot, brother. This is a rebellion and we got 400 years of reason to tear this town down." In terms of Vietnam, Brown denounced America's involvement, in general, and the impact that the war was having on black Americans, in particular. "We go over to Vietnam and fight the racist cracker war," Brown exclaimed, "We got to be crazy ... Our war is here." In making this argument Brown echoed the sentiments of a growing number of black leaders, from Malcom X, who had been one of the first national figures to publicly denounce the war, to Martin Luther King Jr., who in the spring of 1967 had garnered the wrath of most mainstream liberals, black and white, and President Johnson, for condemning the war and terming America the "greatest purveyor of violence" in the world. Picking up on a point made by King, among others, Brown observed that black soldiers were dying at very high rates in the jungles in Southeast Asia; he also asserted that this demonstrated that the United States had "laid out a plan to eliminate all black people ... just like the Germans did to the Jews." In

---

[45] H. Rap Brown "Address," in "A Collation of Transcripts of a Speech Given by H. Rap Brown on July 24, 1967, Cambridge, Maryland," in *Is Baltimore Burning? Maryland State Archives: Documents for the Classroom*, ed. by Lawrence Peskin and Dawn Almes (Annapolis, MD: MSA), available online at http://msa.maryland.gov/megafile/ msa/speccol/sc2200/sc2221/000012/000008/html/speech1.html [accessed September 9, 2014]. (Henceforth referred to as H. Rap Brown, "Address.") This collation includes an audio excerpt of Brown's speech as well as an interview with the radio newscaster who recorded it. "Shots Fired in Cambridge Second Ward," *Baltimore Sun*, July 25, 1967, p. C20; "S.N.C.C. Chief Shot in Cambridge, Md.," *NYT*, July 25, 1967, p. 1; Gail Dean, "Interpretive Signs Now Tell History of Pine Street," *Dorchester Star*, October 21, 2011.

addition, Brown pointed to the hypocrisy of America, which sent black citizens oversees to fight but then denounced black activists who upheld the right of self-defense at home. "If I can die defending my Motherland, I can die defending my mother."[46]

Once during his address Brown pointed to the Pine Street Elementary School, which showed the scars of previous fires, and declared: "You see that school over there – I don't know whether the honkey burned that school or not but you all should have burned that school a long time ago. You should have burned it down to the ground. Ain't no need in the world, in 1967, to see a school like that sitting over there. You should have burned it down and then go take over the honkey's school." Yet, following this inflammatory remark, Brown turned his attention to the role that black "Uncle Toms" played in maintaining the racial status quo and to a description of the way that whites fooled black people into believing they were making progress.[47] (Adjacent to the intersection where Brown spoke was the all-black Elks Lodge, which had burned to the ground on the eve of his address. Some suggested that black militants had burned the lodge to the ground. But more people believed that white youths had torched the building in retaliation for the firebombing of white-owned businesses in the Second Ward.)

Throughout, observed one radio broadcaster, the crowd was "very attentive," responding to Brown's remarks with cries of "tell it like it is" and "Black Power." Brown's call for blacks to "control our community" and his pronouncement that they could not be accused of being thieves since whites had been stealing "everything from us" for centuries, drew especially favorable reactions. Brown also captured the listeners' attention through the manner in which he spoke. As Wayne Page and Patrick Kennicott observed, Brown's address, which he delivered without notes, "came in sporadic torrents," assuming "the flavor of stream of consciousness more than a formal speech." One listener described Brown's style "as that of a 'zestful minister' who was able to 'reach into the minds and souls of the individual and bring out' their emotions."[48]

---

[46] H. Rap Brown "Address"; Peter B. Levy, "Blacks and the Vietnam War," in *The Legacy: The Vietnam War and the American Imagination*, ed. by D. Michael Shafer (Boston: Beacon Press, 1990), pp. 209–232.

[47] H. Rap Brown, "Address." "Shots Fired in Cambridge Second Ward," *Baltimore Sun*, July 25, 1967, p. C20; "S.N.C.C. Chief Shot in Cambridge, Md.," *NYT*, July 25, 1967, p. 1.

[48] Kennicott and Page, "H. Rap Brown" and H. Rap Brown, "Address."

Brown concluded his speech with typical bravado. "Don't be trying to love the honkey to death. Shoot him to death," Brown exclaimed. "Shoot him to death, brother. Cause that's what he's out to do to you." Alluding to the golden rule, Brown added, "Do to him like he would do to you, but do it to him first." Yet, in his closing remarks, Brown offered a final word of caution. "So when you move to get him, don't tear up your stuff." Instead, Brown encouraged his audience to hit the white man where it hurt the most, "in his pocket." When black protesters threatened the white man's money they attacked "the only god" whites had; "you hit his religion." Hence, Brown reiterated, "don't tear up your stuff, don't tear up your brother's stuff, hear?"[49]

"I Don't Give a Damn if the Entire Second Ward Burns"

After Brown finished speaking, most of the crowd dispersed, though about 100–150, primarily young black men, mulled around on Pine Street. Journalists reported that this smaller crowd remained emotionally charged, yet, at the same time, displayed "no overt hostility" to "white newsmen covering the speech." After Brown and the BAF members exchanged addresses and discussed ways to organize black men and women in Cambridge in the future, several young blacks marched toward Race Street in defiance of an order issued by white authorities to remain within the Second Ward. The police turned them back without any incidences of violence. Another teenager, Pamela Waters, decided to return home. Fearing the presence of police on Elm Street, which ran perpendicular to Race and Pine Streets, she requested an escort. Brown agreed to accompany her home. About 25 to 30 others followed.[50]

Well before they set out, law enforcement authorities had prepared for a confrontation. By late afternoon on the 24th, the state police had dispatched twenty-eight men and three canine units to Cambridge, with

[49] H. Rap Brown, "Address."
[50] See "Report of Office of Investigations," March 25, 1968; "Reconnaissance Survey: Field Research Report," Inter-Office Memorandum – Draft, n.d.; "Analysis of Cambridge"; Nathaniel R. Jones to Victor H. Palmieri, 28 March 1968 and Henry B. Taliaferro Jr., to David Ginsberg and Victor Palmieri, 1 November 1967, FBI, Possible Violence, Major Urban Areas: Cambridge, Maryland, n.d., all in *Kerner Commission Records*. See also: Boesel and Goldberg, "Crisis in Cambridge"; "Detroit Smolders in an Uneasy Calm; Guard Patrols Riot-Torn Cambridge," *Washington Post*, July 26, 1967, p. 1; Clayborne Carson and Tom Hamburger, "The Cambridge Convergence: How a Night in Maryland 30 Years Ago Changed the Nation's Course of Racial Politics," http://web.stanford.edu/~ccarson/articles/cambridge_convergence.htm [accessed October 20, 2015].

additional reserves stationed nearby in Easton. The Cambridge Company of the National Guard was mustered to carry out a previously scheduled "routine" training session. All of Cambridge's twenty-eight policemen (there were no women on the force) were ordered into duty; the force's five black policemen were stationed on the edge of the crowd that assembled to hear Brown speak. The remainder of local and state law enforcement personnel was deployed along Race Street. Authorities also ordered all guns and ammunition in local stores locked up. In spite of this strong presence, Cambridge Police Chief Brice Kinnamon and State Attorney William Yates subsequently insisted that they lacked "sufficient men" to "protect the area" (presumably a reference to Race Street which was a major shopping area) or to place Brown under arrest.[51] Yet, given the ratio of armed authorities to those on the streets, approximately one-to-one – this claim was quite problematic.

Before the group of 25 to 30 black men and women reached Race Street, the police ordered them to stop. Then, without warning, Deputy Sheriff Wesley Burton fired two shotgun blasts, one into the ground and then over the heads of the crowd. Some of the buckshot from one of the blasts ricocheted off the pavement and struck Brown. Gladys Ross, another member of the BAF, was injured as well. Police Chief Brice Kinnamon and State Attorney William Yates initially denied that the police had fired their guns. They later retracted these denials, with Yates acknowledging that the police had fired "light charges." While police reported that Brown urged the crowd to "Burn, loot and shoot any officer white or black that stood in their way," in fact, no violence took place. Instead, the group scampered back to Pine Street. Brown was rushed to the hospital, and, after being treated for a superficial wound, was secreted out of town. According to one urban legend, he was hidden in a coffin to avoid detection.[52]

Not long after Brown was shot a white sedan carrying four to six white males sped down Pine Street. When members of the black community called on the police to arrest the drivers, the black officers responded that

---

[51] See "Report of Office of Investigations," March 25, 1968; "Analysis of Cambridge"; Boesel and Goldberg, "Crisis in Cambridge"; FBI, Possible Violence, Major Urban Areas: Cambridge, Maryland, n.d.; "FBI Grabs Brown Sought in Rioting at Cambridge," *Daily Times*, July 26, 1967, p. 1; "Report Says Rap Brown Didn't Cause Md. Riot," *Washington Post*, March 5, 1968, p. 1.

[52] "Analysis of Cambridge"; Boesel and Goldberg, "Crisis in Cambridge"; "Reconnaissance Survey"; "Guardsmen Patrolling Cambridge," *Baltimore Sun*, July 26, 1967, p. 1.

they did not have the authority to do so – recall that Cambridge had an unwritten rule that its black police officers did not arrest white citizens. The same vehicle made at least two other passes through the Second Ward, exchanging gun shots with local residents. With a few exceptions, contemporary police reports and news coverage downplayed the action of these white night riders, with some stating that the occupants threw firecrackers or "may have shot some guns." Yet, Cambridge's black residents contended that the night riders were part and parcel of a larger armed attack which included the shots which injured H. Rap Brown. Gregory Meekins recollected that he was "returning from a party" when the shooting began. James Lewis later testified that he remembered witnessing "a carload of white men speed down Pine Street, shooting." Rather than seeking refuge in the bushes, behind a tree, or a building, Lewis retreated to his upstairs apartment on Pine Street, where he grabbed his shotgun and stood astride his bedroom window to guard against another attack. Lemuel Chester similarly recalled that people "from the other side of town were involved in the fray," adding "it was only by the Grace of God nobody got killed." While there were additional reports of small black crowds and gun shots in the Second Ward, no looting took place.[53]

Contrary to claims that rioting erupted immediately following Brown's speech, government records make clear that the situation calmed to the point that "law enforcement officials," including National Guard Commander General Gelston and the head of the state police, decided to release the National Guard at midnight. At 12:30 a.m., however, white night riders made another pass on Pine Street. This time their car was hit by at least two guns shots. Afterwards, state troopers stopped and searched the car but they released its drivers without charges, stating they had found no weapons. About the same time, rookie officer Russell Wrotten, who was white, was shot while responding to a report that a window had been broken at a laundromat in the Second Ward. In a subsequent trial, Lewis, who was accused of shooting Wrotten, testified that he had not fired his gun and suggested that Wrotten had been shot by the white

[53] "Guard Patrols Riot-Torn Cambridge," *Washington Post*, July 26, 1967, p. 1; "Analysis of Cambridge"; Boesel and Goldberg, "Crisis in Cambridge"; "Reconnaissance Survey"; see *State of Maryland v. James Lee Lewis*, case file, 2118, Dorchester County Circuit Court, MSA; "Cambridge, July 24, 1967," Associated Press, July 24, 1967, Maryland Race Relations, Eastern Shore, Vertical File, Dorchester County Library. On the limitations of black police in Cambridge, see Patricia Bennett, "Role of Negro Police (Cambridge, Maryland)," and "Reconnaissance Survey Field Research Report," n.d., both in *Kerner Commission Records*, reels 12 and 23.

night riders. The state's forensic experts failed to connect the bullets to Lewis's weapon. Nonetheless, Lewis was convicted, though he forever denied the charges.[54]

Even before he learned of this incident, Police Chief Brice Kinnamon, along with other law enforcement officials and political leaders, had listened to a tape recording of Brown's speech. The speech alone left Kinnamon fuming; news that Wrotten had been wounded sent him into a tizzy. He grabbed his rifle and, according to a State Police report, shouted: "We're going to get every son-of-a-bitch down there. I'm getting tired of fooling around." News that Wrotten's wound was minor calmed Kinnamon a bit. Still, Maryland's Attorney General Francis Burch, National Guard General George Gelston, and State Police Captain Paul Randall had to plead with Kinnamon to seal off the Second Ward, the standard operating procedure, rather than "clean[ing] out the area," Kinnamon's personal preference – during protests in the early 1960s, Cambridge's Mayor Calvin Mowbray and state authorities had "had to sit on Kinnamon," to borrow Mowbray's words, to prevent him from using excessive force in response to lawful civil rights demonstrations.[55]

At approximately 2:00 a.m., well over an hour after the guard had dispersed and approximately three hours after Brown concluded his speech, a fire erupted at the Pine Street Elementary School, though the fire siren did not sound for another forty-five minutes. In the interim, city council leader Charles Cornish and businessman Hansel Green, two of the most prominent black residents of the Second Ward, both of whom had reputations as moderates, not radicals, unsuccessfully implored the Rescue and Fire Company to put out the fire. The following morning Green told the *Afro-American* that one "lousy truck" could have stopped the blaze. When Lemuel Chester sought to get the fire company to move in, Chief Kinnamon allegedly retorted: "You goddamn niggers started the fire, now you goddamn niggers watch it burn. I don't give a damn if the entire Second Ward burns." (The *Baltimore Sun* reported that Kinnamon responded: "You people ought to have done something before this. You stood by and let a bunch of goddamn hoodlums come in and let one of my police get shot. Don't come to me with this.") Fire trucks did not even pull out of the station house until 2:45 a.m. and then the RFC merely

54 *State of Maryland v. James Lee Lewis*, case file, 2118, Dorchester County Circuit Court, MSA.
55 "Analysis of Cambridge"; Boesel and Goldberg, "Crisis in Cambridge"; "Reconnaissance Survey."

stationed its equipment on the edge of the Second Ward so as to protect the business district.[56]

Fifty years later, Barbara Pinder recollected that the fire company stood by as the fire spread. They "wouldn't move or take out their hoses," she emphasized; nor would they help black businessmen put out the fire. At one point, she recalled, Hansel Green had pleaded with Charles Cornish to get the fire company to act. "After all, you are commissioner and they'll listen to you," Green implored. Pinder, herself then a teenager, walked with Cornish to see what the policemen and firefighters would say. And as she recalled, they just stood "with their arms folded and said 'we're not going to put it out,'" adding that the "N" people started it and "we're going to let it burn."[57]

Even after state troopers moved into position to protect the firemen, the RFC's trucks remained outside the Second Ward, because, according to Kinnamon, he could not guarantee their safety. Yet, throughout the evening, the crowd remained nonviolent, allowing four white linemen, employed by the local utility company, to clip electrical wiring without harm. In the face of the RFC's recalcitrance to put out the fire, Emmerson Stafford, a longtime black activists, demanded "Just give us some hoses." Others tried to douse the fire with buckets of water and garden hoses. One black resident rhetorically asked a white reporter, "If you aren't scared to come down here, why can't the firemen come in … They're going to let the whole thing burn down." In response to the RFC tepidness, State Police Captain Randall fumed: "Where the hell were the fire trucks?"[58]

Not until 3:25 a.m. did the Rescue and Fire Company proceed into the area, led not by the head of the RFC, but by Attorney General Burch, who personally donned fire gear and commandeered one of the fire trucks. Even then, "some firemen" remained reluctant "to go," not according to Emmerson Stafford because they feared for their safety, but because of

[56] "Analysis of Cambridge"; Boesel and Goldberg, "Crisis in Cambridge"; "Reconnaissance Survey"; "Guard Patrols Riot-Ravaged Cambridge," *Washington Post*, July 26, 1967, p. 1; "Guardsmen Patrolling Cambridge," *Baltimore Sun*, July 26, 1967, p. 1; "H. Rap 'The Lamb' Turns Erring Lion," *Afro-American* (Baltimore, MD), August 19, 1967.
[57] Pinder quoted in "Let it Burn: Civil Unrest 50 Years Later," Kojo Nnamdi Show, WAMU, July 26, 2017, http://thekojonnamdishow.org/shows/2017-07-26/let-it-burn-cambridge-civil-unrest-50-years-later [accessed August 18, 2017].
[58] "Analysis of Cambridge"; Boesel and Goldberg, "Crisis in Cambridge"; "Firemen Watched Cambridge Go," *Evening Sun* (Baltimore, MD), July 26, 1967.

their long-standing animosity toward the black community.[59] When the firemen finally arrived the crowd did *not* harm or impede them. On the contrary, black youths helped them water down the area. But by then, the fire had spread, not to be fully extinguished until dawn. During the wait, William Green allowed members of the crowd to take perishables from his grocery store, which was destroyed by the fire. Police inaccurately reported this action as looting.[60]

"When you See a Lifetime of Work go up in Flames, it Gets to You"

As the Sun rose on the morning of July 25th, residents began to assess the damage. By then the fire had consumed two square blocks and more than twenty buildings, including a dance hall, a grocery store, a record shop, two shoe shine proprietors, the local Democratic Club, two barber shops, a bar-poolroom, a motel, a tailor's shop, and the Zion Baptist Church. One elderly black woman summed up the view of many, declaring: "Lord have mercy. The devil himself has come down on earth today." Reverend Ernest Dupree recalled "I can remember the blaze looking like hell coming on top of us." Marcia Banks, who was ten years old at the time, agreed, stating "it was like the world was coming to an end."[61] (See Figure 2.1.)

Shelter was one of the community's most dire needs. Forty residents lost their homes; at least $300,000 in property damage was incurred. Shirley Ross informed reporters of the *Afro-American* in Baltimore that her family was "completely wiped out...We don't have any clothing, furniture, or food." Mrs. Rosie Cornish and Mrs. Verna Mae Lofton were among those left homeless. When John Bryant, another black resident, told General Gelston that he had nothing to his name, the National Guard commander pulled $2 from his pocket and gave it to Bryant.[62]

59 "Firemen Watched Cambridge Go," *Evening Sun* (Baltimore, MD), 26 July 1967; "Guard Troops Are Pulled Out of Cambridge," *Daily Times*, August 2, 1967, p. 3; "Guardsmen Patrolling Cambridge," *Baltimore Sun*, July 26, 1967, p. 1.
60 "Analysis of Cambridge"; Boesel and Goldberg, "Crisis in Cambridge"; "Firemen Watched Cambridge Go," *Evening Sun* (Baltimore, MD), 26 July 1967; "Guard Troops Are Pulled Out of Cambridge," *Daily Times*, August 2, 1967, p. 3.
61 "Analysis of Cambridge"; Boesel and Goldberg, "Crisis in Cambridge"; "Guardsmen Patrolling Cambridge," *Baltimore Sun*, July 26, 1967, p. 1; "The Minister Donned His Overcoat," *The Morning Herald* (Haggerstown, MD), July 31, 1967; "Cambridge, July 24, 1967," Associated Press, July 23, 1992, Vertical File, Dorchester Public Library.
62 "Firemen Watched Cambridge Go," *Evening Sun* (Baltimore, MD), July 26, 1967.

FIGURE 2.1 The Rev. Conrad J. Branch stands amid ruins of the Zion Baptist Church, destroyed by fire in Cambridge, Maryland, July 25, 1967. By permission of AP Photo.

One of those most affected was Hansel Green whose entire complex of businesses, which included a motel, popular pool room, dance hall, and bar-nightclub complex, was consumed by the fire. One week afterwards, Green fatally shot himself. Green's wife, Lena, explained: "When you see a lifetime of work go up in flames, it gets to you." Green lacked insurance to offset his extensive losses, estimated at between $150,000 and $250,000, and as he told the local newspaper, he could not understand why "such a tragedy should happen to him."[63] Perhaps, if the federal government had treated Cambridge like it treated areas devastated by natural disasters,

---

[63] "Cambridge Riot Figure Takes Own Life," *Afro-American*, August 13, 1967; "Second Ward Resident Gives Out Statement," *CDB*, July 29, 1967. "Services for Greene

and provided federal emergency relief and loans for reconstruction, then Green would not have been so despondent. But as of the late 1960s, the government refused to consider riots to be anything but man made and thus ineligible for such aid.[64]

Much of the rubble remained untouched for weeks, with city officials contending that they could not remove it until insurance adjusters assessed the damage. Two months after the fire, only 14 of 43 residents left homeless by the blaze had found permanent places to live, a situation exacerbated by the pre-existing shortage of adequate housing and an unwillingness of whites to sell or rent to black citizens outside of the Second Ward.[65] The Kerner Commission ranked Cambridge as having experienced a "serious disorder," one level below those in Detroit and Newark and a level above 75 percent of those that took place during the summer of 1967. True, compared to Detroit, Newark, and Watts in 1965, the total amount of property damage in Cambridge appeared small. Yet, if an equal proportion of Detroit's black population had been displaced by the fires, upwards of 7,000 of its residents would have been left homeless.[66]

To insure order, the National Guard rushed 700-strong to Cambridge, reestablishing posts it had occupied from 1963 to 1964. With a ratio of one guardsmen for every fifty residents, "the over-all feeling," observed one reporter "was of a city under armed occupation. Steel-helmeted guardsmen carrying rifles with fixed bayonets, and their clips of bullets in clear sight, were present everywhere" (see Figure 2.2). In spite of or perhaps because of their presence, the situation in Cambridge remained tense. The Black Action Federation held another rally, where it reiterated its demands for better housing, recreation, job training, and broader economic opportunities. Afterwards, some looting and vandalism occurred;

Are Incomplete," *CDB*, August 5, 1967; "They're Bitter, Fearful, Bewildered," *Afro-American*, August 5, 1967; "Cambridge Riot Figure Takes Own Life," *Afro-American*, August 13, 1967; "Second Ward Resident Gives Out Statement," *CDB*, July 29, 1967; "Hansel Green Bidden Farewell," *Baltimore Sun*, August 9, 1967, p. A9: "Eastern Shore Digits Barons Miss Prison," *Afro-American*, April 21, 1956; "Six Wed in Cambridge," *Afro-American*, November 23, 1969.

64 Kerner Commission, *Report*, p. 360. A number of scholars have questioned the distinction between natural disasters and riots. See especially Ted Steinberg, *Acts of God: The Unnatural History of Natural Disaster in America* (New York: Oxford University Press, 2000; 2nd edn., 2006).

65 "Reconnaissance Survey Field Research Report"; "Housing Crisis Grips Cambridge," *Afro-American*, September 23, 1967, p. 1.

66 Kerner Commission, *Report*, p. 113; See also "Staff Paper Explaining Method Used for Selection of Cities for Intensive Studies," n.d., Records of National Commission on Civil Disorders, reel 22.

FIGURE 2.2 Maryland National Guard accompanies fire truck in riot area in Cambridge, July 25, 1967. By permission of AP Photo.

protesters threw rocks and bottles at the National Guard and at cars driven by whites, and an unsuccessful attempt was made to set several buildings on fire. But when National Guardsmen unsheathed their bayonets and sprayed the crowd with tear gas, protesters quickly dispersed without further incident.[67]

Even more so than the National Guard, local authorities sought to squelch the BAF and its supporters. Rather than investigating the culpability of white authorities, local officials set out on a witch hunt to punish black citizens and/or their white sympathizers associated with the revolt. On July 27, the same date as Brown's arrest in Alexandria, Virginia, for inciting a riot, and only two full days since the fire in the Second Ward, James Lewis and Leon Lewis (unrelated) were arrested by Cambridge's police for the nonfatal shooting of Officer Russell Wrotten. The following day, Chauncy Askins, one of the Cromwell's defense witnesses and a member of CNAC, was similarly charged; the day after, Lemuel Chester, one of the leaders of the Black Action Federation, was arrested. Three youths, Dennis Fletcher, Douglas Fletcher, and Gilbert Fletcher, ages fourteen, fifteen, and sixteen, respectively, were arrested and charged with arson for

---

[67] "Cambridge Analysis."

the fire at the Pine Street Elementary School. In short order, authorities detained James DuPont Fletcher and Gladys Fletcher on separate arson charges and Albert Young for the shooting of Officer Wrotten. Four additional black men were arrested for disorderly conduct, two of whom, Martin Tinder and Raydell Smullen, were subsequently charged with discharging a firearm within city limits. Likewise, two CORE activists, Stewart Wechsler and Walter Lively, were charged with inciting a riot and two newspersons, Tony Sargent of CBS and William Schmick, the son of the publisher of the *Baltimore Sun*, with refusing to obey an officer. Ultimately, all of these charges, accept those against the two Lewis's and one of the Fletcher youths, were dropped, though in most of the cases the charges were not dismissed until June 1970, a seeming violation of the right to a speedy trial.[68]

In addition to the aforementioned confrontations, the Black Action Federation continued to demand change, often in a fashion that did not please local or state authorities. In early October, the BAF held a "Black Power Conference" in Cambridge, a miniature version of the one held in Newark weeks before, even though the local elite made clear they did not want it to take place. Some ministers from most of the better known black churches closed their doors to the BAF. When Reverend Ernest Dupree of the Church of God offered his church, his Bishop, James Leonard Eure, of Salisbury, ordered him to padlock its doors or risk being defrocked. In response, Dupree exclaimed that he would not be silenced. "If I can't stand by my convictions, I'm less of a preacher." Nor did Governor Agnew's threats to stop the speech of anyone who sought to incite a riot deter the BAF. Addressing an outdoors assembly of upwards of one hundred,

---

[68] "Reconnaissance Survey Field Research Report"; *CDB*, October 20, 1967, October 23, 1967, November 5, 1967, November 11, 1967, December 12, 1967, and December 13, 1967; "Guardsmen Use Riot Gas to Control an Unruly Mob Here," *CDB*, July 27, 1967; "Four Taken into Custody in Connection with Fires," *CDB*, August 2, 1967; "Negro Is Held in Maryland City on Charge of Attempted Killing," *NYT*, July 28, 1967, p. 14; "Discusses Objective of Group," *CDB*, July 28, 1967; "Analysis of Cambridge"; Research to Stephen Kurzman, Records of the National Commission on Civil Disorders, reel 16; "Guard Breaks Up Crowd in Cambridge," *Baltimore Sun*, July 27, 1967, p. 1; "2 Youths Freed of Fire Charges," *Baltimore Sun*, August 29, 1967, p. C20; *In Re Fletcher*, 251 Md. 520 (1968) 248 A.2d 36, www.courtlistener.com/opinion/1485726/ in-re-fletcher/ [accessed January 14, 2016]; *State of Maryland v. Lemuel Chester*, Case File, No. 2121, Dorchester County Circuit Court, MSA. The dockets of Chester and James DuPont Fletcher and Gladys Fletcher provide no explanation for the delay between their being charged in August 1967 and the decision of the state to drop charges (Nolle Prosse) three years later. No motions for continuance were issued by their defense attorneys or by the State.

Gloria Richardson, Callis Brown, of the New York office of CORE, and James "Dinno" Prettyman, a member of Baltimore-based CIG called on blacks "to unite" and to gather "all our anger...under one roof." Richardson insisted that it was white authorities, not black citizens, who were acting in an inflammatory manner. Rosalie Fletcher of the Black Action Federation condemned Governor Agnew for his refusal to provide aide. "The Governor has high powered aides on his staff. All they have to do is come to Cambridge and see what our needs are." When a sizable proportion of the attendees attempted to march downtown following the speeches, state troopers prevented them from doing so. Outnumbered by law enforcement officials the protesters turned back without incident. In a subsequent press release, the BAF stated that the "power structure" did not want to clean up the debris left from the fire. On the contrary, it wanted the rubble "to stand as a symbol and a warning to those who would practice violence."[69]

Several days after the rally, representatives of the BAF appeared before the town council where they again demanded better housing, jobs, and recreational facilities. "We should have representatives in city jobs. We feel the city owes them to us," declared Elaine Adams, one of the BAF's leaders. "I would like to walk into a city office...and see a black face sitting behind the desk, all ready to greet me," Emmerson Stafford added. "The black people pay taxes too." While neither town council head Charles Cornish nor Mayor Pritchett dismissed the BAF's demands outright, they did not pledge to meet them anytime soon.[70]

Given that the civil rights movement had lost some steam following Richardson's marriage and departure in late 1964, these actions by the BAF suggested that Brown's speech had achieved part of its goal, namely to re-energize the movement in Cambridge. At the same time the intransigence of whites in positions of leadership continued to stand out. At the aforementioned city council meeting, Mayor Pritchett insisted that he would never fire a white person in order to make room for a black person. Police Chief Kinnamon and Mayor Pritchett floated the idea of

[69] "Board to Ask Cambridge to Keep Cool," *Baltimore Sun*, September 29, 1967, p. C24; "Cambridge Meeting Calm; Police Outnumber Militants," *Washington Post*, October 1, 1967, p. C4; "March Halted in Cambridge," *Baltimore Sun*," October 1, 1967, p. 26; "Church Padlocked; B.P. Rally Moved," *Afro-American*, October 7, 1967; "Black Power Rally Here Over Weekend," *CDB*, October 3, 1967; Baltimore, SAC to FBI, Director, "Possible-Racial Violence, Major Urban Areas," July 20, 1967, *Kerner Commission Records*.
[70] "Negro Group Demands Better Housing Jobs," *CDB*, October 3, 1967.

establishing a hundred-person "posse," presumably on the grounds that existing law enforcement forces were too weak to maintain public order. There is also some evidence that local whites sought to work with the National States Rights Party to hold another rally in the area.[71]

Moreover, Cambridge remained central to the nation's consideration of the causes of the revolts. Conservatives, in particular, used Brown's speech and the riot that followed to support their claim that radicals or riot makers were responsible for the unrest. Some liberals, including National Guard commander, General Gelston, and the well-known writer John Barth, a native son of Cambridge, sought to counter this claim. It is to the development of these conflicting narratives that we turn to next.

[71] See Albert Atkinson to Charles Bressler, September 5, 1967, Edward McCabe to Spiro T. Agnew, August 25, 1967, and Charles Bressler to Spiro T. Agnew, September 6, 1967, all in Governor Agnew Papers, Box 14; Spiro T. Agnew to Alexander Trowbridge, September 21, 1967, Alexander Trowbridge to Spiro T. Agnew, October 4, 1967, Spiro T. Agnew to Stewart Udall, October 18, 1967; William J. People to Gilbert Ware, January 9, 1968, Rogers Morton to Gilbert Ware, December 20, 1967, Charles Bressler to William Chaffinich, November 1, 1967, Agil Ware to Spiro T. Agnew, November 1, 1967, Charles Bressler to Spencer Ellis, November 9, 1967, Spiro T. Agnew, "Statement to the Press," October 10, 1967, Rogers Morton to Spiro T. Agnew, December 12, 1967, Edward Van de Castle to George James, March 18, 1967, William Chaffinich to Spiro T. Agnew, 20 March, 1968, all in Governor Agnew Papers, Box 11.

3

Falsely Accused?

Rebellions and revolts are occurring throughout the land, because the United States power structure has been unwilling to yield to the basic demands of its black population and their allies. It has chosen to create scapegoats – to shift the burden of responsibility for the upheavals from the oppressor to the oppressed – rather than undertake the task of correcting centuries of evils.[1]

H. Rap Brown, 1968

Why had the race revolts taken place? Who was at fault? What could be done to make sure they never happened again? And even more broadly, what did they mean? These questions confronted the nation as the unrest of the summer of 1967 died down. President Johnson established the Kerner Commission to answer them; Congress held hearings to do the same; and candidates for political higher office, like Richard Nixon, positioned their campaigns to foment and reap the whirlwinds of the expected backlash. By retaining our focus on Cambridge and several key individuals associated with its riot, particularly H. Rap Brown, Spiro Agnew, Brice Kinnamon, and George Gelston, we can sharpen our understanding of America's reaction to the uprising that had swept across the land. While political elites did not arrive at a consensus as to their cause, offering explanations that varied in emphasis from blaming black radicals like H. Rap Brown to focusing on underlying social and economic ills and cultural pathologies, they tended to agree that "law and order" must be part of the prescribed response. At the same time, conservatives and most

---

[1] H. Rap Brown, "Dear [SNCC] Friends," n.d. Ella Baker Papers, Box 6, Folder: H. Rap Brown, Schomburg Center, New York Public Library, New York.

liberals dismissed charges that white authorities had precipitated much of the violence and that the governments, not radicals, were abridging the legal rights of American citizens. H. Rap Brown, for one, as his attorney William Kunstler asserted, faced "vindictive and unrelenting efforts to destroy him," including the Kerner Commission's decision to withhold potentially exculpatory evidence that could clear him from charges that he had incited a riot. Meanwhile, the needs of many of those who suffered most from the unrest went unattended, suggesting that the nation as a whole made a collective decision to deflect attention away from the structural causes of the revolts in favor of proposals that played better with the white majority.

"We Got Along Fine Until this Happened"

Somewhat surprisingly, on the eve of the summer of 1967, the aforementioned questions did not dominate public discourse in America, in spite of several successive summers of unrest, including revolts in the nation's three largest cities, New York (1964), Los Angeles (1965), and Chicago (1966). One reason for this is that the national media focused its attention on other problems, most notably Vietnam, while simultaneously feeding the public a series of uplifting feature stories lest their mood turn too sour. Illustratively, *Life* magazine's early July 1967 covers focused on the birth of President Johnson's grandchild, the new career of Princess Lee Radziwill (Jacqueline Kennedy's sister), and the effort to negotiate the release of a US official from the "Vietcong." Partly due to the media's coverage, pollsters found that on the eve of the race revolts of the summer of 1967 Americans remained far more concerned with Vietnam (45%) and the high cost of living (16%), than civil rights (9%) – race riots did not even register as one of the most important problems – and that residents of the nation's largest cities overwhelmingly did *not* expect "any serious trouble in their communities in the next six months."[2]

This all changed rapidly with uprisings in Newark, Detroit, and Cambridge. Yet before we examine the public's reactions to this wave of revolts, it is helpful to survey some of the a priori views that Americans held regarding collective violence and conflict. As suggested in Chapter 2,

---

[2] George Gallup, "Most Important Problem, May 27, 1966," in *The Gallup Poll: Public Opinion. Volume III: 1959–1971* (New York: Random House, 1972); www.originallifemagazines.com/LIFE-Magazines-1960s-C488.aspx [accessed October 9, 2014].

it was not uncommon for pundits and politicians to express surprise when riots occurred. Even a prominent sociologist spoke for many when he termed them "a mystery." They were mysterious in his mind and in the minds of many social scientists, and to a certain extent with the public at large, because they did not fit with established assumptions about the nature of American history and its political system. Put somewhat differently, the consensus school of historians and their pluralist cousins in the social sciences, as Hugh Davis Graham insightfully observed, claimed that all Americans shared certain ideals and characteristics that bound them together as one. They believed that there had been little conflict and hence little violence in American history and the conflict that had occurred had taken place for irrational and unnecessary reasons. Moreover, they asserted that the social environment was characterized by abundance and upward mobility, which in turn blunted "class warfare" and that "democratic institutions provided multiple or pluralistic access to policy-making elites." To further borrow Davis Graham's words, most historians and social scientists believed that "Americans agreed broadly on the legitimacy of the constitutional order and the rules of the game in competition over governing."[3]

Consensus and pluralist arguments dovetailed with Gunnar Myrdal's study of American race relations, which he laid out in his monumental work, *An American Dilemma* (1944). Completed during World War II, this instant classic asserted that the American creed, or its fundamental belief in equality, meant that Jim Crow and other forms of racism were anachronistic. Myrdal arrived at this conclusion not by ignoring the depth of racism but rather by insisting that the nation's faith in equality, as embodied in the Declaration of Independence's statement that "all men are created equal" and endowed with certain "inalienable rights,"

---

[3] Hugh Davis Graham, "Violence, Social Theory, and the Historians: The Debate over Consensus and Culture in America," in *Violence in America. Volume 2: Protest, Rebellion, Reform*, ed. by Ted Robert Gurr (Newbury Park, CA: SAGE, 1989), p. 329. Prime examples of this consensus thinking were: Louis Hartz, *The Liberal Tradition in America* (New York: Harcourt, Brace, 1955); Richard Hofstadter, *The American Political Tradition and the Men Who Made It* (New York: Alfred Knopf, 1948); Daniel J. Boorstin, *The Genius of American Politics* (Chicago: University of Chicago Press, 1953); Daniel J. Boorstin, *The Americans*, 3 vols. (New York: Vintage Books, 1965); Robert A. Dahl, *Who Governs? Democracy and Power in an American City* (New Haven, CT: Yale University Press, 1961). Lionel Trilling, *The Liberal Imagination: Essays on Literature and Society* (New York: Charles Scribners, 1950), especially pp. ix–xv; and John Kenneth Galbraith, *American Capitalism: The Concept of Countervailing Power*, rev. edn. (White Plains: NY: M. E. Sharpe, 1956).

would ultimately triumph. Even in the heart of the Deep South, Myrdal predicted that the dilemma between racist views and the American creed would result in ending what he termed "the Negro problem." No great upheaval or revolution was necessary. On the contrary, the forces of modernization which were already underway would suffice.[4]

The prevalence of this consensus viewpoint, which the revolts of the summer of 1964 barely dented, helps explain why so many reacted to Watts with utter surprise. Since the uprisings lay outside of their liberal/consensus framework, politicians and pundits struggled to find ways to incorporate them into their thinking without jettisoning their fundamental faith in the American political system. In contrast, Allen Grimshaw, a burgeoning revisionist scholar who did not share the consensus/pluralist view, believed that collective violence was "simply one of several modes of conflict resolution. The choice of this rather than other modes need not be a mystery; reasons are to be found within the structural arrangements of society itself." For much of American history, Grimshaw explained, with the exception of "a brief period after the Civil War, the pattern of Negro–white relationships, especially in the South, closely approximated the classic accommodative pattern of superordination–subordination," with whites maintaining the dominant or superordinate position. In turn, whites used violence when they perceived threats to this arrangement, in other words, they employed violent means to maintain their status.[5]

Yet, the vast majority of conservatives and liberals proved unwilling to adopt Grimshaw's perspective. Instead, they advanced three not mutually exclusive explanations for the riots. Many blamed black radicals for the turmoil. Without rejecting the role played by radicals or "riot makers," others emphasized the cultural or moral roots of the "disorders," arguing that the violence must have arisen out of the pathology of the black family, out of a culture of poverty, and/or a combination of the two, not out of fundamental flaws in the American system. Still others located the causes of the revolts in the social and economic conditions of America's ghettos, which as the Kerner Commission put it, had been created by white racism. What advocates of all three of these positions

---

[4] Gunnar Myrdal, *An American Dilemma: The Negro Problem in American Democracy* (New York: Harper, 1944). For an excellent discussion of Myrdal, see Nikhil Pal Singh, *Black Is a Country: Race and the Unfinished Struggle for Democracy* (Cambridge: MA: Harvard University Press, 2005).

[5] Allen D. Grimshaw, ed., *Racial Violence in the United States* (Chicago: Aldine Publishing, 1968), pp. 3–6, 14–29, 490.

held in common was a belief that the riots were unproductive and represented a sharp and unfavorable break from American tradition and the civil rights movement. Only a small segment of Americans, mostly those on the left, disagreed, contending that the revolts were consistent with both America's long history of violence and fit within the traditions of the black freedom struggle.[6]

"[Brown was the] Sole Cause of the Riot"

Many political leaders and public intellectuals emphasized that radicals had caused the "riots." Upon creating the Kerner Commission, President Johnson asserted that "the apostles of violence," with their "ugly drumbeat of hatred," had caused the "disorders." To make matters worse, "law-abiding Negro families ... suffered the most at the hands of the rioters," because it was their neighborhoods and dreams of sharing in America's growth and prosperity that was left in shambles. The president reiterated this position in a speech to the International Association of Police Chiefs over a month later. "These wretched, vulgar men, these poisonous propagandists posed as spokesman for the underprivileged capitalized on the real grievances of the suffering people."[7]

The FBI confirmed Johnson's views in a memo written one week after Brown's Cambridge speech. While the FBI reported that it had not uncovered evidence of an "overall conspiracy," it simultaneously emphasized that radicals, like "Stokely Carmichael and Hubert Geroid Brown, commonly known as H. Rap Brown," of SNCC, had "triggered" the "outbreaks" of the summer of 1967 through their "exhortations" of "Black Power." Brown, the memo continued, had delivered a "wildly inflammatory" speech, after which "violence erupted" and "a portion of the Negro section was burned." The following day, the memo observed, the Attorney General had issued a warrant for the arrest of Brown on the charges of "unlawfully inciting" a riot and "maliciously burning

---

[6] Milton Viorst, *Fire in the Streets* (New York: Touchstone, 1981), p. 309. See also: Josh Sides, *L.A. City Limits: African American Los Angeles from the Great Depression to the Present* (Berkeley: University of California Press, 2003).

[7] Lyndon B. Johnson, "Address to the Nation on Civil Disorders," July 27, 1967, Public Papers of the Presidents, www.presidency.ucsb.edu/ws/index.php?pid=28368& st=civil+disorders&st1=; "Remarks Upon Signing Order Establishing Commission on Civil Disorders," July 29, 1967, www.presidency.ucsb.edu/ws/index.php?pid= 28369&st=civil+disorders&st1=; "LBJ Attacks Riot Makers," *Freeport Journal-Standard*, September 14, 1967, p. 1.

the Pine Street Elementary School." The memo concluded by noting that the FBI had apprehended Brown at Washington's National Airport on July 26th, charged him with "unlawful flight to avoid prosecution" and on Maryland's aforementioned felony charges. The memo did not contain a detailed chronology of the events in Cambridge which might have undermined these claims, though lest anyone doubt Brown's nefarious intentions, the FBI memo highlighted that Brown had asserted upon his arrest: "we stand on the eve of the black revolution 'with eye for eye and...life for life," and termed "the current rebellions...a dress rehearsal for the real revolution."[8]

Building on information most likely leaked to them by the FBI, Robert S. Allen and Paul Scott, two widely syndicated columnists, warned local police that they were "no longer dealing with amateurs in riots and demonstrations in their cities." On the contrary, they asserted that the nation faced "hard-core agitators" in city after city that had experienced unrest. The FBI, they continued, had observed "a top aide of Carmichael" urging "Negroes to 'take an eye for an eye, arm for arm, and life for a life.'" While Allen and Scott's column did not name H. Rap Brown as Carmichael's aide, there can be little doubt that he was the person referred to in the FBI's memo. In a subsequent "Inside Washington" column, Allen and Scott explicitly identified Brown as one of the central agitators, adding that Brown was currently "free on bond after being charged...with inciting a riot." Numerous other newspapers similarly cited FBI reports which allegedly claimed that "hard-core agitators" were behind the unrest.[9] Likewise, drawing on information provided to him by FBI sources, columnist Jack Anderson asserted that "Peking's Shadow" was "Behind the Riots."[10] True, Johnson's Kerner Commission ultimately came to a different conclusion, placing much more emphasis on the social and economic conditions of the nation's ghettos than on the actions of black radicals, but Johnson gave at best tepid support for the

---

[8] United States Department of Justice, Federal Bureau of Investigation, "Racial Disturbances," August 1, 1967, in *Civil Rights During the Johnson Administration, 1963–1969*, Part 5, reel 1:00035.

[9] Robert S. Allen and Paul Scott, "Inside Washington," *The Daily Herald*, June 28, 1967, p. 16; "Inside Washington," *The Daily Mail*, August 14, 1967, p. 4; "FBI Report Says Pros Directing Racial Riots," *Daily Times*, June 28, 1967, p. 7.

[10] "A New Red Group Hails Watts Riot," *NYT*, November 21, 1965, p. 72; "Birch Founder's 'Rights' Talk at Howard Draws Laughter," *Afro-American*, November 13, 1965, p. 17; "7 Major Outbreaks Listed in Riots' Report to President," *Afro-American*, October 10, 1964; Jack Anderson, "Peking's Shadow Behind the Riots," *Washington Post*, October 12, 1964.

commission's findings and he did little to undermine the alternative view that "riot makers" had caused the revolts.

The view that "radicals caused the riots" was augmented by hearings conducted by the Senate Judiciary Committee in the immediate aftermath of revolts in Newark, Detroit, and Cambridge. Headed by Mississippi Senator James Eastland, a staunch conservative, the panel invited Cambridge's police chief, Brice Kinnamon, to serve as its *first* witness. The fact that Kinnamon opened the hearings illustrated the significance of Cambridge in the construction of America's understanding of the summer's revolts. Kinnamon testified that Brown was the "sole cause" of the "riot." "It was a well-organized and well-planned affair." Upon completion of his "inflammatory speech," Kinnamon declared, Brown led a group of people toward the business district, "instructing them to burn and tear Cambridge down [and] to shoot any policeman who tried to interfere." "The streets were full of guns seconds after the speech," he added. After playing a recording of Brown's speech, Kinnamon asserted that violence broke out "immediately" afterwards, including the blaze that consumed the Pine Street Elementary School. While Kinnamon did not go as far as he had in an earlier statement to the press, when he proclaimed that Cambridge's riot "was a well-planned Communist attempt to overthrow the government" and that Brown had led "a large armed group down Elem Street...shooting as they advanced," he insisted in his Senate appearance that the disorder was "well organized and well planned" and had the help of outside elements.[11]

Kinnamon also defended the RFC's decision to remain on the perimeter of the Second Ward while the fire grew, on the grounds that the threat to its safety was real. If they had gone into the Second Ward, he told Maryland's Senator Tydings, "some of them would have been shot."[12] Separately, Kinnamon suggested that blacks had set the fire to lure policeman into the Second Ward so that blacks could then "burn and loot"

[11] "Chief Kinnamon Testifies Before the Senate Judiciary Committee," *CDB*, August 13, 1967; US Senate, Committee on the Judiciary, 90th Congress, 1st Session, "Hearings on H.R. 421, Anti-riot Bill – 1967" (Washington DC, GPO: 1967), especially pp. 31–64; "Police Statement," *CDB*, July 28, 1967; "'Outsiders' Called Disrupters of Cambridge Race Accord," *Washington Post*, August 3, 1967, p. 1; "Kinnamon Says Brown Caused Riot," *Baltimore Sun*, August 3, 1967, p. 1; "Police in 3 Cities Say S.N.C.C. Chiefs Incited Rioting," *NYT*, August 3, 1967, p. 1; Brice Kinnamon, "Statement," *CDB*, July 28, 1967.
[12] "Chief Kinnamon Testifies Before the Senate Judiciary Committee," *CDB*, August 13, 1967; US Senate, Committee on the Judiciary, 90th Congress, 1st Session, "Hearings on H.R. 421, Anti-riot Bill – 1967"; Brice Kinnamon, "Statement," *CDB*, July 28, 1967.

the white business district, though he offered no evidence to support this claim. When queried about the proposed "Brown amendment" (named after H. Rap Brown) which, if enacted, would make it a federal crime to cross a state border to incite a riot, Kinnamon expressed his support. But Kinnamon prioritized raising the public's awareness about the danger the nation faced from radicals like Brown over the amendment itself. The "hour is getting late," Cambridge's police chief warned, and if the nation did not re-establish "respect for law and order and for the police," more "riots" would occur.[13]

Moving beyond pinning the blame on Brown and other radicals, Eastland's committee also sought to undermine the contrarian view that social and economic ills underlay the "disorders." Kinnamon played a key role in making this case as well. "The relationship between the Negro community and the white community," Kinnamon testified, was "excellent." Cambridge did not even have a ghetto. Probed about this claim by Senator Everett Dirksen, who noted that all of Cambridge's blacks lived in the Second Ward, Kinnamon asserted that "nothing stopped them from buying homes elsewhere." In terms of high unemployment and poor housing conditions, Kinnamon replied that these problems had been overcome. When asked if Cambridge needed more schools or better recreational facilities, Kinnamon retorted that the city already had the "finest schools" in the nation.[14]

The committee's second witness, Cincinnati police chief Jack Schott seconded Kinnamon's claim, signaling out Stokely Carmichael and H. Rap Brown for the riots in his city. Likewise, Captain John Sarace held Brown and Carmichael responsible for Nashville, Tennessee's riot. One poll revealed that a supermajority of Congress agreed with these views, with 69 percent of Republicans and an equally high number of Southern Democrats, like Senator Eastland, agreeing that "outside agitators" were of "great importance" in terms of causing the riots.[15]

The media's sensational news coverage, especially its reporting on Brown and Cambridge, reinforced the connection between black power

---

[13] "Chief Kinnamon Testifies Before the Senate Judiciary Committee," *CDB*, August 13, 1967; US Senate, Committee on the Judiciary, 90th Congress, 1st Session, "Hearings on H.R. 421, Anti-riot Bill – 1967."

[14] "Chief Kinnamon Testifies Before the Senate Judiciary Committee"; "Hearings on H.R. 421."

[15] "Ford Assails Brown and Carmichael," *NYT*, August 29, 1967; "Congressional Poll on Causes, Prevention of Riots," in *Kerner Commission Records*, reel 27.

FIGURE 3.1 H. Rap Brown, July 27, 1967. Photograph by Marion S. Trikosko, *US News & World Report*. Photograph Collection, Library of Congress.

and rioting. In a contemporary analysis of the press's coverage of Cambridge, David Boesel and Louis Goldberg concluded that "the overall impression one gets is of widespread violence following immediately upon Brown's speech." Newspaper and magazine headlines and accompanying photographs vividly linked the riots to Brown. For instance, a *Newsweek* story entitled "The Firebrand" showed an angry looking Brown, with dark sun glasses and a Band-Aid above his left eye, captioned "Brown: 'Burn America down'" (see Figure 3.1). The article also pictured National Guardsmen marching through the smoke-filled ruins of "this sick city" and photographs of fires smoldering in Cambridge. The average reader could easily miss the fact that the fire did not erupt immediately following Brown's speech and that the Band-Aid over his eye came from a shot by a policeman well before the fire began, or that the remark, "this is a sick city," came from the mouth of Governor Agnew, not Brown.

Likewise, *Life* Magazine's August 4, 1967, issue on the "Negro Revolt," which included numerous horrifying photographs of Detroit aflame, displayed a photograph of H. Rap Brown getting arrested in Alexandria, Virginia with the caption "An advocate of arson who got caught," in extra-large font. As with *Newsweek*'s article, a reader could easily assume that Brown was being charged with inciting the riot that caused the flames in Detroit.[16]

Especially in small town newspapers across the country, the view that Brown and other radicals had caused the riots and deserved to be sent to jail for their crimes predominated. An editorial in Jefferson, Missouri's *News and Tribune*, lambasted Washington's "double standard" for having removed General Edwin Walker from command "because he tried to alert his soldiers to the nature and dangers of communism," while refusing to arrest riot makers like Rap Brown, who has "been preaching 'hate whites' and violence wherever he goes." (Walker, a supporter of the arch-conservative John Birch Society, served as the inspiration for General Jack D. Ripper, the maniacal military leader in Stanley Kubrick's *Dr. Strangelove*.) The Nampa, Idaho, *Free Press* condemned "H. Fink Brown" for "encouraging Americans to rise up against American," and criticized the government for failing to place the "seditious, riot-maker, traitor, and garden variety rat fink" in jail. William Buckley, in a widely syndicated column, quoted Brown's Cambridge speech at length to prove that the riots had been caused by those who sought to transform "local disturbances into wholesale insurrections." "Subtract" the demagogic radicals, Buckley added, from the brew, and the "riots" would have been "defused."[17] Columnist Walter Winchell similarly cast radicals, from Stokely Carmichael and LeRoi Jones (Amiri Baraka) to Cassius Clay (Muhammad Ali) to unnamed "Quaker groups," for the nation's unrest. "And then," added Winchell, "there's H. Rap Brown (watch that word 'Rap' Mr. Printer) [parenthetical in original] whom the

---

[16] Gary Wills, "The Second Civil War: This Time It's Simpler, Black vs. White," *Esquire*, 3:3 (March 1968), p. 71. For an overview of news coverage, see Peskin and Almes, *Is Baltimore Burning?*; "Cities: Man with a Match," *Time*, September 22, 1967; Boesel and Goldberg, "Crisis in Cambridge," p. 127; "Fire this Time," *Time*, August 4, 1967, p. 15; "American Tragedy, 1967: Detroit," *Newsweek*, August 7, 1967, p. 28; "Detroit," *Life*, August 4, 1967.

[17] "Washington's Curious Double-Standard," *The Sunday News and Tribune*, September 10, 1967, p. 4; "He's H. Fink Brown," *Idaho Free Press*, August 29, 1967, p. 4; "Republican Minority Saves This Session of Congress," *The Ogden Standard-Examiner*, December 13, 1967, p. 6; William Buckley, "Civil Rights and Colored TV," The Daily Courier (Connellsville, PA), July 29, 1967, p. 8.

FBI sought on a warrant accusing him of inciting a riot in Cambridge, Maryland."[18]

"Such a Person Cannot be Permitted to Enter a State with the Intention to Destroy and then Sneak Away"

Perhaps no public figure was more responsible for linking Brown to Cambridge's "riot," in particular, and for making the case that radicals caused the Great Uprising, in general, than Spiro Agnew. Elected governor of Maryland in 1966 (he had previously served one term as the executive of Baltimore County), Agnew rose from a position of absolute obscurity to the vice presidency of the United States in a mere two years. Prior to the "Brown riot" he had a reputation as a moderate Republican, in a state where the Republican Party was still viewed as the Party of Lincoln by many black voters. Agnew consolidated his reputation as a Rockefeller Republican during his campaign to become the governor of Maryland in 1966. Agnew's Democratic opponent, George P. Mahoney, ran on the slogan, "Your Home is Your Castle – Protect It," a not-so-thinly-veiled reference to proposed open housing legislation, which Mahoney opposed. In contrast, Agnew cast himself as a responsible moderate who would stand up to the hate mongers. Based on his record and promises, Agnew won the endorsement of the *New York Times*, the Americans for Democratic Action, and the *Afro-American*, all liberal institutions. He also won the overwhelming support of Cambridge's black voters.[19] Indeed, as late as a week before Brown spoke in Cambridge, Agnew was still seen this way by much of the civil rights leadership, in Maryland and nationwide.[20]

On the morning of July 25, Agnew rushed to Cambridge from his vacation home in nearby Ocean City, Maryland. Immediately, he issued a statement expressing his "grief and perplexity at this senseless destruction precipitated by a professional agitator whose inflammatory statements

[18] Walter Winchell, "Black and White," *Lebanon Daily News*, August 3, 1967, p. 53.
[19] Jules Witcover, *White Knight: The Rise of Spiro Agnew* (New York: Random House, 1972), especially chs. 5 and 6. See also Peter B. Levy, "Spiro Agnew, The Forgotten Americans, and the Rise of the New Right," *The Historian*, 75 (Winter 2013): 707–739; "Agnew Wins, Dorchester County Favors Demos," *CDB*, November 9, 1966.
[20] "Dr. Ware Eases Agnew's Burdens," *Afro-American*, April 8,1967; "Transcript – News Conference with Roy Wilkins," July 19, 1967, Papers of Spiro T. Agnew, Archives and Manuscript Department, University of Maryland at College Park, Box 5, Subseries 3; Governor Agnew to William Yates, July 12, 1967, in Governor Spiro T. Agnew Papers, MSA, S1041–1713, Box 14.

deliberately provoked the outbreak of violence." Agnew also announced that he had "directed the authorities to seek out H. Rap Brown and bring him to justice." "Such a person," Agnew exclaimed, "cannot be permitted to enter a state with the intention to destroy and then sneak away." Several days later, Agnew asserted that while he deplored slum conditions and persistent discrimination, these problems did not "give any person or group a license to commit crimes." While promising to work for racial reforms, he declared that he would *not* [emphasis added] meet with those who "engage in or urge riots" and that the state of Maryland would "*not* [emphasis added] allow any person to finish" such "vicious" appeals. In other words, he went on record supporting prior constraint over freedom of speech. In separate public statements, Agnew maintained that irresponsible militants, like Brown, had caused the "riots." Even in his private communications Agnew emphasized the connection between black radicals and rioting. "The appearance of H. Rap Brown and his inflammatory speech (a copy of which we were able to record) caused an outburst of violence and burning" in Cambridge, he wrote to New York Governor Nelson Rockefeller. Brown had been arrested for inciting a riot, Agnew declared, and the case against him "should be successful." Agnew responded similarly to the revolt that erupted in Baltimore following Martin Luther King Jr.'s assassination, admonishing moderate civil rights leaders for not censuring black militants (see Part II).[21]

Agnew's claim that Brown had caused Cambridge's unrest dovetailed with Eugene Methvin's *The Riot Makers* (1970), one of the more popular interpretations of rioting published during the era. Building on a highly publicized 1965 piece he wrote for *Reader's Digest* entitled, "How the Reds Make Riots," Methvin compared black radicals to chemical catalysts. Following Leninist tactics, Methvin asserted, black radicals purposely set out to provoke riots so as to foster a crisis which would lead to a revolution. While Methvin acknowledged that riots were built on a variety of social conditions, he strongly disagreed with the Kerner Commission's claim that whites were responsible for them. Just as emphatically, Methvin insisted it took radicals like Brown to light the match. "Career

---

[21] "Statement by Governor Spiro T. Agnew: Subject Cambridge," July 25, 1967; "Statement by Governor Spiro T. Agnew – Civil Rights and Rioting," July 30, 1967; and "Conference with Civil Rights and Community Leaders," April 11, 1968, all in Governor Spiro T. Agnew Papers, Box. 1, Subseries 3, MSA. Spiro Agnew to Nelson Rockefeller, August 1, 1967, Governor Agnew Papers, Box 14.

protesters and extremists rub raw the sores of discontent and widen social cleavages in the community." To help him prove that radicals intentionally sought to spark riots, he cited statements made by H. Rap Brown, such as "'You gotta stop looting and start shooting!'"[22] (Methvin's book was turned into a film which was widely distributed and shown to law enforcement forces across the nation.)[23]

The first full biography of Brown appeared in the *New York Times* on July 28th and it reinforced the public's view that he had caused the "riot" in Cambridge and that radicals, in general, were responsible for the disorders elsewhere. Brown, "who usually refers to whites as 'honkeys,'" the paper observed, had "urged 400 Negroes to 'burn this town down,'" and a few days later "exhorted a group of 100 Negroes" in Jersey City to "wage guerilla warfare." The same story noted that SNCC's "Angry Rights Leader" had made similar statements in Cincinnati, Houston, Montgomery, and Dayton, all cities that had experienced civil disorders.[24] Throughout the fall of 1967, only one story in the national press offered a more favorable portrait of Brown. Written by Staughton Lynd, a one-time colleague of Brown during Mississippi Summer and a prominent co-activist in the antiwar movement, and published in the *New York Times Magazine*, it countered arguments that "riots" were "irrational," "senseless," and "indiscriminate" events and suggested that Brown enjoyed a "kinship" with the founding fathers for his willingness to risk the threat of imprisonment and death threats in the pursuit of freedom. Yet even Lynd did not probe the actual sequence of events in Cambridge nor counter the view that radicals had incited the revolts.[25] Moreover, the *New York Times* made clear that Lynd's piece did not represent its opinion, publishing letters to the editors and follow-up stories that criticized Lynd

[22] Methvin, *The Riot Makers*, pp. 31, 74–76. "Veteran Journalist Eugene H. Methvin Dies at 77," http://grady.uga.edu/news/view2/veteran_journalist_eugene_h._methvin_dies_at_77 [accessed September 16, 2014; website active at time of access].

[23] National Criminal Justice Reference Service, "The Riot Makers: Abstract," www.ncjrs.gov/App/publications/abstract.aspx?ID=77673 [accessed December 4, 2015]; Frank Carrington, "Review of *The Riot Makers*," *Journal of Criminal Law and Criminology*, 62:3 (1972): 457–458.

[24] "Rap Brown Calls Riots 'Rehearsals for Revolution,'" *NYT*, August 7, 1967, p. 1; "An Affable but Angry Rights Leader: Hubert Geroid Brown," *NYT*, July 28,1967, p. 14; "Verbal Fire Setters," *NYT*, August 8, 1967, p. 38; "S.N.C.C. Head Advises Negroes in Washington to Get Guns," *NYT*, July 28, 1967, p. 14; "Chief of S.N.C.C. Hunted by F.B.I: Missing Leader Accused of 'Inciting to Riot,'" *NYT*, July 26, 1967, p. 1; "Police in 3 Cities Say S.N.C.C. Chiefs Incited Rioting," *NYT*, August 3, 1967, p. 1.

[25] Staughton Lynd, "A Radical Speaks in Defense of S.N.C.C.," *NYT*, September 10, 1967, p. 271.

and Brown's ongoing actions.[26] (For more on Brown's legal travails, see below.)

"Mainly for Fun and Profit"

As we should recall, not only did Kinnamon claim that Brown's speech incited Cambridge's "riot," he contended that the city did not have a ghetto nor unemployment or housing problems. Likewise, one of Governor Agnew's top aides, Charles Bressler, wrote that most of the BAF's assertions about poor treatment of black people in Cambridge were "exaggerated." The economy had grown considerably since the early 1960s, Bressler observed, and statements that poor blacks had not benefited from recently built public housing were unfounded. The Cambridge *Daily Banner* made the same argument, heralding the city's accomplishments, from a dramatic drop in the unemployment rate to the construction of public housing.[27]

Such claims dovetailed with conservative interpretations of the revolts that emphasized that blacks were making economic progress and that many of the revolts had taken place in progressive cities. Writing for the *National Review*, for example, Ernest van Den Haag observed: "Negroes have certainly been discriminated against . . . Yet discrimination has diminished and conditions have rapidly improved since the Second World War." Moreover, Van Den Haag maintained, "there have been more improvements in the last twenty years than in the previous two hundred." Similarly, critics of the Kerner Report pointed out that nationwide "black

---

[26] "Rap Brown Calls Nation on 'Eve' of a Negro Revolution," *NYT*, September 11, 1967, p. 76; "East St. Louis Negroes Throw Firebombs in Fresh Disorders," *NYT*, September 12, 1967, p. 25; "Negroes and Pickets Clash at School," *NYT*, September 13, 1967, p. 35; "2 East St. Louis Negroes Hurt by Firebombs as Unrest Goes On," *NYT*, September 13, 1967, p. 32; "Negro Shot in East St. Louis in 4th Night of Racial Unrest," *NYT*, September 14, 1967, p. 12. "Brown Put in Jail to Await Hearing," *NYT*, September 14, 1967, p. 35; "Volunteers Help to Run Schools," *NYT*, September 14, 1967, p. 52; "East St. Louis 'A Doomed City,'" *NYT*, September 17, 1967, p. 40; "A Hearing is Set on Bond for Brown," *NYT*, September 17, 1967, p. 60; "A Militant Priest Kicks Up a Storm," *NYT*, September 17, 1967, p. E4; "Milwaukee Priest Asks Whites to Help on Open Housing Project," *NYT*, September 18, 1967, p. 36; "Rap Brown is Released on Bail," *NYT*, September 19, 1967, p. 28; "Groppi Ask Fund Cutoff," *NYT*, September 22, 1967, p. 38; Walter Goodman, "Yessir Boss, Said the White Radicals: When Black Power Runs the New Left," *NYT*, September 24, 1967; "Letters: Lynd & Lincoln, Hate & History," *NYT*, October 1, 1967, p. 223.

[27] Charles Bressler to Spiro T. Agnew, September 6, 1967, Governor Agnew Papers, Box 14. *CDB*, July 27, 1967, July 28, 1967, August 30, 1967, and December 22, 1967.

unemployment had declined to 6 percent" and that "poverty was declining at a historically rapid rate." Stephan and Abigail Thernstrom, would
rehash this argument in their 1998 review of the Kerner Report, writing
that "in the quarter-century between the entry of the United States into
World War II and the Voting Rights Act of 1965, the position of black
people in the United States radically improved more than in any other
comparably brief period in US history."[28]

The "fact" of improving conditions or progress for African Americans
underlay one of the other predominant explanations for the revolts, that
they were cultural in origin. The McCone Commission, which California Governor Pat Brown appointed to study Watts, downplayed the role
played by radicals or communists, focusing instead on the rioters themselves, who it claimed were largely young, rootless males, who came from
broken families, had a history of disciplinary problems in the schools, and
had slipped into the ranks of the permanently unemployed. The roots of
black despondency, the report continued, were not to be found in institutional racism but rather, essentially, in the unfortunate history of black
people, who brought with them their rural ways when they migrated to
America's cities in the middle decades of the twentieth century. Rather
than criticize the police or government policies which impeded black
progress, the McCone Commission maintained that "government officials
have [already] done much" and demanded that future "programs must
not be oversold," inferring that the cultural deficiencies of black Americans would diminish the impact of any and all government programs. The
report also suggested that the media and civil rights leaders had exacerbated the situation in Watts via their sensational coverage of the disorders
and their advocacy of "disobedience of the law," respectively.[29]

While few read the entire McCone Report, many picked up its
gist through either news' reports or via popular works that selectively
cited its findings. The *Wall Street Journal*'s headline of the McCone

[28] Fine, *Violence in the Model City*; Thomas Bray, Reading America the Riot Act: The
Kerner Report and its Culture of Violence, *Policy Review*, 43 (Winter 1988): 34; Stephan
Thernstrom, "The Kerner Report," lecture held at Heritage Foundation, March 13, 1968,
www.heritage.org/research/lecture/the-kerner-commission-report [accessed September
9, 2014]; Ernest van den Haag, "How Not to Prevent Civil Disorders," *National Review*,
March 26, 1968, p. 284. For an insightful refutation of these characterizations of recent
migrants to Los Angeles, see Isabel Wilkerson, *The Warmth of Other Suns: The Epic
Story of America's Great Migration* (New York: Random House, 2010).
[29] "Summary of Commission Report on Race Riots in Los Angeles," *NYT*, December 7,
1965, p. 26. For early criticisms of the report, see "Watts Riots Study Depicted as Weak,"
NYT, January 23, 1966, p. 71.

Commission's findings on the Watts rebellion, representatively declared, "Behind the Riots: Family Life Breakdown in Negro Slums Sows Seeds of Race Violence." Below the headlines, the story explained that "the spreading disintegration of the Negro family in the big cities of the North and West," accounted for the violence in Watts which had left thirty-one people dead and over 175 million dollars in property damage. Countless national publications echoed this claim, from the *Washington Post*, which highlighted the "The Illness Behind Watts," to the *Saturday Evening Post* in which Stewart Alsop emphasized the "savage bitterness" and alienation of young black men, as opposed to their poor relations with the police and systematic or institutional racism.[30]

Many popular explanations of the revolts, which built on the findings of the McCone Report and contemporary reporting, cast radicalism and cultural deviancy as two halves of the same coin. *Anarchy, Los Angeles*, a sensational sixty-five page single-edition glossy magazine, which sold over 250,000 copies in less than a month, "characterized" the Watts "conflagration" not as an insurrection but as "hoodlumism" informed by "fun" and "recreation." Acknowledging that there was "no easy answer" to why Watts had exploded, the magazine rejected the proposition that police brutality, "that old bugaboo" had played a role. On the contrary, the magazine asserted, "Los Angeles has probably the finest metropolitan police force in the country," a view which dovetailed with the McCone Commission's depiction of police Chief William Parker. Nor did Watts grow out of long-standing "Negro...frustrations." On the contrary, *Anarchy, Los Angeles* stressed, it was the "lawless fringe" of the community who had been encouraged by "various political and community figures" on the "fringe of the rights cause" to "lash out and take by force that which they are constantly told has been denied them."[31]

In his much ballyhooed study of the urban rebellions of the 1960s, Edward Banfield similarly argued that rioters had rioted "mainly for fun and profit." (For more on Banfield, see Introduction and Part II.) In a piece

---

[30] "Behind the Riots: Family Life Breakdown in Negro Slums Sows Seeds of Race Violence," *Wall Street Journal*, August 16, 1965, p. 1; "The Illness Behind Watts," *Washington Post*, November 21, 1965, p. E1; Rowland Evans and Robert Novak, "Inside Report: The Moynihan Report," *Washington Post*, August 18, 1965. See also the coverage in *Life Magazine*, August 27, 1965, such as the photographs headlined, "Wild Plundering – Grab It and Run."

[31] M. B. Jackson, "The Second Civil War," *Anarchy, Los Angeles* (1965); Strain, *Pure Fire*, p. 133. On the popularity of *Anarchy, Los Angeles*, see Business Bulletin, *Wall Street Journal*, September 19, 1965.

published in the *New York Times Sunday Magazine*, Banfield's colleague, James Q. Wilson, dismissed the notion that "Negroes riot because their lot is deplorable," on the grounds that the "lot of many Negroes has always been deplorable." Wilson also rejected the "relative deprivation" theory, which suggested that blacks revolted because they were deprived relative to other groups. Rather, Wilson asserted that the disorders were more "expressive than instrumental," meaning they were not aimed at achieving any particular political or economic end but at fulfilling personal and emotional needs. And Methvin's aforementioned *The Riot Makers*, while emphasizing the role played by radicals, made clear that one reason they were so successful was because of the "pools of pathology," which included very high rates of divorce, mental illness, and "sub-cultures of violence."[32]

This cultural interpretation gained traction, in part, because it dovetailed with the completion of Daniel Patrick Moynihan's "The Negro Family: The Case for National Action." While some members of the Johnson Administration feared, rightly as it turned out, that the "Moynihan Report" would turn into a "political atom bomb," it became one of the dominant lenses to view the revolts. As *Washington Post* columnists Robert Novak and Rowland Evans put it, this "leaked Labor Department document" "expose[d] the ugly truth about the big-city Negro's plight." In response to the "big-city Negro riots" of the summer of 1964, Novak and Evans continued, Moynihan probed their causes. Rather than radicals or racism in the labor and housing markets, he found that "broken homes, illegitimacy, and female-oriented home life," all rooted in a "tangle of pathology" that could be traced back to the era of slavery best explained the urban ills out of which the revolts erupted. Other writers, such as the aforementioned Methvin, picked up on Moynihan's argument and similarly focused on the "moral foundations of violence." How else to explain disorders in cities like Watts (and later Detroit) which had relatively low unemployment rates, or, as one commentator put it, "no authority with a white face stopped...blacks from casting a vote, or from using the rest rooms at the train station."[33] (As we will see, Agnew and others would

---

[32] James Q. Wilson, "Why We Are Having a Wave of Violence," *New York Times Sunday Magazine*, May 19, 1968, p. 23; Methvin, *The Riot Makers*, ch. 2; Edward Banfield, *The Unheavenly City* (Boston: Little, Brown, 1970).
[33] Office of Policy Planning and Research, United States Department of Labor, "The Negro Family: The Case for National Action," March, 1965, https://web.stanford.edu/~mrosenfe/Moynihan%27s%20The%20Negro%20Family.pdf [accessed February

build on this cultural perspective to hold liberals and their culture of permissiveness responsible for the "disorders.")

Put somewhat differently, statements made by a wide variety of officials, from Cambridge Police Chief Brice Kinnamon to Maryland Governor Spiro Agnew, reinforced by sensational media coverage, which highlighted the fiery rhetoric of black radicals like H. Rap Brown, convinced many Americans – if they needed much convincing – that radicals had caused the revolts and that those who had rioted had done so for fun and profit, not for political reasons. As a poll taken in August 1967 revealed, 45 percent of whites blamed outside agitators for the nation's urban unrest, whereas less than one-third of that number saw either ghetto conditions or "promises not kept" as the cause. A similar poll question revealed that 71 percent of whites believed that the riots were "part of an organized effort," not "spontaneous eruptions." And many whites argued that the main reason for the riots was black laziness, and/or "uneducated people" who did not "know what they are doing," rather than lack of jobs or ghetto conditions. Not surprisingly, the most popular riot-prevention measures were "increasing the size of the police force," "instituting stronger repressive measures," and finding and punishing outside agitators. In contrast, only a very small percentage of white Americans, less than 5 percent, felt that giving black citizens equal opportunities, providing better recreational facilities, or holding more conferences between whites and blacks would prevent further violence.[34]

"It Was Their Way of Getting Revenge. They just Let the Place Burn Down"

Yet, these were not the only explanations given for the revolts of the summer of 1967. Rather, many cast the social and economic conditions of the nation's urban ghettos, not radicals and/or moral failings on the part of blacks, as the primary causes of the uprisings. Or as the Kerner Commission declared in its oft-cited summation of its five hundred plus page report, "What white Americans have never fully understood – but what the Negro can never forget – is that white society is deeply implicated in the ghetto. White institutions created it, white institutions maintain it,

---

4, 2016] (henceforth, "The Moynihan Report"); Viorst, Fire, p. 309. See also: Sides, *L.A. City Limits*.

[34] Hazel Erskine, "The Polls: Demonstrations and Race Riots," *Public Opinion Quarterly*, 31 (Winter 1967): 655.

and white society condones it." (When the commission issued its report, H. Rap Brown noted with some irony that its members "should be put in jail under $100,000 bail each, because they're saying essentially what I've been saying.")[35]

Though few in the nation paid them any heed, black residents of Cambridge clearly agreed that inequality and white racism, not radicals, produced the revolts. "It's not the H. Rap Browns and Stokely Carmichaels that cause the trouble," observed BAF activist Roger Stewart shortly after the "Brown riot," but "it's the kind of conditions that the black people are living in this very day in the Second Ward." Agreeing with this assessment, Gloria Richardson sought to use her connections with Edward Brooke, the only black in the US Senate, whom she's known from her college days at Howard University, to garner the BAF an ear with the Kerner Commission – she was unsuccessful in this endeavor. Somewhat along the same lines, not a single black resident of the city who was interviewed by George Collins blamed Brown for the fire.[36]

On the contrary, Cambridge's black residents emphasized that the RFC's intransigence had caused the crisis. Jack White, a *Washington Post* reporter, for instance, observed that Cambridge's black population remained very bitter over the "refusal of the police chief to let the volunteer firemen go into the area to stop the fire," not Brown's address. In a brief moment of anger, William Green, the brother of Hansel Green who had committed suicide after his business burned down, suggested that Brown and local radicals had caused the "riot." Yet, these words, uttered in a moment of deep grief, belied Hansel Green's own statement, made the day after the fire, that "one lousy truck" could have prevented the destruction of his property and that of many other residents of the Second Ward. "I called [the RFC] three times. My brother called twice. Councilman Charles Cornish called. Still the firemen wouldn't come," Green angrily declared. "The school was burning a long time before the fire began spreading...But they just wouldn't come down here." Herbert St. Clair echoed Green's sentiments. "IT'S A [emphasis in original] damn shame. It was their way of getting revenge. They just let the place burn

---

[35] Kerner Commission, *Report*, p. 2; Brown quoted in, "Rights Leaders Support Criticism of Whites," *NYT*, March 2, 1968, p. 1.
[36] "Church Padlocked; B.P. Rally Moved," *Afro-American*, October 7, 1967; "Black Power Rally Here Over Weekend," *CDB*, October 2, 1967; "Negro Group Demands Better Housing, Jobs," *CDB*, October 3, 1967.

down."[37] Likewise, Maryland's top NAACP leaders, often at odds with Richardson and CNAC, contended that racial inequality not Brown had caused the "riot." Black students were barely "tolerated" at the previously all-white Cambridge High School, observed Juanita Jackson Mitchell, and the Pine Street Elementary School was "a fire trap which should have been closed down long ago."[38] (Ironically, few took note that Cambridge had not experienced a riot by the traditional definition of the term.)

Afro-American journalist George Collins presented probably the most comprehensive refutation of Kinnamon's interpretation of events. While acknowledging that Brown had delivered an inflammatory speech, Collins observed that Kinnamon left out of his testimony several key facts. "Brother Kinnamon 'forgot' about the white night riders" who "raced through Pine Street before the outbreak of violence" and left out of his testimony a remark he had made personally to Collins the night of the unrest, namely: "'the N__s set it, let the damn place burn down.'" Collins challenged Kinnamon's claim that Cambridge did not have a ghetto and that "ninety-nine percent of Cambridge's colored citizens are opposed to this sort of thing." In addition, Collins chided Kinnamon for failing to mention that the Cambridge's government was run by segregationists. Collins, who would go on to become a leading media figure in the Baltimore metro area, concluded with a riff that probably would have made H. Rap Brown proud. "Perhaps it is overly optimistic to expect the boss policeman of Cambridge to tell the nation that his town is a festering sore, reeking with bigotry [and] prejudice ... And that its only concern is to keep colored people locked in the ruins of the slums of Pine Street ... with no hope of ever escaping. No, Chief Kinnamon didn't tell them. But somebody had better tell them – and soon!"[39]

Collins's strongly worded editorial helped illustrate the broad divide that existed between blacks and most whites when it came to understanding the causes of the Great Uprising. In contrast to whites, who blamed outside agitators for inciting the revolts, black men and women listed

[37] "Negro Group Demands Better Housing Jobs," *CDB*, October 3, 1967; "New Cambridge Negro Unit Asks LBJ for Food, Clothing, Shelter," *Washington Post*, July 27, 1967, p. A2; George Collins, "They're Bitter, Fearful, Bewildered," *Afro-American*, August 5, 1967; "Hansel Green Biden Farewell," *Baltimore Sun*, August 9, 1967, p. A9.
[38] "Cambridge Riot Victims Ask for Federal Aid," *Chicago Defender*, August 5, 1967, p. 5.
[39] George Collins, "What Kinnamon Didn't Reveal," *Afro-American*, August 19, 1967. Richard Homan, "Potomac Watch: Rift is Wide in Cambridge," *Washington Post*, August 8, 1967, p. B1. Louis C. Goldberg, "Ghetto Riots and Others: The Faces of Civil Disorder in 1967," *Journal of Peace Research*, 5:2 (June 1968): 116–131.

"prejudice," "ghetto conditions," and a lack of jobs or unfair employment as the main causes. Even greater disparities appeared when asked about police brutality and the criminal justice system – only 8 percent of whites saw police brutality as one of the causes of riots, whereas 49 percent of black respondents did. Likewise, whereas only 34 percent of whites felt that rank and file blacks supported the race revolts, 91 percent of blacks felt they did.[40]

One white official who tended to agree with Collins's interpretation was General George Gelston. Gelston had been the commander of the National Guard when it had been called into Cambridge in 1963–1964 and again in 1967, and he conveyed his views in testimony to the Senate Judiciary Committee. Whereas Kinnamon had contended that H. Rap Brown was the "sole" cause of the riots and that race relations were "excellent," Gelston retorted: "Were there no problem there would be no need for an invitation" in the first place. In support of this alternative perspective, Gelston read at length a letter written by William Adkins, a prominent and well-respected white attorney from Talbot County, which lay just north of Cambridge. "Race relations in Cambridge are not excellent," wrote Adkins. "There are deep-seated feelings of hostility on both sides ... Such progress as has been made ... has done little to improve feelings, since much that was done following 1963 was done not as a recognition of the justice of the Negroes' claims and grievances, but ostensibly as a result of the violence itself." Many racial problems remain, Adkins continued. "Blacks in Cambridge still live largely in a ghetto ... Schools ... are a continuing aggravation ... Little comment need be made about Chief Kinnamon's own swimming pool, which was operated as a totally segregated facility by the Cambridge Volunteer Fire Department."[41]

Gelston also challenged Kinnamon's specific recollection of the events of the night of July 24th. Brown completed his speech at 9:50, Gelston testified, and "nothing happened" until 10:30. While Gelston acknowledged that a brief encounter took place between a group of black activists and police, things remained calm afterwards, he asserted. "From 11:20 until 10 minutes before 12 there was quiet to such an extent" that the commander of the Guard (Gelston), the captain of the state police, and the state's attorney agreed that the "National Guard could be released

---

[40] Erskine, "The Polls: Demonstrations, and Race Riots."

[41] US Senate, Committee on the Judiciary, Hearings on H.R. 421, Anti-Riot Bill – 1967, *Congressional Record*, 90th Congress, 1st Session, Washington, DC: GPO, 1967 "Hearings-Anti-Riot Bill," Adkins quoted pp. 741–744; see also *Congressional Record*, 90th Congress, 1st Session, vol. 113, Part 19, pp. 25404–25406.

and sent home." The fire at the Pine Street Elementary School, Gelston stressed, did not begin until over an hour after the National Guard were released. In other words, contrary to Kinnamon's claims "there was not continuous rioting action following Brown's speech."[42]

Whereas the Senate panel treated Kinnamon as a friendly witness and did not challenge his rendition of the events of the 24th or his broader claim that Brown had caused Cambridge's "riot," it responded quite unfavorably to Gelston's testimony. North Carolina Senator Sam Erwin sought to get Gelston to admit that Brown led a mob downtown after his speech and to establish that the intent of the mob was malicious. Erwin's efforts notwithstanding, Gelston refused to corroborate this claim. On the contrary, Gelston told the committee about the appearances of two other black militants in Cambridge, Dick Gregory and Adam Clayton Powell, earlier in the decade, neither of which led to a unrest. In 1963, Gelston observed, Powell delivered an "inflammatory speech." The following year, Gregory "came down from New York for 4 straight nights." But by personally meeting and maintaining open communication with them, Gelston explained, things "just sort of petered out." In other words, since the appearance of militant speakers in Cambridge had not sparked riots in the past there was no reason to believe Brown's speech had sparked a riot this time around. The committee did not provide Gelston the opportunity to chide Kinnamon for failing to learn or follow this lesson.[43]

Regarding the subject of residential segregation in Cambridge, Senator Erwin and Gelston engaged in a testy exchange. Erwin tried to get Gelston to admit that it was "natural" for people to want to live with other people of the same race. To which Gelston responded, "I don't agree that it happens that way just because people desire it that way." Erwin then countered, "It [segregation] has been going on in this country since the first settlers got in, hasn't it?" "It sure has," Gelston replied. "So if it is not natural, it has been a pretty ingrained practice, hasn't it," Erwin insisted. "Maybe that is the reason for the unrest, that it is not natural," Gelston retorted. At which point Erwin quickly changed the subject to turbulence that had taken place in New Haven, Connecticut.[44]

---

[42] US Senate, Committee on the Judiciary, pp. 730–751; *Congressional Record* – Senate, 90th Congress, 1st Session, Vol 113 Part 19, pp. 25404–25405; State of Maryland, Military Department, "After Action Report – Civil Disturbances Operations," August 25, 1967, in Records of the National Commission on Civil Disorders, reel 28.

[43] US Senate Committee on the Judiciary, pp. 730–737.

[44] US Senate Committee on the Judiciary, pp. 742–744.

Further evidence that Gelston's appearance was not well-received came a few weeks later when Maryland Senator Tydings, one of the members of the Senate Judiciary Committee, entered an editorial into the *Congressional Record* that sharply criticized Gelston "He may know a little something about the army but he certainly does not understand the racial problem," the editorial from the Cambridge *Daily Banner* read. Gelston stated that the riots might have been averted if the city had "given some recognition to Negro grievances," the paper continued. "For his edification we'll outline a few of the things that have been done," and then it proceeded to rattle off the usual litany of alleged improvements that had been made in Cambridge over the past several years, from the establishment of Head Start and jobs training programs to the building of public housing. "Since 1965, the Dorchester County Commissioners have put more cash into the antipoverty program than allocated by any of the other eight counties on the Eastern Shore," the paper added, hardly evidence of neglect.[45]

One contemporary who came to Gelston's defense and who simultaneously challenged the conservative interpretation of racial rioting was the novelist John Barth. A native of Cambridge, Barth's father "Whitey" was a longtime member of the RFC and a judge on the Orphan's Court. In one of his novels, Barth had expressed sympathy for the volunteer spirit of fire association and its members. Yet, Barth, who had moved from Cambridge upon entering college, had taken on many of the liberal ideals of the broader metropolises in which he lived and dislike, if not contempt, for some of the provincial mores of America's small towns. Drawing on Gelston's testimony as well as reportage of several national newspapers, Barth rhetorically inquired: "Mustn't the responsibility . . . be laid as much at the door of Chief Kinnamon and those of his way of thinking as at the door of H. Rap Brown & Co.?" After all, Barth observed, Kinnamon had prevented the Rescue and Fire Company from entering the Second Ward to put out the fire before it spread. Even more stridently, Barth rhetorically interrogated the structural inequality that underlay the racist responses of the state to developments in Cambridge. "One wonders what kind of fireman it is who put out fires only in house of people he approves of; what kind of policeman it is who refuses to protect a law-abiding citizen from the depredations of a lawbreaker because they both happen to be the same color; what kind of state's attorney is it who defines a juvenile as a white child." The last remark was a reference to the disparate treatment

---

[45] "Editorial," *CDB*, August 28, 1967, inserted into *Congressional Record*, 90th Congress, 1st Session, September 13, 1967, p. 25405.

that white and black youths had received in the months before Brown's appearance.[46]

Barth's charges garnered considerable attention from the press, much of it unfavorable, particularly in local newspapers. One letter writer not only defended the RFC, he lambasted Barth for suggesting that one day the community would come to recognize Gloria Richardson as one of its great historical figures, akin to Harriet Tubman. "I have no doubt that Mrs. Gloria Richardson Dandridge will be lectured upon by our own historical society," the letter writer pronounced. "But, Mr. Barth, Hitler and Eichman are lectured upon in Germany, but thank God not in the same esteem as Adenauer."[47] (In the summer of 2008, after the election of its first black mayor, Victoria Jackson-Stanley, Cambridge formally recognized Richardson, declaring August 10th as "Gloria Richardson Day.")[48]

"The Commission Didn't Get It"

While Barth's rejoinder tended to dovetail with the Kerner Commission's conclusion that social conditions, or the ghetto, which had been created and maintained by whites, not radicals, caused Cambridge's "riot," somewhat surprisingly, the Kerner Commission went out of its way to leave details about Cambridge out of its final report, literally relegating it to a series of footnotes and some charts. It did so for a couple of reasons. First, it did not want to undermine the criminal prosecution of Brown. Second, it recognized that Cambridge's revolts did not fit neatly with its depiction of what riots were and why they were taking place. The report's seventy-four page chapter "Profiles of Disorder," for instance, made no mention of events in Cambridge in 1967 and only passing reference to its earlier history of unrest. Nor did the report's extensive index include a single reference to Cambridge in 1967. To be clear, the omission of Cambridge did *not* derive from the commission's lack of knowledge about the

---

[46] John Barth, "Letter to the Editor," *CDB*, August 11, 1967; Peskin and Almes, *Is Baltimore Burning*; Interview with John Barth, by author, Baltimore, Maryland (in author's possession); US Senate, Committee on the Judiciary, pp. 730–745; George Collins, "They're Bitter, Fearful, Bewildered," *Afro-American*, August 5, 1967.

[47] Thomas Hurley, "Letters to the Editor," *CDB*, August 15, 1967. Gail Dean, "Woman Honored for Civil Rights Work," *The Star Democrat* (Easton, MD), August 15, 2008, www.stardem.com/news/article_7fad9e56-1635-52f6-a424-ee3a9fa10a26.html [accessed August 22, 2014].

[48] "Cambridge Honors Gloria Richardson," August 15, 2008, www.myeasternshoremd.com/news/dorchester_county/article_9185f8c3-675f-5bf7-9762-75213f11a2e2.html [accessed September 23, 2016].

community. On the contrary, Cambridge was one of twenty cities, out of 150, which the commission's field representatives visited and one of twenty-three cities its social scientists extensively surveyed. The commission's staff conducted in-person interviews with members of Cambridge's black and white communities, analyzed pertinent social and economic data on the region, and crafted a series of memos on conditions there. General Gelston also testified in hearings held by the commission.[49]

The sum total of this information undermined the standard chronology of events in Cambridge, namely that Brown's speech had caused Cambridge's riot. It also included a bevy of extremely disparaging information about the city's officials and white elite that could have given readers a much fuller appreciation of the entrenched bigotry that underlay the disorders of the 1960s and which suggested that whites, including local authorities, had precipitated the violence and allowed the fire to burn out of control in 1967. "Nineteen sixty-seven was hardly the first time that Kinnamon had displayed a vengeful attitude" toward black activists, the investigators wrote in one internal memo. In 1963 the police chief "had wanted to stop buses full of demonstrators coming to Cambridge and shoot them." At the time, staffers wrote, "the Fire Department [*sic*] had refused to put out blazes" in the Second Ward, except when "threatened" by the mayor – essentially with a replacement by a paid professional force. Kinnamon's assistant, the investigators added, openly referred to blacks as "darkies." The commission's investigators also made clear that power in the city rested with "a small group of influential white citizens," including a prominent attorney, the editor of the city's newspaper, a leading downtown merchant, insurance man, and a manager of one of the largest manufacturing firms. These power brokers, along with the RFC, benefited from the perpetuation of the racial status quo and for years had done their best to resist black demands for reform.[50]

About the same time that the Kerner Commission published its findings, several newspapers reported that the commission had buried an important internal memo entitled the "Analysis of the Cambridge Disturbance." This memo, the newspapers explained, suggested that Cambridge

[49] "Analysis of Cambridge"; "Reconnaissance Survey Field Research Report [Draft]," n.d., reel 23:0326; "Memorandum: Cambridge, Maryland PPR," October 30, 1967, reel 16:042; Kyran M. McGrath, "Memorandum: Cambridge," August 31, 1967, reel 12; "Memorandum: Cambridge, Maryland: A Preliminary Appraisal," November 2, 1967, reel 23; Patricia Bennett, "Role of Negro Police (Cambridge, Maryland)," November 27, 1967, reel 12: 0872, all in *Civil Rights During the Johnson Administration*: Part 5.
[50] "Analysis of Cambridge."

had not experienced a "riot" but only a "low level disturbance." The "leaked" memo, newspapers stated, also suggested that H. Rap Brown had *not* caused the unrest and strongly criticized Chief Kinnamon for going on "'an emotional binge in which his main desire seems to have been to kill Negroes.'" Alvin Spivak, director of information for the commission, responded that the "leaked" memo was one of a number of "very preliminary" reports, a "kind of trial run on a method for conducting the inquiry." He also emphasized that the commission had rejected its findings and suggested that the press should not make too much of it. Unfortunately, the national press never pushed Spivak to document his claims. With the exception of one *Washington Post* story, most coverage by the nation's leading papers relegated the memo to their back pages and did not investigate it further.[51]

In contrast, the black press and the burgeoning radical or alternative press sought to publicize its conclusions. The *Atlanta Daily World* declared: "Riot Commission Accuses Cambridge Police of Helping to Start a Riot." The *Chicago Defender* announced that the "Report Clears Rap Brown" and the *Pittsburg Courier* stated that the commission had uncovered that the police had "panicked" following Brown's speech, clearing the way for Brown's release.[52] Yet in spite of its reputation as a friend of civil liberties and rights, the national media did not, as suggested above, pursue this perspective, preferring instead to champion the Kerner Commission's broader interpretation of the revolts.

Gary Marx, one of the commission's investigators, later postulated that the commission left Cambridge out of its report because it did not fit neatly into the commission's frame of what riots were or what caused them. Cambridge had not experienced a commodity riot but a fairly classic communal riot, which set whites against blacks. Essentially, it was not a far stretch to suggest that Cambridge's 1967 "riot" looked much more like the pogroms of the last years of the nineteenth and early decades of the twentieth century, such as in Wilmington (North Carolina), Atlanta (Georgia), Springfield (Illinois), and Tulsa (Oklahoma), where white

---

[51] Gail Bensinger and Maurine McLaughlin, "Report Says Rap Brown Didn't Cause Md. Riot," *Washington Post*, March 5, 1968, p. A1; "'Ray Memo' to Panel Links Cambridge Riots to Fears of Whites," *NYT*, March 6, 1968, p. 24L; "Riot Report is Disavowed," *Baltimore Sun*, March 5, 1968, p. C9; "Agnew Argues with Report," *Afro-American*, March 9, 1968, p. 32.
[52] "Commission Accuses Cambridge Police of Helping to Start a Riot," *Atlanta Daily World*, March 5, 1968, p. 1; "Maryland Report Clears Rap Brown," March 12, 1968, p. 20; "Says Police Panicked," *New Pittsburg Courier*, May 16, 1968, p. 1.

citizens and authorities went on rampages against blacks, than the typical revolts of the mid-1960s. Marx also suggested that the Kerner Commission avoided discussing Cambridge because it hinted at another underlying cause of the national uprising, namely the Vietnam War. "Wars abroad have been strongly related to violent internal conflicts at home," Marx observed. "That three-quarters of the race riots [in US history] occurred in the one-quarter years devoted to wars" was not mere coincidence. Wars served as "models for violent behavior," tended to raise "black aspirations," and, in the case of the Vietnam War, sapped "vital energy and resources away from the cities in a context of heightened aspirations." Although H. Rap Brown had not used these exact words, he made a similar point in his speech in Cambridge on July 24, 1967. Somewhat paradoxically, conservatives would increasingly find connections between the riots and the war, though in their case the common theme was liberal willingness to appease or embolden radicals (black and antiwar) and an unwillingness to use overwhelming force to maintain order (domestic and international).[53]

Additional unpublished memos suggest that the commission sought to avert discussing Cambridge because it did not want to undermine the criminal case against Brown. Nathaniel Jones, the assistant general counsel of the commission, advised Victor Palmieri, the commission's deputy executive director, to avoid releasing internal memos to Brown's attorneys. He also put forth a legal strategy for doing so, namely invoking executive privilege – more specifically claiming that the commission was exempt from the "Public Information Section of the Administrative Procedure Act." As a result, commission officials withheld potentially exculpatory evidence, such as official timelines which showed that the fire did not erupt until well after Brown had left Cambridge and that the RFC unnecessarily had refused to put out the fire or provide aide to residents who sought to do so. Its determination to hide this information combined with its decision to distance itself from the "Analysis of Cambridge," suggested that both liberals and conservatives prioritized silencing black radicals over maintaining the rule of law.[54]

---

[53] Gary Marx, "Two Cheers for the National Riot (Kerner) Commission Report," in *Black Americans: A Second Look*, ed. by J. F. Szwed (New York: Basic Books, 1970).

[54] For internal discussions of the initial reports, see Henry Taliaferro Jr. to David Ginsburg and Vic Palmieri, Nov. 1, 1967; Nathaniel Jones to Victor Palmieri, March 28, 1967, *Kerner Commission Records*, reel 14.

In addition to hiding the findings of the investigation of Cambridge, the Kerner Commission also essentially censored a more radical interpretation of the riots writ large entitled the "Harvest of American Racism." Written by some of the same social scientists who produced the "Analysis of Cambridge," "Harvest" emphasized that the revolts were political in content and that the proper response was neither law and order or simply more federal funds but rather a fundamental redistribution of power. In addition, "Harvest" explicitly cast the Vietnam War as one of the causes of the revolts and contended that since the war drained funds away from domestic needs, the only way to address the latter would be to end the former. These views proved absolutely unpalatable to David Ginsburg, the director of Kerner Commission, in part because he understood that neither key commissioners nor Johnson would accept them. As a result, he fired the entire staff of social scientists, comprised of 120 men and women, who were associated with it. Recalling the presentation of "Harvest" to the commission, David Boessel, one of its authors, explained: "It was clear" that the Commissioners "didn't get it." They found "Harvest" to be too "politically explosive," because it challenged major assumptions, namely that "riots could not be understood without a conception of black struggle against white domination" and that the "causes were not to be found in the obviously bad living conditions but in the system of the distribution of power in the total society."[55]

"I Know That You are Just a Scapegoat, Unjustly Charged with White Maryland's Wrongs"

Before turning to our second case study, namely Baltimore, it is helpful to briefly survey the plight of H. Rap Brown following his appearance in Cambridge because it sheds a good deal of light on this alternative understanding of the nature and causes of the Great Uprising. More specifically, the state's pursuit of Brown illustrates its desire to deflect responsibility away from its own culpability in creating and maintaining Jim Crow in the North. Two days after his Cambridge address, Brown was arrested outside the nation's capital for inciting a riot. Afterwards, in an

---

55 For Boesel's and Goldberg's recollections, see Andrew Kopkind, "White on Black: the Riot Commission and the Rhetoric of Reform," in *Cities Under Siege*, ed. by David Boesel and Peter Rossi (New York: Basic Books, 1971), pp. 227–249. A condensed version of Kopkind's was article originally published in *Hard Times*, 4 (September 15–22, 1969), pp. 1–4

impromptu news conference, Brown uttered what would become his sig-
natory statement: "Violence is as American as Cherry Pie," which the
press implied meant that he advocated black on white violence.[56] Given
this reading of Brown, not surprisingly, politicians and pundits demanded
his immediate arrest and imprisonment. As a representative letter to the
editor declared, "These people have no right to trial. Either you people in
Congress take immediate steps or we the people will do the job." Weighing in on whether Brown should be released on bail, William Buckley concurred. Since it seemed "perfectly plain that there is clear and present danger that bloodshed and property damage will follow," Buckley declared
that Brown should not be provided bail.[57]

In "Who Are the Real Outlaws?" Brown countered that white condemnation of black violence was hypocritical and self-serving. "They talk
about violence in the country's streets!" "Each time a Black church is
bombed or burned, that is violence in our streets! Where are the troops?
Each time a Black body is found in the swamps of Mississippi or Alabama
that is violence in our land! Where are those murderers? . . . Each time a
police officer shoots and kills a Black teenager that is urban crime!" Just
as importantly, Brown and his attorney, William Kunstler, asserted that
he had not incited a riot nor committed any other crime. Along the same
lines, Brown's personal experience in Cambridge complicated the traditional framing of the revolts, which cast whites as innocent bystanders
and victims. Brown, himself, knew that white authorities had acted as
agents of violence – the deputy sheriff shot him while he was escort-
ing a young woman home, white night riders had caravanned through
the Second Ward, perhaps with guns ablaze, and the chief of police had
allowed the fire to spread in spite of the high cost to black businesses and
residents.[58]

[56] "Congress Mail Heavy on Rioting in Nation," *The Daily Telegram*, August 1, 1967,
p. 1. "Rapp [sic] Brown Sought on Charges of Inciting Cambridge Violence," *Evening
Sun* (Baltimore, MD), July 25, 1967; "Cambridge Riot Beautiful," *Washington Post*, July
27, 1967, p. 3; "Brown Blasts Johnson and Rights Chiefs," *Washington Post*, July 28,
1967, p. A1; "Leader of S.N.C.C. Seized in Virginia," *NYT*, July 27, 1967, p. 1; "S.N.C.C.
Head Advises Negroes in Washington to Get Guns," *NYT*, July 28, 1967, p. 14.

[57] Carolyn Arnesen, "Jail Them," *Wall Street Journal*, August 7, 1967, p. 10; Thurmond
quoted in: "Senator Eastland Raps Rioters," *Fairbanks Daily News-Miner*, August 3,
1967, p. 9; "Good Question," *The Gaffney Ledger*, September 8, 1967, p. 3; "Life
Clouds on Horizon Soon May Engulf U.S. in Anarchy," The Post-Crescent (Appleton,
WI), August 5, 1967, p. 11.

[58] H. Rap Brown, "Who Are the Real Outlaws," in *Die Nigger Die*, pp. 105–107; "We'll
Meet Violence With Violence," *Afro-American*, July 9, 1966, p. 1.

Yet, as Andrew Kopkind wrote, the commission "shrank" from blaming the police and dared not suggest that white authorities may have precipitated the vast majority of the violence. Indeed, a series of reports and subsequent studies by scholars, largely produced by leftists or the black press, suggested that Cambridge was not an outlier. During Detroit's riots, white policemen killed three black men and brutally beat nine other men and women in what became known as the Algiers Motel incident. As John Hersey, author of a prize-winning book on Hiroshima explained, revenge and anger motivated these police killings. Louis Goldberg, similarly uncovered a widespread pattern of white official violence. "Riots," Goldberg observed, often went through different stages. "In the first, widespread and aggressive action by ghetto Negroes overwhelmed local police forces, leaving them virtually powerless to enforce order in the streets. In the second … authorities engaged in harsh retaliatory actions to reassert dominance." In this second state, Goldberg added, "Deep-rooted racial prejudices surfaced. The desire to vent hostility, to re-establish dominance, and to avenge police honor became compelling motives." Subsequent scholarship by Albert Bergesen confirmed that reports of black snipers and the deaths of whites at black hands during the revolts were vastly overstated. In Newark and Detroit, over two-thirds of known deaths were caused by officials (disproportionately white police and troops) shooting at unarmed individuals, including twenty-two men and women who were shot while looting or while fleeing a looting scene, and the bulk of the rest when "authorities fired indiscriminately into crowds," including a four-year-old black girl who was hit in the back.[59]

While this is not the time and place to describe all of H. Rap Brown's legal travails, a brief review is in order because it enhances our understanding of the lengths that the government went to suppress black radicals and divert attention away from its own culpability in the revolts. After being shot in Cambridge, Brown fled, not to avoid arrest – he was

---

[59] Kopkind, "White on Black: The Riot Commission and the Rhetoric of Reform; John Hersey, *The Algiers Motel Incident*, with an Introduction by Thomas Sugrue (Baltimore, MD: Johns Hopkins University, 1997) (originally published by Alfred Knopf, 1998); John Hersey, "The Algiers Motel Incident," *Ramparts*, June 28, 1968, pp. 28–55; Jane Baskin et al., *The Long Hot Summer?*; James Ridgeway and Jean Casella, "Newark to New Orleans: The Myth of the Black Sniper," *Mother Jones*, July 16, 2007, www.motherjones .com/politics/2007/07/newark-new-orleans-myth-black-sniper; Albert Bergesen, "Race Riots of 1967: An Analysis of Police Violence in Detroit and Newark," *Journal of Black Studies*, 12:3 (March, 1982): 261–274; Brad Parks, "Crossroads, Part 2," http://blog.nj .com/ledgernewark/2007/07/crossroads_pt_2.html [accessed May 26, 2015]; Goldberg, "Ghetto Riots and Others."

not under indictment at the time – but rather because he feared for this life. In a sequence of events that can only be described as Kafkaesque, Brown was arrested, released from jail, and rearrested on at least eight separate and unrelated charges over the next four years.[60] This included his arrest for carrying a gun across state lines in spite of the fact that he had a permit to carry and had registered the gun with airline officials before he departed, and had not been under indictment when the plane took off – the official charge was carrying a gun while under indictment. Rather than recognize these unusual circumstances, Judge Lansing Mitchell, who privately declared his intention to "get that nigger," sentenced Brown to five years in jail and a $2,000 fine. Upon his release on $25,000 bail, Mitchell confined Brown to New York City. When Brown broke the terms of this agreement to deliver a speech at a Black Panther rally in Berkeley, California, he was arrested again, this time for violating the conditions of his release.[61]

In 1970, the FBI placed Brown on its ten most wanted list following one of the most bizarre events during the entire time period, namely the detonation of a bomb in a car which was en route to the Hartford County courthouse where Brown's trial was finally to be heard. Even though Ralph Featherstone and William Payne, two of Brown's closest associates, were killed in the blast, authorities insisted that they, along with Brown, were responsible for it. On the same day, a bomb exploded in Cambridge's courthouse. While authorities suggested that blacks had planted it too, neither bombing case was ever solved. Fearing for his life,

---

[60] For timeline on Brown's arrest, see "Narrative Timeline of H. Rap Brown," http://americanascherrypie.tripod.com/id3.html [accessed September 3, 2014; website active at time of access] or "A Chronological Sketch of H. Rap Brown's Cases and Activities," n.d., Ella Baker Papers, Kunstler, My Life, pp. 175–183; Box 6, Folder, H. Rap Brown; Brown, *Die, Nigger Die!* pp. 101–104, 118–120. For newspaper coverage of most but not all of these charges, see "Leader of S.N.C.C. Seized in Virginia," *NYT*, July 27, 1967, p. 1; "Rap Brown is Held in Bail of $25,000," *NYT*, August 20, 1967, p. 1; "Rap Brown Arrested Here for Violation of Bail," *NYT*, February 21, 1968, p. 34; "Rap Brown Pleads Not Guilty to Intimidating F.B.I. Agent," *NYT*, March 14, 1968, p. 47; "Brown Absent in Court; Arrest Ordered," *NYT*, May 5, 1970, p. 40; "Rap Brown Wounded Here in Shootout After Hold Up," *NYT*, October 17, 1971 p. 1; "Brown is Sentenced to 5 to 15 Years in Prison," *NYT*, May 10, 1973, p. 12. Levy, *Civil War on Race Street*, pp. 156–158.

[61] "H. Rap Brown Under House Arrest," *The Movement*, August 1967; "F.B.I. Report on SNCC Travel," January 9, 1968, in *Civil Rights During the Johnson Administration*, reel 18; Brown, *Die Nigger, Die*, ch. 12; "Excerpts from the Vertical File of the Enoch Pratt Free Library," in *Is Baltimore Burning?*

Brown went underground.[62] While authorities cast him as the villain, in fact, well before this incident, the FBI had called for "neutralizing" him. More specifically, in the immediate aftermath of the revolts of the summer of 1967, the FBI established, with the approval of the president and US attorney general, COINTELPRO whose explicit aim was to undermine black militants. Not surprisingly, at the top of its list of targets were H. Rap Brown and Stokely Carmichael (and Martin Luther King Jr.). Within months of its creation, FBI branch offices devised various plans to weaken Brown, including making it difficult for him to obtain bail and secretly sowing seeds of discord between him and other key black radicals. The FBI and special divisions of the New York Police Force also kept tabs on the Black Action Federation and on a coalition of civil rights activists who traveled to Cambridge in the spring of 1968 to demand justice for Brown.[63]

Perhaps no contemporary more forcefully argued that the government's pursuit of Brown was fraudulent than his attorney William Kunstler. Termed by some the "most beloved and hated lawyer in America," for his defense of a wide variety of radicals, from civil rights and antiwar activist, including the Chicago Seven, members of the Black Panther Party, the Weather Underground, and the survivors of the Attica Prison riots, Kunstler cast the government's treatment of Brown as nothing less than proof of its desire to crush the black freedom struggle. From his earliest legal motions related to Brown's arrest for inciting a riot in the days after

---

[62] "Friend of Rap Brown Dies With 2nd Man in Auto Blast," *NYT*, March 11, 1970, p. 1; "Woman Sought In Bombing At Cambridge," *Washington Post*, March 12, 1970, p. A1; "Maryland Hunt Women in Blast," *NYT*, March 17, 1970, p. 32.

[63] US Senate, Select Committee to Study Government Operations with Respect to Intelligence Activities, "Final Report: Book III" (Washington, DC: 1976), p. 20; "Report of Office of Investigation," March 25, 1968, in *Kerner Commission Records*, reel 17; SAC, New York to Director, FBI, April 1, 1968 and SAC, Baltimore, to Director, FBI, April 3, 1968, both in FBI Vault, Black Extremists, Part 2, https://vault.fbi.gov/cointel-pro/cointel-pro-black-extremists/cointelpro-black-extremists-part-02-of/view [accessed September 6, 2017]; for an overview of COINTELPRO see, G. C. Moore to W. C. Sullivan, February 29, 1968, in FBI Vault, Black Extremists, Part 1, https://vault.fbi .gov/cointel-pro/cointel-pro-black-extremists/cointelpro-black-extremists-part-01-of/ view [accessed September 6, 2017]. Beginning in 1967, the FBI kept tabs on Gloria Richardson as well. See Gloria R. Dandridge, FBI File, 100-442421. J. Edgar Hoover, "Memorandum for Mr. Tolson," July 26, 1967 and "SAC New York (100-161140), Counterintelligence Program," September 25, 1967, FBI Papers, Clyde Tolson, Part 1 and Black Nationalist Hate Groups, FBI Vault, respectively. See also Milton Schwartz, NYC Police Department to Dear Sirs, July 29, 1969, and attached photographs, Arnold Goldwag Papers, Box 8, Folder Cambridge, MD: Caravan for Justice for H. Rap Brown.

Cambridge's "riot," to a piece entitled, "J. Edgar Hoover, Frank Hogan, Cambridge, Md., New Orleans Parish, *New York Magazine* vs. H. Rap Brown," which he wrote in 1973, Kunstler contended that the government had pursued an "unabated" vendetta against his client. "His case," Kunstler wrote in 1973, "is a classic example of the perverse use of the legal process to silence a voice that some hate and fear." "No other contemporary American dissenter," Kunstler asserted, had faced such "vindictive and unrelenting efforts to destroy him." Arthur Kinoy, another one of Brown's attorneys, similarly insisted that Brown's treatment demonstrated that the government had undertaken a plan of "mass repression." The government did not "care ultimately whether their convictions [will] stick," in other words whether Brown had incited a riot or not. Rather, it hoped to create an "atmosphere of fear and paralysis…so that the wellsprings of social action can't move in a directed form." Notably, in the Chicago Seven and Attic Prison cases, Kunstler similarly emphasized that it was white authorities who actually committed violent acts not those accused and tried for rioting.[64]

While many cast Kunstler's remarks as hyperbole, a series of reports that emerged in the early 1970s suggested otherwise. In 1971, a young Bob Woodward, writing for the *Montgomery Sentinel*, a small suburban paper, reported that Richard Kinlein, the district attorney of Howard County, Maryland, concluded there had never been enough evidence to try Brown on the inciting riot charges in the first place. The arson charge against Brown, on which the original fugitive arrest had been based, was fabricated, Kinlein told Woodward. Indeed, two years later State Attorney William Yates dropped the inciting to riot charges against Brown. While Yates asserted there was no reason to go forward with the riot trial because Brown was already in prison on separate and unrelated charges, Brown's attorney at the time, Carl Broege, countered that Yates's explanation was specious and that the state's decision to drop the charges proved

<hr/>

[64] William Kunstler, "J. Edgar Hoover, Frank Hogan, Cambridge, Md., New Orleans Parish, New York Magazine vs. H. Rap Brown," *University Review*, March 1973, p. 35; William Kunstler, with Sheila Isenberg, *My Life as a Radical Lawyer* (New York: Birch Lane Press, 1994). See also, William Kunstler, "In Defense of Rap Brown," n.d. Student Nonviolent Coordinating Council Papers, Box 5: Folder 33, Misc. H. Rap Brown. Whereas Brown garnered headline following his address in Cambridge and front page coverage in the months that followed, in 1972, his arrest and trial on armed robbery charges, were buried in the back pages of most newspapers. See, for example: "State Sums Up H. Rap Brown Trial: Is That Improbable," *NYT*, March 27, 1973, p. 34; "H. Rap Brown and 3 Others Go on Trial Tomorrow," *NYT*, January 14, 1973, p. 46; "Rap Brown Convicted of Robbery and Assault," *NYT*, March 30, 1973, p. 14.

that the government had "used Brown as a scapegoat for their own evil" all along.[65]

Whereas state authorities and most of the national press viewed Brown guilty as charged, from the start numerous black activists and the black press presented a much different story, reflecting the conflicting views of the causes of the revolts themselves. Even though many of them disagreed with Brown's fiery rhetoric and/or his advocacy of black power, they considered the government's pursuit of him a greater evil. For instance, Martin Luther King Jr., Fred Shuttlesworth, both of SCLC (Southern Christian Leadership Conference), CORE's Floyd McKissick, Myles Horton of the Highlander Folk School, Tom Gardner of the Southern Student Organizing Committee, and Lawrence Guyot of the Mississippi Freedom Democratic Party, jointly cast the government's treatment of Brown as a threat to everyone's liberty. "If there is anything that history teaches us, it is that those who sit silent while another's rights are violated inevitably come to one of two ends. Either they ultimately compromise their own principles to survive in a police state, or they are eventually crushed themselves when it is too late to resist." A coalition of independent black activists organized and/or participated in "Let Rap Rap" rallies in Brooklyn, Philadelphia, and other communities, where they vociferously lambasted the government for stripping Brown of his most fundamental rights.[66] Similarly, in Chicago, a young Jesse Jackson, one of King's protégées, sought to get all of the government's charges against Brown dropped. "I salute you (Brown), for hurling yourself as a flaming force for freedom against such engrained racism," Jackson declared. (Note the opposite references to fire used by Jackson.)[67]

Likewise, in a multipart story, entitled "The U.S. vs. H. Rap Brown," the *New Amsterdam News* detailed the "inside story of Rap Brown's five-year running battle to stay and speak his mind." Brown, the paper explained, had been hounded by the government from the moment he left Cambridge in July 1967 until his recent arrest in the spring of 1972. Echoing the *New Amsterdam News*' sentiments, the *Afro-American's* John

[65] Bob Woodward, "Rap Brown Indictment Called 'Phony' by State Prosecutor," *Montgomery Sentinel*, January 14, 1971; "Arson Charge Against Brown Termed False," *Washington Post*, January 15, 1971, p. A1; "Md. Drops 3 Charges Against Rap Brown," *Washington Post*, November 7, 1973, p. A1.
[66] "Statement on Behalf of H. Rap Brown," n.d; "Let Rap Rap" [leaflet], n.d. SNCC, "Honky Harassment of H. Rap Brown," March 3, 1968, all in Ella Baker Papers, Box 6.
[67] "Free Rap Brown: Jesse: Plans for Nationwide Campaign," *Chicago Daily Defender*, March 12, 1970, p. 1.

Jasper railed at the "legal hell" Brown had had to endure since he had delivered his address in Cambridge in late July 1967. For years, Jasper contended, Maryland's political leaders, including "Spiro Agnew, the former governor and vice-president (now an admitted crook) who described Rap as a 'mad dog,' milk[ed] the case for all the national and international publicity possible." The "Free State's" (Maryland's nickname) goal, all along, was "to show the nation – and world – how to deal with an 'uppity black boy' . . . who didn't know his place." The black press also challenged claims that Featherstone, Payne, and Brown were responsible for the car bombing, arguing instead that the former two had been assassinated.[68]

In sum, we do not have to agree with Brown's contention that the government had "laid out a plan to eliminate all black people," to do to African Americans "what the Germans did to the Jews," to acknowledge that conservatives and liberals launched an assault on the rights of numerous black citizens, at least in part in order to deflect attention away from their own culpability in causing the riots and from the aggressive and vengeful behavior of state actors during the revolts themselves. Perhaps, the contrarian view of the revolts, both in terms of causation and typology, might have gained more traction if not for the fact that about a month after the Kerner Commission issued its report, Martin Luther King Jr. was assassinated, setting off an even larger wave of revolts than during the long hot summer of 1967. It is to one of the largest of these revolts and the nation's reaction to them that we turn to next.

---

[68] "The U.S. vs. H. Rap Brown," *New York Amsterdam News*, April 1, 1972, p. D8; "U.S. Rap Brown: A Fight for Justice," *New York Amsterdam News*, April 15, 1972, p. A5; John Jasper, "How Md. 'Fraud' Led to Rap Brown's Legal Genocide," *Afro-American*, November 17, 1973, p. 1; "Angela's Free, But Rap's Held in $200,000 Ransom," *Philadelphia Tribune*, August 1, 1972, p. 7; "Slain Friends of Rap Brown to Be Honored," *Philadelphia Tribune*, March 14, 1970, p. 1; "Lanta Man 2nd Victim Maryland Auto Bombing," *Atlanta Daily World*, March 13, 1970, p. 1; "10,000 Nigerians at Ralph Featherstone's Burial," *Philadelphia Tribune*, March 23, 1970, p. 6; "Hunt White Woman Suspect," *Chicago Daily Defender*, March 12, 1970, p. 4.

PART II

BALTIMORE, MARYLAND

4

The Dream Deferred

In [the other] America, thousands of work-starved men walk the streets every day in search for jobs that do not exist...[they] find themselves feeling that life is a long and desolate corridor with no exit signs. In this America, hopes unborn have died and radiant dreams of freedom have been deferred.

Martin Luther King Jr., "The Other America," Baltimore, 1966

A little past 5 p.m. on Monday, April 27, 2015, I departed York, Pennsylvania, where I work and headed south toward Baltimore, Maryland, where I live. Prior to departing, I had done my best to keep abreast of the latest developments in Baltimore, which had been experiencing protests over the killing of Freddie Gray, an unarmed twenty-five-year-old black man by the police. On my ride south, my main source of information was WBAL radio, the most prominent AM station in the area, which had begun a joint broadcast with its television affiliate. From its newscasters I learned that shortly after Baltimore's schools let out on Monday the 27th "rioting" had broken out. At one point one of the station's leading personalities declared, "I can't believe this is happening in Baltimore; I never would have expected this." At the time, I recalled saying to myself: Where has she been living for the past forty years? How can she honestly make such a statement? While moments later she made reference to riots that had occurred in Baltimore in 1968 following Martin Luther King Jr.'s assassination, from the tone of her voice the "Gray uprising" was absolutely disconnected from the past. And there was little in WBAL's coverage, or in much of what was reported on in the ensuing days by most of the major television networks, local and national, that suggested that to comprehend what was taking place in 2015, it was helpful, if not necessary to understand the causes and consequences of Baltimore's Holy Week Uprising of 1968.

Building on our investigation of the revolts in Cambridge, Maryland, Part II of the Great Uprising will explore Baltimore's 1968 revolt. We will begin by following the lead of Thomas Sugrue, who in his path-breaking *Origins of the Urban Crisis* (1990) challenged the conventional wisdom that the urban uprisings of the 1960s produced the decline of Detroit, Michigan, and by extension other American cities. He did so by demonstrating that "white flight" and deindustrialization and persistent white resistance to black calls for better housing, schools, jobs, and public services preceded Detroit's revolt. When coupled with Arnold Hirsch's examination of white resistance to desegregate housing in Chicago, Sugrue's study also demonstrated that the liberal or New Deal coalition did not fall apart in reaction to the urban revolts of the late 1960s. Rather, as Sugrue, Hirsch, and others have showed, it had been frayed along racial lines all along.[1] Likewise, Baltimore's Holy Week Uprising grew out of long-standing black protests for equality and repeated bouts of white retrenchment. White backlash and the collapse of the New Deal coalition did not appear in response to the radicalization of the civil rights movement emblemized by the urban revolts. On the contrary, whites displayed their resistance to fundamentally altering the racial status quo long before 1968. Put somewhat differently, just as in the case of Freddie Gray uprising, the revolts of the 1960s were epilogues not the prologues, conventional perceptions notwithstanding.

Moreover, Baltimore's history suggests that conservative claims that radicals caused the revolts, notwithstanding, the existence of a vibrant black freedom struggle, one which included CORE selecting Baltimore as its "target city" in the summer of 1966, helps explain why it did not experience a riot in the summers of 1966 and 1967. Put somewhat differently, by keeping alive the hope of redressing grievances, black activists, including "radicals" did not cause "riots," on the contrary they helped retain the "peace." Indeed, this counterintuitive explanation will prove most compelling when we take a brief tour of the Cherry Hill neighborhood, the one black community that experienced no rioting in 1968.

After completing our analysis of the origins of Baltimore's revolt, we will examine the revolt itself (see Chapter 5). Unlike Cambridge,

---

[1] Sugrue, *The Origins of the Urban Crisis*, p. 267; Arnold Hirsch, *Making the Second Ghetto: Race and Housing in Chicago 1940–1960* (Chicago: University of Chicago Press, 1998).

Baltimore experienced little interracial or interpersonal violence. Instead, its revolt was characterized by a great deal of property destruction, particularly the theft of nondurable goods and a considerable amount of arson. Or put most simply, Baltimore experienced a fairly typical commodity riot. This said, Baltimore's revolt differed from the typical disorder described by the Kerner Commission and most social scientists. Most notably, it was not sparked by police abuse or a report of police abuse and resulted in far fewer deaths than similarly severe uprisings during the long hot summer of 1967. Both of these differences are worth contemplating because they compel us to rethink some of the common assumptions regarding why riots take place and the nature of the state's response.

We will turn our attention to how the nation responded to the Holy Week Uprising in Chapter 6. Even though the revolts lent weight to the Kerner Commission's findings, the public continued to favor interpretations that placed much more of the blame on radicals and the morally laxity of those who participated in the revolts, as well as culturally permissive liberals who allegedly enabled them, than on structural racism. Baltimore provides a sharp lens through which to focus on this process because of the key role that the governor of Maryland played in shaping the nation's reaction. Spiro Agnew had already gained some notoriety by accusing H. Rap Brown of inciting Cambridge's uprising the summer before. But it was Agnew's contention that black moderates and white liberals, in concert with black radicals, or what he ultimately termed the "radlib" mindset, accounted for his meteoric rise from political obscurity to the vice presidency. Agnew also attracts our attention because of who he was: a self-identified "Middle American," whose politics of resentment struck a responsive chord among a wide swath of the public, which rejected social reform in favor of law and order as the proper response to the Great Uprising.

"Please Don't Make Us Mad on a Hot Day in June"

Over the course of the twentieth century, Baltimore's black community built one of the most significant yet least known freedom movements in the nation. This movement began well before the sit-ins in Greensboro, North Carolina, and remained vibrant on the eve of King's assassination. While it won concessions from the white community, ranging from the desegregation of public accommodations to the appointment of black men and women to top positions in city government,

Baltimore's freedom movement proved unable to fundamentally alter the institutional and structural barriers that underlay the revolts of the 1960s. As in Detroit, the liberal or New Deal coalition, which dominated local politics, remained more firmly committed to maintaining white privileges than to dismantling Jim Crow. Even the most progressive white office holders found themselves largely limited to doling out token reforms, particularly in the areas of housing, education, employment, and the criminal justice system, which in turn left expectations of equality raised but unfulfilled, or as King put it, deferred.

The pillars of Baltimore's struggle to overcome racial inequality were the Jackson and Mitchell families, particularly Lillie M. Carrol Jackson and her daughter Juanita Jackson Mitchell. Over the course of the middle decades of the twentieth century, they built one of the strongest NAACP chapters in the country. They were aided by the Murphy family, which established the *Afro-American*, one of the most prominent black newspapers, in 1892, numerous black churches, as well as by an assortment of left-leaning activists and trade unionists. In the mid-1930s this loose alliance orchestrated a "Buy Where You Can Work" boycott, drives to organize workers at Bethlehem Steel, and campaigns for political representation and legal equality. For example, in 1935, Thurgood Marshall, a native of Baltimore, teamed with Charles Houston to successfully convince the courts to order the University of Maryland to admit Donald J. Murray, a black man, also of Baltimore, to its all-white law school. These actions of the mid-1930s paved the way for additional working- and middle-class assaults on racial inequality staged by other grassroots organizations, ranging from the National Negro Congress to the Mother's Club and to an expansion of the movement in the 1950 and early 1960s.[2]

While the conventional narrative of the civil rights years casts the sit-ins at Woolworth's in Greensboro, North Carolina, as the beginning of the direct action phase of the movement, a more accurate rendition recognizes

[2] Andor Skotnes, "'Buy Where You Can Work': Boycotting for Jobs in African-American Baltimore, 1933-1934," *Journal of Social History*, 27:4 (Summer, 1994): 735-761; C. Fraser Smith, *Here Lies Jim Crow: Civil Rights in Maryland* (Baltimore: Johns Hopkins University Press, 2008); Rhonda Y. Williams, *The Politics of Black Housing: Black Woman's Struggles against Urban Inequality* (New York: Oxford University Press, 2004); Sandy Shoemaker, "'We Shall Overcome, Someday': The Equal Rights Movement in Baltimore, 1935-1942," *Maryland Historical Magazine*, 89 (Fall 1994): 261-273; Barbara Mills, *"Got My Mind Set on Freedom": Maryland's Story of Black & White Activism, 1663-2000* (Bowie, MD: Heritage Books, 2002).

that Baltimore activists staged a successful sit-in five years before North Carolina Agricultural and Technical College students did. In 1955, Helen Hicks, a 4-foot-11 Morgan State student (who went on to earn her PhD at the University of Maryland), led a twenty minute sit-in at the lunch counter of Read's drugstore. During the early 1960s, the local chapter of the Congress of Racial Equality, the Civic Interest Group (CIG), the Interracial Ministerial Alliance (led by the Reverend Marion Bascom), as well as unaffiliated students from Morgan State and several other local colleges and universities orchestrated even larger direct action campaigns, including sit-ins at the Northwood Shopping Center, which lay adjacent to Morgan State, and mass protests at the Gwynn Oak Amusement Park, which lay just outside the city limits.[3]

Among those to chronicle – and participate in – these early protests was August Meier, a pioneer of the study of African American history and a professor at Morgan State from 1957 to 1964. In speeches to students and civil rights groups and in scholarly articles he offered some of the first – and most insightful – analyses of the rise of the sit-in movement, in particular, and the broader civil rights movement, in general. For instance, he placed the rise of the student-based sit-in movement within the context of the decline of colonialism worldwide, structural changes sparked by the New Deal and World War II, and the growth of key civil rights organizations, such as the NAACP and CORE. At the same time, as an activist, Meier helped bridge the gap between those who favored direct action protest and those who did not.[4]

During the same time period, activists also demonstrated against inadequate housing, employment, and education (see Figure 4.1). For instance, on a snowy Easter Day in 1964, the Ministerial Alliance orchestrated a "Freedom March." This event culminated with 4,000 Baltimoreans listening to Dick Gregory declare: "This lets the country know – Please don't

---

[3] Ron Cassie, "And Service For All," *Baltimore Magazine*, January 2015, www.baltimoremagazine.net/2015/1/19/morgan-students-staged-reads-drugstore-sit-in-60-years-ago [accessed September 2, 2015]; "Timeline," Civil Rights Movement Veterans, 1955, www.crmvet.org/tim/timhis55.htm [accessed September 2, 2015]. Smith, *Here Lies Jim Crow*; Mills, *"Got My Mind Set on Freedom."*

[4] August Meier, "Address to the Philomatheans," November 5, 1960 and Epsilon Omega Chapter of Alpha Kappa Alpha Sorority, "Freedom Ball program," October 21, 1960, both in August Meier Papers, Box 64; August Meier, *A White Scholar and the Black Community, 1945–1965* (Amherst: University of Massachusetts Press, 1992); August Meier, "Negro Protest Movements and Organizations," *The Journal of Negro Education*, 32:4 (Autumn 1963): 437–450.

FIGURE 4.1 White picketers protest desegregation of schools in Baltimore in the fall of 1954, following the *Brown* decision. Black parents and their children stand across the street. By permission of AP Photo.

make us mad on a hot day in June."[5] Later that same summer, following the death of Vernon Leopold, a young black man, at the hands of the police, a broad coalition of civil rights forces railed at the persistence of police brutality. Clarence Mitchell III, Lillie May Carroll Jackson, and others gathered testimony from community members that undermined official accountings of his death and requested the creation of a "blue ribbon commission" to examine "unwarranted police killings and brutality in Baltimore." The Baltimore Federation of Civil Rights Organizations, which included the NAACP and the Ministerial Alliance, among others, telegrammed Attorney General Robert F. Kennedy demanding a federal investigation. Fearing that Leopold's death could produce riots like those that had recently occurred in Harlem, Baltimore's mayor, Thomas

5 Barbara Mills, *Got My Mind Set on Freedom*; "4,000 Marchers Brave Snow, Cold," *Afro-American*, April 11, 1964, p. 12; "4,000 Join Baltimore Rights Rally," *Washington Post*, March 31, 1964, p. B2; "March for Baltimore: Press Release," n.d., August Meier Papers, Box 66, Folder 6.

McKeldin, promised emergency action to address some of the squalid housing conditions in the area where the incident had taken place and pressured the governor and police commissioner to investigate ways to improve police–community relations.[6] Based in part on these complaints, a special Police Advisory Committee on Community Relations recommended hiring more black police officers – as of April 1965 only 7.8 percent of the force was black – establishing a "complaint board," which was to include "grassroots people" and expanding police-led recreation committees.[7]

Yet these protests also illustrated the limits of black political power. City comptroller, Heyman Pressman, who had endorsed the previous spring's Freedom March, held independent hearings that blamed public officials for high police turnover and poor morale. At these hearings and in letters to the mayor, many white citizens defended the police and lambasted the city for even considering civilian oversight. John Dietz, for example, wrote: "Always the police are made to appear unworthy, while the lawbreaker or potential lawbreaker is made to look the hero." Rather than establish a community relations or review board, Dietz continued, city officials should "denounce" the "unjustified criticism" of the police by the press. George and Martha Cunningham echoed Dietz's views, contending that a review board "would handicap" the police and "make the lawless more brazen." John Conway, another white city resident, expressed his disapproval of police reform in even more vigorous terms. "Our police dept. is under-staffed and over-burdened with what should be considered unlawful demonstrations. The coon glories in this display of his civil rights . . . Wherever the coon has lived among or close to white neighborhoods, there have been rapes, murders, robberies and general troubles . . . Gentlemen, we've had it – let's cut it short." Along the same lines, the president of the Maryland Criminal Justice Commission called for the department to quit treating blacks with "kid gloves." Given such sentiment, it should not be surprising that charges against the offending police officer were dismissed and that the city council refused to establish

---

[6] "Echoes of the Past," *Baltimore Sun*, April 17, 2016, p. 1; "Negroes Tell Finan Rioting Is Possible," *Baltimore Sun*, September 17, 1964, p. 56; "Mayor Plans Quick Action to Bar Riots," *Baltimore Sun*, July 22, 1964, p. 42.

[7] "Report of the Police Advisory Committee on Community Relations," June 15, 1965, Criminal Justice Commission Collection, Special Collections, University of Baltimore Library. See also: Mayor Theodore McKeldin Papers, Administrative Files, 1963–67, especially folders labeled Police Advisory Committee on Community Relations and Police Review Board, Box 412, Baltimore City Archives, Baltimore, Maryland.

an independent civilian review board.[8] Moreover, as we shall see, residential segregation, employment discrimination, and unequal education remained the rule.

"Unless America Grapples … [with] the Ghettos, We will See Darker Nights of Social Disruption than in Watts"

Among those to lend his support to Baltimore's black freedom struggle was Martin Luther King Jr. While better known for his campaigns in Montgomery, Birmingham and Selma, Alabama, and subsequently Chicago, Illinois, King appeared in Baltimore with regularity. In these visits, King developed a strong relationship with many of the city's black leaders and its ordinary black people. Indeed, though King has been de-radicalized in the public imagination, in the 15 years that he interacted with black Baltimoreans, he often served as a leading edge of the movement, prodding church leaders and members to devote themselves to social activism, promoting direct action protest, demanding attention to employment and housing discrimination as well as segregated public accommodations, and, ultimately, challenging American imperialism and the nation's materialistic values. Following a spring 1966 speech in Baltimore, Reverend Donald Tippitt, for one, described King as the "most prophetic voice in all America, yea, in all the world today." Somewhat similarly, Reverend Bascom, the leader of the Interracial Ministerial Alliance, called him "a brilliant man" whose "greatness … grows larger than life as time goes on."[9]

---

[8] "Echoes of the Past," *Baltimore Sun*, April 17, 2016, p. 1; "Murphy Rejects Public Hearing," *Baltimore Sun*, July 15, 1964, p. 44; "Rights Leaders to See Gelston," *Washington Post*, January 25, 1966, p. C3; "A 600-Page Survey Raps City Police," *Baltimore Sun*, January 10, 1966, p. A1; "Mello Saw a Police Career as 'Opportunity,'" *Baltimore Sun*, November 21, 1965, p. SM14; "'Kid Gloves' Held Used on Negroes," *Baltimore Sun*, April 7, 1965, p. 19; "Finan Opposes Civilian Police Board," *Baltimore Sun*, October 9, 1964, p. 44; "Police Plan is Delayed After Talks," *Baltimore Sun*, July 2, 1965, p. 40; "Police Board Membership is Criticized," *Baltimore Sun*, August 16, 1965, p. 34; "CORE Delegates Knock on Doors in Baltimore Target-City Project," *NYT*, July 3, 1966, p. A1; John L. Conway to Mayor McKeldin, n.d.; George and Martha Cunningham to Mayor McKeldin, July 25, 1965, and John Dietz to Theodore R. McKeldin, September 9, 1965, all in Mayor McKeldin Papers, Administrative Files, Box 412.

[9] Katie Lambert, Jackie Spriggs, and Kerry Zaleski, "Interview with Reverend Marion Bascom," *Chicken Bones: A Journal for Literary & Artistic African-American Themes*, November 6, 2006, www.nathanielturner.com/reverendmarionbascom.htm [accessed November 16, 2016]; "King Forecasts 'Hot Summer,'" *Afro-American*, April 30, 1966, p. 3.

King first appeared publicly in Baltimore in 1953, two years before he emerged as a civil rights leader in Montgomery, when, upon the invitation of Reverend J. Timothy Bodie, an old friend of his father, he presented a guest sermon at New Shiloh Baptist Church. Three years later, King returned to Baltimore to deliver a speech at the Omega Psi Phi fraternity's Annual Convention, where he lent weight to their long-standing support of the NAACP's efforts to end segregated education, which many white Baltimoreans had fought to maintain. Two years later, King returned to Baltimore to receive an honorary doctorate from Morgan State University, where he delivered a rousing commencement address that challenged the graduates to dedicate themselves to fight for equality. Positing that the liberation movements in Africa and Asia as well as the Brown decision signaled a new age, King prodded the graduates to "work passionately and unrelentingly for first-class citizenship." Coming two years before the sit-ins at Greensboro, King's speech made clear that he saw students as the vanguard in this budding movement and that he recognized that the struggle for racial equality encompassed the entire nation, from Stone and Lookout Mountain in Georgia and Tennessee, to "the mighty mountains of New York and . . . the heightening Alleghany's of Pennsylvania."[10]

King's appearances in Baltimore continued apace throughout the 1960s. In 1963, he delivered a keynote address to 8,000 at a Baltimore Freedom Rally, followed by a whirlwind tour of the city, highlighted by an open car tour of Gay Street, in the heart of East Baltimore, the epicenter of the 1968 Holly Week Uprising. In the fall of 1964, King and his top aide Ralph Abernathy spent a day in Baltimore, campaigning against Barry Goldwater, while at the same time condemning the persistence of racism

[10] See "Baltimore '68 Events Timeline," http://archives.ubalt.edu/bsr/timeline/timeline.html [accessed September 2, 2015]; "King Commencement Address," June 2, 1958, http://archives.ubalt.edu/bsr/timeline/afro_speech.pdf [accessed April 22, 2016]; "Dr. King Made Three Major Visits to City," *Evening Sun* (Baltimore, MD), April 5, 1968. On his sermon at New Shiloh Baptist Church, see Martin Luther King Jr. to J. Timothy Boddie, November 24, 1953, https://kinginstitute.stanford.edu/king-papers/documents/j-timothy-boddie; Bayard Rustin to Martin Luther King Jr., December 23, 1963, https://kinginstitute.stanford.edu/king-papers/documents/bayard-rustin-0, [accessed April 22, 2016]; "King Calls for Wider Vote Drive," *Washington Post*, April 2, 1965, p. A1; "King Hailed," *Baltimore Sun*, April 1, 1965, p. 54. On Morgan State, see Ron Cassie, "And Service For All," *Baltimore Magazine*, January 2015, www.baltimoremagazine.net/2015/1/19/morgan-students-staged-reads-drugstore-sit-in-60-years-ago [accessed April 22, 2016] and www.morgan.edu/civilrights/docs/ExhibitProgram_WEB.pdf [accessed April 22, 2016; website active at time of access]. Martin Luther King Jr. "A Great Time to Be Alive: 1958 Commencement Address," www.nathanielturner.com/kingspeaksinbaltimore.htm [accessed November 16, 2016].

FIGURE 4.2 Martin Luther King Jr. meets supporters during a tour of Baltimore, Fall 1964. © Leonard Freed/Magnum Photos.

in the city, or as Abernathy put it: "There is still a trace of Egypt here." Afterwards, King's motorcade stopped in Lafayette Square, in the heart of West Baltimore, the other epicenter of the 1968 revolt, where upwards of 5,000 well-wishers cheered his appearance (Figure 4.2). In 1965, King appeared in Baltimore again, delivering a series of addresses, including one at Coppin State College (a historically black college), another at the Cornerstone Baptist Church, and a third at a testimonial dinner held at the Lord Baltimore hotel. At the last event, he praised clergy members for having overcome their "early reluctance" to support direct action campaigns and received testimonials from a broad array of public figures, including Mayor McKeldin. Outside the hotel, however, the Confederates for Free Segregation carried signs that read, "Down with King" and "There's No Police Brutality in Baltimore," a reference to the aforementioned killing of a black man by police which had sparked protests by the NAACP. Numerous white citizens also wrote to the mayor to voice their sharp criticism of his support for King. For instance, Shirley Lyons characterized King as an "unscrupulous, power hungry" fake, who was the greatest promoter of "bitterness, hatred and violence... known in modern times."[11]

---

[11] "Baltimore '68 Events Timeline"; "Dr. King Made Three Major Visits to City," *Evening Sun* (Baltimore, MD), April 5, 1968; "King Calls for Wider Vote Drive," *Washington*

In 1966, King made two more appearances in Baltimore, one at a national gathering of Methodist clergy and another in November where Baltimore's Community Relation Commission awarded him its "Man of the Decade" prize. At the former, he forecast a "hot summer" because America had failed to grapple with the conditions that had given rise to the previous summers' revolts. In the latter he delivered a speech, entitled "The Other America," where he reflected at length on the underlying causes of these uprisings. Through these words and his ongoing protests against slum conditions in Chicago, King displayed his understanding of the depths of structural and institutional racism and retained his position as one of the clarion voices in the black community, even as more radial activists challenged his philosophy of nonviolence and integration. As the *Afro-American*'s George Collins observed, King "evoked thunderous applause" throughout his "Other America" address, from the audience of 1,200 of "varying religious and racial backgrounds," for championing a crusade against poverty that crushed the hopes of way too many Americans.[12]

King's speech, which he delivered in various forms at different venues in 1966, 1967, and 1968, prefigured the Kerner Commission's proposition that the nation consisted of two societies, one black and one white.[13] "One America," King explained, "is invested with enrapturing beauty. In it we can find many things that we can think about in noble terms...This America is inhabited by millions of the fortunate whose dreams of life, liberty, and the pursuit of happiness are poured out in glorious fulfillment...In this America," he continued, "little boys and little girls grow up in the sunlight of opportunity."[14] In the other America, "we see something that drains away the beauty that exists...In this America, hopes unborn have died and radiant dreams of freedom have been deferred." Moreover, King warned: "Unless America grapple[d] more firmly with the lot of the colored masses in the ghettos, we [would] see darker nights

Post, April 2, 1965, p. A1; "King Hailed," *Baltimore Sun*, April 1, 1965, p. 54; "Dr. King Opposes Goldwater," *Baltimore Sun*, November 1, 1964, p. 26; Shirley Lyons to Mayor McKeldin, May 3, 1965, Mayor McKeldin Papers, Administrative Files, Box 363.

[12] See "Baltimore '68 Events Timeline"; George Collins, "King Hits 'Other America'; Hails Defeat of Backlash," *Afro-American*, November 26, 1966, p. 14.

[13] King's "The Other America" speech is quoted at length in Baltimore Community Relations Commission, "Tenth Annual Report, 1966: A Decade of Progress," pp. 39–42. For a full version of King's "Other America" as delivered in Grosse Point, Michigan, see Martin Luther King Jr., "The Other America," March 14, 1968, www.gphistorical.org/mlk/mlkspeech/ [accessed March 24, 2016].

[14] King, "The Other America."

TABLE 4.1 *Baltimore population and percentage change*

Year	Total Population	% change	White	% change	Black	% change
1950	949,708		723,655		225,099	
1960	939,024	−1%	610,608	−16%	328,416	46%
1970	905,024	−4%	479,837	−21%	420,210	28%
1980	786,775	−13%	345,113	−28%	431,151	3%
1990	736,014	−6%	287,753	−17%	418,951	1%

of social disruption than in Watts last summer." The "power structure," he asserted, needed to go out of its way "now," if it sought to avoid violence; the situation was "urgent," because while black protest in the South had led to advances, the situation had "retrogressed" in the North; it was worse, he asserted, than when over 200,000 had assembled for the March on Washington just three years before.[15]

"[The City Must Stop Practices that] Keep the 'Outs' Out and the 'Inns' In."

While most white Baltimoreans saw their hometown as a place with a progressive racial record, far removed from the bigotry of Birmingham and Selma, Alabama, or even Cambridge, Maryland, which lay across the Chesapeake, King's depiction of two Americas, local activists asserted, clearly applied to their city. Between World War II and 1968, Baltimore's overall population remained fairly stable, yet its racial make-up changed dramatically (see Table 4.1). In 1950 over 700,000 whites lived in the city. Less than a generation later, fewer than 500,000 did. During the same time frame, the number of blacks rose from under 220,000 to over 400,000.[16] When viewed from a metropolitan perspective, the magnitude of this demographic shift appears even clearer. In 1950, the entire population of Baltimore County, which surrounded Baltimore city like a horseshoe, stood at less than 250,000, approximately 20,000 of whom were black. Twenty years later the county's population had risen to over 600,000, all but 20,000 of whom were white.[17] Even within city limits,

[15] King, "The Other America"; "King Forecasts 'Hot Summer,'" *Afro-American*, April 30, 1966, p. 3.
[16] United States Commission on Civil Rights, "Staff Report: Demographic, Economic, Social and Political Characteristics of Baltimore City and Baltimore County" (Washington, DC: GPO, August 1970).
[17] United States Commission on Civil Rights, "Staff Report," August 1970.

as Edwin Orser's fine study on blockbusting documents, Baltimore witnessed a racial sea change as entire sections of the city went from being virtually all white to all black in a very short span of time. These said, overall black residents continued to occupy a disproportionately small share of the entire city. According to one study, in 1965, 380,000 black persons, who represented 44 percent of the city's total population, resided in just 16 percent of the total residential land. At the same time, numerous white working-class communities, particularly those which surrounded the harbor (from Locust Point to Canton), fiercely resisted racial integration, forming neighborhood associations which, among other things, prevented realtors from showing their homes to black men and women and opposing efforts to enact open housing legislation. About the only change that did not take place was that whites did not move into predominantly black neighborhoods.[18]

As an expert witnesses later testified, Baltimore's "index of dissimilarity" stood at 0.83 in 1960 and 0.86 in 1970 on a scale of 0.0 to 1.0 where 1.0 was defined as complete isolation and anything above 0.70 was defined as "hyper-segregation" (see Figure 4.3). One of the reasons for this hyper-segregation was that public housing units, which black citizens disproportionately occupied, were, with a few exceptions, built in black neighborhoods. In turn, this produced a greater concentration of poverty.[19] Moreover, blacks inhabited qualitatively unequal homes. Nearly 50 percent of homes in inner city neighborhoods were rated as "very poor," a situation that the postwar building boom did not alleviate. On the contrary, the qualitative gap between white and black homes widened with the suburban housing boom and the concomitant dearth of new home construction in the city. Without new construction, older housing, especially older rental units in communities disproportionately inhabited by blacks, fell into increasing disrepair.[20] Somewhat

[18] W. Edward Orser, "Flight to the Suburbs: Suburbanization and Racial Change on Baltimore's West Side," *The Baltimore Book: New Views of Local History*, ed. by Elizabeth Fee, Linda Shopes, and Linda Seidman (Philadelphia: Temple University Press, 1991), pp. 203–226; W. Edward Orser, *Blockbusting in Baltimore: The Edmondson Village Story* (Lexington: University Press of Kentucky, 1994). Kenneth Durr, *Behind the Backlash: White Working-Class Politics in Baltimore, 1940–80* (Chapel Hill: The University of North Carolina Press, 2003), [electronic edition], location 2901; "Report," n.d., Public Housing Accommodations-Open Housing, Mayor McKeldin Papers, Box 414.

[19] Testimony of Dr. Gerald R. Webster, *Carmen Thompson et al. v. United States Department of Housing and Urban Development et al.*, Civil Action No. MJG-95-309.

[20] United States Commission on Civil Rights, "Staff Report: Demographic, Economic, Social and Political Characteristics of Baltimore City and Baltimore County," City of Baltimore, "Baltimore Model Cities Neighborhoods: Application to the Department of Housing and Urban Development," n.d.

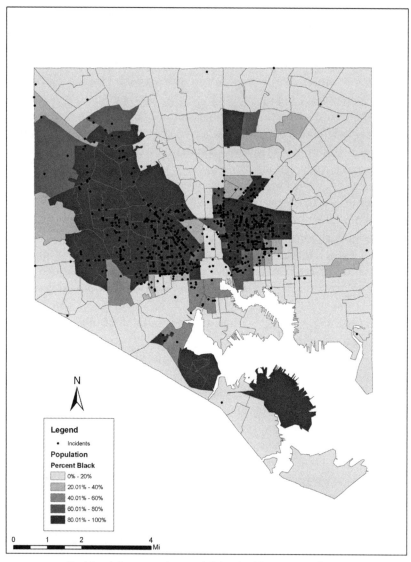

FIGURE 4.3 Residential segregation and "riot incidents" in Baltimore. Map created by author, with special thanks to Kathryn Kulbicki.

paradoxically, while black neighborhoods consisted overwhelmingly of rental units which landlords allowed to deteriorate, white working-class neighborhoods contained some of the highest rates of home ownership of any city in the nation, hovering around 75 percent in the predominantly Polish working-class communities of Southeast Baltimore and Locust

Point, and 70 percent in the white Protestant working-class community of Hampden. While many Jews and middle-class whites moved either to the farther reaches of the city or to the suburbs as the black population spread from the central wards, white working-class Baltimoreans grew even more fiercely committed to maintaining the racial boundaries of their neighborhoods. Or as Kenneth Durr puts it, "the most concrete – and most consequential-boundaries that [white] blue collarites maintained between themselves and black Baltimoreans were residential."[21]

As in many other cities various federal policies exacerbated this situation. For instance, in the postwar period urban planners mapped out concrete highways which they believed would make it easier for suburban residents to commute in and out of the city and to avail themselves of Baltimore's amenities, thus revitalizing downtown business and shopping districts that displayed signs of decline. Invariably, they routed these highways through black neighborhoods. A 1965 study estimated that 25,000 Baltimoreans were displaced between 1951 and 1965, 89 percent of whom were black. Another 13,000 were displaced between 1965 and 1970. While many of these areas were not slums before the urban renewal projects and/or roads were built, they became slums afterwards. Put somewhat differently, by displacing people from their homes, increasing the shortage of good homes for blacks (who were steered by policies, practice, and income disparities away from white neighborhoods) and destabilizing local businesses and community institutions, these "urban renewal" initiatives made a poor situation much worse. Even when the highways were not constructed – in part due to the protests of community neighborhood groups – the long drawn-out process of developing plans, inviting community feedback, and purchasing parcels, produced disinvestment and uncertainty that contributed to urban decline. "In many ways," writes Emily Lieb, "the highway plans and the riots were linked. To the people who lived in the neighborhoods slated for clearance, the expressway proposals made clear that their homes and their schools . . . were less important than an exit ramp. Public policy declared over and over again that Baltimore's black neighborhoods were disposable; in 1968 those who participated in the revolts treated them accordingly."[22]

---

[21] Durr, *Behind the Backlash*, locations 1283–1298 and 1475–1535.

[22] Emily Lieb, "'White Man's Lane': Hollowing Out the Highway Ghetto in Baltimore," in *Baltimore '68: Riots and Rebirth in an American City*, ed. by Jessica Elfenbein, Thomas Hollowak, and Elizabeth Nix (Philadelphia: Temple University Press, 2011), pp. 52–69; Baltimore Urban Renewal and Housing Agency, "Displacement and Relocation, Past and

Moreover, overcrowded and substandard housing contributed to a wide assortment of other social problems. Citywide, the infant mortality rate stood at 28.4 out of 1,000 live births in 1965. Yet in census tracts targeted by the Model City program, which were largely black and poor, infant mortality rates often exceeded 50 per 1,000. The same areas had twice the crime rate as the city as a whole, which was at least twice as high as the surrounding suburban communities. While rising crime rates alarmed whites, we need to remember that blacks were victimized by crime at a far greater rate than whites, making it harder and harder for them to experience the American dream.[23]

Concomitantly, the city began to experience considerable economic pains. Long a blue-collar town, synonymous with work on the docks, garment shops, and steel mills, an increasing percentage of Baltimore's workforce found employment in the service sector, such as in the health care industry and/or in the public sector. Since black workers disproportionately depended on work in the manufacturing, this economic shift had a greater impact on them than it did whites. During the 1960s, the number of men and women employed in manufacturing in Baltimore City declined over 25 percent, in spite of heavy demand for defense-related goods due to the escalation of the Vietnam War. Looked at from a regional perspective, the transformation of the labor market took on even greater significance. Between 1945 and 1968 the total number of jobs in Baltimore City increased 11 percent, the vast majority in sectors of the economy with the lowest rates of black employment. During the same time period, in Baltimore County, where few blacks lived, the number of jobs grew a whopping 245 percent.[24]

Unemployment statistics illustrated the disparate worlds that blacks and whites occupied. Nationally, the unemployment rate which stood at less than 4 percent in 1968 suggested a booming economy. Yet, in Baltimore, the rate for blacks was more than double this and in some inner city

Future, Baltimore, Maryland," March, 1965, in Baltimore Urban Renewal and Housing Agency Records (BURHA), University of Baltimore Library.

[23] International Association of Chiefs of Police, "A Survey of the Police Department, Baltimore, Maryland," 1965; Police Department, City of Baltimore, "Annual Report," 1966; Herbert Lee West Jr., "Urban Life and Spatial Distribution of Blacks in Baltimore, Maryland," PhD thesis, University of Minnesota, 1973; Patrick Sharkey, *Stuck in Place: Urban Neighborhoods and the End of Progress toward Racial Equality* (Chicago: University of Chicago Press, 2013).

[24] United States Commission on Civil Rights, "Staff Report"; City of Baltimore, "Baltimore Model Cities Neighborhood: Application to the Department of Housing and Urban Development" (1967); Kenneth Durr, *Behind the Backlash*, p. 199.

census tracts unemployment hovered just below 30 percent or at Great Depression levels.[25] Even in segments of the labor market where things looked bright on the surface, such as at Bethlehem Steel Corporation, they appeared gloomy beneath it. As a report by the US Civil Rights Commission observed, blacks were "virtually unseen" in office work but were found abundantly in the most dangerous and worst-paying jobs.[26]

Some social scientists predicted that black people, like other migrants, would move up the social ladder over time. One way they would do so would be by becoming increasingly embedded in the business community, as small businesspersons and entrepreneurs. Yet, studies of Baltimore – and other cities – revealed that blacks owned a disproportionately small share of small businesses. In 1972 (the date for when the best data is available), when blacks made up more than of 46 percent of the population, they owned only 12.3 percent of the businesses, overall, including only 6 of 1,396 manufacturing firms and 5 of 1,700 wholesale establishments. In retail, blacks were heavily concentrated in a cluster of enterprises: beauty and barber shops, liquor and food stores, and to a lesser extent bars and restaurants. Few owned businesses in one of two of the main shopping areas that served black residents, Mondawmin Shopping Center or the Gay and Monument Street corridor, not to mention the fancier downtown department stores, where more expensive durable goods, like furniture and clothing, were sold. One reason for the concentration of blacks in these smaller businesses was that they lacked savings and faced a higher cost of entry in terms of insurance and borrowing rates.[27]

At the same time, black citizens remained vastly underrepresented in City Hall. As of May 1966, only two of twenty-one city council members were black, even though blacks comprised about 40 percent of the city's overall population. This pattern of underrepresentation persisted after the Holy Week Uprising – Baltimore did not elect its first black mayor until 1987. One reason for this was that district lines were drawn in ways that diluted the black vote. In addition, Baltimore held local elections in "off years," when voter turnout was traditionally low, especially among poorer and less educated men and women, who were disproportionately black. Party affiliation intertwined with race to maintain white political

[25] United States Commission on Civil Rights, "Staff Report."
[26] Maryland Commission on Human Relations, "Systematic Discrimination: A Report on Patterns of Discrimination at the Bethlehem Steel Corporation, Sparrows Point, Maryland" (1970); "Negro Workers Picket Steel Firm," *Washington Post*, January 20, 1968, p. C5.
[27] West, "Urban Life and Spatial Distribution of Blacks in Baltimore," pp. 12, 62–66.

power, as became evident in the vote for city council in the fall of 1967. In this election, Robert Douglass, a moderate who won the support of the powerful Mount Royal Democratic Club, became the first black person to represent the majority black Second District on the city council. Yet, in the same election, Walter Lively, a black activist and the Republican nominee, lost by a wide margin to his white Democratic rivals, Joseph Mach and Clement Pacha, even though both of these white officials were well-known opponents of open housing laws. One of the reasons Lively lost was because the plurality of blacks voted for a straight Democratic ticket.[28] Furthermore, as the proportion of black voters grew, whites deployed extra legal measures to maintain their power, such as turning away qualified voters on questionable grounds from polling places. These irregularities, combined with the aforementioned gerrymandering of district lines, in the estimation of a special advisory committee to the US Civil Rights Commission, "served to increase the level of tension between blacks and whites." If the city wanted to "avoid conflict," the commission added, "it will have to give black America the opportunity to hold office, without resorting to devices," which "keep the 'outs' out and the 'inns' in."[29]

White control of City Hall in Baltimore, like in Cambridge, had real world ramifications in terms of services, jobs, and the pace of change. Although headline stories cataloged breakthroughs that black citizens made in the public sector, from the first black police sergeant in 1947 to the first black housing inspector in 1951 and the first black judge in 1957, overall, blacks remained underrepresented in government jobs.[30] Whereas blacks made up over 40 percent of the city's population, less than 18 percent of the entire Baltimore government's workforce was black in 1966. No blacks worked in eighteen distinct governmental divisions; between

[28] "Judge Rules on Districts Before City Council Primary," *Baltimore Sun*, August 14, 1971, p. B18; *Vernon N. Dobson et al. v. The Mayor and City Council of Baltimore City et al. and John C. Donahue, President et al.*, United States District Court for the District of Maryland 330 F. Supp. 1290, 1971, US Dis. Lexis 11931, August 23, 1971. City Council, Newspaper Clipping, Vertical File, Enoch Pratt Free Library, especially: "Negroes Hoping to Move Toward Greater Municipal Participation," "GOP Puts Lively in Council Race," "Racial Issue Hangs Heavily Over Second District Campaign," "Members of Newly Elected Council," and "Council Adds Two Negroes."

[29] Maryland State Advisory Committee to the US Commission on Civil Rights, "Report of An Investigation of Alleged Voting Irregularities in Baltimore's Seventh Congressional District," 1970.

[30] On strides made by blacks, see "Toward Equality: Baltimore's Progress Report" (Baltimore, MD: Sidney Hollander Foundation, 1960).

90 percent and 100 percent of employees in nineteen other divisions were white; only one division counted more than 15 percent of its employees as black. Whereas other migrant groups had been able to leverage their political power to garner government jobs, which in turn allowed them a modicum of economic security, black citizens remained economically vulnerable, in part, because they lacked political power.[31]

Along the same lines, construction sites paid for with federal, state, and city funds disproportionately benefited white workers who had access to the skilled trades while blacks did not. One survey of building contractors doing business with the city found that blacks made up 75 percent of all unskilled positions but only 10 percent of the top-skilled ones. There were no journeymen or apprentices in the Iron Workers Union and only 124 blacks working as skilled workers on projects funded by the city, in total, out of nearly 800 openings. Acknowledging the severity of this problem, in 1967 Baltimore's Community Relations Commission recommended implementing a "massive affirmative action program." Yet this proposal had minimal impact on municipal hiring until after the uprising and by then broader structural forces were beginning to diminish the number of government jobs or construction work paid for with federal, state, or local dollars.[32]

Moreover, even though Mayors McKeldin and D'Alesandro III retained reputations as racial liberals, they proved unable to get the city council to support fair housing bills or to implement various federally funded reforms, such as legal aid. One of the reasons they proved unable to do so was because of fierce resistance from white voters to such reforms. The Taxpayers Interest League, for instance, termed all efforts to compel property owners to sell or rent to all people regardless of color a violation of the Fourteenth Amendment and the right of association. Henry Miller, who lived in the Patterson Park neighborhood, which as we shall see proved fertile to the likes of National State's Rights Party, termed open housing legislation "one of the most dictatorial pieces of legislation I have ever heard [of]. It reminds me of Communist Russia and Nazi Germany." Much to his chagrin, McKeldin found that he could not even count on the support of his fellow Rockefeller Republican, Spiro

---

[31] Baltimore Community Relations Commission, "Annual Reports" (1965, 1966, and 1967); Mayor McKeldin Papers, Baltimore Community Relations Folder, Box 63; Gilbert Ware to Spiro Agnew, September 17, 1967, Governor Spiro T. Agnew, General File, 1967–68, S1041–1713, Box 14, "Civil Rights: Re: Dr. King's Assassination."

[32] Baltimore Community Relations Commission, "Annual Report, 1967"; "Baltimore CRC Newsletter," July/August, 1967, Mayor McKeldin Papers, Box 363.

Agnew, who while still serving as the executive of Baltimore County, simply wrote, we face "different" problems. Baltimore City's population is 40 percent black; in contrast, Agnew stated matter-of-factly, the county "has few Negroes."[33]

Dreams deferred characterized the educational experience of Baltimore's black citizens as well. While city officials did *not* join southern communities in decrying the Brown decision – it implemented a freedom of choice plan instead – the school system remained segregated. As of 1966, 90 percent of black students still attended majority black schools and two-thirds of white elementary students attended schools that were 90 percent white. This at time when the school aged population was about half black and half white. Several white working-class communities opposed even token desegregation in a manner that reminded observers of the massive resistance of the Deep South. Recognizing these deficiencies, Thomas D'Alesandro supported busing during his 1967 mayoral campaign and nominated Thomas Sheldon as his superintendent, who historian Howell Baum described as a leader who had a radical plan. Yet, Sheldon's term did not begin until after the Holy Week Uprising, or put differently not until faith in school integration had essentially evaporated.[34]

Moreover, in two important elections, the Democratic presidential primary in 1964 and the gubernatorial election in 1966, large swaths of Baltimore's white voters demonstrated their racist views by supporting two icons of white supremacy, George Wallace and George Mahoney. In 1964, Wallace vied with Senator Daniel Brewster, President Lyndon Johnson's stand-in, for the Democratic presidential nomination. Largely on the backs of black and Jewish voters, Brewster defeated Wallace in Baltimore city by 40,000 votes. Yet he lost to Wallace in the white working-class wards. Writes Kenneth Durr, "In East and South Baltimore blue-collar wards 1, 23, and 24 combined, Wallace got 64 percent of the vote. In South Baltimore, the margins for Wallace ran in the high 60 percent range. In the Second Precinct of Ward 21, where school desegregation protests had [taken place], Wallace got 71 percent. In Ward 24's Fourth Precinct – the site of Southern High School [another site of anti-desegregationist

[33] "Core Says Baltimore Lagging," *Washington Post*, May 8, 1966, p. B4; Taxpayers Interest League to Mayor McKeldin, July 13, 1966; Henry Miller to Mayor Theodore McKeldin, March 4, 1967; Memo Re: Telephone Conversation with Spiro Agnew, March 16, 1964; all in Mayor McKeldin Papers, Box 414.
[34] Howell Baum, "How the 1968 Riots Stopped School Desegregation in Baltimore," in *Baltimore '68*, pp. 154–179; Howell Baum, *"Brown" in Baltimore: School Desegregation and the Limits of Liberalism* (New York: Cornell University Press, 2010).

FIGURE 4.4 Alabama Governor George Wallace campaigns in Maryland for GOP nominee Barry Goldwater, October 19, 1964. AP Photo.

protest] – Wallace took 67 percent."[35] The strong support for Wallace was particularly astounding considering the opposition he engendered from the working class's most important institutions, organized labor and the Catholic Church (see Figure 4.4).[36]

Two years later, much of Baltimore's white working class displayed just as strong support for George Mahoney, the candidate who ran for governor on the "your home is your castle – defend it" slogan. Mahoney lost the state primarily because his Republican opponent, Spiro Agnew, won by overwhelmingly large margins in the surrounding lily-white suburban counties and among blacks statewide. But Mahoney won Baltimore even

[35] Durr, *Behind the Backlash* [Kindle edition] Location 2629–2652.
[36] "Brewster Beats Wallace," *Baltimore Sun*, May 20, 1964, p. 1; "Maryland's Vote Held Anti-Negro," *NYT*, May 21, 1964, p. 1; "Vote Called a Disgrace," *Washington Post*, May 25, 1964, p. C7; "Opposed by Catholic Paper," *NYT*, March 21, 1964, p. 10.

though he garnered nary a black vote. Once again white working-class voters defied the entreaties of their union and church leaders, casting an estimated 71 percent of their ballots for Mahoney. Ironically, the same wards would soon become much more receptive to Agnew, with large numbers of their residents shedding their identification with the Democratic Party for the first time in their lives.[37]

Blacks also encountered a rising number of blatant examples of white supremacist actions in the streets. In the spring of 1965, a mob of whites successfully pressured a black woman to move out of the home she had rented in the all-white Woodberry neighborhood. In July 1966, writes Kenneth Durr, the "NSRP's [National States Rights Party] Reverend Connie Lynch, a self-proclaimed inciter of race riots ... appeared on a stage [in Patterson Park] adorned with the symbol of the NSRP, a Confederate flag with a Nazi SS lightning bolt superimposed on it," where he "denounced CORE, communists, Jews, the NAACP, [and] the Supreme Court." While only about 500 attended his first rally, two days later a larger rally of approximately 1,000, primarily white working youths, took place. At the rally some chanted "kill the niggers." Afterwards, a mob of whites attacked black residents in East Baltimore.[38]

While far right groups like the KKK and NSRP never represented the views of the majority of white people, nor the majority of white workers, public polls demonstrated the degree to which whites and blacks held divergent views of racial matters. As part of its investigation the Kerner Commission employed a group of social scientists from Johns Hopkins University and the University of Michigan's Survey Research Center to conduct in-depth surveys of fifteen cities, including Baltimore.[39] Summarizing their findings, the Johns Hopkins team wrote: "Blacks ... see the cause of the civil disorders as defects in the *system* [emphasis added] that

---

[37] Durr, *Behind the Backlash* [Kindle edition], Location 2823 to 2905.

[38] John Barrett to Samuel Daniels, Memorandum on Woodberry Situation, March 5, 1965 and Gene Noble and James Barrett to Samuel Daniels, Memorandum on Woodberry Situation, March 4, 1965, both in Mayor McKeldin Papers, Box 363; Durr, *Behind the Backlash* [Kindle edition], Location 2772 to 2812; Rhonda Y. Williams, "The Pursuit of Audacious Power: Rebel Reformers and Neighborhood Politics in Baltimore, 1966–1968," in *Neighborhood Rebels: Black Power at the Local Level*, ed. by Peniel E. Joseph (New York: Palgrave Macmillan, 2010), pp. 221–222.

[39] Angus Campbell and Howard Schuman, "Racial Attitudes in Fifteen American Cities," in *Supplemental Studies for the National Advisory Commission on Civil Disorders*, (Washington, DC: GPO, 1968), pp. 1–67; Peter Rossi, Richard Berk, Bettye K. Eidson, *The Roots of Urban Discontent: Public Policy, Municipal Institutions, and the Ghetto* (New York: John Wiley & Sons, 1974); Richard Berk, "The Role of the Ghetto Retail Merchants in Civil Disorders," PhD dissertation, Johns Hopkins University, 1970.

surrounds the black community while whites tend to blame personal characteristics of blacks." Surveys of subgroups reinforced this central finding. For instance, white and black merchants who operated stores in black communities held vastly different views of black residents, with the majority of white merchants believing that blacks were "as well off" as white in terms of "educational opportunities," "treatment by the police," "medical care," and "recreational opportunities," and faced "less well off" opportunities only in the realm of housing. Large majorities of blacks, in contrast, felt they were "less well off" than whites in all of these areas except medical care. Likewise, by a nearly two-to-one margin, employers (who were presumed to be white), felt blacks were either treated better, equal to, or the same as whites of the same income, as those who felt they were treated worse. In contrast, large majorities of blacks perceived racial discrimination as a major concern, both in terms of obtaining employment and when it came to getting promoted. Perhaps just as tellingly, over three-quarters of all African Americans believed that big companies "hire a few Negroes only for show purposes, to appear to be non-discriminatory." While blacks in Baltimore had significantly better views of the police than did blacks in the other cities, they held much less favorable views of the police than did whites.[40]

Given the degree and persistence of the racial divide in Baltimore, one has to wonder why it did not experience a revolt in 1964, when uprisings took place in Harlem, Rochester, and Philadelphia, or during the long hot summer of 1967, when hundreds of cities, including Newark, New Jersey, did. Baltimore's Human Relations Council suggested that "luck" combined with the enlightened leadership of Mayor McKeldin, "a man who communicated his sincere commitment to equal opportunity to the people, enlightened leadership by police officials ... and businessmen, who actively supported a significant summer [of 1967] crash employment program," accounted for the lack of "rioting."[41] Yet, a more likely if counterintuitive explanation emphasizes Baltimore's long history of civil rights activism as the key to averting disorder. Put somewhat differently while Agnew subsequently claimed that radicals, enabled by culturally permissive liberals, caused riots, the opposite was the case. By providing

[40] Campbell and Schuman, "Racial Attitudes in Fifteen American Cities"; Berk, "The Role of the Ghetto Retail Merchants in Civil Disorders."
[41] Baltimore Human Relations Commission, "Annual Report, 1967," p. 2; Gary Reynolds to John Spiegel, Brandeis Lemberg Center, June 30, 1967, Mayor McKeldin Papers, Box 395.

constructive alternatives or keeping the dream alive, black activists did not cause "riots," rather they forestalled them.

"Black Power at Its Best"

In 1966 CORE selected Baltimore as its first "Target City," allowing the organization to test its new black power philosophy on the ground. When Baltimore's Mayor McKeldin asked "why us?" CORE's local activists James Griffin and Sampson Green responded: because the city had "slapped [blacks] in the face" by refusing to enact a fair housing law and because after years of activism CORE had concluded that without more pressure there was good reason to wonder whether the situation was "ever going to [change]." CORE's newly minted national director Floyd McKissick added, CORE targeted Baltimore because it is "a racist city, in every sense of the word...where Negroes are denied admission to public accommodations...[where] there is a school problem...a housing problem...and...police brutality."[42] In addition, CORE targeted Baltimore because it already had an active local chapter in the city. Even before the project officially began, this chapter had garnered a good deal of favorable media coverage by staging demonstrations against both housing units and taverns that continued to discriminate against non-whites. In addition, an affiliate of CORE, the Maryland Freedom Union (MFU), had launched efforts to organize poor black workers. These efforts afforded CORE the opportunity to pursue black economic empowerment, as opposed to desegregation, as one of the main thrusts of black power. (For more on MFU, see below.)[43]

[42] "CORE Says Baltimore is Lagging," *Washington Post*, May 8, 1966, p. B4; McKissick quoted in: "Baltimore Target City," *U.S. News & World Report*, May 23, 1966. Louis C. Goldberg, "CORE in Trouble: A Social History of the Organizational Dilemma of the Congress of Racial Equality Target City Project in Baltimore, 1965–67," unpublished PhD dissertation, Johns Hopkins University, 1970.

[43] "Baltimore CORE Gaining Momentum," *Chicago Defender*, June 24, 1967, p. 2; Callender quoted in: "CORE's Target City," *The Emporia Gazette*, June 1, 1966, p. 2; "White Racists Spark Violence in Baltimore," *The Pantagraph*, July 29, 1966, p. 1; Who will Trigger a Riot?" *Afro-American*, May 28, 1966, p. 5; "6 CORE Members Nabbed in Sit-in," *Baltimore Sun*, May 24, 1966, p. 8; "CORE Confronts KKK-Bar Integrated," *Baltimore Sun*, June 2, 1966, p. 4. "Rights Group to Stress New Militant Stand," *Chicago Defender*, July 2, 1966, p. 2; "Harambee City: Congress of Racial Equality in Cleveland and the Rise of Black Power Populism," http://harambeecity.lib.miamioh.edu/home-page [accessed June 23, 2016; website active at time of access], especially documents on the Maryland Freedom Union, Baltimore and Cleveland Target City Projects, and Baltimore Target City Project. Williams, "The Pursuit of Audacious Power."

To help kick start its Target City campaign, CORE convened its 1966 national convention in Baltimore. Though scheduled to speak, Martin Luther King Jr. did not attend, allegedly because of prior commitments – some suspected he did not come because of his disagreements with CORE's new endorsement of self-defense and turn away from integration as a goal. But a wide array of other civil rights stalwarts, from Stokely Carmichael to Fannie Lou Hamer, did. Over the course of the convention, delegates sought to flesh out the meaning black power, which Carmichael had only recently popularized. Rejecting claims that black power "implied a drive for black supremacy," Carmichael stressed that black power meant that black people needed to "stand up and get things for themselves." Carmichael, Hamer, and CORE's new leader, Floyd McKissick, also made clear that they sanctioned self-defense as "a right." In a pamphlet entitled "Breaking the Noose," convention delegates further defined black power as winning livable welfare benefits, unionizing low-wage disproportionately black workers, establishing freedom schools that would "teach Negro history and culture," registering black voters, and attacking the "abuses of urban renewal."[44]

While the national press tended to highlight CORE's controversial stances, particularly its support of armed self-defense and opposition to the Vietnam War, these positions did not deter many local civil rights groups from supporting the project. The Interdenominational Ministerial Alliance endorsed CORE's goal of obtaining the black community's "proper share of the total economic and political power." Reverend Edwards added that one of the advantages of CORE's philosophical shift was that it allowed individuals who were not committed to nonviolence to participate in demonstrations. Rather than finding CORE's opposition to the Vietnam War offensive, the Civic Interest Group and several other interracial groups welcomed CORE to the antiwar movement. Even Mayor McKeldin offered CORE the keys to the city and displayed a willingness to work with rather than against the organization, because he saw cooperation as a key to averting riots.[45] At the same time, some

---

[44] "We'll Meet Violence With Violence," *Afro-American*, July 9, 1966, p. 1; "CORE Adopts new Resolution; End Non-Violence," *Chicago Defender*, July 5, 1966, p. 6; "CORE Says: Fight Fire With Fire," *New Journal and Guide*, July 9, 1966, p. 1; Goldberg, "Core in Trouble."

[45] "CORE Calls Baltimore Target City," *Washington Post*, April 15, 1966, p. C2; "CORE Picks Baltimore for Session," *Washington Post*, June 19, 1966, p. B7; "Baltimore Picked by CORE," *NYT*, April 15, 1966, p. 20; "Key Leaders in Baltimore for CORE Meeting," *Afro-American*, July 9, 1966, p. 10; "CORE Plan Upsets Baltimore Mayor," *NYT*,

moderate civil rights groups opposed Target City, with Juanita Jackson Mitchell warning that "Black Power will lead us to the wrong path of freedom."[46]

As suggested above, one of CORE's initiatives involved the Maryland Freedom Union's efforts to organize black workers, many of whom were women. (Technically, the MFU was organizationally distinct from CORE, though there was considerable overlap in terms of personnel and focus.) MFU sought to organize unions from the grassroots up and to reach workers often considered un-organizable by the mainstream movement, such as nursing home, health care, and retail workers. Ola Johnson, a nursing home worker who rose to a leadership position within MFU, described it as an example of "Black Power at its best." The drive to organize retail workers in West Baltimore, for instance, brought together the community in its various roles – as consumers, as residents, and as workers. "The black people of Pennsylvania Avenue were behind us," she explained. In turn, Johnson contended, MFU helped black workers gain a living wage, something that most considered an impossible dream when the drive began.[47]

Concomitantly, black steel workers, with MFU support, began to orchestrate protests against both Bethlehem Steel, the largest employer in the city, and the United States Steelworkers, one of the most powerful unions in the nation. Employment in the steel mills, especially Bethlehem's

April 17, 1966, p. 60; "CORE Is Given Key to City," *Washington Post*, July 4, 1966, p. A6; "CORE Will Insist on Black Power," *NYT*, July 6, 1966, p. 1; "Advice to Dr. King," *Afro-American*, July 16, 1966, p. 14. Mills, *"Got My Mind Set on Freedom"*; Smith, *Here Lies Jim Crow*, especially chapters 3, 4, and 5. James Williams, "Sightseeing: Changing Moods in the Movement," *Afro-American*, July 16, 1965, p. 5; James Williams, "Everybody is a Race Expert," *Afro-American*, October 30, 1965, p. 5; "Sightseeing: You Can't Win, So Join Them," *Afro-American*, August 6, 1966, p. 5; Rhonda Williams, "The Pursuit of Audacious Power," pp. 218–227; UPI, "New Core Militancy Aimed at Baltimore," *Tyrone Daily Herald*, July 2, 1966, p. 1; "Negro Clergy Scorn CORE's 'Black Power,'" *The News* (Frederick, Maryland), July 8, 1966, p. 1; David Glenn to Mayor McKeldin, April 27, 1966 and Interdenominational Ministerial Alliance to Mayor McKeldin, May 5, 1966, both in Mayor McKeldin Papers, Box 361.

46 "NAACP Raps 'Black Power' Concept," *Chicago Defender*, July 6, 1966, p. 6; "Morgan President Urges Students to Reject Black Power," *Afro-American*, October 15, 1966, p. 17; "NAACP Aide Criticizes 'Black Power' Rallying Cry," *Washington Post*, July 9, 1966, p. B3. "King Refuses to Join Attack on 'Black Power' Advocates," *Afro-American*, October 22, 1966, p. 1.

47 Michael Flug, "The Maryland Freedom Union: Collective Action," *News & Letters*, n.d., http://harambeecity.lib.miamioh.edu/files/original/7de4ecb59eb472de6fcf40fed12 f5468.JPG [accessed June 23, 2016; website active at time of access]; "Negroes Gain Union Right," *Baltimore Sun*, July 14, 1966, p. A13; CORE, "Target City Pamphlet," n.d., Mayor McKeldin Papers, Box 381.

massive Sparrows Point plant, had been one of the strongest magnets of the Great Migration of blacks to Baltimore. Compared to the meager earnings available to blacks in the rural South, employment in the steel industry seemed to many, at first, a godsend. Blacks also knew that they had played a key role in winning union recognition from the steel industry. Yet, by the mid-1960s, it was becoming increasingly clear to many black steelworkers that their dreams had been deferred. While over ten thousand blacks worked for Bethlehem, very few found employment in either skilled blue-collar jobs and fewer still in white collar managerial ones. As of 1968, blacks held only about 3 percent of supervisory positions, even though they made up 38 percent of Bethlehem's work force in Baltimore. Instead, they were "concentrated" in substantially lower paying and the most dangerous positions. Blacks were "traditionally excluded" from apprenticeships and compelled to take tests to qualify for positions currently held by white steelworkers, even though the latter never had to take such tests.[48]

Moreover, this labor market segmentation, black activists contended, emanated from the discriminatory practices of *both* the Bethlehem Steel Corporation and the local branches of the US Steelworkers Union. As Lee C. Douglass, the leader of the Shipyard Workers for Equality, a grassroots organization of black Baltimore steelworkers and an affiliate of CORE and the MFU, put it, discrimination existed in "all the bread and butter areas dealing with jobs." Supported by the national leadership of CORE and U-JOIN, an offshoot of SDS (Students for a Democratic Society), black steelworkers staged a series of protests, including freedom marches at the Sparrows Point plant, at the corporation's headquarters in Bethlehem, Pennsylvania, and outside the Department of Labor in Washington, DC. At one rally in Baltimore, Lincoln Lynch, CORE's associate national director, made clear that the union shared responsibility with the company for these discriminatory practices. If the "United States Steelworkers doesn't have your best interests at heart," he declared, "then to hell with the United States Steelworkers." On a separate occasion, CORE's new leader Floyd McKissick demanded that the federal government withdraw its $50 million worth of federal

---

[48] "Bethlehem Accused by U.S. of Job Bias at Sparrows Point," *Baltimore Sun*, February 3, 1968, p. B20; Maryland Commission on Human Relations, "Systematic Discrimination: A Report on Patterns of Discrimination at the Bethlehem Steel Corporation, Sparrows Point, Maryland" (1970); "Charge Steel, Metal Firms with Bias," *Call and Post*, November 19, 1966, p. 10B; "Discrimination at Steel Co. Questioned," *The Oil City Derrick*, October 22, 1966, p. 13.

contracts with Bethlehem until it demonstrated a "commitment" to racial equality.[49]

In 1967, the Target City project essentially came to an end, with CORE focusing more of its energies on a second Target City project in Cleveland than on Baltimore. In his dissertation, "CORE in Trouble," CORE veteran Louis Goldberg demonstrated that a lack of coherent planning and organizational disputes between the national office and local activists hampered the project from its start.[50] This said, the broader local crusade to attain greater black economic and political power did not come to an end with the termination of the Target City project. MFU activists continued to organize poor black workers, including health care workers, who as we shall see, would enjoy unprecedented victories after Holy Week 1968. Concomitantly, a variety of activists pushed for greater black political influence. The so-called Goon Squad, composed of ministers, lawyers, educators, and civil rights activist (sometimes one-and-the same), turned the firing of Joseph Howard, a black prosecutor who had railed at the "unequal treatment of black and white rape victims," into a cause célèbre, culminating with his election as a city judge the following year.[51] Burgeoning grassroots black and female-led welfare rights groups organized protests against welfare cuts; and the Activists for Fair Housing, another offshoot of CORE, pressured City Hall to enact open housing legislation. If the government did not meet the demands of these various groups, warned welfare activist Margaret McCarty, "Long, hot, angry summers" lay ahead. Phillip Jenkins agreed, suggesting in his poem, "Nice Little Nigger," that blacks were tired of being "conned" by those who counseled patience and accommodation.[52]

---

[49] "Steelworkers Union Meeting Bars C.O.R.E.," *Baltimore Sun*, April 15, 1967, p. B18; "Point Pushes Negro Advancement," *Baltimore Sun*, April 28, 1967, p. C9; "CORE Rally Scores Bias," *Baltimore Sun*, April 29, 1967, p. A9; "Point Chosen For National CORE Fight," *Baltimore Sun*, May 6, 1967, p. B22; "CORE Seeks Labor Action," *Baltimore Sun*, December 14, 1967, p. A20; "Negro Workers Picket Steel Firm," *Washington Post*, January 20, 1968, p. C5; "Bethlehem Accused by U.S. of Job Bias at Sparrows Point," *Baltimore Sun*, February 3, 1968, p. B20; "Steelworkers Taking Point Fight to D.C.," *Afro-American*, February 3, 1968, p. 30; Lee Douglas Jr., "Letter to the Editor," *Baltimore Sun*, August 7, 1968, p. A10. See also, Michael Flug, "Organized Labor and the Civil Rights Movement of the 1960s: The Case of the Maryland Freedom Union," *Labor History*, 31:3 (Summer 1990), pp. 322–346.
[50] Goldberg, "CORE in Trouble"; Barbara Mills, *Got My Mind Set on Freedom*.
[51] Rudolph Lewis, "A Christian Goon Squad in Black Baltimore," *Chicken Bones: A Journal for Literary & Artistic African-American Themes*, July 4, 2011, www.nathanielturner.com/christiangoonsquadblackbaltimore.htm [accessed November 18, 2016].
[52] McCarty quoted in, Rhonda Williams, "Nonviolence and Long Hot Summers: Black Women and Welfare Rights Struggles in the 1960s," *Borderlands*, 4:3 (November 3,

Black civil rights activists also helped elect Thomas D'Alesandro III to mayor on a very progressive platform in the fall of 1967 – D'Alesandro won well-over 90 percent of the black vote. Moreover, after his election, black militants pushed him to the left. For example, a coalition of black and white leftists prodded D'Alesandro to apply for federal Model City funding and, after he did so, called for grassroots community involvement in the program. Without full participation by the poor themselves, Walter Lively inveighed, "nothing more than a junk heap of shattered hopes, broken promises and another grab bag for governmental big shots and traditional government agencies" would result. Or as McCarty put it, "if poor people's ideas were not incorporated, they did not want the program." Moving beyond words, in February 1968, a coalition of about twenty civil rights, Black Power, and neighborhood organizations formed a "takeover" committee and demanded control of the Model Cities Agency itself. When negotiations between this coalition and Mayor D'Alesandro hit a roadblock, Target City veteran Danny Grant threatened to "destroy the program" and to go to Washington, DC, to press the coalition's demands with federal officials. In response, D'Alesandro implemented a compromise, which sought to provide "maximum participation of the poor at every phase in the planning of the Model City program."[53]

Yet, CORE and other activists enjoyed no such luck with Governor Spiro Agnew, who went out of his way to demonstrate that he would do nothing to legitimate advocates and associates of Black Power, even those who might have genuine grievances. When Agnew's top civil rights advisor, Gilbert Ware, suggested that he could enhance his image by paying "personal ostentation free visits to the ghetto," to show militants that he was not their "foe," and counter recent claims that he had "overstated the case against Rap Brown," – Agnew adamantly rejected his counsel, exclaiming: "There is absolutely no way to overstate the case against Rap

2005); Phillip Jenkins, "Nice Little Nigger," January 1967, Mayor McKeldin Paper, Box 381; "Activists for Fair Housing," leaflet, n.d., Mayor McKeldin Papers, Box 357.

53 "2nd District Politics Alters Focus," *Baltimore Sun*, July 8, 1967, p. A9; "A Visit With Ruth Turner in New York Brings Report of CORE's Target City," *Call and Post*, December 24, 1966, p. 3A; "4 in CORE Arrested at Mach's Café," *Baltimore Sun*, November 21, 1967, p. C24; "Open Tavern Bill Fails by a Single Vote," *Baltimore Sun*, June 20, 1967; "D'Alesandro Named Baltimore Mayor; Democrats Sweep," *NYT*, November 8, 1967, p. 34; "D'Alesandro Slate Leads in Baltimore," *Baltimore Sun*, September 8, 1967, p. A1; "D'Alesandro Elected Mayor of Baltimore," *Washington Post*, November 8, 1967, p. A8; "D'Alesandro Beats Sherwood and Carries Entire Democratic Ticket to Victory at City Hall," *Baltimore Sun*, November 8, 1967, p. AE1; "D'Alesandro Defeats Angelos in Primary," *Baltimore Sun*, September 8, 1967, p. AAA1; "D'Alesandro, Sherwood Win Primary," *Baltimore Sun*, September 8, 1967, p. A1; Rhonda Williams, "The Pursuit of Audacious Power," pp. 230–232.

Brown."[54] Furthermore, on the eve of the Holy Week Uprising, Agnew engaged in a showdown with students at Bowie State College, one of Maryland's historically black colleges. Though the campus had a reputation for moderation not militancy, tensions rose after Agnew dismissed student complaints regarding the intolerable conditions on campus, which they termed "the cesspool of the State College system" – including poor food, awful dormitories, underpaid faculty, and mismanagement by the registrar's office. On March 27, 1968, following a couple of weeks of protest, student body president Roland Smith and other student activists decided to organize a peaceful boycott of classes. Rather than meet with students, Agnew sent one of his aids, Charles Bressler, who exacerbated the situation through his flippant and insensitive remarks. When students threatened to burn the school down if Agnew did not meet with them, Bressler suggested they should do so because it would "save the state" and taxpayers hundreds of thousands of dollars. After Bressler departed, students occupied the entire campus. In response, Agnew closed the college, ordered state police to arrest the students, and blamed "outside influences" for the turmoil. "This is not a racial dispute" but rather a question of "respect for...the law," Agnew proclaimed at a press conference on April 4, 1968, a statement he knew would further inflame the situation but which he also hoped will garner him support from the state's white voters.[55]

Blacks in Baltimore learned of the arrest of Bowie students and King's assassination at about the same time. Agnew's characterization of the protests as having nothing to do with race was condescending at best. Placed within the context of the broader political climate of the early spring of 1968, Agnew's response to the Bowie State protest confirmed not only how little political power they enjoyed but also the depth of white resistance to implementing substantial racial reforms. After all, Agnew had been the moderate candidate in 1966 and he owed his election to black voters. Baltimore's uprising probably would have taken place without the showdown at Bowie State. Still, it was Agnew, not black radicals, who threw fuel on the fire on the eve of the revolt.

---

[54] Ware and Agnew quoted in Rhonda Williams, "The Pursuit of Audacious Power," pp. 232–233.

[55] Witcover, *White Knight*, pp. 10–16; "Bowie State Boycott Closes Most Classes," *Washington Post*, March 28, 1968, p. A1; "Bowie State Is Closed by Agnew," *Baltimore Sun*, April 5, 1967; "Historic Protest Remembered in Bowie State Play," *The Sentinel*, November 24, 2015, www.thesentinel.com/pgs/index.php?option=com_k2&view=item&id=1883:historic-protest-remembered-in-bowie-state-play&Itemid=766 [accessed May 27, 2016].

Before turning to the revolt, itself, it is helpful to briefly explore the history of Cherry Hill, the single black neighborhood in Baltimore that experienced no looting or arson following King's death. By reinforcing a sense of community and showing that one could fight City Hall, local activists in Cherry Hill kept the dream alive. Put somewhat differently, Cherry Hill's story confirms that grassroots activism, not the strong arm of the law or the absence of radicals, provided the best insurance against rioting.

"I Think It Is Interesting During the Riot in the 60s, there Was not a Single Window Broken, not a Single Incident of Looting"

In the aftermath of World War II, with the black population of Baltimore outgrowing the "ghettos" of East and West Baltimore, the city government, with the support and aid of the state and federal government, decided to develop a largely uninhabited section known as Cherry Hill into an all-black neighborhood. Even though whites from adjoining communities protested this decision, authorities considered it far preferable to the other alternative, namely constructing desegregated public housing in white communities. During the late 1940s and 1950s close to 20,000 blacks, from varying socioeconomic classes and backgrounds moved into a mixture of public and private housing in Cherry Hill. Many of the residents saw themselves as "pioneers" who had created not just a place to reside but a community they considered their own. They helped establish a branch of the public library, gathered at the local shopping center, playgrounds, and a recreational center. They also organized little league teams, political clubs, and churches, and played a seminal role in maintaining local schools.[56] This high level of civic activism prompted one Cherry Hill resident to describe the community as "the closest neighborhood I have ever lived in." Or as Cathy Brown, a longtime resident of Cherry Hill put it, "I think it is interesting during the riot in the 60s, there was not a single window broken, not a single incident of looting, and we had 17,000 people living here then ... I think this [says] a lot about the kind of neighborhood this is."[57]

---

[56] "Cherry Hill: Oral History Project Interviews, April–May, 2000" (copy in possession of author); "A City Within a City on Banks of Patapsco," *Afro-American*, August 26, 1967, p. B10.

[57] John R. Breihan, "Why No Rioting in Cherry Hill?" *Baltimore '68*, pp. 39–50; Interview of Ms. Kathy Brown by Dawn McEwan and Bob Merchant, May 4, 2000, in "Cherry Hill: Oral History Project Interviews," April–May 2000, Tape 7 (in author's possession).

This is not to suggest that Cherry Hill's residents lived in the Promised Land, that they were immune from the racist structures that limited blacks economically and politically. Political gerrymandering left the residents underrepresented in city and state government. Geographical isolation made it more difficult for residents to commute to various jobs. By all standard socioeconomic measurements, income and poverty levels, educational achievement, and percentage of residents on public assistance, Cherry Hill was virtually indistinguishable from the "ghettos" of East and West Baltimore. Nonetheless, residents retained a sense of hope, to a large part because of the level of civic engagement, including grassroots organizations, that were willing and able to demand (and win) meaningful victories.[58]

The protests of one grassroots group, INCITE, proved telling. Learning of the city's plans to build an incinerator on land long set aside for a public park, a group of activists, including members of CORE, "laid siege," to borrow the *Baltimore Sun's* words, to a meeting of Baltimore's Park Board. At one point, Cherry Hill activists got into a testy exchange with Park Board president Samuel Hopkins. "This board is supposed to be the servants of the people...not subject to your whim," declared Madeline Murphy, one of Cherry Hill's leaders. Another Cherry Hill resident exclaimed that she was "sick and tired" of the city's broken promises. With INCITE leading the way, Cherry Hill residents engaged in a sustained and ultimately successful effort to stop the construction of the incinerator. They wrote letters to the editor, staged public protests, lobbied state and local representatives, and warned of greater turmoil if the city did not rethink its plans. And when the city decided not to build the incinerator, activists continued to raise their voices in objection to other environmental injustices, such as the construction of a scrap metal plant which would "significantly polluting [*sic*] the air" and the refusal of the city to clear out disease and garbage-ridden swamps which lay adjacent to Cherry Hill.[59]

58 "Cherry Hill: Oral History Project Interviews, April–May, 2000" (copy in possession of author); DeWayne Wickham, *Woodholme: Growing Up Alone: A Black Man's Story* (Baltimore, MD: Johns Hopkins University Press, 1995); Williams, *The Politics of Black Housing*, pp. 62–63, 145–148, 217.
59 "Park Unit Hears Cherry Hill Protest of Incinerator Plan," *Baltimore Sun*, July 13, 1966, p. C28; Clarence Jones, "No Incinerator," *Baltimore Sun*, August 18, 1966, p. A10; "McKeldin Backs 'Flats' Location: Takes Side in Cherry Hill Incinerator Fight," *Baltimore Sun*, September 3, 1966, p. B20; Clarence Jones, "Cherry Hill Incinerator," *Baltimore Sun*, September 8, 196, p. A14; Madeline Murphy, "Cherry Hill," *Baltimore Sun*, July 14, 1967, p. A8.

INCITE's efforts, both in terms of personnel and methods, overlapped with other grassroots activism in Cherry Hill, in many cases led by and for women. Madeline Murphy explained that Cherry Hill's residents united to "develop solutions and paths of actions," aimed at addressing the needs of the community. To fight crime, they prodded the police to open a store front in Cherry Hill's shopping district, part of the broader initiative to develop better relations between local black youths and the police. At the same time, tenant groups, allied with church leaders and social service workers stopped the city from allowing liquor stores from operating. The local Welfare Rights Organization not only demanded greater respect for black women on welfare, and better benefits, but an end to the Vietnam War which, in their words, was disproportionately taking away their sons. Cherry Hill residents also investigated ways to increase their political power. To these ends, in the fall of 1967, the Cherry Hill Coordinating Council invited longtime SNCC stalwart Julian Bond to deliver a keynote address at its twentieth anniversary celebration. At the time, Bond was involved in a struggle to maintain his seat in the Georgia State legislature. In the speech, Bond cited the Lowndes County Freedom Organization, which had established its own political party known as the Black Panther Party, as one example of historically disenfranchised blacks attaining power. And while the standard narrative of civil rights years tends to emphasize the divisions between advocates of nonviolence and self-defense, Rhonda Williams observes that a number of Cherry Hill activists found ways to marry the traditions of Malcolm X and King, and in doing so, "offered an alternative to upheaval."[60]

Activism alone did not account for the lack of "rioting" in Cherry Hill; geography also played a key role. Looting in East and West Baltimore, which erupted following King's assassination, could not spill over into Cherry Hill because of its physical isolation. To do so the looters would have had to navigate the inner harbor or adjacent white neighborhoods and physical barriers.[61] Along the same lines, Cherry Hill's commercial establishments differed spatially from those in other sections of the city.

[60] Williams, *The Politics of Black Housing*, pp. 62–63, 145–148, 217; Williams, "Nonviolence and Long Hot Summers"; "Celebrations Set by Cherry Hill," *Baltimore Sun*, September 24, 1967, p. 17; "Earn Power, Group Told," *Baltimore Sun*, September 25, 1967, p. C10. "Poverty Unit To Move Into New Sections," *Baltimore Sun*, January 19, 1968, p. B18; "Meeting 'leak' Irks Cherry Hill Leader," *Afro-American*, March 30, 1968, p. 32; "Come and Talk It Over," *Baltimore Sun*, February 11, 1968, p. M4; James David to Mayor McKeldin, December 8, 1965, Mayor McKeldin Papers, Box 377.
[61] Breihan, "Why No Rioting in Cherry Hill?"

In most of Baltimore's neighborhoods, merchants lined specific shopping fares or roads, such as Pennsylvania Avenue or Gay Street. In contrast, Cherry Hill's clothing stores, small supermarket, and pool hall were clustered in a shopping center. Up through at least the mid-1960s, Cherry Hill's residents gathered at this shopping center on Friday nights and perceived it as their village square. This perception of the shopping center as a sort of modern-day commons mitigated against vandalism and looting. There is also some evidence that the shopping center had a higher percentage of black-owned businesses than elsewhere, though a number of key stores were owned by white and they were not targeted during the revolt.[62]

As suggested above, Cherry Hill's actions or lack thereof during the uprising smashes another parcel of conventional wisdom, that a firmer hand by the state, ranging from a stronger show of force to shooting looters, would have prevented looting. As will be discussed more fully in Chapter 6, in the aftermath of the Holy Week Uprisings a major debate erupted over whether authorities had responded properly to the rioting. Chicago Mayor Daley's order to shoot to maim looters and kill arsonist won him a good deal of support. In contrast, Attorney General Ramsay Clark's criticism of Daley and support for limited use of force earned him the venom of a large segment of the population. Spiro Agnew's metamorphosis from a relatively unknown Rockefeller Republican to the second highest public official in the land, rested to a large part on his get tough persona as well. Yet the case of Cherry Hill suggests that the use of force does not directly correlate to a lack of rioting. No federal troops or National Guardsmen were rushed into the neighborhood. Nor did police or state troopers increase their presence. On the contrary, community activism and engagement, and a record of meeting at least some of the demands of these activists, not shotguns and bayonets, proved the best way to maintain the peace.

[62] Breihan, "Why No Rioting in Cherry Hill?"

5

The Holy Week Uprising of 1968

He preached nonviolence and look at him now.

Black Steelworker, Baltimore, April 5, 1968[1]

While this chapter will focus on Baltimore, it is important to remember that the Holy Week Uprising was widespread. Between the evening of April 4th, when James Earl Ray shot Martin Luther King Jr. and Easter Sunday April 14, 1968, looting, arson, or sniper fire occurred in 196 cities in thirty-six states plus the District of Columbia. Fifty-four cities suffered at least $100,000 in property damage, with the nation's capital and Baltimore topping the list at approximately $15 million and $12 million (81 million in 2015 dollars), respectively. Thousands of small shopkeepers saw their life's savings go up in smoke. Combined forty-three men and women were killed, approximately 3,500 were injured, and 27,000 were arrested. Not until over 58,000 National Guardsmen and regular Army troops joined local state and police forces did the uprisings cease.[2] Put somewhat differently, during Holy Week 1968, the United States experienced its greatest wave of social unrest since the Civil War.

---

[1] "Baltimore Shocked, Angered, Hurt, Grieved by Death of Dr. King," *Afro-American*, April 6, 1968, p. 1.

[2] Thomas F. Parker, ed., *Violence in America, Volume 2: 1968–72* (New York: Facts on File, 1974), pp. 15–29; *Riot Data Review*, 2 (August 1968); Kevin Maroney to Ramsey Clark, April 15, 1968, "Riot Statistics, 1967–1968," Personal Papers of Ramsey Clark, Box 75, Lyndon B. Johnson Library, Austin, Texas; "Attachment A," Lyndon Johnson Aides: James Gaither, Lyndon Johnson Library; Box 37, Riots 1968: Dr. King [2]. National Guard Association of the United States, "Use of National Guard During Civil Disorders in 1968," January 1, 1969, National Guard Files, Baltimore Armory, Baltimore, MD, Civil Disturbances, 1968 July/December.

Somewhat surprisingly, this wave of the Great Uprising has received remarkably little attention. With the exception of *Ten Blocks from the White House*, collectively written by the reporters of the *Washington Post* in the immediate wake of King's assassination, scholars have virtually ignored them. In 2008, Clay Risen, a journalist, composed *A Nation on Fire*, yet his work hardly dented the general treatment of the race revolts of the era, which focuses on those that took place in Watts, Newark, and Detroit in 1965 and 1967, respectively. As a result, the Kerner Commission's claim that the "disorders" were triggered by incidents involving the police has continued to hold sway, in spite of the fact that this obviously was not the case in April 1968. The overweighting of the riots of the long hot summer of 1967 has also produced another assumption that proves problematic when examined from the perspective of Baltimore, namely that the National Guard were trigger-happy. On the contrary, National Guard units and federal troops responded with a good deal of restraint in 1968. Paradoxically, this helped produce major debates regarding whether their hands had been tied and if a greater use of force could have prevented much of the destruction. Finally, while the student and youth protests of 1968, such as those at Columbia University and during the Democratic convention in Chicago, clearly were significant events, there can be little doubt that historians have paid too much attention to them. For instance, in his popular text on the 1960s, Terry Anderson devoted about a paragraph to King's deaths and the uprisings that followed but nine pages to the disturbances at Columbia and Chicago. Relatively speaking, the Holy Week Uprisings had a much more profound impact, leaving a lasting impact on millions of ordinary Americans which they could still vividly recall forty to fifty years later as if the revolts had just taken place. And one of the reasons that authorities reacted so aggressively to the aforementioned student and youth protests was because they feared they might reignite much larger revolts in adjoining black ghettos in New York and Chicago. Localized campus rebellions or youth "festivals" could be contained, they reasoned, but renewed urban revolts posed a much more significant challenge to the social order.[3]

---

[3] Ben Gilbert and the Staff of the *Washington Post*, *Ten Blocks from the White House: Anatomy of the Washington Riots of 1968* (New York: Praeger, 1968); Risen: *A Nation on Fire*; Medrika Law-Womack, "A City Afire: The Baltimore City Riot of 1968: Antecedents, Causes and Impact," MA thesis, Morgan State University, 2005; Anderson, *The Sixties*; Gitlin, The Sixties; Jerry L. Avorn, *Up Against the Ivy Wall: A History of the Columbia Crisis* (New York: Atheneum, 1969).

"If We Could Make It to Sunday Morning"

Just five days before Martin Luther King was assassinated President Johnson (LBJ) shocked the nation by declaring that he would not seek renomination. Citing his desire to overcome and heal the divisiveness in the land, Johnson also initiated a bombing halt in Vietnam. Though blindsided by his announcement (which was not part of the prepared remarks he released to the press), more than one of his associates observed that it had left the president reinvigorated. As his longtime aide Horace Busby observed: "His demeanor was that of a new man. His conversation began to quicken with talk of what could be achieved over the balance of the year. There was a fresh excitement and an old bite in his tone as he declared: 'We're going to get this show on the road again.'" Not only did LBJ feel renewed, his approval ratings, which had sunk to a low of 35 percent, jumped to 50 percent between April 1 and April 4.[4]

When combined with Eugene McCarthy's "upset" victory in the Democratic presidential primary in New Hampshire and Robert F. Kennedy's declaration of his presidential candidacy, Johnson's announcement created a renewed sense of optimism, even among segments of the black population. During the late winter and early spring of 1968, a broad coalition of new leftists, labor unionists, and religious groups, united behind the United Farm Workers of America's national grape boycott, highlighted by Cesar Chavez's three-week long hunger strike. Many of these groups rallied in support of Martin Luther King Jr.'s foray into Memphis, Tennessee, where he demonstrated his solidarity with striking sanitation workers and looked forward to the forthcoming Poor People's Campaign in Washington, DC. Protests in the streets of Prague, Czechoslovakia, often referred to as Prague spring, reinforced this sense of optimism.[5]

King's assassination burst this temporary bubble. Not long after President Johnson informed the nation of King's death, revolts erupted in cities across the nation, most notably in Washington, DC and Chicago, Illinois. At a special morning meeting at the White House, LBJ met with many of the nation's civil rights leaders, where he recited a telegram from

4 Lyndon Baines Johnson, "Address to the Nation, March 31, 1968," in *Public Papers of the Presidents*, www.presidency.ucsb.edu/ws/index.php?pid=28772&st=&st1= [accessed October 13, 2014]. Risen, *A Nation on Fire*, pp. 27, 89.
5 "North Vietnam and U.S. Agree to Contact; Johnson Consults Saigon; To Go to Hawaii," *NYT*, April 4, 1968, p. 1. William Chafe, *The Unfinished Journey: America Since World War II*, 5th edn. (New York: Oxford University Press, 2003), pp. 333–356.

Dr. Martin Luther King Sr., which stated: "Please know that I join in your plea to American citizens to desist from violence and permit the cause of nonviolence for which my son died not be in vain." After reading this, LBJ turned to the civil rights leaders and declared: "'If I were a kid in Harlem, I know what I'd be thinking right now. I'd be thinking that the whites have declared open season on my people, and they're going to pick us off one by one unless I get a gun and pick them off first.'"[6]

Without a doubt, the overwhelming feeling in Baltimore's black community following King's death was one of deep sorrow mixed with anger. Forty years later, Robert Birt, a black teenager who grew up in the Latrobe Housing Projects in East Baltimore, distinctly recollected telling his mother that "this is something I will never forget," adding that he even recalled the weather. "It was warm." Juanita Crider, a seven-year old girl who lived in East Baltimore in 1968, came home from school on the evening of the 4th and remembered seeing her grandmother crying and muttering "Dr. King is dead, what are we gonna do?" Like many other black families, Crider's had pictures of King, John F. Kennedy, and Jesus Christ on their mantel piece. Dorothy Hurst, a member of CORE, stated that it felt like "part of you died." Lilly Hyman, an eighteen-year-old high school student who lived in Edmonson Village, termed King's death absolutely devastating. "It was almost like the world was ending." Devon Wilford-Said, who had met King when she was in elementary school, expressed a similar sentiment, adding that news of his death set off "flash backs of seeing him . . . and of the people gathered around cheering."[7]

Like Wilford-Said, Harold Knight, a black high school student, had had the opportunity to meet King. In Knight's case the encounter proved life-changing, convincing him to follow in King's footsteps, first by enrolling at Morehouse College, King's alma mater, and then by dedicating his own life to the ministry and the fight against racial injustice. Yet in April 1968, this road was still well into the future, and he recalled that King's death "shattered" his world and left him pondering where both he individually and blacks collectively would "go from here." Homer Favor, a black civil rights activist, who, in his own words cried like a baby when his wife informed him that King had been murdered, felt like he had taken

[6] King Sr. and Johnson quoted in, Risen, *A Nation On Fire*, p. 89.
[7] Interviews with Juanita Crider, Dorothy Hurst, Devon Wilford-Said, and Lillie Hyman, http://archives.ubalt.edu/bsr/oral-histories/oral-histories1.html [accessed October 13, 2014 and October 21, 2014]. For a good overview of King's final year alive, see Tavis Smiley, *Death of a King: The Real Story of Dr. Martin Luther King Jr.'s Final Year* (Boston: Little, Brown, 2014); and Branch, *At Canaan's Edge*.

a body blow. Fatefully, Favor added, King was supposed to have spoken in Baltimore on March 28th to build support for his upcoming Poor People's Campaign but his visit was canceled due to his commitment to help striking sanitation workers in Memphis, Tennessee.[8]

Alongside these feelings of sorrow appeared ominous signs of trouble. Birt's mother did not want him to attend school on Friday, April 5, because she "felt that something wasn't right." Some of the employees of Ted Lewis, a white merchant, warned him to clear out because there were rumors spreading that his furniture store, on Gay Street, was going to be burned down. Herman Katkow, also white, who owned a dress shop on Pennsylvania Avenue, received a phone call from a man who declared "they're gonna come up and they're gonna ransack all of the stores . . . and we better get out right away before . . . we suffer physical harm to ourselves." And some black business people began to put "Soul Brother" signs or black cloth on their homes and places of business, presumably to protect them from looters.[9]

Sensing the community's anger yet wanting to avert violence and looting, such as had erupted already in Washington, DC, most of Baltimore's established civil rights groups emphasized the need to honor King's commitment to nonviolence. Juanita Jackson Mitchell asserted that King's assassination would "challenge our youth to continue the fight for freedom with love." Verda Welcome, one of the state's few black state representatives, described King's death as a "tragic loss" and reminded citizens of King's words "that we can achieve nothing by lawlessness." Madeline Murphy emphasized that King, "who preached nonviolence," was the victim of "senseless" white violence, and called for blacks to "knock on every door" to "mobilize for freedom."[10]

Yet representatives of more militant civil rights groups proclaimed that King's death proved the need for a different approach. "The shooting of King demonstrated how white America will not tolerate non-violence . . . and clearly points out that we have to reorganize our thinking," declared James Griffin of Baltimore CORE. SNCC field representative Robert Moore stressed that King's assassination showed that

---

[8] Interviews with Home Favor, and Harold L. Knight, http://archives.ubalt.edu/bsr/oral-histories/oral-histories1.html [accessed October 13, 2014 and October 21, 2014].

[9] Interviews with Ted and Jane Lewis, Herman and Ethel Katkow, and Yvonne Hardy-Phillips, http://archives.ubalt.edu/bsr/oral-histories/oral-histories3.html [accessed October 13, 2014].

[10] "Baltimore Shocked, Angered, Hurt, Grieved by Death of Dr. King," *Afro-American*, 6 April 1968, p. 1.

blacks had to defend themselves, adding that "White America has a plan of genocide for America." Based on the reports of the *Afro-American*, the views of these last groups appeared to hold sway on the streets. As one black steelworker informed an *Afro's* reporter, "I always admired King...he was a great man. But...nonviolence just ain't the way." To which one of his friends added, "It's just a sign to fight – to let go. This proves that nonviolence don't work. He preached nonviolence and look at him now."[11]

The response of black Baltimoreans to King's death tended to parallel the actions of blacks in Omaha, Nebraska, Cincinnati, Ohio, and Milwaukee, Wisconsin, three cities that historian Ashley Howard has insightfully written about in "Prairie Fires," a study of the urban rebellions in the Midwest. In these three cities, Howard argues, most blacks who participated in the revolts were working class. They saw taking to the streets as a legitimate form of political protest, justified by their subordinate economic, political, and sociocultural position and their inability to effect change. In contrast, most black elites opposed looting and firebombing and other acts of property destruction and acted largely as "counter-rioters" during the uprisings.[12]

Sensing that the potential for violence was high, Governor Agnew placed Maryland's National Guard and the Maryland State Police on alert and signed a recently enacted law that gave him sweeping powers in case of a state of emergency. The City of Baltimore opened a special Emergency Headquarters Command Post, where Police Commissioner Pomerleau and other top officials gathered to implement a pre-established civil defense plan, known as Operation Oscar. In time, this command post would coordinate a vast array of agencies and operations, ranging from the actions of the police, fire, and other first responders to the establishment of shelters and distribution of food. Somewhat serendipitously, the city's Office of Disaster Control and Civil Defense, which was founded in the early years of the Cold War to develop and coordinate a civil defense plan in case of nuclear attack, had orchestrated operation Hi-C, its first practice response to a riot-related civil disaster, just a week before King's assassination.[13]

[11] "Baltimore Shocked, Angered, Hurt, Grieved by Death of Dr. King."
[12] Howard, "Prairie Fires"; Seligman, "'But Burn – No,'" pp. 230–255.
[13] Police Department, City of Baltimore, Maryland, "1968 Riots: Action Reports, April 5, 1968–April 12, 1968," http://archives.ubalt.edu/bsr/archival-resources/documents/baltimore-police-reports.pdf [accessed October 10, 2014] (henceforth: "Action Reports"); Col. Edwin F. Gates, "Request for Ammunition from Civilian Agency," April 6, 1968, in Ramsey Clark Papers, Box 16, Folder: Baltimore, Chicago, Memphis

Believing that the riots of the previous summer had been precipitated by radicals, city authorities and the FBI began to carefully monitor and arrest local activists. On the afternoon of April 6th, police arrested James Ford, of CORE, on charges of assault. Ford's colleague, Walter Dixon, was accused of firebombing a lumberyard. Stuart Wechsler, also of CORE, who had been charged with inciting a riot in Cambridge the year before (the charge were dropped) was taken into custody. So too were Danny Grant and Yosef Karrem of CORE. Walter Lively, a leader of U-JOIN, an SDS affiliate, was kept under surveillance.[14] Simultaneously, the FBI closely monitored Stokely Carmichael's moves and some law enforcement officials reported that he had plans to come to Baltimore from Washington, DC, a story which the talk radio station WAYE passed along to its listeners even after it proved unfounded.[15]

At the same time, there were reasons to believe that Agnew would never need to use his new powers and that the Emergency Command Post would prove an unnecessary precaution. The previous fall Baltimore had elected Thomas D'Alesandro III as mayor. The son of a former congressman and mayor of Baltimore and the brother of future Speaker of the House Nancy Pelosi, D'Alesandro III had served on the city council during the 1960s where he had earned a reputation as a racial liberal. His election in 1967 was noteworthy because he won 93 percent of the black vote. During the campaign, Howell Baum writes, D'Alesandro defended "busing to relieve overcrowding and to remove children from deficient schools" – a position that garnered him the enmity of many working-class whites. D'Alesandro enjoyed strong relations with the interdenominational and interracial ministerial alliance and with the local NAACP. At his inauguration, D'Alesandro nicknamed Baltimore the "city of hope" and vowed "to root out every cause or vestige of discrimination." Afterwards, he appointed blacks to several key posts, including George Russell and Marion Bascomb as the city's first black city solicitor and fire commissioner, respectively.[16]

Riots; Robert H. Osborne, "Report on Baltimore Civil Disorder Relief and Support Activities," June 15, 1968 (City of Baltimore). For an electronic copy of this report, see http://archives.ubalt.edu/bsr/archival-resources/documents/June-15-1968.pdf [accessed October 17, 2014].

[14] "Action Reports."

[15] Jane Motz, "Report on the Baltimore Civil Disorders, April 1968" (Baltimore: Middle Atlantic Region of the American Friends Service Committee, 1968); "Summary Reports," 6 April, 1968, Ramsey Clark Papers, Box 75, Folder, "Summaries – Riots – April 8, 1968."

[16] Howell Baum, "How the 1968 Riots Stopped School Desegregation in Baltimore," p. 159; Michael Olesker, *Journeys to the Heart of Baltimore* (Baltimore,

Immediately following King's assassination, D'Alesandro, took great solace in the fact that Baltimore, unlike Washington, DC, had remained peaceful. On Friday, April 5, he traveled to Annapolis to meet with General George Gelston, head of the National Guard, and Governor Agnew. While the three prepared for unrest, D'Alesandro remained confident that Baltimore would avert an emergency. "My hope, at that time," he recalled years later, "was that if we could make it to Sunday morning," when many of Baltimore's black residents went to church, "then we would have made it." And the situation in Baltimore remained calm on Thursday, Friday, and most of Saturday. In an effort to help, D'Alesandro called for a special day of prayer on Sunday and designated Monday as a "city-wide day of mourning for Dr. King."[17] A number of Baltimore's most prominent black leaders displayed their solidarity with the new mayor. George Russell, for instance, emphasized that King's death was a time to renew his commitment to using nonviolence to "correct injustices in our society."[18]

In its recently released report, the Kerner Commission had observed that poor relations with the police stood as the most common spark of the revolts of the long hot summer of 1967. Historians of the urban rebellions of the 1960s have echoed these findings. Yet, as late as March 1968, in an article entitled "How Baltimore Averts Riots," *Reader's Digest* contended that the city had far fewer worries on this front than did most others. "Last summer, many of America's large cities exploded with race riots – but not Baltimore ... How is it that nothing happened" the article's author asked? "No man knows all the answers to that question but a large share of the credit must go to the Baltimore Police Department ... and to a novel concept of a police department as a social-service agency." To foster better race relations, the department's new commissioner, Donald Pomerleau, mandated that every police officer take a course in black history. He expanded the size of the Community Relations Department and "told them to penetrate the Negro community, not with a gun and nightstick but with service." He established "storefront service centers" and promoted two blacks, Flan Couch and Major William Harris, both

---

MD: Johns Hopkins University Press, 2001), pp. 264–265; Interview with Marion Bascomb, http://archives.ubalt.edu/bsr/oral-histories/transcripts/bascom.pdf [accessed October 21, 2014].

[17] Interview with Thomas D'Alesandro, by Fraser Smith, Baltimore, Maryland, May 2007, http://archives.ubalt.edu/bsr/oral-histories/transcripts/dalesandro.pdf [accessed October 14, 2014]; Olesker, *Journeys to the Heart of Baltimore*, pp. 264–266.

[18] "Baltimore Shocked, Angered, Hurt, Grieved by Death of Dr. King," *Afro-American*, 6 April, 1968, p. 1.

Morgan State graduates, to head these initiatives. Building on efforts launched by General George Gelston, who had served as Baltimore's temporary police commissioner, Harris reached out to black activists, such as members of CORE who had named Baltimore their "Target City" in 1966. An article in the *Wall Street Journal* similarly singled out Baltimore's police force for praise, noting that the aforementioned community relations unit composed of nine black and nine white officers, half of whom had degrees in sociology, checked in with local civil rights groups on a daily basis, and provided services to youngsters throughout the city, from visiting schools to "discuss youngsters' grievances" to helping teenagers find rides home. This said, King's death, which many blacks believed was abetted by law enforcement authorities, such as J. Edgar Hoover's FBI, reinforced black Baltimore's distrust of the larger criminal justice system. Moreover, in the wake of the revolt, the city's police force, like others around the country, became increasingly militarized and subordinated such community relations efforts.[19]

Many residents went about their normal business on April 5th and 6th, following King's death. Schools and businesses remained opened; public transit continued to run; department stores remained busy as residents readied themselves for Easter Sunday, and baseball and music fans looked forward to the opening of the Baltimore Oriole's baseball season, and/or the forthcoming appearances of James Brown and an array of other black performers. Tom Carney, white, who lived in the Catholic neighborhood of Pigtown, adjacent to Camden Yards, the current home of the Baltimore Orioles, recalled that he attended his Friday classes at the recently opened University of Baltimore County. Though he noticed that a number of his fellow black classmates were upset, he did not think much of it at the time. Bill and Carle Evitts, two white graduate students at Johns Hopkins University, though saddened by King's death, shopped for supplies for their regular Friday evening

---

[19] Floyd Miller, "How Baltimore Fends Off Riots," *Readers Digest*, March 1968, pp. 109–113; "Uneasy Cities: Race Violence Erupts Amidst Efforts to Avert Trouble This Summer," *Wall Street Journal*, June 15, 1967, p. 1; "Come in and Talk it Over," *Baltimore Sun*, February 11, 1968, p. M4. "Police to Seek Fund Approval for Riot Gear," *Baltimore Sun*, May 15, 1968, p. C28; "Confused Coordination and Officials Looking Aside Responsible for Unprepared Local Riot Control," *The Daily Record*, June 14, 1968, p. 1; "Armored Truck Loan Plan Set By Police," *Evening Sun* (Baltimore), August 14, 1968, p. C2; "City Equipped with Riot Helmets," *Baltimore News American*, August 30, 1968, p. C1; Agenda, Community Meeting, April 16, 1967, and Pamphlet, "Western Police Community Relations Council," April 12, 1967, both in Mayor McKeldin Papers, Box 363.

bridge game, assuming it would take place without interruption. And Lynnwood Taylor, a sixteen-year-old black junior at Forest Park High, went ahead with his plans to attend his prom on Saturday night, April 6, at the civic center, in spite of the fact that he felt devastated by King's assassination.[20]

Just as significantly, spontaneous and organized efforts on the part of civil rights activists did not result in any conflicts. On Friday, April 5, students at the historically black Coppin State College "refused to follow the regular academic routine." In response, administrators canceled classes. Protests at Northwestern High School, a racially mixed school, resulted in a twenty-five minute silent prayer at the school's auditorium. A half-dozen longshoremen stopped work at noontime to pay tribute to King, as did workers at the Social Security administration's headquarters in nearby Woodlawn. Religious leaders, from Cardinal Sheehan to Rabbi Israel Goldman, expressed their "profound sorrow" and announced special memorial services. Parren Mitchell and David Glenn, heads of the Community Action Agency and Community Relations Commission, respectively, reported that their staff members had been on the streets all day and found that "every rumor" of trouble had proven false. The following day, an assortment of activists organized a noontime memorial service for King at Lafayette Square in West Baltimore. Approximately 250 attended and, according to police reports, it concluded around 1:30 p.m. "with no incidents," convincing Commissioner Pomerleau he could leave the Emergency Command Post.[21]

Yet, the lack of incidents ultimately proved to be the proverbial calm before the storm. Ironically, based on the city's initial response, or lack thereof, to King's death, a good many of Baltimore residents may have awakened on Palm Sunday, April 7, thinking that, D'Alesandro's wish had been granted – that the city had made it to Sunday without trouble. The first two morning editions of the *Baltimore News American* made no mention of any unrest, presumably because they went to press the evening before. Instead, the *News American*'s headlines emphasized that

[20] Interviews with, Ted and Jane Lewis, Thomas Carney, and Bill and Carole Evitts, Lynwood Taylor, http://archives.ubalt.edu/bsr/oral-histories/oral-histories2.html [accessed October 13, 2014].
[21] "After Action Report: Task Force Baltimore, April 7–13, 1968, Warren Christopher Papers, Lyndon B. Johnson Library, Austin, Texas, Box 12, Civil Disturbances 1968 #2"; "City to Mark Monday as Day of Mourning For Dr. King, Schools, Offices, Will Close," *Baltimore Sun*, April 5, 1968, p. 38; "Baltimore Sad but Peaceful As Negro and White Mourn," *Baltimore Sun*, April 5 1968, p. 38.

America's "Military Spending May Top World War II Record Year," a proclamation that some of Baltimore's defense-related workers probably viewed favorably.[22] Radio and television reporting on the outbreak of the uprising appears to have been delayed as well. John Darlington, a member of the National Guard, got a call to report to the Fifth Armory regiment early on the evening of April 6th. While driving downtown, he learned nothing about the outbreak of violence in East Baltimore (see below), because, according to him, the mayor had prodded the stations to keep these reports "out of the public venue."[23] Believing that all remained normal, the Pats sisters went off to synagogue on Sunday morning and Reverend John Yost prepared for his Palm Sunday sermon.[24] Even after the revolt was self-evident, television stations continued to temper their coverage with everyday feature stories, such as one narrated by Susan White on whether it was advisable to dye baby chicks for Easter. White protested against having to do this story but was told it was necessary to "show the viewers that life goes on."[25]

Yet, in reality, Baltimore's Holy Week Uprising was already well underway and it is doubtful that church leaders could have kept it from spreading even if the city had made it to Sunday without any incidences. As Rev. Marion Bascom later explained, "it would take a lot more to alleviate racial tensions building on Baltimore streets. Simply delivering a calming Sunday morning sermon would not quell the growing rage of the city's black citizens." Moreover, Bascom added, there were always more people in the streets on Sunday morning than attended church.[26]

"They Killed Martin Luther King... They Had to Shut the City Down!"

Beginning around 5:15 p.m. on Saturday, April 6, people began to gather on the 400 and 500 blocks of North Gay Street in the heart of East

---

[22] *Baltimore Sun*, April 6, 1968, p. 1; *Baltimore News American*, April 7, 1968, p. 1.

[23] Interview with John Darlington, http://archives.ubalt.edu/bsr/oral-histories/transcripts/darlington.pdf [accessed October 16, 2014].

[24] Interview with John Yost, http://archives.ubalt.edu/bsr/oral-histories/transcripts/yost.pdf [accessed October 16, 2014] and Interview with Pats Family, http://archives.ubalt.edu/bsr/oral-histories/transcripts/pats.pdf [accessed October 16, 2014].

[25] Interview with Jack Bowden and Susan White-Bowden, http://archives.ubalt.edu/bsr/oral-histories/transcripts/bowden.pdf [accessed October 21, 2014].

[26] Bascom quoted in: WYPR, "'68: The Fire Last Time, Part II." For a transcript of this radio show, see http://archives.ubalt.edu/bsr/archival-resources/documents/wypr-part-2.pdf [accessed July 15, 2016].

FIGURE 5.1 Fire and looting erupt on Gay Street in East Baltimore on the evening of April 6, 1968. By permission of AP Photo.

Baltimore. As orders were issued for all off-duty police to report to their respective districts, the crowds grew in size, some store windows were broken and a fire bomb was thrown into a vacant house. Officer Melvin Howell recalled driving from the Central District headquarters to the Gay Street area and being informed by a foot patrolman who was already on the scene that several black males had started to shout and "used rocks to break out the windows" of a nearby drugstore, and "then all of sudden a crowd [estimated to be about 150 strong] started gathering." When police arrived and blocked off the immediate area, the crowd surged up Gay Street and looting and burning commenced, including fires set at two furniture stores (see Figure 5.1).[27] Robert Birt captured the irony of the moment. "Mayor D'Alesandro...got on the radio...and made a nice liberal speech...He said he thought it was commendable how Black

27 "After Action Report: Task Force Baltimore, April 7–13, 1968"; City of Baltimore, "Report of Baltimore Committee on the Administration of Justice Under Emergency Conditions," May 31, 1968; Melvin Howard, "Civil Disorders in Baltimore City," http://baltimorecitypolicehistory.com/citypolice/baltimore-city-police-history/riot-1861–1968.html [accessed October 17, 2014].

citizens of Baltimore in this trying time didn't resort to an explosion of mass anger." But then, Birt recalled, just as he finished saying this "I started to notice some things were happening. It's almost as if the riot was beginning just as he was commending us for not doing it."[28]

By some reports, the crowd quickly grew to over 1,000 men and women. Like a slow moving wave, it rode its way up Gay Street and spilled over to Hartford Road and Greenmount Avenue. Herbert Hardrick, a black soldier who was home on leave after completing basic training, was shooting pool at Peterson's Pool room, at the virtual nexus of Gay and Hartford, when "a guy walked into the pool room and said, 'Y'all sitting around drinking and celebrating. They've killed our soul brother and leader, get the sticks and let's go.'" Yvonne Phillips recalled seeing smoke and her cousin, Shorty, running into her mom's store declaring, "I hear they're coming, I hear they're coming" and witnessing a "horde of people coming through."[29] Gerard Gassinger, who owned a furniture store at Gay Street and Paterson Park Avenue, about two miles from where the first crows had gathered, was at home when Daisy May, one of his sales ladies, called to report that his store was being looted. "About 350 looters [were] in the store," she exclaimed, and implored him "not to come to the store" because "they will kill you."[30] "As the disorders continued to increase," recalled John Peterson, "so did the level of violence, becoming much more destructive as rock throwing turned into looting, looting into firebombing and anti-establishment anger was vented in angry confrontations with police and attacks on firefighters."[31]

One person who participated in this early wave of the revolt was Robert Brady, a twenty-one-year-old black steelworker. As the Sun began to set on Saturday, April 6, 1968, Bradby was relaxing at a bar in East Baltimore. From inside the bar he could see a raucous crowd, which, when he left the bar, he did his best to avert. To his surprise, however, gunshots rang out, nearly hitting him. Presumably, the shots were fired either by the owner of Gabriel's Spaghetti House, John Novak, or by Clarence Baker, a forty-seven-year-old white bartender, both of whom

[28] Interview with Robert Birt, by Nyasha Chikowore and Maria Paoletti, July 7, 2007, Baltimore, Maryland, in *Baltimore '68: Riots and Rebirth in an American City*, pp. 248–249.

[29] Interviews with Herbert Hardrick and Yvonne-Hardy-Phillips, http://archives.ubalt.edu/bsr/oral-histories/oral-histories3.html [accessed October 13, 2014].

[30] Gerard P. Gassinger, "Riot Diary," http://archives.ubalt.edu/bsr/archival-resources/reports.html [accessed October 13, 2014].

[31] John Peterson, *Into The Cauldron* (Clinton, MD: Clavier House, 1973), pp. 36–37.

feared that the crowd was about to ransack their business.[32] These gunshots, Bradby later admitted, angered him and he responded by concoct-
ing an improvised Molotov cocktail and throwing it into the restaurant.
On one level, his reaction was spontaneous and apolitical. Yet on another
level, there can be little doubt that Bradby's anger over King's death and
the long-standing discrimination he had faced as a black person in Baltimore motivated him to attack one of the white-owned businesses in the
neighborhood. Bradby's Molotov cocktail resulted only in a small fire,
which, by all accounts, was about to go out when another man threw
a bigger firebomb into the building. As a result, the fire spread. By the
time firemen arrived much of the building had been destroyed. Unbeknownst to Bradby, Louis Albrecht, a fifty-eight-year-old white resident
of Baltimore, who, ironically, had sought refuge in the restaurant, died in
the blaze.[33] Around the corner another dead body, William Harrison, an
eighteen-year-old black man was later located, shot dead, presumably by
Clarence Baker, the white bartender at Gabriel's Spaghetti House, who
mistakenly believed that Harrison had been one of the men who had firebombed the restaurant. Upon learning of the death of her son four days
later, Harrison's mother exclaimed, "I don't understand how something
like this could happen." Harrison worked only a block away from the
Spaghetti House and he may have gotten caught up in the wave of looting that swept down Gay Street or he may simply have been on his way
home from work – he lived less than a mile away. Along with Albrecht,
he was one of six fatalities during the uprising.[34]

In response to the surging crowds on Gay Street, Police Commissioner
Pomerleau ordered K-9 units to deploy downtown and Governor Spiro
Agnew declared a state of emergency, which established an 11 p.m. to
6 a.m. curfew and banned the sale and distribution of alcoholic bever-
ages. The Maryland State police mobilized upwards of 300 men to assist
in the protection of the state office buildings; State Attorney General
Burch prepared to assist in the maintenance of order; and Gene Noble,

[32] "Stenographic Transcript in the Case of *State of Maryland v. Robert Bradby*," Criminal
Court of Baltimore, Part V, June 5, 1969, T495–1103, Case #3330, MSA, Annapolis,
MD. See also: *State v. Robert Badby*, Post-Conviction Files, 1972, Baltimore Criminal
Court, 92105–92106, MSA.
[33] "Stenographic Transcript in the Case of *State of Maryland v. Robert Bradby*"; "Police
Charge 2 in Arson Death," *Baltimore Sun*, April 26, 1968, p. C28.
[34] "First Looter Shot to Death," *Baltimore News American*, April 8, 1968, p. 1; "Federal
Troops Leaving the City, Order Restored, York Says," *Evening Sun* (Baltimore, MD),
April 12, 1968, p. 1; "Son's 'Riot' Death Baffling to Mother," *Afro-American*, April 27,
1968, p. 28.

of the Community Relations Commission, organized black clergyman to "attempt to quiet crowds on Gay Street." By ten o'clock, with reports of fires, looting, and fighting coming into the Command Post with regularity, Mayor D'Alesandro advised Agnew that things were "getting worse" and requested that the governor send in the Maryland National Guard.[35] By 11 p.m., about five hours after the first disturbances, approximately 2,000 guardsmen began to take positions on the perimeter of the troubled areas.[36]

At first it seemed that the arrival of the National Guard might quell the unrest. Or as guardsmen John Peterson put it: "the appearance of a disciplined body of troops had its quieting effect on the neighborhood and the troops met only occasional resistance." By the end of the night, officials reported that the city was "relatively calm." At 2 p.m. on the 7th, Fire Chief Thomas declared that all fires in the city were "under control." Accordingly, Police Commissioner Pomerleau recommended waiting to see the "results of the 4.00 p.m. curfew" before pushing the governor to request federal troops. Yet, as the evening of the 7th approached, looting and arson re-escalated. Just as importantly, the uprising spread beyond the Gay and Hartford Street corridors to the black community in West Baltimore. Ruth Stewart, a young black mother of two, recalled returning to her West Baltimore residence from work at Johns Hopkins University Hospital, in East Baltimore, when she observed the outbreak of looting. "Just like everybody…all of a sudden came together." Residents pulled their cars up to stores and took everything. "You could see people coming out on the streets with TV's and stuff." The situation was "scary," Stewart emphasized, because "you didn't know whether you would live or die" (see Figure 5.2).[37]

Eventually, fourteen distinct neighborhoods and at least a half-dozen commercial districts experienced at least twenty incidences of looting, vandalism, or arson. Every major black section of the city, with the exception of Cherry Hill in southwest Baltimore, was affected. Over the next four days, there were over 1,700 fires and upwards of 8,000 calls for service.[38] Just as importantly, the crowds grew savvier in their

---

[35] "After Action Report: Task Force Baltimore, April 7–13, 1968,"
[36] "Action Reports."
[37] Interview with Ruth Stewart, http://archives.ubalt.edu/bsr/oral-histories/oral-histories4 .html [accessed October 13, 2014]; Peterson, *Into the Cauldron*, pp. 46–47; "Action Reports."
[38] "Action Reports"; Baltimore Fire Department to LNO G2, n.d. Maryland National Guard Papers (unprocessed collection), 5th Armory Regiment, Baltimore, Maryland.

FIGURE 5.2 "Woman Pleads for People to Stay Out," Eager Street at Broadway, in East Baltimore, April 8, 1968, *Baltimore News American* collection, Special Collections, University of Maryland Libraries. By permission of the Hearst Corporation.

interactions with authorities. "I had expected to see great masses of people in the streets" and to employ "standard riot control formations to clear them out," recalled Captain Jean Gilman. Instead, Gilman observed, troops encountered the equivalent of "guerilla warfare with small groups starting fires and running; throwing bottles and running, cutting or disconnecting firehouses and running, in the front and out the back of a store, grabbing what they could, and running. It's damned near impossible for troops in battle dress to handle that sort of thing."[39]

Faced with this escalating situation, Governor Agnew formally requested federal troops and President Johnson signed orders to deploy them and to federalize the National Guard. Even before the order became official, Lieutenant General Robert York and Fred Vinson, of the Justice Department, had reconnoitered Baltimore and readied units from the

[39] Peterson, *Into the Cauldron*, p. 57.

FIGURE 5.3 National Guard cordon off business-residential section of Baltimore, April 8, 1968. By permission of AP Photo.

82nd Airborne to occupy the city. As federal troops arrived, announcements were made that schools would be closed on Monday, April 8. With the prospect of food shortages due to looting, food distribution centers were opened at nearly twenty places in the city. All department stores were closed, as were 95 percent of all smaller shops in the city. Five utility substations were placed under guard. Johns Hopkins Hospital staffers were asked to stay on duty all night, in part due to the extremity of the emergency and in part because it lay adjacent to some of the most widespread unrest which made it risky for personnel to travel home. A request went out for an additional 2,000 troops stationed at Andrews Air Force base. All told, 10,956 troops deployed in Baltimore (see Figure 5.3).[40]

"Situation Reports" which flowed into the White House provided a keen sense of the speed with which circumstances changed in Baltimore.

[40] LTG Robert H. York, "After Action Report: Task Force Baltimore, April 7–13, 1968," Warren Christopher Papers, Civil Disturbances 1968 #2; "Executive Order: Providing for the Restoration of Law and Order in the State of Maryland," April 7, 1968, White House Central File, HU2-ST20-ST21, Box 26, Lyndon Johnson Library.

Whereas one report issued on the afternoon of the 6th relayed that a peace rally had taken place in Baltimore "without incident," a separate report, issued about six hours later, stated that twenty fires had erupted, that "firemen [were being] pelted with bricks and stones," and that stores were being "ransacked."[41] By 4 a.m. on the 7th, situation reports noted that Baltimore had recorded five deaths, 300 fires, and 404 arrests. Subsequent reports, issued as the sun began to set on April 8th, observed that over 2,200 individuals had already been arrested and 500 individuals had been injured. By the evening of the 8th, government officials estimated that one-quarter of the city had been impacted by the revolt, recorded looting at a "warehouse known to contain guns and ammunition," and warned that whites had gathered at Patterson Park "geared to march to the ghetto to have it out."[42]

The Maryland National Guard's "Staff Log" presented compelling evidence of the escalation of Baltimore's uprising as well. Ironically, nearly two days after King was shot, General Gelston and other law enforcement officials remained just as concerned about the outbreak of violence in other parts of the state as they were about Baltimore. Between midnight and mid-afternoon on the 6th, local police sealed off the Second Ward of Cambridge, the site of the "Brown riot" the summer before, and Army commanders approved an Air Transport for a trip of officers to the Eastern Shore. Maryland National Guard commanders contemplated sending forces to Prince George and Montgomery Counties on the outskirts of Washington, DC, lest the uprising in the nation's capital spread to its nearby suburbs. But then at 7 p.m. on the 6th all Maryland Army and Air Force National Guards were ordered to mobilize for "probable deployment" in Baltimore. Within thirty minutes of this order, command headquarters was receiving calls from officers, who were in route to duty at the Armory, of "unruly mobs" and Molotov cocktails being "thrown thru store windows" on Gay Street. Not long after this, reports arrived of over thirty individuals being treated for gunshot wounds at Johns Hopkins University and of sniper fire pinning down fire fighters who sought to put out a blaze. (Many of these reports ultimately proved untrue.)[43]

[41] "Situation Reports," Ramsey Clark Papers, Box 67, Summaries – Riots – April 8, 1968; City of Baltimore, "Report of Baltimore Committee on the Administration of Justice Under Emergency Conditions," May 31, 1968; "Daily Staff Journal/Duty Officer's Log," April 5, 1968–April 10, 1968, National Guard Files.
[42] "Situation Reports," Ramsey Clark Papers, Box 67, Summaries – Riots – April 8, 1968.
[43] "Daily Staff Journal or Duty Officer's Log," April 5–April 10, 1968."

One National Guardsmen who experienced the rapid shift in Baltimore's plight was Joe DiBlasi, a white student at the University of Baltimore. At about the same time that Robert Bradby was having a drink in East Baltimore (see above), DiBlasi was returning to his home near South Baltimore from a routine National Guard drill session in Parkville, Maryland, one of the nearby suburbs. Though he witnessed a few kids throwing rocks at cars, he did not expect such juvenile pranks to escalate into anything substantial. No sooner had he returned home, however, than he received a call from the National Guard ordering him to report to the federal Armory as quickly as possible. Subsequently, DiBlasi was placed in charge of a squad of twelve men and given orders to take up a position at the corner of North and Pennsylvania Avenues, near the historic center of the Baltimore's African American community where jazz legends such as Cab Calloway used to play. From his post, DiBlasi witnessed looting, burning buildings, and defiant crowds. Looking back, DiBlasi emphasized the surreal nature of the event. "You would just look around and say, 'how can this be happening?'" a statement that reflected the degree to which white citizens had managed to deny or repress their knowledge and responsibility about the vast racial divisions that existed in Baltimore.[44]

The speed with which the unrest spread caught many Baltimore residents off guard. Barbara Gaines, a black high school student in 1968, was returning to her home in Edmondson Village on the far west side of city on the evening of April 7th when she first experienced the revolt firsthand. Upon exiting her bus she witnessed tens of people running across the street "back and forth like they lost their minds ... yelling, 'They killed Martin Luther King; They killed Martin Luther King!'" The black community was so enraged, she explained, that it felt that "they had to shut the city down!" "Gates were being pulled off of the department store doors ... Cigarettes were flying," liquor lay everywhere, inside and outside the liquor stores. Blacks tore up "every establishment that was owned by a white person or a Jewish person," she continued. Not just teenagers looted, Gaines recalled. "There were adults rioting. You know, parents, mothers, fathers." "It was a free for all," with everything being taken until there "was nothing left in them [the stores]."[45]

[44] Interview with Joseph John DiBlasi, http://archives.ubalt.edu/bsr/oral-histories/transcripts/diblasi.pdf [accessed May 13, 2016].
[45] Interview with Barbara D. Gaines, n.d., http://archives.ubalt.edu/bsr/oral-histories/transcripts/gaines.pdf [accessed October 10, 2014].

Jazz singer Ruby Glover was out with friends and several coworkers "having a wonderful time" at a Pennsylvania Avenue club on the
evening of the 7th when soldiers burst through the establishment's doors
to enforce the curfew which the governor had imposed on the city. On
stage and in the middle of her performance, Glover was unaware that
she was violating the curfew. "All hell has broken loose," she recalled, as
the troops hustled everyone out of the club. "It looked like everything
was on fire," she stated. "It appeared that everything that we loved and
adored and enjoyed was just being destroyed." Sunday, April 7th was
Palm Sunday, and Lutheran minister, John Yost, was in the midst of his
eleven o'clock morning sermon when he heard frightening noises nearby.
Yet, Yost and his parishioners were spared because National Guardsmen
and State Troopers had cordoned off the downtown/midtown section of
the city where his church was located, and at virtually no time during
the uprising did the participants in the revolt challenge these unofficial
boundaries.[46]

For Louis Randall, one of the first African Americans to graduate from
the University of Maryland Medical School, three years after the *Brown*
decision, the outbreak of the revolt was just as dramatic. As he vividly
recalled over forty years later he was delivering a baby at Provident hospital, in West Baltimore, when he heard the sounds of windows being broken. From the hospital he could smell the acrid smoke from stores being
burned. As soon as he could, Randall rushed home and then dashed off
to his office building, which he had recently opened with several other
black doctors. Like many other African American business owners, Randall placed a "Soul brother" sign on his door to make clear to would-be
looters that his was a black-owned business. Still, not trusting the sign
alone, Randall vigilantly stood guard, gun in hand, hoping he would not
have to shoot anyone in order to preserve what he had worked so hard
to achieve.[47]

One of the most perilous moments of the uprising occurred on the
afternoon of the 9th due to miscommunications between federal, state,
and local authorities. At midday about 200 men and women began
to assemble at Lafayette Square, in West Baltimore, for a peace rally.
Unknown to federal officers, Maryland National Guard commander

[46] Michael Yokel, "100 Years: The Riots of 1968," *Baltimore Magazine*, www
.baltimoremagazine.net/2007/5/100-years-the-riots-of-1968 [accessed, October 11,
2014].
[47] Interview with Louis D. Randall, November 30, 2006, http://archives.ubalt.edu/bsr/
oral-histories/oral-histories3.html.

General George Gelston had given his approval for the gathering. After General York instructed commanders that they lacked a permit to assemble, federal forces began to disperse the crowd. Local commanders requested the right to unsheathe their bayonets should the crowd resist. As the crowd proceeded to march down Pennsylvania Avenue, the chance for a confrontation peaked. Fortunately, for all involved, Major William "Box" Harris, the top black police officer in the city, appeared. After fielding a barrage of jeers, Harris announced, to cheers, that the rally would be allowed to take place after all.

Detached observers, perhaps influenced by classical studies of crowd behavior, such as Gustave Le Bon's, often described riots as having a carnival-like atmosphere. Morris Janowitz, whose report on the long hot summer of 1967 was published on the eve of King's assassination, highlighted "repeated reports of the carnival and happy day's spirit that pervades the early stages of the commodity riots."[48] Daniel Berger, a reporter for the Baltimore *Evening Sun*, recalled seeing a group of children, "jumping up and down with glee" in a riot-torn neighborhood in East Baltimore. Even when a police car cruised by, he reported, the children continued to jump up and down.[49] Tom Ward, a white attorney who joined a team of television reporters to survey the scene in West Baltimore on April 8th, described the atmosphere as "an eerie combination of resignation and Roman holiday."[50] Somewhat along the same lines, conservatives claimed that many of those who participated in the revolt were motivated by opportunism, not social injustice, and some firsthand reporting lent weight to this claim.[51]

Yet other observers saw the uprising as a clear protest against the persistence of racial inequality. Father Richard Lawrence, an activist priest whose Catholic church served many blacks, recalled encountering one of his parishioners on the streets after the revolt had begun. "Father you don't understand, I know you've been with the demonstrations and all

---

[48] Gustave Le Bon, *The Crowd: A Study of the Popular Mind* (1891), available at: www.gutenberg.org/cache/epub/445/pg445.html; Janowitz, *Social Control of Escalated Riots*, p. 13; Stephen Reicher and Jonathan Potter, "Psychological Theory as Intergroup Perspective: A Comparative Analysis of 'Scientific' and 'Lay' Accounts of Crowd Events," *Human Relations*, 38 (February 1985), pp. 167–189.

[49] Daniel Berger, "The Elements of Riot," *Baltimore Sun*, April 9, 1988, Vertical File, Baltimore Riots, Enoch Pratt Free Library, Baltimore, Maryland.

[50] "Recalling the Baltimore 1968 riots," *Baltimore Sun*, April 3, 1988, p. 27.

[51] Interview with Jewell Chambers, Interview with Devon Wilford-Said; Interview with Larry Wilson, http://archives.ubalt.edu/bsr/oral-histories/transcripts/wilson.pdf [accessed October 16, 2014]; Interview with Ruth Stewart.

that sort of thing," the parishioner explained to Lawrence. "But you were born white and you really can't totally understand. I mean I've done this civil rights thing too, you know it, I've been there; I've been in the marches, I've been in the rallies, you name it. Nobody's listening," his parishioner continued. "Murdering Dr. King was just the last straw that nobody's listening. We can go on demonstrating as long as we want, nobody will listen. I don't know what to try next, but maybe blood flowing in the streets is what it takes. Maybe some of his blood, with some of my blood flows in the streets, then maybe the man will listen. Maybe not, but I've got nothing else left to try ... I don't care if I get killed, I've got two kids and I'm not going to have them come up in the world I came up in. I'm just not going to have it."[52] Moreover, as Ashley Howard has argued, many working-class blacks, especially young men who felt emasculated by a society that did not allow them to serve their prescribed role, that of economic provider, protectors of their female kin, and as citizens, saw the looting and burning of stores as a legitimate form of political protest. They did not loot for the fun of it but rather as an expression of their legitimate grievances against a racist world.[53]

In Baltimore as in other cities, local residents targeted businesses with which they had grievances. Jewell Chambers, then a young reporter with the *Afro-American*, recalled some who rushed into stores exclaiming that they were going to get rid of their "book," meaning that they owed the merchant of the looted store a debt for previously unpaid goods and they intended to steal the equivalent amount while they had the opportunity to do so. Devon Wilford-Said recollected that when the revolt began her mother implored her to stay inside. But when Wilford-Said "went shopping" at Crowns, a store with a reputation for treating black people poorly, her mother proved "alright" with her disobedience because "she wanted us to get even too." And most, though not all, black-owned businesses were spared.[54] It should be added, that this desire to "get even" grew out of the historical experiences of African Americans, who first in slavery and then as sharecroppers in the South had been cheated out of the fruits of the labor by their owners and white merchants.

---

[52] Interview with Richard Lawrence, http://archives.ubalt.edu/bsr/oral-histories/transcripts/Lawrence.pdf [accessed October 20, 2014].

[53] Ashley Howard, "Prairie Fires," especially pp. 191–192, 223–228.

[54] Interview with Jewell Chambers, http://archives.ubalt.edu/bsr/oral-histories/transcripts/ChambersTranscript.pdf [accessed October 16, 2014]; Interview with Devon Wilford-Said; Interview with Larry Wilson, http://archives.ubalt.edu/bsr/oral-histories/transcripts/wilson.pdf [accessed October 16, 2014]; Interview with Ruth Stewart.

Furthermore, blacks targeted white-owned businesses because they saw white merchants as outsiders whose interests did not align with those of the black community.[55]

At the same time, the Holy Week Uprising engendered a great deal of fear, fear of getting shot, of being bayonetted by the Guard, of losing one's home, of not being able to find food or prescription medicine.[56] Frieda Halderon, a black mother of five who lived in East Baltimore, worried about the "safety" of her own family, "because when you hear gunshots, shootings, all you're telling yourselves is, 'Duck down, don't go near the window, don't go near the doors.'" Halderon also recalled worrying that her husband, who worked at Bethlehem Steel, would get arrested on his way back from work which went on curfew notwithstanding. Jewell Chambers remembered one man standing at the corner of North Avenue and Baker Street directing traffic into an already looted bar while simultaneously imploring looters not to "be lighting no matches cause I live upstairs."[57] Ruth Stewart, a mother of two young children, acknowledged that she stole diapers, carnation milk, vitamins, and other things, not because she wanted to get back at any particular merchant but since she felt she had to have "what was going to help me and my family...survive." Rosalind Terrell, a young black mother with one son, recalled the fear and humiliation of having to navigate the lines of policemen and army troops who demanded that she show her pass on her way to and from work. "It reminded me of slavery," Terrell emphasized. "Although I knew that it was a security issue, but to me it was really a humiliating kind of thing to have to show a pass to come in and out of my own neighborhood."[58] Jo Ann Robinson, a history graduate student, echoed Terrell's sentiment. "We were at 2649 Maryland Ave and right up the street the National Guard set up an encampment," Robinson recalled. "You just looked out your window and realized you were living under martial law."[59]

Indeed, fear was one of the central memories of the revolt on the part of virtually all involved. For firefighters the uprising proved a particularly

---

[55] For a contemporary study of Black views of white merchants, see Berk, "The Role of the Ghetto Retail Merchants in Civil Disorders."

[56] Interview with Jewell Chambers.   [57] Interview with Jewell Chambers.

[58] Interview with Ruth Stewart; Interview with Frieda Halderon, http://archives.ubalt .edu/bsr/oral-histories/transcripts/halderon.pdf [accessed October 16, 2014]; Interview with Rosalind Terrell, http://archives.ubalt.edu/bsr/oral-histories/transcripts/terrell.pdf [accessed October 16, 2014].

[59] WYPR, "The Fire Last Time: Part 2," http://archives.ubalt.edu/bsr/archival-resources/ documents/wypr-part-2.pdf [accessed July 16, 2016].

frightening experience. As one firefighter recalled, "Every piece of equipment in the city and I believe some in the county were in use. There we
so many fires that there wasn't [*sic*] enough companies to fight the fire as
a unit." Units had to fight large blazes understaffed; firemen worked with
little sleep and food, and at times feared that they would be attacked by
"mobs of hundreds of people" who gathered around. Unlike the RFC in
Cambridge, which refused to extinguish a small fire which grew into a
very large one (see Part I), Baltimore's firefighters persevered, and in the
process they discovered, as one firefighter put it, that "the rock and bot-
tle throwing stopped as the people realized we were there to save their
houses."[60] Among the most memorable fires were those that took place
on Lombard Street, on "Corned Beef Row," a Jewish section with some
of the Baltimore's most famous delicatessens. On the morning of April
6th, the merchants of this section paid for a special advertisement in the
Baltimore Sun to express their sorrow over the "loss of the great civil
rights leader, Dr. Martin Luther King Jr." This one-quarter page advertisement, did not, however, protect them from the community's wrath.[61]
Conventional wisdom, notwithstanding, it was not the blazes of Baltimore's Holy Week Uprising that spelled the demise of "Corned Beef
row." In the aftermath of the revolt, most reopened, but other long-term
forces, ranging from the rise of suburban shopping malls to urban renewal
which changed city streetscapes, resulted in the closing of many of the
shops.[62]

[60] "Being in the Baltimore City Fire Department and the 1968 Riots," http://doubledogged
.blogspot.com/2007/02/being-in-baltimore-city-fire-department.html [accessed October
17, 2014]; a sense of the dangers faced by firefighters can also be gleaned from archived
film footage. See https://archive.org/details/Reel614 [accessed October 17, 2014; website
active at time of access].

[61] http://doubledogged.blogspot.com/2007/02/being-in-baltimore-city-fire-department
.html [accessed October 17, 2014]; images of the fires on Corned Beef row can be found
at: Baltimore '68: Riots and Rebirth, especially http://archives.ubalt.edu/bsr/images/
newsamerican.html [accessed October 17, 2014]; Police Department, City of Baltimore,
Maryland, "1968 Riots: Action Reports, April 5, 1968–April 12, 1968," http://archives
.ubalt.edu/bsr/archival-resources/documents/baltimore-police-reports.pdf; "Lombard
Street Merchants Association: Advertisement," *Baltimore Sun*, April 6, 1968, p. B9.

[62] Elizabeth Nix and Deborah Weiner, "Pivot in Perceptions: the Impact of the 1968 Riots
on Three Baltimore Business Districts, in *Baltimore '68: Riots and Rebirth in an Amer-
ican City*, pp. 180–297. Baltimore Urban Renewal and Housing Agency, "The Older
Community Shopping Center As Seen by the Baltimore Consumer," April 1965, in
Baltimore Urban Renewal & Housing Authority Collection, University of Baltimore
Library.

Fear was just as predominant a part of the experience for many merchants as it was for firefighters. For the Pats sisters, all in their teens at the time, the revolt was a traumatic event, though one which they did not utter a word about in public for nearly forty years. Sharon, Betty, and Ida Pats, all white, had gone to bed on the night of Saturday, April 6th, two days after King's death. Earlier in the day, a female black neighbor had warned their family that they "better get out." And Sharon Pats (Singer) later recalled that things had been tense in the neighborhood ever since King's assassination. Nonetheless, when the Pats girls awoke on Sunday morning, they felt secure enough to drive to Hebrew School and to go shopping. Not until Sharon steered her family's car down North Avenue did she realize that much of her neighborhood was in smoke. Winding her way around crowds of people, Sharon quickly picked up the rest of her family and drove away.[63] Shortly afterwards, the Pats's home and business was looted. A day later it was burned to the ground. It "was the end of [our] life as [we] knew it," stated Sharon; Betty Pats (Katznelson) elaborated: "My mom was out of her job and what she did. My dad was out of his job and what he did... Nothing was right." Ironically, Sharon added, prior to the revolt there was a great deal of excitement about the prospect of renewing the neighborhood, with funds raised by the Mid-City Development Corporation. But, as Ida Pats put it, the redevelopment "never materialized."[64]

Stuart Silberg, white, was the owner of Manhattan Drugstore, a full service restaurant and a pharmacy, one of the largest in East Baltimore. Shortly after the looting began, the plate glass window of his store was smashed and an improvised Molotov cocktail was thrown inside the restaurant. Though the flames did not consume the entire building, they caused considerable damage. Before the fire began to spread, "several men came into the store with a gun and held it to his head, and told him he would die if he didn't follow directions and allow them to take whatever they wanted." Silberg's son hypothesized that the store would have suffered even greater damage if it was not located so close to Johns Hopkins Hospital, which enjoyed a heavy police and troop presence. Underinsured and traumatized by the incident, Silberg did not attempt to rebuild; instead he went to work at another pharmacy, before opening a smaller

[63] Interview with Sharon Pats Singer, Ida Pats, and Betty Pats Katznelson, February 20, 2007, http://archives.ubalt.edu/bsr/oral-histories/oral-histories4.html.
[64] Interview with Sharon Pats Singer, Ida Pats, and Betty Pats Katznelson.

store in Pikesville, the Jewish section on the suburban outskirts of the city. All of his employees lost their jobs. The store's customers, Silberg's son added, "were shocked and unhappy." Moreover, the "riot" left his mother traumatized and his father jaded and "it took a long time [for him] to recover."[65]

At the same time, there were instances where black employees protected their white employers. For instance, when someone threw a gasoline bomb into George Constantinides's Cleaners on Harford Road, his black employees whisked him away to a nearby home and called his family to inform them that he was safe. Two days later when Constandinides's nephew came to bring his uncle home, Constantinides displayed empathy for those who had burned his place, asserting that if they had "known him…they wouldn't have burned him out."[66]

Close to 80 percent of all establishments that suffered damages were owned by whites, a disproportionate number by Jews. Some of these Jewish merchants were holocaust survivors. Thomas Ward, a lawyer who represented a lot of Jewish store owners, recalled that one of his clients, whose store was looted and destroyed during the riots, had met his wife in the concentration camps. "He and his wife both had their tattoos from the SS Gestapo on their arms. He was relocated to the United States…started a little grocery store and they burnt him down…None of them every wanted to go back and none of them did go back." Others had fled Russian pogroms earlier in the century or descended from those who did. A number of commentators explicitly compared what had happened to Jewish merchants during the riots to what had happened during the Russian pogroms.[67] This said, a post-riot study by the Baltimore Jewish Council disputed the conventional wisdom that Jewish merchants had been targeted because of black anti-Semitism. Damage to stores owned by Jews was proportionate to the total number of stores that they owned. Or as the report concluded, "Senseless vengeance against merchants *who happen to be* Jewish is quite different than vengeance against merchants *because* they are Jewish" (emphasis in original).[68]

[65] Interview with Stuart Silberg, http://archives.ubalt.edu/bsr/oral-histories/transcripts/silberg.pdf [accessed October 21, 2014].

[66] WYPR, "The Fire This Time, Part III," http://archives.ubalt.edu/bsr/archival-resources/documents/wypr-part-3.pdf [accessed July 15, 2016].

[67] See Baltimore *Jewish Times*, April 12 and 19, 1968; Interview with Thomas Ward, http://archives.ubalt.edu/bsr/oral-histories/transcripts/ward.pdf [accessed October 20, 2014]; Baltimore Jewish Council, "Statistical Analysis of the Baltimore Riots, April 1968."

[68] Baltimore Jewish Council, "Statistical Analysis."

"In the Event that You Cross Howard and Franklin Streets...They Are Going to Kill You All"

While many had good reason to fear for their lives, one of the central paradoxes of the Holy Week Uprising was that Baltimore experienced far fewer fatalities than did places that revolted during the long hot summer of 1967. Six individuals were killed, five blacks and one white. In contrast, thirty-four men and forty-three women had been killed in Watts and Detroit the year before. Fatalities were also far lower in Washington, DC, Chicago, and other large cities that experienced revolts in the spring of 1968 than in cities that experienced uprisings in the preceding years. Somewhat along the same lines, even though they had to face large and unruly crowds, most often with unloaded weapons, few National Guardsmen or federal troops suffered serious injuries.[69] And while close to 1,000 businesses were affected and hundreds were ransacked or torched, public and community buildings, including symbols of the establishment, such as schools, government buildings, and churches, were largely spared.[70]

Based on the fact that there were substantially more fatalities in 1967 than in 1968, Edward Banfield concluded that the former were significantly more severe. But Banfield, among others, failed to consider other explanations for why there were fewer fatalities. Indeed, by all other measurements – arrests, property damage, days of unrest, number of troops – the Holy Week Uprisings were just as, if not more, severe.[71] The main reason Baltimore experienced fewer fatalities was that federal authorities altered the way they responded to the revolts. This change came about based upon studies of the 1967 uprisings conducted by both the Kerner Commission and by the military itself. Cyrus Vance, who headed the military's study, developed detailed procedures for responding to urban "disorders" and, building on these procedures began conducting intensive riot-training programs for law enforcement officials across the nation. Branches of the military, including the National Guard and Army, did

---

[69] *Riot Data Review*, 2 (August 1968); Thomas F. Parker, ed. *Violence in America, Volume 1: 1956–1967* (New York: Facts on File, 1974); Janowitz, "Social Control of Escalated Riots," The University of Chicago Center for Policy Study, in White House Central File, Lyndon B. Johnson Library, HU2, Box 7, Folder March 1, 1968–April 7, 1968.

[70] The Maryland Crime Investigating Committee, "A Report of the Baltimore Civil Disturbance of April, 1968," June 4, 1968.

[71] Edward Banfield, *The Unheavenly City Revisited* (Boston: Little Brown, 1974), p. 232; Carter, "Explaining the Severity of the 1960s Black Rioting"; *Riot Data Review*, 1–3 (May 1968–February 1969).

the same. Most importantly, military authorities decided to deploy troops with orders that they were not to load their weapons and that they were to refrain from shooting looters. Put somewhat differently, Vance promoted a policy of "containment," one that resembled America's foreign policy in the postwar era. Some have even suggested that this policy dovetailed with America's actions abroad in another way – the battleground was in colonized territories, from French Indochina to East and West Baltimore. In both cases, the goal was to keep the "contagion" from spreading. Or as "Little Melvin," who was one of Baltimore's best-known criminals and somewhat of a folk hero, warned his fellow blacks, "in the event that you cross Howard and Franklin Streets," which demarcated downtown, "they are going to kill you all."[72]

This new approach saved lives, but ironically garnered much public wrath and galvanized conservative attacks on liberalism for being soft on lawbreakers.[73] In addition, the relative lack of fatalities in Baltimore failed to undermine one of the most enduring images of the riots of the 1960s, that of the trigger-happy National Guardsmen. Because the National Guard had provided little riot training prior to the long hot summer of 1967, its soldiers gained a deleterious reputation. The shooting of students by National Guardsmen at Kent State in 1970 reinforced this image. Yet, an examination of the actions of the National Guard and federal troops during the Holy Week Uprising in Baltimore reveals an alternative perspective, namely one of considerable restraint in the midst of stressful circumstances. Father Richard Lawrence, an activist Catholic priest and longtime CORE member, described the Guard's performance in Baltimore and offered an adept explanation for it. "I was on the street when the National Guard began to arrive," Lawrence recollected. "And do you know who was in the National Guard in 1968? Danny Quayles by the thousands, suburbanite kids with influential daddies...so they wouldn't have to go to Saigon." (Dan Quayle served as vice-president from 1989 to 1993. During the presidential campaigns, he was criticized for taking

---

[72] LTG Robert H. York, "After Action Report: Task Force Baltimore, 7–13 April, 1968," Warren Christopher Papers, Civil Disturbances 1968 #2; Ben Franklin, "Patrol of Negro Peacemakers Sent Out in Baltimore," *NYT*, April 10, 1968; Interview with Melvin Douglas Williams, http://archives.ubalt.edu/bsr/oral-histories/oral-histories4.html.

[73] Paul J. Scheips, *The Role of Federal Military Forces in Domestic Disorders, 1945–1992*, (Washington, DC: Center of Military History, 2005), pp. 205–230; *Kerner Report*, ch. 12, especially, fn. 1, p. 329–332; "Testimony of General George Gelston," Meeting of National Commission on Civil Disorders, September 20, 1967, *Civil Rights During the Johnson Administration*, Part 5: reel 3.

advantage of his connections – his father was a rich and powerful publisher – to get into a unit of the National Guard rather than fighting in Vietnam.)[74] Tight, white, suburbanite, most of them had never been in the ghetto, much less patrolled one. When they "rolled down Pennsylvania Ave...their eyes were as big as saucers, they were so scared the uniform of the day should've included rubber pants." But, rather than get in shoot outs with imaginary snipers, as had Guardsmen during the long hot summer of 1967, "their discipline held, and I'll tell you a reason why it held. George Gelston...the General of the National Guard...he knew what he had. So...[he] ordered [that their] weapons...be carried unloaded" and that their weapons may be loaded only on direct command of a commissioned officer."[75] Wilson Thornton Jr., a black National Guardsmen who had been born and raised in Baltimore, confirmed Lawrence's assessment. After convoying down from the armory in Pikesville, his unit was stationed on Pennsylvania Avenue, where it encountered people who "were looting, running up and down the street with boxes of Kotex...cutting the firemen's hoses." Following the terms of engagement laid down by their commanding officers, Thornton's unit, among others, did not shoot or, in most cases, seek to arrest those who were breaking the law. Rather, simply through their presence they hoped the area would quite down.[76]

This analysis also reminds us that most of those who responded to orders to control the civil disturbances were young men at the time and their experiences remained among the most vivid and perhaps formative they ever had. "If you were on Pennsylvania Avenue during the riot and weren't scared, then you were a damned fool," Private August Ziegler recalled. "We're standing there just about as naked as a man can be – no ammo, no gas, no communications, bayonets sheathed – with the nearest help the two guys at the end of the next block...And these young toughs knew we had nothing. 'What-ta-ya gonna do with that toy gun, mother fucker, we know you ain't got no bullets...' They had absolutely no fear of us...One of them got nose to nose with me and the son-of-a-bitch spat right in my face...What really got to me," Ziegler added, "was that I could feel myself getting mad and thinking to myself how much of this shit are we supposed to take. But looking back I realize that if I had struck out at them, they would have been all over us before we could have gotten

[74] On Quayle, see Calvin Trillan, "Uncivil Liberties," *The Nation*, October 10, 1988, p. 298; Mark Hosenball, "Pulliam Strings," *New Republic*, October 31, 1988, pp. 18–20.
[75] Interview with Richard Lawrence.
[76] Interview with Wilson Thornton Jr., http://archives.ubalt.edu/bsr/oral-histories/transcripts/thornton.pdf [accessed October 20, 2014].

FIGURE 5.4 Black soldier stands guard during uprising in Baltimore. *Baltimore News American* collection, Special Collections, University of Maryland Libraries. By permission of the Hearst Corporation.

help. Even if we had ammunition," "the gang or mob" probably would not "let you load it." Put somewhat differently, Ziegler concluded, the lack of ammunition probably saved his life.[77]

Black National Guardsmen faced particularly difficult circumstances, having to deal with verbal taunts and other tests of their discipline (see Figure 5.4). "House nigger," a crowd of blacks yelled at Sergeant Robert Jones, the only black member of his platoon. "You black mother fucker, you're on the wrong side!" it continued. "It was hard to go against your own people," Jones recalled of this situation. "But it was a job that had to be done." In the case of Lieutenant Robert Douglas, who commanded a company of soldiers in one of the city's hottest spots on the night of April 6th, the challenge came in a nonverbal form, when a black man "undid his trousers, took out his penis and shaking it at Douglas shouted, 'prick, prick, prick.'" To make matters worse, Douglas had to rush from this

[77] Ziegler quoted in Peterson, *Into the Cauldron*, pp. 69–70.

incident to guarding fireman besieged by a crowd and by alleged snipers. When Douglas and another unit charged into a building in search of the latter, they encountered "a number of kids with broom sticks, pretending they were guns, and aiming them out the windows and doors at the troops and firemen." Michael Agetstein recalled a similar circumstance, whereby he spotted a pistol "being aimed at him" from a second story window. "To this day," recalled Agetstein, "I don't know what kept me from firing. But as I kept the window in my rifle sights, the head and shoulders of what must have been a six-year-old boy appeared holding what I was later to learn was a toy pistol. I shook so bad after that I could hardly take the clip out of my rifle."[78] Unlike in Newark and Detroit, none of the fatalities in Baltimore in 1968 were the result of gunshots by a National Guardsmen or federal soldiers.

Situations like those described above, tend to confirm Ashley Howard's suggestion that one way that working-class blacks asserted their masculinity was by confronting authorities. Already alienated from non-violent protest, because they felt it "reproduced the same degrading rituals of domination and submission that suffused the master/slave relationship," the revolts provided black men with an opportunity, even if a temporary one, to "take back control." In normal circumstances, police controlled black communities, frisking young black men, in particular, with impunity and demanding deference at all times. During the revolts, in contrast, young black men flipped the script, attaining deference from armed officials.[79]

Armed whites played a role in the uprising as well, reinforcing the military's strategy of containing the revolt to black neighborhoods. Frank Bressler, for one, organized an armed posse of mostly Jewish businessmen in the largely Jewish Park Heights section of Baltimore. "Many of us were ex-military people," Bressler explained, so we set up "a military type of defense" to protect our homes and our businesses. They raised money, bought more guns and ammunition, distributed the weapons, and "set up defenses" throughout upper northwest Baltimore. Armed with a gun and a short-wave radio and the conviction that he had the constitutional right to defend his property, Bressler spent several nights at his business, prepared to fire at anyone who tried to enter. Through his employees, most of whom were black, Bressler let it be known that he and tens of other business owners would shoot anyone who broke into

[78] Peterson, *Into the Cauldron*, pp. 48, 101, 105–106.
[79] Ashley Howard, "Prairie Fires," pp. 221–242.

their establishments. And though some looting spread up Park Heights Avenue, Bressler remains convinced that the show of force "saved north-west Baltimore from destruction."[80]

Likewise, in Little Italy, a nearly all-white neighborhood, shopkeepers armed themselves and threatened to shoot anyone who ventured into their neighborhood. Or as future governor Marvin Mandel put it: collectively they made clear that "Anybody comes across the line, we're gonna take care of 'em."[81] On April 9th a white mob assembled near Patterson Park and vowed to have it out with blacks. Consistent with its policy of containment, however, federal troops and National Guard units made clear that they would not allow the whites to cross into the black section of town.[82]

Arrest records and the sites of most of the riot-related incidents confirm that Baltimore's revolts remained very local affairs. The vast majority of those imprisoned were arrested within ten blocks of where they lived. Incidents of looting, arson, and vandalism took place almost exclusively in black neighborhoods, to a large degree because, as suggested above, authorities quickly cordoned off downtown and led blacks to believe that they would be shot, if they ventured outside of their own communities.[83] Unlike Chicago, where most blacks lived on the south side and whites on the north side of the city, Baltimore had two ghettos, in West and East Baltimore, which lay on the edge of a downtown corridor. Some people referred to the layout of Baltimore as the parenthesis of poverty, with white businesses and residences located inside the parenthesis or on the exterior sections of the city and in the suburbs. White fears that the "Mau Mau were coming to the suburbs," to borrow Stokely Carmichael's words, not only proved unfounded, only a very small proportion of establishments in neighborhoods that were predominantly white experienced looting or damage. Even in predominantly white neighborhoods that abutted predominantly black ones, invisible demarcation lines, which informed blacks to stay out, remained firm during the

---

[80] Interview with Frank Bressler, n.d., Baltimore '68: Riots and Rebirth Project, http://archives.ubalt.edu/bsr/oral-histories/transcripts/bressler.pdf [accessed October 10, 2014].

[81] Interview with Marvin Mandel, http://archives.ubalt.edu/bsr/oral-histories/transcripts/mandel.pdf [accessed October 21, 2014]; "After Action Report – Task Force Baltimore, April 7–13, 1968."

[82] See Summary Reports of Riots, April 8, 1968, Ramsey Clark Papers.

[83] Stephen J. Lynton, "Arrests Present a Profile of City Rioters," *Baltimore Sun*, April 22, 1968, p. C1.

revolts (see map in Figure 4.3). For instance, Tom Carney, who grew up in "Pigtown," a predominantly Catholic neighborhood that lay adjacent to Camden Yards, the current home of the Baltimore Orioles, recalled being able to smell the smoke from adjacent, largely black neighborhoods in the city where looting was taking place. Yet, as he put it, the "rioting" did not take place "in our neighborhood."[84]

Arrest records also provide an approximation of who participated in the revolt. Over the course of the week, the city arrested 5,512 men and women, the vast majority of whom were charged with violating curfew. The plurality of arrestees were over the age of thirty. Ninety-two percent of the arrestees were black; 85 percent were males; 63 percent of all of the arrestees were charged with curfew violations; and an additional 7 percent with disorderly conduct. Some 910 men and women were charged with larceny but many of these charges were later dropped because of the difficulty of proving them in a court of law. Only thirteen men (no women) were charged with arson, few of whom were convicted. In Detroit, 89 percent of arrestees were male and almost all were black; in a larger sample of nineteen cities, 19 percent of the charges were for violating curfew, 31 percent for breaking and entering or trespass, 0.4 percent were for arson and only 0.1 percent for homicide. Put somewhat differently, as Robert Fogelson and Robert Hill demonstrated in their study "Who Riots?" the "rioters" were not the "riffraff," or "unattached, juvenile, unskilled, unemployed, uprooted, [and] criminal." Rather, they were more likely to be over the age of thirty than juveniles and employed as blue-collar workers than unemployed.[85]

Anecdotal evidence, culled from oral histories and newspaper stories, reaffirm these findings. The aforementioned Robert Bradby, who was charged with and convicted of murder during the uprising, worked at Bethlehem Steel. (After being released from jail, Brady found employment as a school bus driver.) Ruth Stewart, who acknowledged that she stole diapers, carnation milk, vitamins, and other things for the survival of her young children, was a student at the time – her husband was in the army,

---

[84] Interview with Tom Carney, December 5, 2006, http://archives.ubalt.edu/bsr/oral-histories/transcripts/carney.pdf [accessed October 11, 2014].

[85] Robert M. Fogelson and Robert B. Hill, "Who Riots? A Study of Participation in the 1967 Riots" in *Supplemental Studies for the National Advisory Commission on Civil Disorders* (Washington, DC: GPO, July 1968), pp. 221–223. The Maryland Crime Investigating Commission, "A Report of the Baltimore Civil Disturbance of April, 1968," June 4, 1968, pp. 24–26; "Arrests Present a Profile of City Rioters," *Baltimore Sun*, April 22, 1968, p. C20.

serving in Germany. (She later worked as a school teacher.) Glenn Cook, who was taking a semester off from Columbia University, was working at Bethlehem Steel as well, when he was arrested for possession of a Molotov cocktail on April 7. Leonard Carter, convicted of looting a bakery, worked as a laborer at the Department of Education. Likewise, Charles H. Muller, who broke a window at a liquor store, had worked for one of the local antipoverty agencies.[86]

As the revolt spread the city jail began to overflow. At one point, arrestees refused to enter their jail cells, compelling authorities to rush state troopers to the city prison to restore order. Eventually, the city decided to turn the Civic Center into a temporary "detention center." Opened in the fall of 1962 after over half-a-century of haggling, the Civic Center had been hailed as a "symbol of the new spirit" in the community, as a centerpiece of the revitalization of its downtown. It served as the home of the city's professional hockey and basketball teams, including Earl the Pearl Monroe, often considered one of the new "black" athletes. The Civic Center regularly hosted the Ringling Brothers circus and the Ice Follies, and top musical performers, including Dionne Warwick who wowed a sold-out audience there on Sunday, March 29, 1968. During the revolt, however, the center came to symbolize the lack of fundamental progress that the city had made in recent times, looking more like an internment camp than an engine of economic growth and cultural unity.[87]

The magnitude of the arrests severely strained the criminal justice system. Even though the Kerner Commission had rejected responding to "riot" emergencies by "short-cutting ... procedures for the protection of individual rights," in fact, widespread "short-cutting" took place in Baltimore.[88] Elsbeth Levy Bothe, a young attorney with the ACLU, recalled

---

[86] Newspaper reports on the trials of arrestees provide only sporadic information on the employment histories of defendants. On Bradby's subsequent employment, see "Edgewood High Students Hurt on Bus Trip to Disney World," *Baltimore Sun*, April 5, 2003, http://articles.baltimoresun.com/2003-04-05/news/0304050100_1_harford-county-edgewood-high-florida-highway-patrol [accessed August 19, 2015]. "Riot-Linked Term Raised Twelve-Fold," *Baltimore Sun*, May 2, 1968, p. C26; "33 Charged in Riots Still Await Trial," *Baltimore Sun*, November 28, 1968, p. C36; Interview with Ruth Stewart. On the working-class make-up of those who participated in the revolts, nationally, see Ashley Howard, "Prairie Fires," especially ch. 4.

[87] John C. Schmidt, "After Fifty-Years-A Civic Center," *Baltimore Sun*, 21 October 1967, p. A1; "Dionne and Company Thoroughly Enjoyable," *Baltimore Sun*, 30 March, 1968, p. 22.

[88] Kerner Commission, *Report*, pp. 345–346; The Maryland Crime Investigating Committee, "A Report of the Baltimore Civil Disturbance of April 1968" (June 4, 1968); Motz, "Report on Baltimore Civil Disorders, April 1968."

that the city's chief jailer had no intention of stopping arrests from being made just because the prison was overflowing. Or as a correction's official informed Bothe, "'They can stand on their heads!'" When Alan Bloom, a young recent graduate from the University of Baltimore Law arrived at the courtroom, he could not believe the chaos of the scene. Usually there were at most three or four prisoners in a courtroom, he recalled, but during the uprising he saw fifty to seventy prisoners surrounded by National Guardsmen armed with rifles and fixed bayonets, even though the vast majority of defendants were charged only with curfew violations.[89] (For an assessment of the city's reaction, see Chapter 6.)

The uprising also impacted emergency personnel, including those responsible for distributing food and key social services. As early as the evening of April 7th, representatives of the mayor's office, Red Cross, Department of Education, Public Welfare, and Salvation Army met to coordinate their activities. They set up food kitchens, shelters, and an emergency transportation system to get displaced people to these centers. For example, Baltimore's residents were transported by school buses to public schools, where they were fed by school cafeteria workers. The Community Action Agency distributed surplus food – 82,000 pounds of which came from the US Department of Agriculture – and clothing at its centers.[90] Private citizens supplemented these public efforts. Ed Fischel, a member of Loyola College's "Students for Social Action," recalled loading up a station wagon of blankets, clothes, and food and driving it down to St. Vincent de Paul in the midst of one of the most burned out sections of the city. Though frightened by the surrounding flames and National Guardsmen who lined the streets, Fischel felt so moved by the favorable reception he received from the parish's priest and from people in the neighborhood that he made additional trips with more supplies.[91] Baltimore Colt stars, Lenny Moore and John Mackey, both black, also played a prominent role in the relief effort. Moore, for example, journeyed down to the Civic Center where an estimated 2,500 riot-related arrestees

---

[89] Interview with Alan Bloom, http://archives.ubalt.edu/bsr/oral-histories/transcripts/bloom.pdf [accessed October 17, 2014]; Interview with Elsbeth Levy Bothe, http://archives.ubalt.edu/bsr/oral-histories/transcripts/bothe.pdf [accessed October 17, 2014].

[90] See Photo, "Study in Contrasts," April 9, 1968, and http://archives.ubalt.edu/bsr/images/newsamerican.html and WMAR-TV film footage, http://archives.ubalt.edu/bsr/images/footage.html [both accessed October 20, 2014].

[91] Interview with Ed Fishel, http://archives.ubalt.edu/bsr/oral-histories/transcripts/fishel.pdf [accessed October 20, 2014].

were being detained. "Most of those people hadn't eaten in 24 hours," and he feared that "all hell was about to break lose." Taking advantage of his status, he contacted Mayor D'Alesandro's office and, along with Mackey, developed a plan for ameliorating the situation.[92]

As early as the night of April 8th, Attorney General Fred Vinson suggested that the end was in sight.[93] At about the same time, Mayor Thomas D'Alesandro privately informed one of LBJ's top aides, Joseph Califano, that the "deployment of Federal troops on the streets...saved the city."[94] The number of incidents dropped on April 9th, allowing the Baltimore Orioles to play their opening game on April 10th, one day later than originally scheduled. One final byproduct of the uprising was the cancelation of a concert by the king of soul, James Brown. Scheduled to appear at Baltimore Civic Center on April 12th, Brown chose not to perform, in part, because it was being used as a make-shift jail. According to some analysts, Boston's decision to allow Brown to go ahead with his show on April 6th helped Boston avert significant turmoil following King's death.[95]

But the end of the revolt marked only the beginning of the renewed debate over its causes, which in turn informed the public's discourse over the proper response. Even more so than in the summer of 1967, Maryland's Governor Spiro T. Agnew played a key role in shaping this debate. Moving beyond accusing radicals of inciting riots, Agnew blamed black and white moderates for the turmoil. It is to this response that we turn to next.

[92] Ron Snyder, "To the Rescue: Colts Moore, Mackey, Unsung heroes of '68 Riots," *Baltimore Examiner*, April 4, 2008, p. 8.

[93] Fred Vinson, "Press Conference," April 8, 1968, White House Central Files, Box 26, File HU2/st21, President Lyndon Johnson Papers.

[94] Joe Califano to Lyndon Johnson, April 8, 1968, *Civil Rights During the Johnson Administration*, Roll I:5.

[95] National Public Radio, "The Night James Brown Saved Boston," www.npr.org/templates/story/story.php?storyId=89273314 [accessed July 15, 2008].

6

One Nation, Two Responses

> I remember that Dr. King was killed. White people remember looting.
> Larry Gibson

In so far as historians have considered the impact of King's assassination and the revolts that followed, many have concluded that these comingled events represented a watershed in American history, the point where the liberal coalition that had enacted the civil rights acts of the mid-1960s came to an end. Or as Steven Gillon explained: "Any hope of forcing white America to confront the deep racial divide in the country – however slim to begin with – died that night." Even before King's death, President Johnson had responded tepidly to the Kerner Commission's findings and "denounced the notion that America was moving toward two societies as a 'catchy but insidious slander.'" After King's assassination, he grew increasingly withdrawn, rejecting calls to reinvigorate the War on Poverty and push through the equivalent of a domestic Marshall Plan. Yet, we need to ask, did the Holy Week Uprisings, themselves, foreclose the opportunity to address the racial divide which the Kerner Commission had identified as the cause of the revolts, most notably in its famous line, "Our nation is moving toward two societies, one black, one white – separate and unequal?" Or was white retrenchment and the politics of resentment, which foreclosed on responding favorably to the commission's recommendations, made or constructed by those who sought to benefit politically from the unrest?[1]

---

[1] Gibson quoted in Smith, *Here Lies Jim Crow*, p. 236. McLaughlin, *The Long Hot Summer of 1967*; Kerner Commission, *Report*, "Introduction"; Steven Gillon, "'Separate and Unequal': Revisiting the Kerner Commission," *Huffington Post*, May 13,

Retaining our focus on Baltimore, this chapter will suggest that the latter was the case. Conservative politician and pundits, along with complicit liberals, intentionally framed or used the Holy Week Uprisings in such a way to insure that the Kerner Commission's recommendations would meet their demise. Simultaneously, they conflated the racial revolts with the antiwar movement, crime, and the rise of the counterculture, women's and "third world" movements, to bolster the politics of resentment and white retrenchment. While some pundits suggested that this was a natural course of events and/or a result of a paradox, namely that the "Negro riots because whites do not do enough, and whites do not do enough because Negroes riot," to borrow the *New York Times*' words, this construction obscures white responsibility for creating the conditions against which blacks revolted against in the first place and white resistance to substantially altering the racial status quo before and after the uprisings.[2]

At the same time, the Holy Week Uprisings also produced a different response, one which rejected the notion that the revolts betrayed the black freedom struggle and required a restoration of "law and order" above all else. In Baltimore, as in many other communities, the uprisings led to the rise of an increasingly assertive Black Power movement that sought greater economic and political power. This Black Power surge was not atypical. On the contrary, it represented what some scholars have termed a broader black nationalist renaissance. Put somewhat differently, from the perspective of many ordinary black men and women, the Holy Week Uprisings did not represent a watershed in which some great era came to a lamentable end, rather the revolts marked a new and positive phase in a long struggle to achieve equality.[3]

"This Masochistic Group Guilt For White Racism Pervades Every Facet of the Report's Reasoning"

One of the central figures in the construction of the conservative response to the Holy Week Uprisings was Maryland's Governor Spiro Agnew.

1975, www.huffingtonpost.com/steven-m-gillon/separate-and-unequal-revi_b_7268382 .html [accessed March 22, 2016]. On the idea of establishing a domestic Marshall Plan, see "'Marshall Plan' for Slums Urged," *Afro-American*, August 19, 1967, p. 1.

[2] Joseph, *Waiting 'Til The Midnight Hour*, p. 162.

[3] Peniel Joseph, ed., *Neighborhood Rebels: Black Power at the Local Level* (New York: Palgrave Macmillan, 2010); Thompson, *Whose Detroit?*; Winston A. Grady-Willis, *Challenging U.S. Apartheid: Atlanta and Black Struggles for Human Rights, 1960–1977* (Durham, NC: Duke University Press, 2006); Clarence Lang, *Grassroots at the Gateway: Class Politics and the Black Freedom Struggle in St. Louis, 1936–1975* (Ann Arbor: University of Michigan Press, 2009); Alex Poinsett, *Black Power Gary Style: the Making of Mayor Richard Gordon Hatcher* (Chicago: Johnson Publishing, 1970).

While Agnew had gained some notoriety following Cambridge's riot in the summer of 1967, it was his reaction to the revolts following King's assassination that catapulted him into a national spokesperson for the burgeoning New Right and landed him a spot on the GOP's presidential ticket. Seven days after King was shot, with some federal troops still deployed in Baltimore, Agnew invited the city's black leaders to a special meeting. Given Agnew's earlier record as a racial moderate, they arrived expecting some soothing words and perhaps an endorsement of policies akin to those recommended by the Kerner Commission. Instead, Agnew delivered a blistering speech that simultaneously alienated his audience and made him a folk hero to millions of so-called Middle Americans.[4]

Arriving late, the usually punctual Agnew began his speech *sans* the standard niceties. "Look around you and...you'll observe who is not here," Agnew declared. "You will *not* find the circuit-riding, Hanoi visiting type of leader...The caterwauling riot-inciting, burn-America-down type of leader is conspicuous by his absence. That is no accident, it is just good planning. And in the vernacular of today – 'that's what it's all about, baby.'" These radicals, Agnew continued, caused the riot. "Tell me one constructive achievement of [H. Rap] Brown...They do not build – they demolish." To bolster his argument Agnew quoted Stokely Carmichael and H. Rap Brown at their most inflammatory, such as Brown's declaration: "'Get yourselves some guns. The honky is your enemy...This city [a reference to Detroit in the wake of its 1967 riot] will look like a picnic after black people unite to take their due.'"[5]

These opening remarks suggested that Agnew intended to blame radicals for the unrest, which was consistent with his claim that H. Rap Brown had incited a riot in Cambridge the summer before. Many others, including Baltimore's Mayor Thomas D'Alesandro, insisted that the riots had been well organized. William Boucher, executive director of the Greater Baltimore Committee, similarly testified that he was "certain that a substantial degree of organization was involved in the riots." And in the weeks to come, in Baltimore and nationally, many Americans, from prominent politicians to media pundits would contend that black activists

---

4 Levy, "Spiro Agnew"; Alex T. Csicsek, "Spiro T. Agnew and the Burning of Baltimore," in *Baltimore '68*, pp. 70–85; Witcover, *White Knight*, pp. 3–9, 178–192.
5 Spiro T. Agnew, "Statement at Conference with Civil Rights and Community Leaders," State Office Building, Baltimore, Maryland, April 11, 1968, in *Addresses and State Paper of Spiro T. Agnew, Governor of Maryland, 1967–69*, ed. by Franklin Burdette (Annapolis: State of Maryland, 1975), p. 758; "After Action Report, Task Force Baltimore, April 7–13, 1968."

had fomented the revolts.[6] Agnew did nothing to undercut this belief even though he knew that claims that Brown and Carmichael had caused Baltimore's riot lacked credibility. Brown was in jail at the time of King's assassination and Carmichael was attending King's funeral when looting broke out in Baltimore. Agnew not only ignored these facts, he fed the rumor mill by declaring that he had information that showed that Carmichael helped plan the riot.[7]

Yet it was not this attack on black militants that angered Baltimore's black leaders or attracted the attention of the national press and Richard Nixon. Rather, Agnew distinguished himself by redirecting attention away from the radicals to moderate blacks, and by inference, liberals in general. Even though many of those present had spent hours on the streets trying to convince looters to disperse and had been longtime supporters of King and his nonviolent methods of effecting change, Agnew insisted that they shared much of the blame for the destruction that had wracked Baltimore and by extension hundreds of other American communities. Specifically, Agnew accused Baltimore's black leaders of having cow-towed to black radicals. "When white leaders openly complemented" black leaders for criticizing an inflammatory statement that one black radical made several weeks prior to the riot, Agnew explained, "you ran … You were stung by insinuations that you were Mr. Charlie's boy," by epithets like "Uncle Tom." This "silence" Agnew exclaimed, "magnified" the invective of the radicals.[8] (The claim that they refused to condemn an inflammatory statement by a black radical was a reference to Robert Moore, a SNCC activist who had worked in Lowndes County, Alabama, alongside Carmichael and Brown. In February 1968, Moore set up a SNCC office in Baltimore, where, among other things, he called the "war on crime" a "war on the black community." When State Senator Clarence

---

[6] Spiro T. Agnew, "Statement at Conference with Civil Rights and Community Leaders." US Senate, Committee on the Judiciary; Anthony Platt, ed., *The Politics of Riot Commissions, 1917–1970: A Collection of Critical Reports and Essays* (New York: Collier Books, 1971); "Were Riots Organized," *U.S. News & World Report*, April 22, 1968, p. 12; J. L. McClellan, "How Riots are Stirred Up," *U.S. News & World Report*, May 6, 1968, pp. 68–71; Leo Fait to Herbert Myerberg, May 1, 1968, in http://archives.ubalt.edu/bsr/archival-resources/documents/box-8-police-judicial%20response.pdf [accessed January 26, 2016]; William Boucher quoted in Greater Baltimore Committee, "Minutes," April 19, 1968, http://archives.ubalt.edu/bsr/archival-resources/documents/gbc-riots.pdf [accessed March 25, 2016].

[7] Levy, "Spiro Agnew"; Csicsek, "Spiro T. Agnew and the Burning of Baltimore," pp. 70–85.

[8] Spiro T. Agnew, "Statement at Conference with Civil Rights and Community Leaders."

Mitchell lambasted Moore for, in his words, appealing to the criminal element, many other activists in the community, including members of the Interdenominational Ministerial Alliance and U-JOIN leader Walter Lively, defended his critique of the police.)[9]

Before concluding his address, Agnew assured those still in the audience that he too sought to eliminate prejudice and favored the establishment of equal opportunity. But rather than dwell on his own record of working with Maryland's black leadership to promote this agenda, Agnew returned to his main theme, the culpability of liberals. "I am sure that these remarks come as somewhat of a surprise to you, that you expected nebulous promises and rationalizations and possibly a light endorsement of the Kerner report." "This I could not do," Agnew insisted, because, "some hard things need to be said." Concluding with a statement that would prove ripe with irony, Agnew asserted that he was "committing political suicide" by being so forthright. Indeed, in an insightful essay, journalist Gary Wills suggested that Agnew intentionally delivered a provocative speech in order to attract attention to himself.[10]

Most of Maryland's blacks, many of whom had supported him when he ran for governor in 1966, were aghast at Agnew's remarks. No sooner had he finished berating them, Reverend Marion Bascom recalled, than "simultaneously, we got up and started walking out." At the time, Bascom described Agnew "as sick as any human in America," and years afterwards he remained livid over Agnew's accusation that black leaders had caused the riot, detailing the risks they had taken to stop it.[11] After walking out, Bascom and others assembled at the Douglas Memorial Church where they drafted a statement that declared that the governor had "failed to demonstrate enlightened and concerned leadership." Those who did not walk out were just as indignant. Samuel Daniels, the former director of Baltimore's Human Relations Commission, called the speech "insulting." Juanita Jackson Mitchell, who stayed to "hear Agnew out," engaged

9 Rudolph Lewis, "Forty Years of Determined Struggle: A Political Portrait of Robert Moore," *Chicken Bones: A Journal*, www.nathanielturner.com/fortyyearsof determinedstrugg.htm [accessed June 3, 2016]; "Sen. Mitchell Blasts Moore," *Afro-American*, February 10, 1968, p. 1; "S.N.C.C. Aide is Criticized by Mitchell," *Baltimore Sun*, February 9, 1968, p. C26; "Anti-Crime Plans Termed 'War on Black Community,'" *Baltimore Sun*, February 8, 1968, p. C22
10 Spiro T. Agnew, "Statement at Conference with Civil Rights and Community Leaders"; Gary Wills, "The Agnew Controversy Refuses to Die," *Esquire*, February 23, 1969.
11 Interview with Marion Bascom; Interview with Homer Favor, both in: http://archives.ubalt.edu/bsr/oral-histories/index.html.

in a sharp exchange with the governor afterwards. While she deplored the violence, Mitchell asserted that it was the city and government that had "made our children burners and looters."[12]

Nor did this anger subside in the days that followed, in spite of efforts by some to smooth over hard feelings. Thirty Catholic priests from the region joined the Ministerial Alliance in condemning Agnew's speech for insulting those who had worked for years "to rid Baltimore of the evil effects of racism." In an open letter entitled "What It's Really All About Ted (Agnew's nickname) Baby," published in the *Afro-American*, a coalition of Baltimore's black leaders lambasted the governor for thinking he had the right "to hand pick our leaders and issue them ultimatums," chided him for ignoring the real grievances of the students at Bowie State, and made clear they would no long defer to his or anyone else's paternalism, or as they put it: "In short, Ted baby, our young people – and old ones – are no longer willing to be 'good old boys and girls' ... It's not that kind of party anymore. And that's what it's really all about, Ted baby!" (see Figure 6.1). Similarly, William Lively, who Agnew had refused to invite to the speech on the grounds that he was one of the "caterwauling, riot-inciting, burn-American-down type(s)," declared that "Agnew is the only outside agitator around," adding that the governor was "exploiting the disorder in Baltimore, just as he did in Cambridge last year." Moving beyond words, the recently formed Maryland Action Group, led by Leo Burroughs Jr., a veteran of the locally based Civic Interest Group, placed a white sheet and a bullwhip on the fence outside the governor's mansion in Annapolis. "The white sheet symbolizes his [Agnew's] movement toward the Klan, Burroughs explained. "The bullwhip symbolizes the slave–master posture."[13]

Yet Agnew's speech resonated with much of the larger public. According to one account, in the two weeks following the speech, Agnew received close to 9,000 phone calls, telegrams, and letters, nearly 90 percent of them favorable. The Baltimore *Evening Sun* reported that Agnew enjoyed "surprisingly strong support from the white middle class across the State." If Agnew thought he had taken a political risk by insulting Baltimore's "Negro" leaders, these communications suggested otherwise. Whereas the national media criticized Agnew for speaking so bluntly, small town

[12] Gene Oshi, "Negroes Quit Conference With Agnew," *Baltimore Sun*, April 12, 1968, p. C22; "Agnew Insults Leaders," *Afro-American*, April 13, 1968, p. 1.
[13] Newspaper Clipping File: Agnew Riot Statement and African American Community Leaders, http://archives.ubalt.edu/cj/pdf/agnew.pdf [accessed April 22, 2016]; "What It's Really All About, Ted Baby," *Afro-American*, April 13, 1968, p. 4.

FIGURE 6.1 Political cartoon, "An Oasis of Sanity." The cartoon, which appeared in the *Afro-American* (Baltimore) on April 20, 1968, contrasts Agnew's hysterical response to the revolts to that of the Kerner Commission. Also portrayed are: President Johnson, far right, and leading members of Congress, at table in rear. By permission of the *Afro-American* (Baltimore).

newspapers and letter writers applauded his forthrightness, with David Kahne writing that he hoped it would inspire a new trend in the nation. Arthur Gutman, an insurance agent from Baltimore agreed, adding, "I would vote for you for President." Among the complimentary messages a number came from prominent conservatives, such as Arizona's Governor Jack Williams and California's William Knowland.[14]

---

[14] David Kahne to Spiro T. Agnew, April 16, 1968; Arthur Gutman to Spiro T. Agnew, April 15, 1968; Governor Jack Williams to Spiro T. Agnew, April 23, 1968, all in Governor Agnew Papers, MSA, SC2221-12-41 and S1041-1713.

In the aftermath of the Holy Week Uprising and his speech to Baltimore's black leaders, Agnew focused not just on violence and the rise of
crime but on the alleged cultural roots of the rise of disorders in American society. Cultural permissiveness, not social and economic hardship,
Agnew insisted, underlay the "riots." Nowhere did Agnew make this case
more clearly than in his critiques of the Kerner Commission. Before the
National Governor's Conference Agnew lambasted the commission for
blaming "everybody but the people who did it. This masochistic group
guilt for white racism pervades every facet of the Report's reasoning."
"If one wants to pinpoint one indirect cause...it would be...that law-
breaking has become a socially acceptable and occasionally stylish form
of dissent." Blacks in the 1930s, Agnew contended, rioted less not because
they were better off but because the "climate was less permissive."[15]

Agnew was hardly alone in condemning black radicals as well as liberals for the latest round of urban unrest. Georgia Governor Lester Maddox, for one, a symbol of white supremacy in the South, stated that he had
advised the president "on numerous occasions" that liberal programs had
inspired, encouraged, and "often times" protected and financed "lawless
agitators" who "would bring waves of violence, burning, looting and violent death." Rather than calling for more reforms in the wake of King's
death, Maddox implored LBJ to "denounce the...fraudulent recommendations of the riot probe commission that even now encourage increased
violence."[16] South Carolina's Strom Thurmond suggested that King and
his philosophy of civil disobedience had caused the "riots," writing: "Are
we not witnessing the whirlwind sowed years ago when some preachers
and teachers began telling people that each man could be his own judge
in his own case."[17]

Agnew's focus on the cultural roots of the disorders dovetailed with
Daniel Patrick Moynihan's "culture of poverty" thesis, which, as we have
seen, many conservatives and liberals championed. Moynihan's "message
that culture, not economics, was the driving force in poverty," writes

[15] Spiro T. Agnew, "Statement to Executive Session," National Governors' Conference,
Cincinnati, Ohio, July 23, 1968. See also: Spiro T. Agnew, "News Conference," June
20, 1968 and Spiro T. Agnew, "News Conference," August 1, 1968, all in *Addresses
of Spiro T. Agnew*. Witcover, *White Knight*, p. 178; "Agencies Probing City's Rioting,"
Evening Sun (Baltimore, MD), April 13, 1968, p. 20.
[16] Lester Maddox to Lyndon B. Johnson, April 9, 1968, Lyndon B. Johnson Papers, WHCF,
Box 193.
[17] Thurmond quoted in Rick Perlstein, *Nixonland: The Rise of a President and the Fracturing of America* (New York: Scribner, 2008), p. 257; Douglass E. Kneeland, "Agnew
Stresses Equality to V.F.W.," *NYT*, August 22, 1968, p. 27.

Richard Perlstein, "delighted conservatives," because it largely absolved whites of complicity in the recent urban racial disorder. It also had the advantage of not being rooted in some form of biological or genetic determinism as had many traditional racist claims. Yet, Moynihan's critics saw his interpretation as just the newest of many "scientific" rationalizations of white supremacy which blamed blacks for their second class status rather than persistent, systematic, and ongoing racially discriminatory policies.[18]

Agnew's views also prefigured Edward Banfield's influential analysis of the urban revolts. Too often scholars have assumed that Banfield made his famous claim that blacks rioted "mainly for fun and profit" prior to the Holy Week Uprisings. While Banfield's largely theoretical work utilized examples drawn almost exclusively from studies of Watts and Detroit, in other words before 1968, in fact, he did not fully spell out his views until 1970, the year his very influential book *The Unheavenly City* was published. Put somewhat differently, rather than seeing Agnew's proclamations as an outgrowth of Banfield's publication, it is more accurate to consider Banfield's theories as scholarly window dressing for Agnew's stump speeches.[19]

Banfield and Agnew's analysis went hand in hand in one additional way; both cast the media as part and parcel of the culturally permissive liberal establishment. The media, Banfield argued, encouraged rioting via its "sensational coverage [which] appealed directly to the criminal element." By legitimizing rioting, he asserted, liberal intellectuals and moderate civil rights activists increased the probability of their taking place. This claim echoed Agnew's assertion that the media's coverage of Richard Nixon's November 3, 1969 "Silent Majority" speech, in particular, and of everything from the Vietnam War to race relations, in general, reflected the unacceptable bias of a "small fraternity" of privileged men "whose views did not represent those of the majority of Americans." Termed at

---

[18] Moynihan, "The Moynihan Report"; Perlstein, *Nixonland*, p. 394.
[19] Banfield, *The Unheavenly City*, pp. 212–223. For a critical review of Banfield's book, see Jeff Greenfield, "Urban Problems – Once Over Lightly," *NYT*, September 1970, p. BR8; and Duane Lockard, "Review of *The Unheavenly City*," *Transaction* (March–April, 1971), p. 69. For more favorable views, see "Britain's Riots," *Wall Street Journal*, July 14, 1981, p. 30; and Thomas Sowell, "'The Unheavenly City Revisted,'" *The American Spectator*, February 1994; Robert Nisbet, "Book Review: The Unheavenly City," *The Intercollegiate Review*, Fall 1970, pp. 3–10; T. R. Moarmor, *Commentary*, July 1, 1972; and Mike Konczal, "Rioting Mainly for Fun and Profit: The Neoconservative Origins of Our Police Problem," http://rooseveltinstitute.org/rioting-mainly-fun-and-profit-neoconservative-origins-our-police-problem/ [accessed January 26, 2016].

the time the most anti-media presentation by a political leader in American history, Agnew's attach, on those he subsequently designated as the "nattering nabobs of negativism," still resonates fifty years later in conservative lambasts of the "lame-stream media."[20]

A bit less obviously, Agnew's speeches and the favorable responses they garnered reflected the nation's growing concerns about gender. Americans had been experiencing a crisis of masculinity for over a century and the drive to appear manly had influenced politicians as far back as Teddy Roosevelt. The rise of the women's liberation movement as well as the counterculture reignited fears about the decline of masculinity and Agnew's appeal rested, in part, on his ability to cast himself as a "real man" as opposed to liberals, who he described as unmanly or "effete." This was especially the case with regards to whether or not troops and police should be allowed to shoot rioters, with Agnew's (and Daley's) pro-use of force stance portrayed as the manly position and the liberal non-use of lethal force as the unmanly one. Moreover, in short order, in terms that presaged the rise of an antifeminist movement, personified by Phyllis Schlafly's anti-ERA crusade, Spiro Agnew would portray feminists as part and parcel of the "radlib" menace which, in his estimation, threated the very existence of the American republic. (When Agnew faced demands that he should resign from the vice presidency, Phyllis Schlafly proved one of his staunchest defenders.)[21]

Agnew was a master at conflating the different social movements of the latter half of the 1960s, besmirching them all via sharply barbed rhetorical attacks, and via his persona. Or, to borrow an insight from Richard Hofstadter, via his willingness and ability to play status rather than interest politics, to self-identify with the so-called "Middle Americans" (later termed the silent majority by Nixon) – those who opposed urban and

[20] Banfield, *Unheavenly City*, pp. 225–233; Spiro T. Agnew, "Address to Midwest Regional Republican Committee Meeting, Des Moins Iowa, November 12, 1969, in *Impudent Snobs: Agnew vs. Intellectual Establishment*, ed. by John Coyne Jr. (New Rochelle, NY: Arlington House, 1972), pp. 265–270. See also Levy, "Spiro Agnew."

[21] Spiro T. Agnew "English Anyone?" in *Exploring Language*, ed. by Gary Goshgarian, 8th edn. (New York: Longman, 1998), pp. 409–411; Matthew J. Lassiter, "Inventing Family Values"; and Marjorie J. Spruill, "Gender and America's Right Turn," both in *Rightward Bound: Making of American Conservative in the 1970s*, ed. by B. Schulman and J. Zelizer (Cambridge, MA: Harvard University Press, 2008); Charlotte Curtis, "Judy Agnew – From Obscurity to National Spotlight in 10 Minutes," *NYT*, August 9, 1968; "Obituary: Judy Agnew, Wife of Vice President," *NYT*, June 28, 2012, p. B15. For more on Agnew's resignation, see Peter B. Levy, "Go Quietly or Else: The Resignation of Vice President Spiro T. Agnew," *Maryland Historical Magazine*, 110:2 (Summer 2015): 226–251.

campus unrest, supported American troops in Vietnam, and openly displayed their support for their country, flag, and traditional family values – Agnew came to embody the conservative critique of radicals and their liberal enablers. In contrast, many other politicians in the postwar era played down their identity – for example, Kennedy had to transcend his Catholicism and Johnson his southern ties. Or as Arthur Schlesinger, who was no fan of Agnew astutely put it: Agnew "grew up during the Depression, dropped out of college, served bravely in the war and studied law in night school. Nothing was easy for him." In time, Schlesinger continued, "he has emerged as hero, or villain, not in the battle of programs but in the battle of life styles ... With his Lawrence Welk records and his Sunday afternoons with the Baltimore Colts, Mr. Agnew was the archetype of the forgotten American who had made it."[22] Conservative columnist John Hay agreed, adding that it was Agnew's penchant for making political gaffes and his relative plebian background, which liberal commentators ridiculed, that made him so attractive to Middle America. "He is the personification of the 'American Dream' of success and affluence," and while he is criticized "for achieving the goals and respecting the standards his generation was taught and urged to achieve and respect, the fact remains that those same standards and values continue to be respected by an overwhelming majority of the American people who refuse to concede that either God or the American Dream is dead and are convinced that an affluent 'square' society, pursuing a course somewhere down the middle of the road is more desirable than anarchy."[23]

This said there was one thing missing from Schlesinger's and Hofstadter's point about Agnew's ability to appeal to identity politics; they left out that Agnew was also white and race played a crucial role in who he was and the reasons why other whites identified with him. He had fought in a segregated army, lived in white suburbs, and championed white cultural heroes, like Lawrence Welk. In addition, as a

[22] Arthur Schlesinger, "The Amazing Success Story of 'Spiro Who?'" NYT, July 26, 1970, www.nytimes.com/books/00/11/26/specials/schlesinger-spiro.html [accessed January 18, 2013]. For an historian who emphasizes Agnew's role in promoting identity politics, particularly the burgeoning ethnic rights politics of the early 1970s, see Kenneth Durr, *Behind The Backlash: White Working-Class Politics in Baltimore, 1940–1980* (Chapel Hill: University of North Carolina Press, 2003), chs. 5 and 6.

[23] Gary Wills, "The Agnew Controversy Refuses to Die" and John Hay, "The Rebuttal," both in *Esquire*, February 23, 1969, in Spiro T. Agnew, Vertical File, Enoch Pratt Free Library, Baltimore, Maryland. See also Rudy Abramson, "Agnew Suburbia's Regular Guy," *Pacific Stars & Stripe*, September 7, 1968, pp. 10–11, from Spiro T. Agnew, Vertical File, Richard Nixon Presidential Library, Yorba Linda, CA.

Greek-American, Agnew symbolized the bulging white middle class with ethnic roots, whose economic fortunes rested to a large degree on privileges reserved for white Americans, from home loans guaranteed by the federal government to educational benefits, which in Agnew's home state flowed disproportionately to white schools. No wonder he and millions of other whites continued to believe in traditional values. The system had worked for them while it simultaneously shrouded the degree to which it fostered caste privileges.[24]

"An American Citizen's First Right Is Safety for Himself and His Family"

Agnew not only helped frame the public's understanding of what had caused the "riots," he played a key role in shaping how Americans should respond to them, in particular, and to the broader rise in disorder and crime in general. As noted earlier, in the immediate aftermath of King's assassination, a national debate erupted over whether the government had used enough force or not. On one side stood Chicago's Mayor Richard Daley who, during the riots in the Windy City, had ordered police to shoot to kill arsonists and maim looters. On the other side stood Attorney General Ramsey Clark who defended the policy of the restrained use of lethal force. Public opinion surveys and investigative reporting revealed that most Americans not only blamed radicals for the unrest, they believed that the government should have responded with greater force. A CBS poll revealed that "90% of whites believed the police should be tougher in responding to riots." Similarly, 62 percent of a nationwide sample supported shooting looters. Thomas B. Edsall, who would later write a well-respected study of white backlash, found similar sentiment in Baltimore. Leonard Kerpelman, a former civil rights lawyer, for instance, told Edsall that he believed that the National Guard "should have shot to kill." Numerous small business owners joined together to sue the city for failing to use "all reasonable diligence to prevent the uprising." Vincent Cala, a former city official and activist within the Republican Party, organized a "Citizens National League" to lobby lawmakers to empower

---

[24] Ira Katznelson, *When Affirmative Action Was White: An Untold History of Racial Inequality in Twentieth-Century America* (New York: W. W. Norton, 2006); David Roediger, *Working Toward Whiteness: How American Immigrants Became White: The Strange Journey from Ellis Island to the Suburbs* (New York: Basic Books, 2006); Lizabeth Cohen, *A Consumer's Republic: The Politics of Mass Consumption in Postwar America* (New York: Vintage Press, 2003).

law enforcement officials to respond with greater force in future outbreaks. We "will urge city councilmen, State lawmakers and congressman to allow the laws of this country to again be enforced." Similarly, Baltimore's State Senator Joseph Berrelli, who represented the First District of Baltimore, comprised primarily of white residents, submitted a "Scavenger" bill, which would make it easier to prosecute looters and increase their penalty upon conviction.[25]

During the revolt Agnew had done little to suggest that he opposed the official government policy, yet afterwards, when asked about his position regarding shooting looters and arsonists, he made clear that he stood with Daley. While he felt it was improper to shoot a twelve-year-old youth who was seen with a box of matches, he endorsed Daley's order that authorities had the obligation to shoot someone who had "hurled a Molotov cocktail" into a building. When probed by the press if this meant he favored shooting unarmed looters, Agnew emphasized that if criminals were allowed to flee from the police, "the whole system of law and order will break down." "Nobody will ever submit to arrest if they believe nothing will happen if they run." Put somewhat differently, Agnew insisted that authorities could employ "any means necessary – and . . . that includes shooting" an unarmed suspect.[26]

As the summer turned to fall, both before and after Richard Nixon surprised virtually everyone by nominating him to serve as his running-mate, Agnew maintained this line. As he informed over 4,000 members of the American Legion at their annual convention, "Confronted with a choice, the American people would choose the policeman's truncheon over the anarchists' bomb."[27] Before an equally appreciative audience of orthodox Greeks, the vice presidential nominee attacked the "insidious relativism" that had handcuffed the ability of the National Guard and

[25] Thomas B. Edsall, "White Liberals Concerned, Outraged Over Rioting," *Evening Sun* (Baltimore, MD), April 11, 1968, p. F12.
[26] On support for Agnew's tough stance, see Paul Kach to Spiro T. Agnew, May 16, 1968 and Robert Campbell to Spiro T. Agnew, May 30, 1968; Henry Finklestein to Spiro T. Agnew, May 7, 1968, all in Governor Agnew Papers; see also "Transcript of News Conference," April 18, 1968, in Addresses and State Papers of Spiro T. Agnew, Governor of Maryland 1967–69, Archives of Maryland online, www.msa.md.gov/megafile/msa/speccol/sc2900/ sc2908/000001/000083/html/index.html [accessed August 19, 2010]. For a description of the national debate, see "Clark Opposes Force in Riots," *Baltimore Sun*, April 18, 1968, p. A1; "Agnew Expands Views on Shots at Looters," *Evening Sun* (Baltimore, MD), August 2, 1968, p. D14; "Agnew: Let Police Fire at Looters," *Washington Post*, August 2, 1968, p. A1.
[27] Agnew and Ready quoted in William Morrissey, "The Police vs. Terrorists: It's All in How It's Handled," *Baltimore Sun*, September 6, 1970, p. K1.

police to protect the community. Imagine the plight of the "agonizing police officer who couldn't bring himself to kill a looter over a pair of shoes," Agnew declared. "Where does this line of reasoning end? Do you kill a thief over a pair of boots? A diamond ring? When a person is looting another's property can his depth of involvement be measured by the monetary or material value of his loot?" Without explicitly answering these rhetorical questions, he implied that the scale of justice should tilt toward the protection of property over human life.[28]

Likewise, in reference to the riots that had taken place during the Democratic convention, Agnew praised the actions of Chicago's police. "The riot in downtown Chicago was deliberately planned," asserted Agnew. "Some rioters," he alleged, "wore razor blades attached to their shoes, for kicking policeman." The following day, Agnew returned to this same theme, delivering an "11-page speech on law and order," with the crowd of close to 25,000 white Chicagoan suburbanites responding particularly enthusiastically to Agnew's assertion that "an American citizen's first right is safety for himself and his family, and that right shall be secured." (This attack on the demonstrators in Chicago illustrated Agnew's conflation of different social movements.)[29]

Opinion polls demonstrated the degree to which Agnew's views resonated with much of the white public. In a retrospective analysis, sociologists Howard Schuman and Maria Krysan argued that 1968 represented a turning point in white attitudes regarding race relations and civil rights. In 1963, at the height of the nonviolent phase of the movement, Schuman and Krysan write, only 19 percent of whites blamed "blacks themselves" for their disadvantages. A far larger plurality, 43 percent, blamed whites. By the late spring of 1968, in contrast, 58 percent of whites blamed "blacks themselves for their disadvantages," a dramatic shift that persisted for at least thirty years. Likewise, a survey of whites who worked but did not live in Baltimore's "ghettos," found that the majority believed that "rioting was caused more by the agitation of militants than problems of poverty and unemployment." The same survey revealed that the majority of whites felt that blacks had "already achieved as much equality as he [*sic*] deserves." This does not mean that Schuman and Krysan viewed the uprisings as creating white backlash. Rather, they suggested that these poll numbers displayed a "reversion

[28] "Riot Study Criticized by Agnew," *Washington Post*, July 31, 1968, p. C1.
[29] "Agnew Hits Democrats on Law Issue," *Washington Post*, September 16, 1968, p. A2; "Politics: Agnew Opens His Campaign," *NYT*, September 5, 1968, p. 40.

toward assumptions that were even more widespread earlier." In other words, only during a very brief window, between roughly 1963 and 1967, did whites display a greater openness to viewing themselves as culpable and to supporting substantial remedies to the persistence of racial inequality.[30]

One of the by-products of this conservative retrenchment, one which many liberals, including President Johnson supported, was a self-declared "war on crime," which included both stiffer penalties and the militarization of police forces around the country. By mid-May 1968, for instance, Baltimore's city council had appropriated funds that enabled its police forces to purchase additional "riot gear," including tear gas grenades. The Maryland Crime Investigating Committee recommended supplying police forces with "mace" which the newspaper described as "an innocent-looking black squirt can...which propels a stream of super tear gas for a distance of 20 feet." A few months later, the city arranged to "borrow" armored vehicles which had "gun ports on both sides," during future "emergency situations."[31]

In addition to more arms, local citizens favored empowering the police to the fullest degree possible. For instance, a twenty-eight-person commission of Baltimore citizens, led by Comptroller Hyman Pressman, declared that "just as in time of war against a foreign enemy, we must adopt the same methods and means to fight and defeat this domestic enemy." This included the expansion of "stop and frisk" procedures. By the early 1970s, Baltimore, like many other cities across the nation, had procured a fleet of helicopters. Especially given their cost, at upwards of $100,000 a piece, the efficacy of these machines in fighting crime was problematic, and some local politicians like councilwoman and future Senator Barbara Mikulski insisted that "if the battle against crime is to be won it will be won in the streets by the community itself and not by modern technology." Nonetheless, the desire to have a greater arsenal of weapons to contain urban disorders convinced the city to go ahead with their purchase. Notably, one of the first places where state helicopters were deployed was in Hartford

---

[30] Howard Schuman and Maria Krysan, "A Historical Note on Whites' Beliefs About Racial Inequality," *American Sociological Review*, 64 (December, 1999): 847–855; Berk, "The Role of the Ghetto Retail Merchants in Civil Disorders."

[31] "Police to Seek Fund Approval for Riot Gear," *Baltimore Sun*, May 15, 1968, p. C28; "Confused Coordination and Officials Looking Aside Responsible for Unprepared Local Riot Control," *The Daily Record*, June 14, 1968, p. 1; "Armored Truck Loan Plan Set By Police," *Evening Sun* (Baltimore, MD), August 14, 1968, p. C2; "City Equipped with Riot Helmets," *Baltimore News American*, August 30, 1968, p. C1.

County, to hover over the courthouse where H. Rap Brown was supposed to be tried for inciting a riot.[32]

Moreover, in the wake of the initial revolts, the federal government established the Law Enforcement Assistance Administration (LEAA), which initiated, in its own words, "the first national attack on crime in the history of the nation." Jettisoning the traditional wall between the federal government and state and local law enforcement agencies, the LEAA spent $63 million in this war on crime in its first year of existence, an amount which skyrocketed to $699 million in less than four years. Maryland, for example, received $50,000 for combating "riots and civil disorders." A good deal of the LEAA's funding went to training the paramilitary forces, often known as SWAT teams. These units received "specialized military training to deal with riots, hostage situations, and terrorists." Only later did these SWAT teams focus more of their attention on the war on drugs.[33]

Somewhat along the same lines, in the wake of the revolts, Americans also debated what rights rioters should or should not enjoy, a debate which prefigured the adoption of increasingly harsh sentence guidelines for an assortment of crimes, including nonviolent drug offenses. In a study of the performance of the justice system during Baltimore's uprising, the American Friends Service Committee concluded that the justice system had absolutely failed. With its jails overflowing, the study noted, the city had incarcerated men and women at the civic center, which lacked places to sit or sleep, adequate toilet facilities, and a shortage of food. Because of the sheer mass of arrestees, "constitutional rights were knowingly ignored." Suggestions to release the prisoners on their own recognizance were rejected; so as to attain speedy trials, defense attorneys recommended that "their clients waive the right to hear the testimony of their accuser, to cross-examine opposing witnesses, [and] to present witnesses

---

[32] "Police Seek Men, Money," *Baltimore Sun*, February 7, 1969, p. C8; "Police Win Round on Copters," *Baltimore Sun*, February 6, 1973, p. C7. Ironically, Mikulski ultimately voted for procuring the copters. "Rap Brown Stays Away from Trial," *Baltimore Sun*, April 21, 1970, p. A1. WYPR, "'68 The Fire Last Time: Five Part Documentary Series," http://archives.ubalt.edu/bsr/links/wypr.html [accessed March 6, 2016], especially" Part 5: Lessons Learned"; Karena Rahall, "The Green to Blue Pipeline: Defense Contractors and the Police Industrial Complex," *Cardoza Law Review*, 36 (2015). "Military Policing Urged," *Baltimore Sun*, February 20, 1972, p. A26. "Army Troops Vanquish 'Rioters' in 'Riotsville, U.S.A.,'" *Baltimore Sun*, October 5, 1967, p. A5; "Use of Firearms in Riots Deplored," *NYT*, November 26, 1967, p. 37. Kerner Commission, *Report*, chs. 11 and 12.

[33] Susan Welch, "The Impact of Urban Riots on Urban Expenditures," *American Journal of Political Science*, 19:4 (November 1975): 741–760; LEAA, "3rd Annual Report: Fiscal Year 1971" (Washington, DC: GPO, 1972).

in their own defense." If a defendant objected to these concessions, he or she was "held over for bail," which was "impossible" to obtain "because bail bondsmen were not available." Prosecutors and judges also threatened defendants with more serious charges if they did not plead guilty to lesser crimes. The Friends' report added that since the court could not prove looting charges (technically larceny), judges imposed "rather heavy penalties for curfew violations."[34]

Published weeks after King's assassination, the Friends' report probably underestimated the degree to which the system had failed. Months later, many of those convicted of the most serious crimes, such as arson and murder, had their convictions overturned or their sentences dramatically reduced because of miscarriages of justice during the revolts. In mid-November 1968, after Agnew had been elected vice-president, Louis Price, who had been convicted on arson charges, was freed from prison when the State Attorney's office acknowledged that it "had found inaccuracies in the testimony of a former police officer," the only eyewitness to the alleged crime. At the trial, Officer Gregory Ferrell claimed that he saw Price depart the headquarters of the Student Nonviolent Coordinating Committee and encourage a crowd to "burn and loot and warn merchant to close their shops or be burned out." Only when faced with "gaps" in the Ferrell's testimony did the state order Price's release, and even then the judge refused to grant a motion for a new trial on the lesser disorderly conduct charges.[35] The following spring, The Maryland Court of Special Appeals similarly overturned the arson conviction of an eight-year-old black youth who had been sentenced to eight years in jail. In issuing its opinion, the Appeals Court noted that the state had not offered any expert testimony regarding the cause of the fire nor shown that the youth had precipitated the blaze.[36] Likewise, in 1972, four years after being sentenced to life in prison, Robert Bradby was acquitted of murdering Louis Albrecht. (Bradby's arson conviction was upheld and his sentence was reduced to ten years.)[37]

Yet neither these reversals nor the Friend's report convinced the majority of whites that the government had acted too harshly. The Friends

[34] Motz, "Report on the Baltimore Civil Disorders," April 1968.

[35] "Court Frees Man Accused in Charges Related to Riot," *Baltimore Sun*, November 16, 1968, p 15.

[36] "Arson Term Overturned," *Baltimore Sun*, March 20, 1969.

[37] "Man Acquitted In Fire Death, Once Pleaded Guilty," *Baltimore Sun*, April 5, 1972; and "Firebomb thrower's term cut to 10 years after appeal," *Baltimore Sun*, May 11, 1972, p. 16.

acknowledged this by explicitly lamenting the public's (white) willingness to accept increasingly severe measures, from the "enactment of stop-and-frisk laws" to the militarization of police forces. Unlike the Friends, the Committee on the Administration of Justice under Emergency Conditions found that the city had performed "admirably."[38] A separate published report by the "Maryland Crime Investigating Commission" concluded that in case of a future outbreak of violence, force should be used "whenever force is necessary to accomplish the preservation of the law and order." The crime commission even suggested that the failure to use lethal force had allowed the "riot" to escalate. This commission also approvingly quoted a pledge made by Newark's director of police that next time around, "there won't be any fooling around." Next time, "fifteen minutes after the crowd starts gathering, we'll have 100 men there, armed with shotguns. We will disperse the crowd, and our patrols will keep it dispersed."[39] Given that the authorities had used deadly force during Newark's revolts and killed tens of men and women, a number of whom were clearly innocent bystanders, it remains unclear what the police director meant when he suggested that they had "fooled around" in 1967.

"[The Poor] Refuse to Sit in the Corner While Others... Decide Their Welfare"

When Spiro Agnew addressed Baltimore's black leaders in the wake of King's assassination and the Holy Week Uprising, he sought to undermine the Kerner Commission's argument that social and economic ills had caused the revolts and to promote a more forceful response to the disorders sweeping America. Claims that he was jeopardizing his political career notwithstanding, he also had good reason to believe that his denunciation of black radicals would resonate with the broader, predominantly white public. Perhaps Agnew also hoped that his dose of tough love would prod black moderates to condemn black radicals. After all the civil rights movement had not been united prior to King's death; most moderate groups had opposed the rise of Black Power, including CORE's

---

[38] "Report of the Baltimore Committee on the Administration of Justice Under Emergency Conditions" (City of Baltimore, May 31, 1968); for an electronic copy of report, see http://archives.ubalt.edu/bsr/archival-resources/documents/may-31-1968.pdf [accessed October 17, 2014].

[39] Maryland Crime Investigating Commission, "A Report of the Baltimore Civil Disturbance of April, 1968," June 4, 1968, http://archives.ubalt.edu/bsr/archival-resources/documents/baltimore-civil-disturbances.pdf [accessed January 26, 2016].

decision to select Baltimore as its "Target City" in 1966. However, this ploy utterly backfired. Not only did the black leaders who assembled for Agnew's speech condemn the governor's pronouncements, the black community in Baltimore united afterwards and it did so around essentially a Black Power agenda. As Rev. Marion Bascom of the Interdenominational Ministerial Alliance observed, Agnew's attempt to "deliberately ... divide us," produced the opposite results. Or as Parren Mitchell, brother of Clarence Mitchell Jr., the so-called 101st Senator, put it: Agnew's rebuke "provided the platform on which a much tougher, more militant Black group ... could come into existence."[40]

Put a bit differently, most blacks responded much differently to King's death and to the uprisings that followed than did most whites. Not only did they reject the argument that the nation should respond to the uprisings by adopting ever more forceful measures, they tended to move beyond the Kerner Commission's recommendation, which, at its best, called for increased federal funding to address the social and economic ills that undergirded the revolts. This is not to suggest that they opposed what many termed a domestic Marshall plan but many *also* demanded a restructuring of society. Only by attaining more political and economic power, the power to check the abuses of the police and to control the destinies of their communities, from the public housing projects where they lived to the schools in their neighborhoods, and by taking greater pride in who they were as a people, could blacks overcome a system which had demeaned them for centuries. Moreover, this newfound unity around a militant platform was not unique to Baltimore, suggesting that those who cast King's death as the demise of the movement have misinterpreted the civil rights years.[41]

While Baltimore's black residents united around a Black Power platform, broadly defined, they did not coalesce around a single organization or leader. Instead, in the wake of the uprisings, the black freedom struggle took on a much more decentralized structure. As a result, Baltimore's story is a bit more difficult to see and tell than in places where single organizations and/or leaders predominated, such as the Black Panther Party in Oakland and Amiri Baraka in Newark. Nonetheless, the decentralized structure of Baltimore's Black Power movement, its lack of a unifying

---

[40] Bascom and Mitchell quoted in Williams, "The Pursuit of Audacious Power," pp. 234–235. See also Joseph, Neighborhood Rebels; Thompson, *Whose Detroit?*; Grady-Willis, *Challenging U.S. Apartheid.*

[41] Marable, *Race, Reform, and Rebellion*, pp. 118, 128–176; Woodard, "Message from the Grassroots," p. 93; Woodard, *A Nation within a Nation.*

organization of figure, should not mislead us into concluding that the movement was in disarray or went into retreat.[42]

One organization that emerged following King's death was a newly formed chapter of the Black Panther Party (BPP). Founded in the fall of 1968 with an office on Eager Street, near the epicenter of the previous spring's revolt, the branch included a number of Vietnam veterans, including Marshall Conway. Conway, who, in his own words, "had tried SNCC and the Republic of New Africa," dedicated himself to the BPP because he felt it "would have an impact on the lives of people." As in other cities, the Panthers focused much of their attention on providing free breakfasts for poor youths and combating police abuse. Even though the Panthers were strongly opposed by the local NAACP, with Lillie M. Jackson comparing the BPP to the KKK, a number of the NAACP's traditional allies supported the Panther's efforts. Most notably, the Sharp Street United Memorial Methodist Church, Jackson's place of worship, allowed the BPP to use its facilities for its breakfast program and when Jackson sought to evict the Panthers, Reverend Clifford convinced its board of trustees not to do so on the grounds that the BPP's efforts paralleled its mission of community service. Likewise, when the BPP came under attack by local, state, and federal authorities, a broad coalition of leftists, black and white, ranging from peace activists allied with the Berrigan brothers to the ACLU, came to its defense.[43]

As in other cities, the Panthers attracted new members via its militant positions and look and feel. As Steve McCutchen observed, the BPP's colors, in other words its clothing, language, and use of symbols, "impressed people." While the Baltimore chapter did not "patrol or monitor the police," presumably because Maryland's law banned individuals from openly carrying guns, it did espouse self-defense and touted the national organization's reputation for standing up to the cops. One of the main

---

[42] Thomas Anthony Gass, "A Mean City: The NAACP and the Black Freedom Struggle in Baltimore, 1935–1975," PhD dissertation, Ohio State University, 2014; Lee Sartain, *Borders of Equality: The NAACP and the Baltimore Civil Rights Struggle, 1914–1970* (Jackson: University Press of Mississippi, 2013).

[43] Judson L. Jeffries, "Revising Panther History in Baltimore," in *Comrades: A Local History of the Black Panther Party*, ed. by Judson L. Jeffries (Bloomington: Indiana University Press, 2007), pp. 15–46; Judson L. Jeffries, "Black Radicalism and Political Repression in Baltimore: The Case Study of the Black Panther Party," *Ethnic and Racial Studies*, 25:1 (January 2002): 64–98; Marshall Conway, *Marshall Law: The Life & Times of a Baltimore Black Panther* (Edinburg: AK Press, 2011); "Panthers Supported in Baltimore," *Washington Post*, December 22, 1969, p. B7. On Jackson and the BPP, see Gass, "A Mean City," pp. 422–423.

ways that the Panthers spread their message and recruited new members was by selling its newspaper, *The Black Panther*. Indeed, even though Baltimore's chapter never had many official members, it sold thousands of copies of this paper – by one account Baltimore sold the third highest number of papers of any branch in the nation – suggesting that its reach was far greater than its membership – only New York and Chicago received more Panther papers than Baltimore.[44]

Some Panther members also worked with the newly formed "Soul School," which had been founded by veterans of the civil rights movement with the goal of instilling a sense of pride in the black community.[45] One of the Panthers members was Paul Coates, who along with his wife mentored their son, Ta-Nehisi Coates, on a variety of black nationalist and Afro-centric traditions.[46] Long before Ta-Nehisi became one of America's best-known black intellectuals, however, the Panthers had disappeared from Baltimore, a byproduct of external repression and internal disagreements. Judson Jeffries writes, the "police went to great lengths to put the Panthers out of business," and other state agencies did the same. This included winning a court-ordered injunction that prohibited the BPP from selling its newspaper and banning its members from speaking at public schools to planting informants and provocateurs within the organization. This repressive effort culminated with a mass raid on the BPP's homes and office on May 1, 1970. Even before this raid, the police had arrested Marshall Conway and charged him with murdering a policeman, a charge he denied but refused to fight in court because he considered the proceedings to be illegitimate.[47]

[44] Steve D. McCutchen, "Selections from a Panther Diary," in *The Black Panther Party Reconsidered*, ed. by Charles Jones (Baltimore: Black Classic Press, 1998), pp. 115–134. On the sale of Panther newspapers in Baltimore, see US Congress, *Hearings Before Committee on Internal Security, House of Representatives, 91st Congress, 2nd Session, 1970* (Washington, DC: GPO, 1971), p. 4992.

[45] Jeffries, "Revising Panther History in Baltimore"; Jeffries, "Black Radicalism and Political Repression in Baltimore"; Conway, *Marshall Law*; "Black Panthers Step Up Activity," *Baltimore Sun*, January 1, 1969, p. C16; "School Talks By Black Panther Banned," *Baltimore Sun*, March 28, 1969, p. A9; "Panthers Supported in Baltimore," *Washington Post*, December 22, 1969, p. B7; "Soul School and Black History," http://therealnews .com/t2/index.php?option=com_content&task=view&id=31&Itemid=74&jumival= 13339 [accessed March 28, 2016]; "Baltimore Organization Educates Community Through Roots and Culture," https://warptown.com/baltimore-organization-educates-community-through-roots-and-culture/ [accessed September 8, 2017].

[46] Ta-Nehisi Coates, *The Beautiful Struggle: A Memoir* (New York: Spiegel & Grau, 2008).

[47] Jeffries, "Revising Panther History in Baltimore"; Jeffries, "Black Radicalism and Political Repression in Baltimore"; Conway, *Marshall Law*. FBI material on the Baltimore

To truly appreciate the impact of the Black Panthers in Baltimore, in particular, and the black power surge which it represented, we must recognize the multiple ways it resonated with many black people. Even when the local chapter of the Panthers disintegrated due to state repression, its ideas were championed by others. One clear example of this was the impact that the Panthers and Black Power had on black youths. Nkenge Touré, born Anita Stroud in 1951, who joined the Panthers in the late 1960s (probably 1969), recalled that the first time she saw the iconic photo of Huey Newton armed with a rifle and a spear she was "just in awe." At the time, she was a student at the newly desegregated Eastern High School, where, due to the extent of discrimination and prejudice on the part of students, teachers, and administrators, she decided to form an underground club called the "Black Voice." In the wake of King's assassination, Touré recalled, black students who joined this group, including herself, became increasingly militant. For instance, she helped organize a walkout after a confrontation with a white teacher. When authorities arrested Touré and seven other female students for this action, the broader community rallied to their defense – they were called the "Eastern Eight," which put them in the same company as the Chicago Seven, plus Bobby Seale, the "New York 21," and the "New Haven or Connecticut Eight," all nationally known political prisoners. To display their support for the "Eastern Eight," some sympathetic students set fire to Forest Park School, prompting its temporary closure.[48]

Touré's actions, as suggested above, were representative of a broader phenomenon that this study cannot do justice, namely the wave of black

branch of the Panthers includes: FBI Director to SAC, Baltimore, March 14, 1968; FBI Director to SAC, Baltimore, March 28, 1968; FBI Director to SAC Baltimore, n.d.; FBI Director to SAC Baltimore, September 5, 1968; FBI Director to SAC Baltimore, September 30, 1968; FBI Director to SAC, Baltimore, October 14, 1968; FBI Director to SAC, Baltimore, December 2, 1968; FBI Director to SAC Baltimore, March 3, 1969; all in COINTELPRO, Black Nationalist Hate Groups, https://vault.fbi.gov/cointel-pro/cointel-pro-black-extremists/cointelpro-black-extremists-part-10-of [accessed various times]; "Panthers Supported in Baltimore," *Washington Post*, December 22, 1969, p. B7; McCutchen, "Selections from a Panther Diary," pp. 125–127.
48 "Voices of Feminism Oral History Project: Nkenge Toure, Interview by Loretta Ross," December 4–5, and March 23, 2005, Washington, DC, www.smith.edu/libraries/libs/ssc/vof/transcripts/Toure.pdf [accessed June 24, 2016]; "Black Pupils Air Baltimore Demand," *Washington Post*, February 17, 1970, p. C1; "100 Arrested at Baltimore High School," *Washington Post*, February 19, 1970, p. E1; "School Fire Blamed on Arson," *Baltimore Sun*, April 7, 1970, p. C22; "Expelled Senior Misses Hearing," *Baltimore Sun*, May 1, 1970, p. A10. See also Leah Worthington, "Black Panther Women: Armed with Politics and Guns in the Winston-Salem, Philadelphia, and Baltimore Branches," MA thesis, University of Charleston, South Carolina, 2016.

student activism that swept across the nation in the late 1960s and early 1970s. Partly inspired by black college student protests, reinforced by King's assassination, the Holy Week Uprisings, and the rise of the Black Panther Party, these protests illustrated that the movement did not decline after Holy Week 1968. As Charles Billings demonstrated, a substantial percentage of black students identified with black nationalist objectives, found violence to be a "valuable" or acceptable means to achieve one's goals, and believed that the "system" was "breaking up." Even among nonactivists, Billings found a sizable number who shared these sentiments.[49]

Other sources similarly recognized the breadth of the high school rebellion. For instance, in a story that contextualized the Touré-led walkout at Baltimore's Eastern High School, the *Afro-American* reported that "nearly one in five of the nation's high schools had some kind of demonstration last year [fall 1968–spring 1969]." While multiple issues, from dress codes and the Vietnam War precipitated many of these protest, "racial issues were involved in 30 per cent" of the total. In addition, the *Afro-American* observed, in the late 1960s and early 1970s, the incidences of interracial violence in high schools rose precipitously, in part because black students became increasingly assertive and demanded equal treatment and respect. For example, at Northern High School in Baltimore, a school of 2,800 students, 85 per cent of whom were white, black students formed a group named "Black Awareness" which sported buttons that read "end discrimination" and organized meetings to protest against the general attitude of teachers, administrators, and students, including the administration's decision to prohibit them from holding a talent show. As William Golden, one of the few black teachers at Northern and a supporter of the Black Awareness group, stated, the protest over the talent show was "just the tip of the iceberg." Students wanted to hold the show in order to "bring some pride to our people." But they also sought to raise white awareness of many other forms of "subtle" and "latent" forms of discrimination, from threats to transfer black protesters out of Northern to the intimidation of teachers, like himself, who dared stand up for their rights.[50]

49 Billings, "Black Activists and the Schools."
50 "Violence Plagues Nation's Schools as Fall Semester Shakily Commences," *Afro-American*, October 4, 1969, p. 14; "High Schools Act to Defuse Protests," *Washington Post*, September 21, 1969, p. 1; "'We Have Never Had Any Racial Problems,'" *Afro-American*, April 26, 1969, p. 11. On the flag-burning at Northern High School, see

Activists, Inc. displayed the surge of black militancy in Baltimore in the post Holy Week Uprising period as well. Formed prior to King's assassination, Activists, Inc. became increasingly assertive and attracted a growing number or supporters in the immediate aftermath of his death. In addition to calling for greater black representation in City Hall, on community action or poverty initiatives, and in developing educational offerings aimed at enhancing black pride and skills, Activists, Inc. demanded better health care for black Baltimoreans. "Nowhere has the damage to black bodies and minds been more direct" than in the area of health, the group asserted. While rarely considered one of the primary goals of the Black Power movement in Baltimore, attaining better health care by empowering black people became one of the more resonant rallying cries. Activists, Inc., for instance, called for giving black people a greater voice in government and private health organizations, increasing "black ownership of nursing homes, drugstores, medical equipment supply stores, and other health related enterprises," and, in concert with the Maryland Freedom Union and ultimately Local 1199 (see below), organizing black health care workers.[51]

Alongside the Black Panther Party and Activists, Inc. stood a number of more traditional organizations and figures which shared a common interest in enhancing black political and economic power and black pride, even if they simultaneously disagreed with the Panther's emphasis on self-defense and calls for worldwide revolution. This included the aforementioned Marvin Bascom and Vernon Dobson, two of the leaders of the Ministerial Alliance, and Larry Gibson, a recent graduate of Columbia University Law School – often this group was called the "goon squad." While black ministers like Dobson had played a role in the fighting for civil rights for years, in the wake of the uprisings, they became increasingly assertive, rallying residents around the campaigns of black candidates for local, state, and federal office, and, as we will see, promoting black economic initiatives. For instance, with the help of Gibson,

Interview with Nia Redmond, http://archives.ubalt.edu/bsr/oral-histories/transcripts/redmon.pdf.

[51] "Activists Question New School Nominees," *Afro-American*, December 28, 1968, p. 32; "New School Concept to Be Unveiled," *Afro-American*, September 28, 1968, p. 32; "Activists Demand Role in Health," *Afro-American*, April 6, 1968, p. 32; "School Head's Pay Anger Activists," *Afro-American*, May 4, 1968, p. 32; "Model Cities Board Chairman Hits Role of 'Establishment,'" *Afro-American*, May 11, 1968, p. 32; "Crosse Withdraws to Boost Mitchell," *Afro-American*, July 27, 1968, p. 1. On Activists, Inc. and the state of the movement in Baltimore on the eve of King's death, see Mills, *Got My Mind Set on Freedom*, pp. 636–668.

Dobson successfully promoted the election of Joseph Howard as the first black judge in the city over the objection of the party's bosses, white and black. While the "goon squad" could not muster enough votes to elect Parren Mitchell to Congress in 1968, it enjoyed more success the second time around. Among those who joined the campaign to elect blacks to office were Walter Lively, the leader of U-JOIN, James Griffin, a veteran of CORE, and Walter Carter, sometimes termed Baltimore's Martin Luther King for his years of extensive activism in the city.[52]

For a variety of reasons, the push for black political power proved less successful in Baltimore than in a number of other comparable cities. While Gary in Indiana, Cleveland in Ohio, and Newark in New Jersey, for instance, elected black mayors not long after their uprisings, Baltimore did not elect its first black mayor until 1987 and did not gain a majority on the city council until well into the 1990s – this in spite of the fact that blacks comprised a majority of the city's residents as early as 1975. Yet this does not mean that attaining political power did not animate blacks in Baltimore as much as it did blacks in other communities, from Lowndes County in Alabama to Detroit in Michigan. Rather, it revealed that whites in Baltimore were able to develop more sophisticated defenses of their power than whites in these other places.[53]

The push for political power was paralleled by efforts to attain more black economic power. In addition to working with the goon squad which sought to elect more black officials, Vernon Dobson joined forces with an assortment of other prominent Baltimore black leaders to support a chapter of the Opportunities Industrial Center (OIC), a national organization established by Philadelphia's Reverend Leon Sullivan. Begun in 1964, the OIC provided vocational training, fostered business and housing co-ops, and sought subcontracts for black-owned business from large multinational corporations. The OIC's efforts played a role in prodding the Nixon administration to adopt the "Philadelphia Plan," which became a model for affirmative action around the nation. Among the OIC's best-known Baltimore members was Henry J. Parks, the owner of Parks Sausage Company, the first black-owned business to be listed on the New York stock exchange. At a meeting held in Baltimore in December 1968, Sullivan

[52] Smith, *Here Lies Jim Crow*, pp. 214–223; "Election Retrospect: Workers of All Nationalities Helped Bring Howard Victory," *Afro-American*, November 16, 1968, p. 14. For a thorough history of Blacks and Baltimore politics, see Marion Orr, "Black Political Incorporation – Phase Two: The Cases of Baltimore and Detroit," PhD dissertation, University of Maryland, College Park, 1992.

[53] Orr, "Black Political Incorporation."

pledged to help Baltimore's branch of the OIC apply for federal funds, under the Model Cities program. A month later, Baltimore became the ninth city in the nation to receive such a grant, which was to be used to fund educational projects, economic development, and youth programs.[54]

The seeds of Baltimoreans United in Leadership Development or BUILD, a grassroots organization which built upon the principles of Saul Alinsky and dedicated itself to empowering poor neighborhoods, can also be found in the black power surge of the very late 1960s and early 1970s. Beginning in the late 1970s and early 1980s, BUILD challenged the neoliberal redevelopment model that Baltimore's leaders, especially D'Alesandro's successor Donald Schaefer pursued. The most notable example of Schaefer's policy, which the national media celebrated as evidence of Baltimore's successful revival, was the construction of the Inner Harbor, a glitzy combination of shops, restaurants, and museums – including the National Aquarium. Yet echoing both the Black Power movement's critique of the urban redevelopment programs of the 1950s and 1960s and employing some of its same confrontational methods, BUILD countered that the so-called renaissance had not helped working-class and poor Baltimoreans, who were disproportionately black, but rather benefited suburban whites, tourists, and real estate developers. Moreover, BUILD argued that public dollars could be better spent developing human capital, by investing in neighborhood schools and job training. Not surprisingly, many of those who helped establish BUILD in 1977, had been active in the black power surge of the late 1960s and early 1970s, most notably Dobson and Wendell Phillips. BUILD also grew into a prominent force on the local scene because it drew on the strengths and traditions of black female activism, which surged in the wake of King's death.[55]

---

[54] On the OIC, see http://explorepahistory.com/hmarker.php?markerId=1-A-368 [accessed March 24, 2016]; Matthew J. Countryman, *Up Country*, pp. 110–117; Jessica Ann Levy, "From Protest to Entrepreneurism: Leon H. Sullivan, Opportunities Industrialization Centers, Inc., and the Black Empowerment in the United States," Association for the Study of African American Life and History (ASALH), September 23–27, 2015, Atlanta, Georgia (unpublished paper in author's possession). On Russell's participation in OIC, see "OIC Founder's Actions Seen Backing Stand of Workers," *Afro-American*, December 14, 1968, p. 1; on Parks, see www.blackpast.org/aah/parks-henry-green-jr-1916-1989-0 [accessed March 24, 2016]; "Baltimore Model Cities Plan Approved," *Baltimore Sun*, January 18, 1969, p. B20. See James Dilts, "Whatever Happened to Model Cities?" *Baltimore Sun*, October 26, 1969, p. D3.

[55] Orr, "Black Political Incorporation," ch. 7; "BUILD Turns 20 with Gusto," *Baltimore Sun*, February 10, 1977, p. 1B; "Saul Alinsky Legacy Alive in City's BUILD," *Baltimore Sun*, May 31, 1980, p. A16.

Since arrest records and contemporary reportage showed that the overwhelming majority of those who looted stores and committed other acts of violence or destruction were men, it is tempting to suggest that women disapproved of the revolts. Yet, it is worth considering Ashley Howard's proposition that women participated in different ways due to gender roles and expectations, and that afterwards they took the lead in adopting more militant means to combat racial inequality.[56] In their words and deeds black women averred that racism, which manifested itself in housing and welfare policies as well as everyday interactions with white merchants, caused the rebellions, not the "dysfunctional" Negro family. Whereas paleo- and neoconservatives decried expanding welfare benefits and other federal programs because it rewarded "rioters," black women in Baltimore asserted that decent housing, meaningful child support, and living wages were human rights that should not be left up to the whim of state agents or exploitative employers. Put somewhat differently, black female activists argued that it was not the cultural mores of black Americans that needed changing but rather the fundamental belief systems and social structures of American society.[57]

Rhonda Williams's *The Politics of Black Housing* makes clear that the struggle of black women in Baltimore for better housing, welfare rights, and overall dignity began well before the 1960s. Yet, she also observes that it was in the wake of Holy Week Uprising that grassroots groups, composed of public and private housing tenants, emerged as a bona fide force. For instance, beginning at the tail end of the decade, black women in Baltimore joined hands with national tenant organizations to demand better treatment. This included the establishment of resident advisory boards, hiring of blacks to manage public housing projects, and staging of rent strikes against landlords who refused to bring their homes up to code. Simultaneously, organizations led by women lobbied city authorities to apply for federal funding to upgrade public housing and formed housing associations which demanded and won a greater say in running their complexes. Moreover, using public housing projects as a base, poor black woman in Baltimore established locally based welfare rights organizations which became part of a national welfare rights movement. As part of this movement they decried the nation's obscene spending on the

---

[56] Ashley Howard, "Prairie Fires," especially ch. 5.

[57] For an excellent discussion of the discourse on poverty, see Amy Nathan Wright, "Civil Rights 'Unfinished Business': Poverty, Race, and the 1968 Poor People's Campaign," PhD dissertation, University of Texas at Austin, 2007, pp. 35–45.

Vietnam War relative to expenditures at home for public welfare and
Medicare, staged demonstrations and lobbying efforts in state capitals,
and participated in the Poor People's Campaign (PPC) in Washington,
DC.[58]

Amy Nathan Wright has observed that "the media's negative
portrayal...ensured that the popular view of the PPC was that of a failed
campaign." But a closer examination of the PPC suggests that it represented a remarkable effort. It united blacks of different backgrounds and
political and institutional affiliations around what remains arguably the
most pressing problem that faces the nation, persistent intergenerational
poverty, especially among people of color. In seeking to raise public awareness about poverty while simultaneously empowering the poor themselves, the PPC was a part of and not separate from the black power/black
nationalist surge that followed the Holy Week Uprisings. Its failure to
achieve their empowering aim ultimately says more about the breadth of
white resistance to fundamentally altering the racial status than it does
the alleged weakness of the black freedom struggle in the wake of King's
death.[59]

While Ralph Abernathy, Andrew Young, and contingents from Mississippi who rode the so-called "mule train" to Washington, DC, received
the lion's share of the contemporary press' coverage, thousands of black
Americans from cities that had experienced racial revolts participated in
the PPC as well. Hundreds if not thousands of black Baltimoreans, especially black women, lent their support to the campaign and filled the ranks
of those who protested in the nation's capital. On May 15, just over a
month after its Holy Week revolt subsided, between 300 and 500 men
and women gathered at the War Memorial Plaza, adjacent to Baltimore's
City Hall, to display their support for King's final dream. Displaying signs
that read: "I'm Tired of Being Broke," "We Demand Jobs or Money," and
"Hear Us Today or in November," and singing freedom songs from "Ain't
Nobody Gonna Turn Us Round" to "O Freedom," they listened to leaders of the SCLC and the locally based Interdenominational Ministerial

[58] Williams, *The Politics of Black Housing*, especially part III and Epilogue.
[59] Wright, "Civil Rights 'Unfinished Business,'" pp. 223, 528–529. For a fairly traditional
description of the problems faced by the Poor People's Campaign, see Peter Ling, "King's
Assassination Hurt the Poor People's Campaign," in *The Assassination of Martin Luther
King, Jr.*, ed. by Noah Berlatsky (New York: Greenhaven Press, 2011), pp. 103–110;
Gordon Keith Mantler, "King's Assassination Provided a Window of Opportunity for
the Poor People's Campaign," in *The Assassination of Martin Luther King, Jr.*, pp. 111–
122.

Alliance extol the upcoming demonstrations in the nation's capital. In Baltimore, as in the nation, it is unlikely that the different wings of the movement would have joined hands for such an effort before King's death. But after the uprising, activists from CORE and SNCC to the Ministerial Alliance and the local branch of the NAACP proved willing to unite.[60] One Baltimore resident who participated in the rally was a middle-aged black mother of six who went into labor during the event. She informed organizers that her child would be named "Uhuru," the Swahili word for "freedom." Ida Stallings, another woman who attended the rally with her three children, declared that she was participating in the Poor People's Campaign because "I know what poverty is and I want something better."[61]

Spiro Agnew, in contrast, had nothing but negative things to say about the campaign. He accused extremists with having taken over the movement, suggested that "a lot" of people with "Cadillacs" were participating in the "so-called poor people's" demonstrations, and afterwards declared that "Chicago tactics" should have been used against the protesters. Asked to clarify how he would have responded to the assemblage had he been president, he declared: "I think I would have taken the same steps that were taken in Chicago to make certain they didn't use public property as a private hotel." In Chicago, the police had forcibly removed protests form public parks in what many termed a "police riot." Public polls showed that the vast majority of whites sided with Agnew. Sixty-one percent of whites opposed the PPC; only 21 percent supported it.[62] The same polls revealed 80 percent of blacks had a favorable opinion of the PPC.[63]

Agnew's diatribe, notwithstanding, on Solidarity Day, which was held on Juneteenth (June 19), a symbolic day in African American history,

[60] Laura Pearlman, "More Than a March: The Poor People's Campaign in the District," *Washington History*, 26:2 (Fall 2014): 24–41.
[61] "March Activity Starts Here with Plaza Rally," *Afro-American*, May 18, 1968, p. 3; "Poor's March Stops in City for a Night," *Baltimore Sun*, May 17, 1968, p. C26; Mills, *Got My Mind Set on Freedom*, pp. 636–668.
[62] "Governor Agnew Raps Poor's Campaign," *Washington Post*, June 16, 1968, p. A15; "Agnew Says Poor March Called for 'Chicago' Tactics," *Baltimore Sun*, September 22, 1968, p. A1. Poll Shows Races Divided on Poor People's Campaign," *Baltimore Sun*, June 10, 1968, p. A5. Among those to "march in the mud" of Resurrection city was Reverend Walter L. Hildebrand, the pastor of Bethel AME Church. See "New Pastor Hopes Bethel Will Continue Service in the Inner City," *Afro-American*, June 15, 1968, p. 32.
[63] "Poll Shows Races Divided on Poor People's Campaign," *Baltimore Sun*, June 10, 1968, p. A5. "Three Faiths Back March," *Baltimore Sun*, May 7, 1968, p. A8.

an estimated 2,000 Marylanders joined approximately 60,000 men and women from other parts of the nation to listen to speeches from an array of activists, ranging from SCLC stalwarts Ralph Abernathy and Jesse Jackson, to Reies Tijerina and Walter Reuther. Many arrived on one of thirteen buses that departed from Lafayette Square, one of the centers of Baltimore's Holy Week Uprising. Among those to ride in this caravan were members of the Baltimore branch of the CORE, a congregation of black steel workers, and high school students from several Baltimore City schools.[64] One notable Baltimore native who joined them, Clarence Mitchell Jr., compared the PPC to the movement that had produced the *Brown* decision. Even though he had clashed sharply with militants prior to Baltimore's revolt, afterwards, he pledged to support "direct action until the issue of poverty is dealt with."[65] Likewise, Baltimore's NAACP and many church groups clearly moved to the left. Rev. Walter Hildebrand, the newly appointed pastor of Bethel AME Church, a bulwark of Baltimore's black community since its foundation in 1795, "walked in the mud at Resurrection City," to demonstrate his church's renewed commitment to pressure the "power structure of society . . . to do the right thing" and to "make . . . our Democratic ideals real to young people who dislike pretense and sham!"[66]

Also present on Solidarity Day but less noticed were hundreds of women, including some who belonged to Baltimore's chapters of the National Welfare Rights Organization. For example, just before the Juneteenth Solidarity Day, the Poor People's Campaign's newspaper warned: "Women Plan to Display Women Power, Watch Out America!" Afterward, the newspaper explained in militant language that if the government tried to shut down Resurrection City, as it had done during the Bonus March in the early 1930s, women would surround the city and force policemen to confront them first.[67] Building on momentum

[64] "2,000 Marylanders Travel to Washington for Rally," *Baltimore Sun*, June 20, 1968, p. A1; "Model Cities Group Forms," *Baltimore Sun*, February 27, 1968, p. A8; Activists, Inc. "Baltimore Under Siege: the Impact of Financing on The Baltimore Home Buyer, 1960–1970," September, 1971, copy available at: http://cdm16352.contentdm.oclc.org/cdm/singleitem/collection/p16352coll6/id/24/rec/9 [accessed March 25, 2016]; "Students Back Up Washington March," *Afro-American*, May 4, 1968, p. 32.

[65] "Poor's Pleas Bridging Gap," *Afro-American*, June 22, 1968, p. 16; "Hundreds Rally for Poor March," *NYT*, May 16, 1968, p. C20.

[66] "New Pastor Hopes Bethel Will Continue Service in the Inner City," *Afro-American*, June 15, 1968, p. 32.

[67] "'Woman Power' Major Factor in Solidarity Day Activities," *Afro-American*, June 22, 1968, p. 16. Wright, "Civil Rights 'Unfinished Business,'" pp. 276–277, 410.

generated by the PPC, various women-led groups, such as the Associated Negro Appeal, Inc. (ANAI) adopted a more militant posture afterwards, particularly when it came to involving the poor themselves in developing programs aimed at meeting the needs of the black community. "They [the poor]" the ANAI declared approvingly, "refuse to sit in the corner while others who have neither experienced their problems nor suffered the torture of poverty and deprivation decide their welfare." And, by inference, the ANAI expected to involve poor people, especially women, in their efforts going forward.[68]

In the wake of the Holy Week Uprising, black women also pushed for better wages and conditions and union recognition. With the help of the Maryland Freedom Union (MFU), they sought to organize a chapter of Local 1199 of the Health and Hospital Workers Union at Johns Hopkins University, one of the most powerful institutions in the city.[69] Martin Luther King Jr. had called Local 1199 his favorite union and following his death Coretta Scott King spent much of her time and energy in helping it grow, first in Charleston, South Carolina, and then in Baltimore. At an August 1969 rally in Baltimore, Coretta Scott King explained that "her interest in the union campaign was especially strong because most of the 2½ million nonprofessional hospital workers are women…most of them black" (see Figure 6.2). Many of these women, she added, were the main providers for their families and they were "sick and tired of working full-time jobs for part-time pay." Ten years earlier the Building Service Employees International had failed to win union recognition at the hospital. In contrast, in the wake of the uprising and with the support of a coalition of activists, including King, veterans of CORE and SNCC, and white progressives who appreciated the way that Local 1199 married civil rights and antiwar activism, the union succeeded, winning recognition not only at Johns Hopkins but also at Maryland General and Lutheran Hospital. One of Local 1199s key organizers was Robert (Bob) Moore, the very same individual whom Spiro Agnew had singled out as the person Baltimore's civil rights leaders had allegedly refused to condemn because they were fearful of being called "Uncle Toms." One of Moore's co-organizers was Fred Punch, a native of New York who warned that blacks would tear the town down if the hospitals did not recognize the union. Given that Johns Hopkins Hospital lay on the edge of the epicenter of the Holy

[68] "A.N.A.I. to Help Poor," *Afro-American*, August 17, 1968, p. 13.
[69] Flug, "Organized Labor and the Civil Rights Movement of the 1960s."

FIGURE 6.2 Coretta Scott King protests with striking hospital workers in Charleston, SC, in the summer of 1969. She similarly rallied with striking hospital workers in Baltimore later that fall. AP Images.

Week Uprising, this was a warning which Hopkins's leaders evidently felt they could not ignore.[70]

During this same time period, one of the other main sites of employment, namely the docks, also displayed the impact of the black power surge. The Longshoremen's union in Baltimore had been segregated into two locals, one black and one white, essentially since their original charter in the early decades of the twentieth century – Local 829 was the white local and Local 858 was the black local. After the Civil Rights Act of

[70] "From Orderly to Organizer," *Afro-American*, November 8, 1969, p. 20; Robert B. Moore, "Community Unrest: The Rise of Baltimore Local 1199," *Chicken Bones: A Journal* www.nathanielturner.com/communityunrestbaltimore1199.htm [accessed April 8, 2016]; Leon Fink and Brian Greenberg, *Upheaval in the Quiet Zone: A History of the Hospital Workers' Union Local 1199* (Urban: University of Illinois Press, 2009); Punch quoted in: A. H. Raskin, "A Union with 'Soul'" *NYT*, March 22, 1970, p. 231; "Hospital Local 1199 Leaders in Civil Rights, War Protests," *Afro-American*, July 1970, p. 7; "Mrs. King Urges Pro-Union Vote," *Baltimore Sun*, August 27, 1969, p. C28; Greg L. Michel, "Union Power, Soul Power: Unionizing Johns Hopkins University Hospital, 1959–1974," *Labor History*, 38:1 (Winter 1996–1997), pp. 28–66; Robert Moore, "Memoir," www.crmvet.org/vet/moorebob.htm [accessed June 3, 2016].

1964 made such segregated workforces illegal, the International Long-shoremen's Association (ILA) sought to figure out the best way to comply with the law. Leaders of Local 858, the black local, favored desegregating both locals; in contrast, Local 829, the white local, favored merging the two. While he envisioned merging the two unions in the future, Hershey Richardson, president of Local 858, stated he felt it was important to maintain separate locals in the short term. This position reflected the broader civil rights movement's increasing suspicion about the value of integration, more specifically that the merger would diminish black power on the docks, which translated into control of hiring halls, the composition of work gangs, and nature of the union's leadership. Regarding union leadership, William Parrish, the business agent of Local 858, noted that when segregated locals in New York merged, black leadership was eliminated. "And when you eliminate the black leader you eliminate the power of the black people behind him. We don't want that to happen in Baltimore." In reference to the impact that a merger would have on work itself, an anonymous black longshoreman warned it would result in black dockworkers getting all of the "dirty" work. Hiring practices by management, presumably with the complicity of the ILA, which largely blocked blacks from obtaining managerial and supervisorial positions, reinforced black distrust of merging the locals as the best way to comply with the 1964 Civil Rights Act. And as another black dockworker observed, "The merger don't mean a thing if we don't have no black superintendents on the docks."[71]

Assessing the long-term impact of this surge in militancy in the wake of the Holy Week Uprisings is beyond the scope of this chapter. Nor is it the claim of this chapter that this activism represented a brand new

---

[71] *United States of America v. International Longshoremen's Ass'n*, 319 F. Supp. 737 (D Md. 1970), http://law.justia.com/cases/federal/district-courts/FSupp/319/737/2134932/ [accessed June 3, 2016], *United States v. International Longshoremen's Association*, 460 F. 2nd 497 (1972), http://openjurist.org/460/f2d/497/united-states-v-international-longshoremens-association-i-l-a#fn1_ref [accessed June 3, 2016]; "Justice Department Directs ILA to Cease Discrimination," *Baltimore Sun*, April 18, 1969, p. C28; "Integration of ILA Backed," *Baltimore Sun*, October 26, 1966, p. A12; "Integration in ILA Backed," *Baltimore Sun*, October 26, 1966, p. A12; "Black Dock Chiefs Angry," *Baltimore Sun*, April 5, 1972; "Plea Arouses Waterfront Race Tension," *Baltimore Sun*, October 13, 1966, p. C7; "Longshore Unions Split is Reported," *Baltimore Sun*, August 2, 1968, p. C7; "Negro Asks U.S. to View Port Hiring," *Baltimore Sun*, February 16, 1968, p. C7; "Container Exhibit Spurs Dock Workers," *Afro-American*, November 2, 1968, p. 32; "'Mixed feelings' about Merger," *Afro-American*, October 10, 1970, p. 15; "Dockworkers Find No Help in Order to Merge Locals," *Afro-American*, May 10, 1969, p. 19.

phenomenon in Baltimore. On the contrary, as we have seen, Baltimore's freedom movement had a long history. Rather, the goal of this section is to make clear that blacks responded quite differently to King's death and the revolts that followed than did the majority of whites. Much of the activism, from the protest of welfare mothers and the formation of the Black Panther Party to the challenges mounted by students, demonstrated that Baltimore's black community was more than willing to disrupt the racial status quo rather than accommodate calls for law and order in the aftermath of the uprising. Moreover, in words and deeds, black Baltimoreans rejected claims that the revolts were caused by moral failings. On the contrary, as strikes by black female health care workers suggested, they believed that poor wages not poor behavior caused poverty.[72]

Meanwhile, forty-five miles north, in York, Pennsylvania's white leaders, emboldened by Nixon and Agnew's call for law and order, refused to address many of the same conditions that underlay Baltimore's revolt. They even ignored the Pennsylvania Human Relations Commission's strongly worded recommendations to implement meaningful racial reforms or risk their own revolt. Perhaps they did so because they conceived of racial revolts as a problem of large cities, not smaller and midsize communities. Or perhaps they reasoned that they did not need to placate the local civil rights movement because, unlike in Cambridge and Baltimore, blacks in York made up a much smaller percentage of the population and thus lacked even the chance to impact policies at the polls. Regardless, as we shall see, this choice proved a very risky one.

---

[72] King quoted in Wright, "Civil Rights 'Unfinished Business,'" p. 233.

PART III

YORK, PENNSYLVANIA

7

The Promised Land

For where does one run to when he's already in the Promised Land?
Claude Brown, *Manchild in the Promised Land* (1965)

Shortly after sundown on July 21, 1969, Lillie Belle Allen was murdered in York, Pennsylvania. Born and raised in Aiken, South Carolina, Allen, age twenty-seven, had set out the day before with her father and children for Brooklyn, New York, where her older brother Benjamin resided. She planned a brief stop in York along the way to visit her sister Hattie. Having tired of the "southern way of life," her sister later recalled, Lillie Belle was strongly considering moving north. As Allen and her family headed toward York, the nation celebrated mankind's first successful moon landing and Neil Armstrong's unprecedented lunar walk. Unbeknownst to Allen, racial tensions had boiled over in York shortly before she departed Aiken. By the evening of July 21st, dozens of men and women, black and white, had already been shot, including Officer Henry Schaad, a rookie policeman. He would later die from the gunshot wound he incurred on July 18. Yet Allen and her family had little if any sense that they were in danger when they set out to buy some food after a relaxing day in the countryside at her brother-in-law's favorite fishing spot. As they approached the railroad tracks that crossed North Newberry Street, however, members of various white gangs yelled out to each other, "Here comes the niggers" and aimed an arsenal of weapons at their car. Hattie Dickson, Allen's sister, who was driving her father's Cadillac, did not hear any of the warning calls but she distinctly remembers seeing a white man with a gun pointed in her direction. "Lord," she yelled, "they're getting ready to shoot!" In a panic, Hattie tried to turn around.

When the car got stuck on the railroad tracks, Lillie Belle Allen exited the passenger side door with the intention of taking over the driving. But no sooner had she done so than she was met by a fusillade of gunshots. Gary King later testified: "So many bullets…hit the white Cadillac…it was just like somebody sat it out in a field for target practice." Dickson later termed her sister's death a "modern-day lynching," a mob attack on an innocent female with complicity from the police.[1]

Largely ignored by the press and historians and conveniently forgotten by many of York's citizens, Allen's death and the turmoil that surrounded it captured international attention over thirty years later when in mid-May 2001 its two-term mayor, Charlie Robertson, white, was charged with Allen's murder. According to one source, over eighty newspapers worldwide as well as all of the major television networks ran stories on Robertson's arrest. From as far away as Alberta, Canada, to London, England, the story that a mayor of a US city had killed a "preacher's daughter" made headlines. As *Newsweek*, reported: "Mayor Charlie Robertson of York, Pa., should have been a shoo-in this fall for a third term. For the past decade, York has cheerfully prospered under his leadership, and the town of rolling green hills and integrated neighborhoods is still undergoing a $100 million building boom. But…last week, just as the mayor was celebrating a tight Democratic primary victory, police put him in handcuffs." Specifically, authorities charged Robertson, who had been a police officer in 1969, with supplying the bullets that others had used in Allen's murder and inspiring white gang members to defend their turf, which included North Newberry Street. The mayor acknowledged that he had shouted "white power" at a gathering in a nearby park the night before Allen's shooting, but denied having provided one gang member with a 30.06 rifle and encouraging him to "kill as many niggers as you can." He also rebuffed suggestions that he had stated if he "wasn't a cop [he'd] be leading commando raids against Black neighborhoods," as attested to by another witness. Ten other white men were indicted for Allen's murder alongside Robertson. Subsequently, two black men were indicted for

---

[1] William Keisling, *The Wrong Car: The Death of Lillie Belle Allen: A Police Murder Mystery* (Yarbird, Kindle edition, 2002); *Commonwealth v. Robert N. Messersmith, Gregory H. Neff, Charles Robertson, et al.*, Court of Common Pleas of York County, Pennsylvania (henceforth *Commonwealth v. Robert Messersmith et al.*), see especially: "Testimony of Hattie Dickson," "Testimony of Steven Noonan," and "Testimony of Debra Taylor." "Witness Testifies in Race-Riot Slaying," *The Augusta Chronicle* (Georgia), February 28, 2001, p. B3.

the murder of Officer Henry Schaad, whose case, like Allen's, had gone unsolved.[2]

York's revolt and the trials that took place over thirty years after Allen's and Schaad's deaths, provide a third opportunity to reappraise the Great Uprising, to reconsider what took place and why. Most simply, this chapter reaffirms that the revolts of the 1960s, as the Kerner Commission postulated, grew out of the social and economic conditions of America's urban ghettos. But hindsight also allows us to see that in York, as in Cambridge and Baltimore, the Great Uprising grew out of long-standing black struggles to achieve equality and out of white resistance to substantially alter the racial status quo.

York also challenges those who have cast the urban revolts of the 1960s as commodity as opposed to communal riots. On the contrary, in the summer of 1969, blacks in York demonstrated their willingness to defend their homes and selves with arms if necessary from attacks by white civilians and authorities. Likewise, whites in York deployed weapons, including armed personnel carriers and an assortment of high powered rifles because, as suggested above, they sought to maintain the racial order. Put somewhat differently, blacks wanted to change their place, socially, economically, politically, and culturally, and whites resisted such efforts. Indeed, years later white policemen acknowledged that they saw nothing wrong, then or since, with providing guns and ammunition to white gang members so they could protect "their neighborhoods," whereas they never gave a thought to granting blacks the same right. Concomitantly, these same police officers forcefully removed blacks from parks, from corners, and from the downtown streets and, in doing so, conveyed the

---

[2] William Costopoulos with Brad Bumsted, *Murder Is the Charge: The True Story of Mayor Charlie Robertson and the York, Pennsylvania, Race Riots* (Philadelphia: Camino Books, 2004). For international coverage of Robertson's indictment, see "Another 1960s Race Death Trial," *The Weekend Australian*, May 19, 2001, p. 17; "Old Wounds of Racism Reopened," *The Globe and Mail* (Canada), May 18, 2001; "Mayor Fights Poll – and Murder Charge," *The Guardian* (London), May 18, 2001, p. 3. For national coverage, see Amy Worden, "Mayor of York Withdraws From Race," *Philadelphia Inquirer*, May 25, 2001, p. 1; "Indicted York Mayor Says He Won't Step Down," *Philadelphia Inquirer*, May 18, 2001, p. 1; "3 Agree to Testify in Racial Killing," *Philadelphia Inquirer*, June 26, 2001, p. 1. For contemporary coverage of the riot, see "Gunfire Renews as Cyclists Scatter People in York, Pa." *NYT*, July 21, 1969, p. 23; "Woman Killed in York, Pa.," *NYT*, July 22, 1969, p. 33; "Calm Prevails in York, Pa., As Guard and Police Patrol," *NYT*, July 24, 1969, p. 34; "Strain and Calm in York, PA: Guard and Curfew Restore Order on the Surface," *NYT*, July 27, 1969, p. 45.

message that whites, and whites alone, had the right to determine what spaces blacks could occupy and when.

Finally, York's revolt prods us to rethink the places where the Great Uprising occurred. Riots in large metropolises attracted a great amount of national attention at the time and have generated sustained interest by historians and social scientists. York's revolt, in contrast, was largely ignored at the time and, until Mayor Robertson's arrest, forgotten. Without considering riots in York and places like it, in midsize cities with populations between 25,000 and 150,000, where the plurality of the revolts occurred and, in many cases, blacks made up only a small minority of the population, we cannot understand fully the nature and impact of the Great Uprising, including the failure of Americans to grapple with the nation's urban and racial ills. Efforts to do so had always rested on a fragile coalition, and as the history of York demonstrated, they gave way to a desire to deny and repress public memory of the revolts and the conditions that had given rise to them.[3]

"A Time when Racism Was Everywhere"

Because the roots of the unfulfilled expectations and frustrations of African Americans who migrated north originated in the south, our journey to understand York's revolt begins with a brief detour to Aiken, South Carolina, years before Lillie Belle Allen commenced her summer trip. Between 1920 and 1970 hundreds of thousands of South Carolina's blacks left their "native" soil, joining millions of other African Americans in the Great Migration to the north (also west and urban south). A significant percentage of those who did so ended up in Pennsylvania. Of those who moved to York, a disproportionate number came from Aiken and Bamberg counties, South Carolina. They were pushed out by an array of well-known factors, ranging from poverty and unequal education to political powerlessness and the indignity of Jim Crow. But one factor stood out: white violence. Aiken was a Ku Klux Klan stronghold. Its members regularly terrorized blacks, making sure that they stayed in their "place," namely at the bottom and silent.[4]

---

[3] One of the few works to look at rioting in a small or midsize community is: Goodman and Sugrue, "Plainfield Burnings."
[4] I. A. Newby, *Black Carolinians: A History of Blacks in South Carolina from 1895 to 1968* (Columbia: University of South Carolina Press, 1973). "IN MOTION: The African-American Migration Experience," www.inmotionaame.org/home.cfm; jsessionid=f830167081139479995 2260?bhcp=1, especially the charts linked to "The

A particularly notorious lynching in 1926 drove home this feature of white supremacy. As the NAACP's Walter White wrote in *Rope and Faggot*, the brutal triple murder or lynching of Bertha, Damon, and Clarence Lowman of Aiken on October 8, 1926, was conducted with the full knowledge of "members of the South Carolina legislature, relatives of the Governor, lawyers, farmers, business men, and politicians," not to mention the newly minted sheriff, who was an open leader in the Klan. By the time of the killings, Sam Lowman, the son of slaves and the patriarch of the family and the father of three who were slain, had learned to read and write and become a self-sufficient farmer, an owner of a Ford touring car, and a registered voter. Put somewhat differently, Lowman and his family were guilty of demonstrating "too much independence" and for this reason Bertha, Damon, and Clarence Lowman were sent to their graves.[5]

Twenty years later, in the immediate aftermath of World War II, white supremacists in the region again used the weapon of violence to remind blacks of their second class status. In this instance, Sergeant Isaac Woodard, a black World War II veteran who was headed home after three years of serving his country, was "beaten with a nightstick and blinded" by Aiken's white chief of police. As with the Lowman lynching, a trial followed. Not surprisingly, justice again proved it was *not* color blind, as an all-white jury, to the cheers of a jam-packed courtroom, acquitted the police chief, Linwood Shull, of all charges. Internationally, Woodard's case, along with those of a handful of other black soldiers who were viciously attacked upon their completion of their service, became a *cause célèbre*. Folk singer, Woody Guthrie, for one, released a song entitled "The Blinding of Isaac Woodard." And President Harry Truman appointed his Commission on Civil Rights, in part, in reaction to this atrocity. But for African Americans who resided in Aiken, these acts were small solace and they had little if any impact on their daily lives.[6]

Great Migration (1916–1930)" and "The Second Great Migration (1940–1970)." Jim Kalish, *The Story of Civil Rights in York, Pennsylvania: A 250 Year Interpretive History* (York, PA: York County Audit, 2000), pp. 20–21. Voni B. Grimes, *Bridging Troubled Waters* (York, PA: Wolf, 2008); Wilkerson, *The Warmth of Other Suns.*
[5] Walter White, *Rope and Faggot*, reprint (New York: Arno Press, 1969), pp. 29–33; Elizabeth Robeson, "An 'Ominous Defiance': The Lowman Lynchings of 1926," in *Toward the Meeting of the Waters: Currents in the Civil Rights Movement in South Carolina during the Twentieth Century*, ed. by Winfred B. Moore Jr. and Orville Vernon Burton, (Columbia: University of South Carolina Press, 2008), pp. 65–92; I. A. Newby, *Black Carolinians.*
[6] Mary Dudziak, *Cold War Civil Rights: Race and the Image of Democracy* (Princeton, NJ: Princeton University Press, 2000), p. 23.

Whether the Lowman's lynching or Woodward's blinding affected members of Lillie Belle Allen's extended family remains unclear. But white violence undoubtedly was one of the forces that pushed black residents of Aiken to join the Great Migration, and the promise of a more just society was just as certainly one of the factors that pulled them northward. It would be naïve to suggest that African American migrants expected the North to be a place of milk and honey, but, in the least, they believed they were escaping law enforcement authorities who were one and the same with the Ku Klux Klan. York, like the other cities, also attracted Aiken's black citizens by offering economic opportunities unavailable in the South. In 1950, for instance, the medium per capita income of black persons in York was nearly double what it was for blacks in Aiken County, $1,353 to $758.[7]

While we do not know how Aiken's black residents first learned that there were jobs in York, during the 1920s and even more so during World War II and after, the "White Rose City," as it was known, had a wide array of openings, especially in its many manufacturing establishments, such as American Chain and Cable Company and Schmidt and Ault Paper, all of which paid much better than work in South Carolina. True, not all of York's firms opened their doors and many black workers were relegated to low skilled and poorly paid service positions, such as porters, custodians, and day laborers. Nonetheless, the pull of these jobs, along with the relative greater sense of social freedom that existed in the North compared to the South, was strong enough to ensure a steady stream of newcomers. As a result, York's black population rose steadily from under 2,000 in 1920 to over 6,500 fifty years later, a 300 percent increase. Even though they constituted a much smaller percentage of the total population than in Baltimore and Philadelphia, which lay to the south and the east, York's blacks built a vibrant community, which included churches, fraternal associations, and social clubs. Crispus Attucks (CA), a social service association named after the black revolutionary hero who died at the Boston Massacre, for instance, played a central role in the life of much of York's African American community, sponsoring separate all-black scouting troops, basketball teams, and pre-school programs. Julie Hines-Harris, for instance, recalls attending choir rehearsals at church on Monday or Tuesday, student council at CA on Wednesday, working on the CA's newspaper on Thursday, and participating in Teen Town dances on

---

[7] *U.S. Census of Population: 1950: South Carolina* (Washington, DC: GPO, 1951); *U.S. Census of Population: 1950: Pennsylvania* (Washington, DC: GPO, 1951).

the weekends. In 1943, motivated by their desire to eradicate Jim Crow in the city's schools and public facilities, York's black community also established their own branch of the NAACP. Just as importantly, black people developed close interpersonal ties that helped them grapple with economic hardships during the depression and after.[8]

This said, in the areas of housing, recreation, employment, education, and, especially, relations with the police and "City Hall," many of York's blacks found that they had migrated to the Promised Land that wasn't. Interviews conducted with York's black residents years after the Great Migration, revealed widespread prejudice. While York did not sport Jim Crow signs, interviewees recalled that many white establishments did not serve them or compelled them to buy their food inside but eat it outside or to "take it out with you." Fred Jenkins found the duplicitous or hypocritical nature of racism in York particularly troublesome. In the South, he explained, they'd tell you: "I don't want you. Where[as] here [in York], they would use underhanded [means] to get rid of you." Or as Stephan Freeland, one of those accused of shooting Officer Schaad put it in 2003, "That was a time when racism was everywhere... What the people felt was going on in the southern counties, it wasn't only going on down there, it was going on right here."[9]

By 1970, blacks constituted 13 percent of York's population, the vast majority of whom lived in two of the city's sixteen census tracts, #10 and #7. Housing in census tract #10, which as of 1960 was the only majority black tract, was, in a word, abysmal. Out of a total of 1,121 housing units in 1960 nearly a third were rated as either deteriorated or dilapidated. The medium value of units in the tract in 1970 stood at $6,100, a third less than the city average, and the vast majority of blacks in the city could not afford to own a home. Instead they were compelled by

[8] Teresa McMinn, "Codorus Street Reunion Plans to Give People a Look Back – and Ahead," *York Daily Record*, July 22, 2012; Panel Discussion, February 8, 2014, York County Heritage Trust; Debora Hamm, Interview by Author, Baltimore, Maryland, December 20, 2013; Kiara Banks, "A Community Story: The Bambergers Migrate North and Beyond," *Journal of York County Heritage* (September 2012), pp. 29–31. Julia-Hines Harris, Interview by Michael Breeland, York, Pennsylvania, December 4, 1987, York College Oral History Center.

[9] "Testimony of Stephen Freeland," *Commonwealth of Pennsylvania v. Stephen D. Freeland*; *Commonwealth v. Leon F. Wright*, York, PA, March 2003. See also "Photos," York's African-American Historical Preservation Society, www.facebook.com/yorksblackhistory/ [accessed December 2, 2016]; Fred Jenkins, Interview, York, Pennsylvania, November 9, 1982, York College Oral History Center; Interview with Annie Gordan, York, Pennsylvania, April 8, 1983, York College Oral History Center.

FIGURE 7.1 Housing conditions in York's black community. By permission of the York History Center.

economic circumstances and de facto segregation to live in rental units, many of which lacked adequate heating and/or plumbing – 77 percent of the residents of census tract #10 were renters, compared to 51 percent of the residents of the city overall. Many black homes were located in back alleys behind major streets, in flood-prone areas. For instance, in 1972, Hurricane Agnes flooded 86 percent of the homes in census tracts #10 and #16 (see Figure 7.1). Urban renewal left blacks fending for a declining stock of urban housing which they could afford and/or which realtors and rental agents were willing to show them in the first place. The destruction of the Codorus Street and the Freys Avenue communities, two centers of black life, a by-product of the city's limited urban renewal program, left close to 200 black families looking for a place to live in a housing

market that already inadequately met their needs.[10] Moreover, throughout the era, City Hall proved unresponsive to the black community's call
for better housing, reluctantly applying for federal funds for public housing, if at all, and enforcing housing codes just as ineffectively.[11]

To make matters worse, the housing travails of York's black community occurred in the midst of a suburban boom, and in York County, as
elsewhere in the 1950s and 1960s, the suburbs were virtually all white.
In 1960, 99.9 percent of those who lived in York's suburbs were white;
ten years later the number stood at 99.6 percent. In contrast to the deteriorating and overcrowded housing in the inner city, homes in the suburbs were replete with modern amenities and saw their values steadily
increase. For instance, during the mid-1960s, the total value of property in
York Suburban School district, which abutted the city, skyrocketed from
$4.75 million to $136 million. During the same time period, property values in the entire city, which had far more residents, grew only $17,000.
This suburban boom was fed by the out-migration of whites from York
City and by government policies which underwrote white suburbanization nationwide.[12]

When adjusted for York's changing boundaries, the city lost 8,464
whites between 1960 and 1970, continuing a trend that had begun in
1950. The city's declining white population, which peaked at 56,699 and
fell to 43,556 by 1970, belies the common belief that the riots caused
white flight, unless one were to assume that the vast majority of those
who fled did so in the five months following York's revolt (see Figure 7.2).
What these demographic statistics tend to mask is that a significant segment of the white population suffered from some of the same housing
woes as York's black population and may have underlay a good deal of
the white anxiety of the period. For instance, census tract #16, where the

---

[10] City of York, "There and Back Again: A Plan for Improvements," n.d.; York Planning
Commission, "An Analysis of Socio-economic Factors and Housing," 1973; York Planning Commission, "York County Comprehensive Plan: Population," all in HUD Papers,
RG 207, Boxes 1857 and 2541, National Archives, College Park, MD.
[11] Pennsylvania Human Relations Commission (henceforth PHRC), "Investigatory Hearing
Report, 1968," in Raymond P. Shafer Papers, General File, MG209, Carton 42, Pennsyl-
vania State Archives, Harrisburg, PA.
[12] See Douglas S. Massey and Nancy A. Denton, *American Apartheid: Segregation and the
Making of the Underclass* (Cambridge, MA: Harvard University Press, 1994); Kenneth
T. Jackson, *Crabgrass Frontier: The Suburbanization of the United States* (New York:
Oxford University Press, 1978); Arnold Hirsch, *Making the Second Ghetto: Race and
Housing in Chicago 1940–1960* (Chicago: University of Chicago Press, 1998). "County
Property Values Go Up," *York Gazette and Daily* (henceforth *YGD*), July 2, 1968.

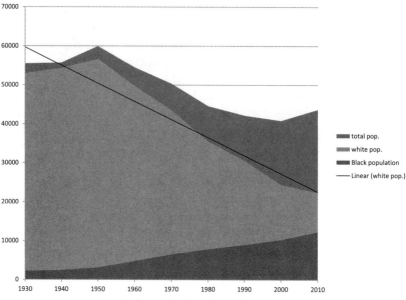

FIGURE 7.2 York population change, by race, 1930–2010.

Newberry Street Boys who were associated with Allen's murder resided, tied with census tract #10 for last in terms of "substandard" housing. As of 1960, over half of the homes in this tract were rated as deteriorated or dilapidated, a significantly greater proportion than that in tract #10.[13] Just as significantly, housing prices in the city faced downward pressures at a time when homes were the primary investment of many Americans.

While the overall employment situation in York remained strong through most of the 1960s (which helps explain the continued in-migration of blacks to the city), persistent discrimination at the workplace combined with shifts in the labor market, both spatially and occupationally, added to the growing frustrations of many black Yorkers and perhaps some younger white city residents. Throughout this era, York remained a blue-collar town, especially for men. Partly fueled by defense spending and by the competitiveness of many of the local firms, manufacturing jobs grew at a steady pace, from 36,160 in 1960 to 42,292 in 1970, a 20 percent increase. An even faster rise in white-collar and service work combined with the fact that York had a relative diverse mix

---

[13] York Planning Commission, "An Analysis of Socio-economic Factors and Housing"; York County Planning Commission, "Comprehensive Plan," 1978, both in HUD Papers, RG 207, Box 405.

of industries – from machinery and metal fabrication to paper and food production – resulted in low unemployment rates, a mere 3.2 percent for the city in 1970.[14] Yet these statistics masked the economic circumstances for many African Americans. Twice as many blacks as whites were unemployed in York, and twice as many city residents could not find jobs as those who lived in the suburbs. Blacks held poorer paying jobs, resulting in substantially lower median income for black families. Even much higher participation rates by black women failed to close these economic gaps. One reason for this disparity was outright discrimination. A survey of ninety-nine employers conducted in 1961 found that 75 percent did not have any black employees and 10 percent declared they would not hire blacks workers "under any circumstances." While the 1964 Civil Rights Act made such blatant discrimination illegal, blacks in York still encountered barriers to obtaining skilled and well-paying jobs. In 1968, the Pennsylvania Human Relations Commission observed "striking examples of black college graduates denied employment at commensurate skill levels" and far fewer chances for "advancement" once they obtained a job.[15] Or as one interviewee recollected years later, "white folks weren't ready for blacks to get ahead. They wanted to keep us in our place."[16]

Blacks also tended to work at older less productive and ultimately less profitable firms (or branches), thus placing them at greater risk for seasonal layoffs and, in the long run, more susceptible to deindustrialization. With lower rates of education (see below), black men and women had less of an opportunity to buffer themselves from the changing economy by finding employment in the more rapidly growing sectors of the labor market. They also accumulated fewer savings to weather downturns. This proved particularly true for blacks who resided in census tracts #7 and #10, where the poverty rate stood at 34 percent, more than triple the city average and almost seven times higher than the county overall.[17]

While not from South Carolina, one of the black persons who migrated to York was Daisy Myers and her story provides a sense of the racial

---

[14] York County Planning Commission, "Comprehensive Plan," 1978; US Bureau of the Census, *Census of Population and Housing, 1970: Census Tracts, Final Report PHC (1)-237 York, PA.* SMSA (Washington DC: GPO, 1972).

[15] York County Planning Commission, "Comprehensive Plan," 1978; US Bureau of the Census, *Census of Population and Housing, 1970* (Washington, DC: GPO, 1971); PHRC, "Investigatory Hearing Report, 1968."

[16] Anon., interviewed by Di Neesha Harris, December 2013, York, Pennsylvania (in author's possession).

[17] York County Planning Commision, "Comprehensive Plan," 1978; US Bureau of the Census, *Census of Population and Housing, 1970*; PHRC, "Investigatory Hearing Report, 1968."

situation in York at mid-century. In 1957, Myers gained national fame
when she and her husband, William Edward Myers, a native of York,
Pennsylvania, became the first black family to move to Levittown, Pennsylvania. In spite of its reputation as an affordable respite for working-
and middle-class families, the Myers were met with fierce resistance. Some
even called Myers the "Rosa Parks of the North," for the dignified fashion in which she and her husband faced down white mobs. But before she
moved to Levittown, Myers had already encountered the sting of racism
in York.[18]

Born and raised in Richmond, Virginia, Myers attended all-black
schools and churches and lived in a largely all-black neighborhood and
thus, as a youth, in her own words, was largely sheltered from many of
the worst attributes of white supremacy. After a brief stint in New York
City, where she pursued a graduate degree at New York University, she
came to associate the North with, in her words, an even "freer life." Yet,
when she married William Myers and moved to York, his hometown, in
1951, she quickly learned that this was not always the case. Even though
both she and her husband had college degrees, real estate agents in York
steered them away from the homes they wanted to buy. After being reluctantly hired by the city's housing agency, which did not know that she was
black when she applied, she was passed over for a supervisory position in
favor of less-qualified white applicants. Rather than accept this slight, she
resigned, much to the surprise of her boss who expected that she would
not protest such mistreatment. Before departing for Levittown, she fre-
quently encountered outright bigotry on the part of her fellow workers
and other white locals who complained about "niggers [who] were gonna
[*sic*] live side by side" with them. She also grew sickened by the deplorable
conditions that many black people in York had to live in because of housing discrimination.[19]

Even though black children enjoyed much better educational opportunities in York than black children did in the South, unequal education
remained the rule. Myers herself initially was unable to secure a job as a
teacher in spite of her advanced training. Until *Brown v. Board of Education*, blacks in York attended segregated elementary schools – either James
Smallwood or Aquilla Howard. After *Brown*, these schools closed. Still

---

[18] Daisy D. Myers, *Sticks 'n Stones: The Myers Family in Levittown* (York: York Heritage
Trust, 2005).
[19] Daisy D. Myers, Obituary, www.legacy.com/obituaries/york/obituary.aspx?n=daisy-d-
myers&pid=154941095 [accessed July 6, 2015]; Myers, *Sticks 'n Stones*.

racial discrimination pervaded the system. By and large blacks were not hired to teach in "white" schools. McKinley Elementary School, which was 54 percent non-white in 1968, did not have a gym or library and the student to teacher ratio was higher than at the "white" schools. At Hanna Penn Junior High School, which was integrated, the Human Relations Commission found "a racist attitude on the part of teachers," as evidenced by "frequent recourse to corporal punishment" and by a refusal to accord black students with proper recognition. Julia Hines-Harris, for one, was denied a Daughters of American Revolution (DAR) award, even though she scored the highest on the DAR. test, because she was black. Instead, her eighth-grade teacher gave the award to a white student who scored third on the exam – a Jewish student was passed over for the award as well. At William Penn High School (WPHS), black faculty and staff were underrepresented, making up only 3 percent of the employees, whereas black students comprised 23 percent of the student body. Guidance counselors steered blacks away from attending college and disproportionately placed black students in low level classes. In 1967, for example, only 14 of 400 non-white students took the College Board examination. Sam Manson recalled that an "overwhelming number of Black students were assigned to … special education and low academic level classrooms in the basement also known as the dungeon of the building." Nonetheless, the educational system proved more responsive to black demands for reform than did other sectors of York society. Most notably, in the immediate aftermath of Martin Luther King Jr.'s assassination, black students at WPHS forged a protest movement that won significant concessions from the city, from the hiring of more black staff and teachers to the introduction of African American history into the curriculum.[20]

Throughout the 1960s, an era of heightened expectations, poor relations between black Yorkers and the police and City Hall stood out. After holding investigatory hearings, the Pennsylvania Human Relations Commission (PHRC) concluded that "The Police Department of the City of York," seemed more concerned with maintaining "the status quo than maintaining peace." The PHRC observed that police department's

[20] PHRC, "Investigatory Hearing Report, 1968"; Dwayne Wright, "Black Pride Days, 1965–1970: A Critical Historical Ethnography of Black Student Activism, Curricular Reform, and Memory at William Penn Senior High School in York, Pennsylvania," PhD dissertation, University of Georgia, 2005, p. 82; Jeffrey Werner, "A Peaceful Mourning: The York High Students' Reaction to Martin Luther King's Assassination and Its Significance When Contrasted with York City," Senior thesis, York College, 2008 (in author's possession). Interview with Julia Hines-Harris.

FIGURE 7.3 York's mayor John Snyder walks city streets with his German Shepherd dog. By permission of the York History Center.

deployment of the canine corps displayed the racist attitudes of many on the force, and substantiated the black community's complaint that the police used dogs "to instill fear in Black Youths."[21] To make matters worse, York's Mayor John Snyder refused to address concerns about the police. Snyder, who became York's mayor in 1961 and was re-elected in 1965, openly referred to blacks as "darkies" and regularly walked the streets with a German Shepherd dog which he used to intimidate black youths (see Figure 7.3). He defeated Henry Leader, the brother of Pennsylvania's governor, George Leader, by allying with the York County's conservative Democratic Committee – George Leader was one of Daisy

---

[21] PHRC, "Investigatory Hearing Report, 1968"; For an early example of police misuse of dogs see *YGD*, July 20, 1963; and Jim Kalish, *Civil Rights in York.*

Myers' most prominent supporters. In the summer of 1963, following the mauling of two black men, already in custody, by police dogs, black Yorkers staged a protest at City Hall. Coming in the immediate aftermath of the vicious use of German Shepherds in Birmingham, Alabama, which generated a national outcry, one might have expected Mayor Snyder to reconsider his decision to deploy police dogs. Instead, Snyder defended their use. (For more on these protests, see below.)[22]

And then there were the white gangs of York. On one level, York's youth gangs, most notably the Newberry Street Boys, the Girarders, the Swampers, and Yorklyn Boys, were social in nature. They joined together neighborhood youths who hung out at their "club houses," played sports (and drank) and proudly wore their colors and insignias at school and on the streets. On another level, the gangs exemplified the prevalence of racial segregation and served as conveyors of white supremacist attitudes. The Newberry Street Boys spray-painted their clubhouse with the slogan "white power" and along with other white gangs attacked black people who ventured into "their" neighborhoods, with the explicit purpose of keeping them from "getting their foot in the door." Randy Graham recalled that as a 16-year-old white gang member he went to the York Fair looking for blacks to fight. "They were black. We were white. If there were blacks somewhere, we were fighting them." Only years later did Graham express deep regret for his attitudes and actions, but at the time, he observed, he had been taught that blacks were not equal and he did not question this claim. The gangs also sought to keep white youths from crossing cultural boundaries that either explicitly or implicitly undermined white solidarity. Craig Ilgenfritz, a white youth who grew up in the predominantly black Freys Avenue neighborhood and favored soul music, like Marvin Gaye, recalled being chased and beaten by members of the Newberry Street Boys because they saw him as a "flip over of Uncle Tom."[23]

[22] Kalish, *Civil Rights in York*; p. 56; PHRC, "Investigatory Hearing Report, 1968"; PHRC, "Press Release," n.d., Raymond Shafer Papers, General File, MG 209, Carton 42; "Mayor's Dog Probe Fizzles, But He's For Them Anyway," *YGD*, June 7, 1968, p. 1. Debbie Noel, "The Grapes of Wrath," *York Dispatch*, September 21, 2005; Keisling, *The Wrong Car*, Kindle edn. Location 1042–1044; Interview with William Althouse by Jason Feldman, December 2014, York, Pennsylvania (in author's possession); Interview with Bennie Carter by James Virden, March 19, 2013, York, Pennsylvania (in author's possession).
[23] Craig Ilgenfritz, Interview by author, York, Pennsylvania, June 11, 2014; Debbie Noel, "The Grapes of Wrath," *York Dispatch*, September 21, 2005; Karen Rice-Young, "Ten

One particular boundary white gangs fiercely guarded was the one between the sexes; they did not tolerate interracial dating. Members of the Girarders, for instance, called Mark Eissler, a white York College student who was dating black women, a "nigger lover" and then nearly knocked him unconscious. York police harassed black men seen with white woman in town.[24] This obsession with interracial dating, among other things, reflected the gendered concerns of white gangs. In addition to defending physical spaces they deemed white, gang members socialized young men into strict gender roles, which included the notion that white women needed the protection of white men from black men and/or that white men owned white women. Looking back, some black women suggested that white gang members left them alone, most likely because white men did not see black women as a threat to the "natural" hierarchy which placed white men at the top.[25]

While white gang members were known to fight each other, during periods of racial turmoil they put aside their rivalries. Rick Knouse, one of the co-defendants in the Allen murder trial and a member of the Girarders gang, testified that when the trouble started in July 1969 members of the Newberry Street Boys (NSB) "came and asked for help in their neighborhood, and so we went over there." Whites associated with the Girarders and Yorklyn Boys gathered with the NSBs at a white power rally the night before Lillie Belle Allen was killed and joined forces with them the day of her murder. On both occasions they shared a common racially charged language, referring to blacks as "niggers" and championing "white power." During the same time period, members of York's police force, many of whom lived in these same white neighborhoods, riled up white gangs with dire warnings of black attacks. Phil Grosklos testified that he went down to Newberry Street armed with a shotgun after the police alleged that "Black Panthers" with machine guns were in the area and that whites needed to defend their neighborhoods. Or as one anonymous NSB member put it: "the gang had been under the advisement of the police department since the trouble started." They had told people that the police "wouldn't interfere with their defending their turf,"

Days: The '69 Riots in York, PA: An Oral History," Senior thesis, York College, April 24, 1992 (in author's possession); Testimony of John Altaberry, *Commonwealth of Pennsylvania v. Robert Messersmith et al.*

[24] "Student Assaulted by 'Gang in York,'" *YGD*, September 12, 1969; Craig Ilgenfritz, Interview by author.

[25] Anon., interviewed by Di Neesha Harris, December 2013, York, Pennsylvania (in author's possession).

because, simply stated, the "cops are on our side." Somewhat similarly, Police Officer McMaster later testified that he did not think that his fellow officers were doing anything wrong when they provided ammunition to white gang members during the 1969 revolt because the gang members claimed they intended to use it to protect their homes.[26] McMaster and his fellow white officers never considered providing weapons or ammunition to blacks so they could do the same.

"They Might as well Proclaim this a City where Race Hatred Reigns"

York's revolt, like those elsewhere, was viewed by contemporaries and by subsequent generations as a surprising or unexpected event that emerged out of the frustration and alienation of black youths who, heretofore, had not been engaged in the struggles for racial equality. Alternatively, many whites interpreted the revolts as evidence of the sudden rise of militants or radicals who had no or few connections to the mainstream struggle for civil rights. Yet, a closer examination of York suggests that the Great Uprising did not represent a sharp break from the past. On the contrary, it can best be understood as part of a long continuum of struggle. Put somewhat differently, blacks in York had a tradition of protesting against racism and white privilege. This tradition or history was not well known and it is still difficult to parcel together. Persistent employment discrimination and residential segregation, the slow and uneven pace of school desegregation, police abuse and inequities in the criminal justice system, prodded the black community to repeatedly demand change. The unresponsiveness of City Hall and the political and economic elite to these demands gave rise to a more militant posture in the latter half of the 1960s, a shift that represented a logical next step not a rupture from the past.[27]

As far back as the earliest years of the Republic, York's small black community had established their own churches, a sign of their determination not to accept second class status. With the support of a select number

[26] *Commonwealth of Pennsylvania v. Charlie Robertson et al.* especially opening statements and testimony of Steven Noonan, Robert Stoner, Steven Rinehart, Stewart Aldinger, Sterling Frederick Flickinger, Greg Neff, Richard Hansford, Dennis McMaster, and Rick Knouse. Rice-Young, "Ten Days"; "Police Role Scrutinized," *York Dispatch*, October 9, 2002.
[27] For a critique of the conventional wisdom that the urban revolts of the 1960s represented a dramatic break or turning point, as opposed to one more stage in the long term struggle of the black community, see Theoharis, "'Alabama on Avalon.'"

of whites, including some Quakers and perhaps Thaddeus Stevens, who taught briefly in York, blacks in York County created numerous "stops" on the underground railroad, many of them in "freedman enclaves," such as "Croties' Row," not far from where many blacks would reside one hundred years later. In the latter half of the nineteenth century, York even had a black baseball team, the "Colored Monarchs," who competed in the Eastern Interstate League. York native, George Bowles, the first black person to graduate from William Penn High School, earned a medical degree from Harvard University in the early 1900s and by the 1930s had become one of the most respected public health authorities in the nation. Nationally, he expended much energy combating tuberculosis and other public health scourges that disproportionately impacted African Americans. Back in his home town, he helped found the Crispus Attucks Center (1931) and, in concert with several local churches initiated the tradition of celebrating "Interracial Day" during "Negro History Month." In 1930, for instance, Bowles delivered a memorable "Interracial Day" address at the Heidelberg Reformed Church, where, among other things, he chided whites for their alleged surprise over the extent of racial discrimination. Black demands were not that radical, he insisted, they simply wanted "fair play and equal opportunity." During the same time period, "Negro" women's clubs and local black churches, accumulated the resources – financial, organizational, and cultural – which served as the foundation for a broader assault on the racial status quo during the 1960s.[28]

One example of the extent of black organization in York appeared in 1935. At the time, the city's elementary schools were segregated but its middle and high schools were not. When rumors surfaced that some whites favored extending Jim Crow to all grades, York's Inter-Racial Commission, which included Dr. Bowles and representatives of the black churches, protested vociferously against such a move. "We are absolutely opposed to any segregation. We are suffering it now!" exclaimed Dr. Bowles. Echoing Bowles's sentiments, Reverend T. E. Montouth declared, "When you are trying to force on us more segregation we resent it.

---

[28] Jim Kalish, *The Story of Civil Rights in York*, quoted Bowles, p. 26; "York, PA," *Afro-American*, August 21, 1921, p. 11; "Pennsylvania: York, PA," *Afro-American*, February 1, 1924, p. 2; "York, Pennsylvania," *Afro-American*, February 1, 1930, p. 16; "York," *Afro-American*, May 14, 1931, p. 5; "Open Doors of Business, Says Dr. [Mordecai] Johnson," *Afro-American*, February 14, 1931, p. 4; "Anne W. Brown Sings at York Bi-Racial Meet," *Afro-American*, April 28, 1934, p. 8; "Pennsy Solons Speak at York," *Afro-American*, June 6, 1936, p. 12.

Negroes of York stand together against segregated schools."[29] In the face of such protest, the middle and high schools remained desegregated.

With World War II, which reignited the Great Migration and galvanized black calls for "double victory" against Nazi racism abroad and Jim Crow at home, protests against racial inequality in York, as elsewhere, picked up. In 1942, a coalition of blacks and whites, including Chester Hayes, the director of Crispus Attucks, and Rabbi Alexander Goode, initiated a panel discussion entitled "The Church and Racial Tensions" which criticized various institutions, from labor unions and charitable organizations to certain "unnamed" churches for not applying the golden rule. Local historian Jim Kalish writes that speakers "correlated the problems of inadequate housing, absence of health care ... with racial discrimination. They reported that Negro boys and girls were merely tolerated at schools ... [and that white] parents mislead their children about racial differences," in line with the way that race was discussed in Nazi Germany. The following year, Bowles helped found a local branch of the NAACP, which began to pressure the city on inadequate housing, unequal educational opportunities, and residential discrimination. Blacks and their white allies in York also pushed for making the Fair Employment Practices Committee (FEPC) a permanent agency and, failing that, the enactment of state laws that outlawed employment discrimination.[30]

In spite of the rising tide of anti-communism on the home front, which proved devastating to many progressive organizations, antiracist activism did not abate in the immediate postwar years. Local activists, in concert with members of the National Negro Congress, held a mass meeting at William Penn High School to try to reverse the US Senate's decision to disestablish the FEPC. The group called for "vigorous efforts" to keep this agency alive, which had been crucial to the employment advances made by African Americans during World War II. The rally also included a stirring reading of the Gettysburg Address by Charles Grayson, one of York's prominent black residents, and speeches by local black ministers.

---

[29] "Speedy Action of York Citizens Blocks Race Teacher's Support of Jim Crow in Jr. High School," *Pittsburgh Courier*, August 17, 1935, p. 4.

[30] Kalish, *Civil Rights in York*, pp. 24–35; "Brown's Bill Wins 'First Round,'" *Pittsburgh Courier*, March 31, 1945, p. 1. The literature on the impact of World War II on African Americans is vast. See, for example, Richard Dalfiume, "The Forgotten Years of the Negro Revolution," *Journal of American History*, 55:1 (June, 1968): 90–106; Richard Dalfiume, *Desegregation of the United States Armed Forces: Fighting on Two Fronts, 1939–1953* (Columbia: University of Missouri Press, 1969).

In 1947, the local branch of the NAACP and black clergyman prodded the state to pursue cases of racial discrimination against local restaurants and fraternal associations. Two years later, broader protests developed over the refusal of local pools to admit black patrons. When the city council chose to close rather than desegregate the pools, national forces turned up the heat. In a biting story, one black journalist termed York a "hot bed of racism."[31]

In 1948, Henry Wallace's Progressive Party held its state convention in York, where the one-time vice-president railed at segregation and discrimination. While Wallace's sharp criticism of President Truman's foreign policy and his willingness to accept the support of members of the Communist Party of the United States led members of the NAACP and many labor unions in York and across the nation to break ranks with him, somewhat surprisingly he enjoyed very strong support from one of York's most prominent businessmen, J. W. Gitt, the publisher of the *York Gazette and Daily* (*YGD*). In fact, the *YGD* was the only commercial paper in the nation to endorse Wallace for president. Even before 1948, Gitt had taken several very progressive positions on racial matters, including advocating the establishment of a permanent FEPC and the desegregation of the military.[32]

In 1950, one of York's black residents, Lieutenant Leon Gilbert, gained national fame (or infamy), when he was court-martialed for disobeying the orders of his white commander and sentenced to death. Gilbert's plight generated international attention, including a visit from Thurgood Marshall, the NAACP's chief legal counsel, who took on Gilbert's case as well as those of a number of other blacks charged with offenses while serving their country in Korea. Marshall uncovered widespread evidence

---

[31] "Wisconsin Matron Studies Pool Feuds," *Afro-American*, August 20, 1949, p. 16; "Ministers Urge Swimming Pools Be Opened to All Citizens," *Afro-American*, December 3, 1949, p. A16; "Jim Crow Guide to the U.S.A.," *YGD*, March 11, 1950, p. 13; "Race Bar Ends At York, Pa. Public Pool," *Chicago Defender*, August 9, 1947, p. 3; "Jim Crow Takes Dive in Pa. Pool," *Cleveland Call and Post*, August 9, 1947, p. 1B.

[32] "FEPC Group Mass Meeting Set for Tonight," *YGD*, February 12, 1946, p. 2; "Fighters for FEPC," *YGD*, February 14, 1946, p. 30; "Pa. Grand Jury to Hear Case of Restaurant Bias," *Afro-American*, April 26, 1947, p. 15; "York Cafes Must Serve Elks or Face Law Suits," *Afro-American*, May 17, 1947, p. 1; "Pa. Equal Rights Law Flouted as Jury Frees Two Violators," *Afro-American*, August 30, 1947, p. 15; "Minister Forced to Pay Costs in Equal Rights Case," *Pittsburgh Courier*, August 30, 1947, p. 21; "Rev. Jackson Backs Wallace Movement Here," *Philadelphia Tribune*, March 9, 1948, p. 1; Mary Hamilton, *Rising From the Wilderness: J. W. Gitt and His Legendary Newspaper: The Gazette and Daily of York, PA* (York: York Heritage Trust, 2007). "Fighting Editor Hits School Bias," *Afro-American*, May 19, 1951, p. 13.

of discrimination against black soldiers, from the training they received stateside and the equipment they received to disparate penalties for alleged offenses. When General Douglas MacArthur rebuffed Marshall's attempt to visit black soldiers in Korea, Walter White, the head of the NAACP, composed a militant telegram protesting his conviction. Gilbert's case was even more poignant because he came from a family that had dedicated itself to serving their nation. Gilbert's father, Leon Sr., served in the army for fifteen years, including a stint during World War I. Gilbert himself had served during World War II and re-enlisted when the Korean War broke out (as did his brother).[33]

What few knew at the time was that Gilbert's wife, with the aid of the Civil Rights Congress (CRC), a radical organization, not Marshall, initiated the effort to free her husband. William Patterson, the head of the CRC and the author of "We Charge Genocide," a biting indictment of the United States, corresponded directly with Gilbert's wife almost from the moment of her husband's arrest. After visiting him in his Japan stockade, Kay Gilbert proclaimed that her husband had been sent on a "suicide mission," by "an officer [white] who had 'not kept his head.'" To garner further attention and sympathy for her husband's "fight for freedom," nationwide and in York, Kay Gilbert went on a hunger strike. Moreover, the coalition that developed around Lieutenant Gilbert's case revealed the support networks that had grown over the years in York. Black churches and veterans groups, athletic teams sponsored by the Crispus Attucks Center, and kin and peer groups, rallied to his defense. The Charles E. Williams post of the American Legion, the all-black branch in York, held fund-raising drives and testified to Gilbert's patriotism. With the help of Gilbert's former employee, Gilbert's wife retained the service of two white York attorneys, who worked overtime to help secure his release. Ultimately, these forces along with Thurgood Marshall prodded Truman to

---

[33] White quoted in, Carl Rowan, *Dream Makers, Dream Breakers: The World of Justice Thurgood Marshall* (Boston: Little, Brown & Co., 1993), p. 163; for a historical discussion of Gilbert's case, see Kim Phillips, *War! What Is It Good For? Black Freedom Struggles and the U.S. Military from World War II to Iraq* (Chapel Hill: University of North Carolina Press, 2014), pp. 135–138; "Lt. Gilbert's Story: Condemned Officer Not Afraid to Die," *Afro-American*, November 25, 1950, p. 1; "'Thought I Was Right,' Condemned Soldier Says," *Atlanta Daily World*, October 17, 1950, p. 1; "NAACP to Push Case of Lieut. Gilbert," *Cleveland Call*, December 9, 1950, p. 3B; "American Legion Ask Full Investigation of Gilbert Court Martial," *New Journal and Guide*, November 4, 1950, p. 1; "Spare Mate's Life, Wife Begs Truman," *Philadelphia Tribune*, September 26, 1950, p. 1. William T. Bowers et al. *Black Soldiers/White Army: The 24th Infantry Regiment in Korea* (Washington, DC: US Army-Center for Military History, 1996).

stay Gilbert's death and to reduce his sentence to twenty years, of which Gilbert served five.[34]

Even before Gilbert's arrest, a loose coalition of left-leaning blacks and whites had displayed an increasing militancy in York. In the spring of 1950, the Progressive Party held a Conference for Jobs, Peace, and Civil Rights at York's William Penn High School. At the conference, headlined by a keynote address by Earl Dickerson, a black city councilman from Chicago and a former member of the FEPC, blacks, and whites rallied for civil rights.[35] About a month later, Crispus Attucks released the "Survey of Local Negro Employment in Non-Agricultural Industry in York County." The report revealed widespread employment discrimination, which relegated blacks to unskilled jobs in manufacturing and routinely passed them over for positions in favor of white candidates with the same or lesser qualifications. Several employers suggested that white workers who resented "Negro advancement" caused the discrimination; others blamed labor unions for restricting blacks to unskilled positions. At a mass meeting, Reverend Thomas Montouth built on the findings of this report to rail at the "poor industrial job opportunities for Negroes in York." To improve the situation, local black leaders demanded the enactment of a "strong law which forbids discrimination in industry" and an "extensive program of education and vocational guidance" to increase the number of qualified applicants.[36]

It should not be surprising that veterans, who had fought for their country, first to defeat racist Nazism in Germany and then to protect

---

[34] "Truman Orders Stay of Death for Lieutenant Leon Gilbert," *Atlanta Daily World*, November 28, 1950; "Exclusive Interview with Lt. L.A. Gilbert in Stockade," *New Journal and Guide*, December 2, 1950, p. 11; "Military," *Crisis*, January 1951, p. 39; "'Fight Goes On' Gilbert Tells Lawyer; Sobs Love for Folks," *New Age*, December 2, 1950, p. 1; "Prayers, Protests for Doomed Soldier," *New York Amsterdam News*, September 30, 1950, p. 5; "Gilbert Plans Appeal," *New York Amsterdam News*, December 2, 1950, p. 1; Peace Conference Opens in York," *Philadelphia Tribune*, May 13, 1950, p. 9; "Spare Mate's Life, Wife Begs Truman," *Philadelphia Tribune*, September 26, 1950, p. 1. "Freedom Is Asked for Lt. Gilbert," *Philadelphia Tribune*, September 8, 1951, p 1; "Gilbert's Life Spared," *Pittsburg Courier*, December 2, 1950, p. 1. Also see "Fight For Racial Justice," Lt. Leon A. Gilbert Correspondence," and Lt. Leon A Gilbert, Clippings, all in Papers of the Civil Rights Congress, New York Public Library, Archives Unbound. Especially: John Bolton to Kay Gilbert, January 5, 1951; Kay Gilbert to William Patterson, December 22, 1950; William Patterson to Kay Gilbert, September 17, 1952; William Patterson to Leon Gilbert, December 29, 1952; Leon Gilbert to Morris Greenbaum, January 16, 1951; and Judson Ruch to Morris Greenbaum, August 20, 1951.

[35] "Peace Conference Opens in York," *Philadelphia Tribune*, May 13, 1950, p. 9.

[36] Kalish, *Civil Rights in York*, pp. 37–39; "News from York, PA," *Philadelphia Tribune*, August 1, 1950, p. 14.

freedom in Korea, proved receptive to such proclamations. At the same time, the newsletter of the Crispus Attucks Center suggested that young people were growing increasingly impatient with the pace of change too. Barbara Johnson, a black teenager, questioned the unwritten rule that kept black and white youths from dating one another. Charles Woodyard complained of the lack of African American history in the high school curriculum. "To be proud of ourselves as a race we must know and be proud of our achievements."[37] This burst activism paid off with a few notable victories. York closed its two black elementary schools following the *Brown* decision; at about the same time, the YMCA, which previously had resisted the desegregation of its pools, dropped all restrictions to black membership.[38] One youth who graduated from William Penn High School in 1958 was Ronald McKinley Everett. While the extent of his activism in the 1950s remains unknown, Everett, who changed his name to Maulana Karenga, became one of the nation's most prominent black radicals in the mid-1960s, the founder of US (and Kwanzaa), an organization that promoted cultural nationalism.[39]

While the black freedom struggle hit a lull in the latter half of the 1950s, it re-emerged stronger than ever in the early 1960s. In the national black press, York's residents praised the sit-inners for their willingness to "risk everything...for what they consider most valuable." Simultaneously, with the help of key white allies, particularly Dorie Leader, black activists researched and published an extensive "Community Audit of Human Rights," which in turn bolstered demands for a variety of reforms. Citing "the United Nations Universal Declaration of Human Rights and the Constitution," writes Kalish, the report documented "discriminatory practices by real estate agents, bankers [and] physicians [as well as]...nonprofit agency directors, retail store managers [and] restaurant owners." One example of systemic discrimination was York Real Estate Board's decision to refuse to admit William Barber, a black man,

---

[37] Johnson and Woodyard quoted in, Kalish, *Civil Rights in York*, pp. 39–40.

[38] "Mr. Montouth Replies," *New Journal and Guide*, April 9, 1960, p. 9; "York YWCA Opens Membership to All," *Afro-American*, October 16, 1954, p. 11; York YMCA Drops All Races Bars," *Afro-American*, April 2, 1955, p. 15; Jim Kalish, *Civil Rights in York*, pp. 41–43.

[39] See "Kwanzaa's Roots Stretch from York to Africa," www.ydr.com/local/ci_27218710/kwanzaas-roots-stretch-from-york-africa [accessed July 20, 2015]; "Kwanzaa's Founder Graduated from William Penn," www.yorkblog.com/yorktownsquare/2006/12/11/kwanzaas-founder-graduated-from-william-penn/ [accessed July 20, 2015].

as a member. As the former assistant executive director of the York Redevelopment Authority, Barber clearly had the qualifications to join the board but he was denied membership by a vote of twenty-three to three "because members feared that he would sell homes in all-white neighborhoods to Blacks."[40]

Local black groups regularly invited guest speakers to York, including Philadelphia's Reverend Leon Sullivan, to generate support for protests against local conditions. At the same time, by participating in civil rights demonstrations elsewhere, local activists bolstered the sense that York's efforts were part of a broader struggle. For instance, a sizable contingent of York's black residents participated in the 1963 March on Washington and a smaller contingent traveled to Selma, Alabama, in 1965 and brought back stories regarding these events to the local black community. The issue that generated the most vociferous and widespread activism was the deployment of dogs and abusive actions on the part of York's police. As Maurice Peters, an employee with the Post Office and the head of the Peaceful Committee for Immediate Action (PCIA) put it, the city failed "to understand the urgency in rising racial tensions as a result of the brutality of certain police officers." Years earlier, Peters had staged a single-person swim-in against the city's segregated schools. His son, Maurice Peters Jr. would become a distinguished medical doctor and, in the 1980s, a member and leader of the Nation of Islam. In 1963, the PCIA held a series of mass meetings and orchestrated marches downtown, ending at the steps of City Hall (see Figure 7.4). There, marchers carried banners descrying the use of police dogs, compared York to Birmingham, Alabama (the notorious site of vicious attacks by German Shepherd dogs on nonviolent protesters), and sang freedom songs. To bolster their spirits, they invited Hal Brown, a native of York who had become a CORE leader in California, to speak. He urged his former friends and neighbors to "tell the white establishment" that they were not satisfied with the racial status quo. While men led the protests and gave most of the speeches, women in York, as elsewhere, swelled the ranks of those who marched in the streets and, most likely, did the legwork to orchestrate the protests in the first place. This wave of protests culminated with a rally of 1,500 at Penn

---

[40] Kalish, *Civil Rights in York*, pp. 44–47. A fourteen page summary of the report was released in 1961, York County Council for Human Relations, *ABC's of Good Will for Yorkers* (1961). "Local Civil Rights Pioneer Doris "Dorrie" Leader dies at age 89," *York Dispatch*, September 12, 2012; Molefi Kete Asante, *Maulanga Karenga: An Intellectual Portrait* (Cambridge: Polity Press, 2009).

FIGURE 7.4 Civil rights protest on steps of City Hall, York, PA. Unfortunately, there are no good photographs of the larger rally in Penn Commons. By permission of the York History Center.

Commons in late October 1963. Given that York's black population stood at about 5,000 at the time, this represented a remarkable turnout.[41] This would be the equivalent to approximately 300,000 blacks marching in New York City.

In a letter to the editor, Carmine Molinaro adeptly captured the state of race relations in York at the time. The police department's use of dogs, which led to the indiscriminate biting of three black men, precipitated

[41] Brown and Kalish quoted in Jim Kalish, *Civil Rights in York*, pp. 52–53. York's black population was just over 4,700 in 1960. "York, Pa. Civil Rights Leader Took Plunge Against Discriminatory Ban at City Pool," www.yorkblog.com/yorktownsquare/2010/02/23/maurice-peters-abdul-alim-muha/ [accessed July 14, 2015]; "York Negroes Plan City Hall Protest," *The Gettysburg Times*, July 23, 1963, p. 6; "Penn Park Negro Unity Rally October 1963," in "Photos, York's African-American Historical Preservation Society," www.facebook.com/yorksblackhistory/ [accessed December 2, 2016].

the protests, Molinaro wrote. But the decision of the city to maintain a canine force and the divergent views that blacks and whites had of the dogs illustrated the deeper problem. While York's Mayor John Snyder contended that the city used the canine corps to "control crowds and riots," in York, as in Birmingham, Molinaro expounded, both Bull Connor and York's Director of Public Safety deployed dogs to "show their might"; their goal was social order not "social justice." To make matters worse, Molinaro continued, when the PCIA convinced Mayor Snyder to meet with its leader Maurice Peters, Snyder used the occasion to try to intimidate Peters and then rebuffed all of the PCIA's complaints. He did so, Molinaro added, with impunity, because he understood that he enjoyed the support of the majority of York's white residents, including one who responded to the PCIA's nonviolent protests by suggesting that the nation should put blacks in "reservations," just like it had done to the Indians.[42]

While the vast majority of the protesters were black, the local movement enjoyed the support of some key white allies, including some members of the local clergy and the aforementioned Dorrie Leader and J. W. Gitt. Throughout this period, Gitt's newspaper, the *York Gazette and Daily*, covered the civil rights movement in York and across the nation and, much to the consternation of the local elite, ran exposes on the depth of racial discrimination in York. This included a gripping photo essay on housing conditions in the black community. Writes Mary Hamilton: "When Henry Schmidt," one of York's scions and an associate of Gitts's at the exclusive all-white and all-male downtown Lafayette Club, "told him he could not enjoy his breakfast looking at those pictures in the paper, Gitt retorted, 'Then why in hell don't you do something about it?'" Moreover, Gitt's paper ran a string of stories and editorials that aimed at shaming the city's leaders into doing something about both police abuse and the systemic discrimination in housing and employment. Some of these editorials were written by Robert Maynard, a black journalist who Gitt hired to work for his paper in 1961. Unbeknownst to the public, Gitt had Maynard publish these articles anonymously – without a byline – in order to protect him from "harassment from the police and KKK."[43] (Maynard went on to become one of the most prominent black journalists in the

---

[42] Carmine Molinaro Jr. "Letter to the Editor," *The Daily Courier* (Connellsville, PA), August 5, 1963, p 11.
[43] Hamilton, *Rising From the Wilderness*, pp. 194–195, 210–211.

nation, first as a correspondent for the *Washington Post* and then as the publisher and owner of the *Oakland Tribune*.)[44]

One example of the synergy between Gitt's paper and black activists came in the summer of 1965. Following another set of attacks by police officers on members of York's black community, Gitt ran a column that condemned the city for having failed to reform the police department, adding that York "could be headed for some bad trouble." When the local NAACP organized a week of protests in front of City Hall, several *Gazette and Daily* reporters joined them. They were confronted by an equally large group of counter-protesters, who took on the name the "Committee to Support Local Police Officers." In contrast to the black demonstrators, this organization called on city leaders to offer commendations to the police officers who were accused of abuse. George Chantiles, a town council member whose brother was one of the accused officers, evicted *Gazette and Daily* reporters from his court room during hearings regarding this incident. Later that fall, after being re-elected by a sizable margin, Mayor Snyder promoted a citywide referendum to formally repeal a previously enacted ordinance which called for the creation of a police advisory board to which Snyder had never appointed anyone to anyway. With the logistical support of many police officers, over 2,700 residents signed the petition, prompting the city council to repeal their previous measure. To which, Charles Gitt, J. W.'s son, editorialized: "They might as well proclaim this a city where race hatred reigns."[45]

The traditional narrative of the civil rights years has paid little attention to either the state of race relations or the struggles against inequality in small and medium size cities, particularly those north of the Mason–Dixon line. Yet, York's story suggests that tens of thousands of blacks who resided in such places faced persistent discrimination and realized few reforms in spite of decades of protest. Even the contemporary shift of attention from the Deep South to the "north," which accompanied the outbreak of riots in Harlem, Watts, Detroit, and Newark, failed to garner York or places like it much attention, which in turn may have further encouraged the white elite to continue to equivocate. But in York,

[44] Bruce Lambert, "Obituary: Robert C. Maynard, 56, Publisher Who Helped Minority Journalists, *NYT*, August 19, 1993, www.nytimes.com/1993/08/19/obituaries/robcrt-c-maynard-56-publisher-who-helped-minority-journalists.html [accessed June 9, 2017].

[45] Hamilton, *Rising From the Wilderness*, pp. 211–212, ch. 18, n.61; "Suspend Cop in Kid Nab," *Afro-American*, July 30, 1966, p. 12.

as across the nation, blacks grew increasingly militant, threatening they would give the city "one last chance" to address their concerns. The failure of the white community to respond constructively to even such heightened rhetoric, not to mention the warnings of the statewide Human Relations Commission, as we shall see in the following chapter, virtually insured that York would experience one of the most severe revolts of the entire Great Uprising.

8

Fighting Back

If we must die – oh, let us noble die . . .
Pressed to the wall, dying, but fighting back!
Claude McKay, "If We Must Die," 1919

As uprisings swept the nation, York's political leaders failed to implement reforms aimed at improving relationships between law enforcement authorities and the black community. Faced with the intransigence of the white community, a number of York's black citizens allied with more radical civil rights groups, particularly those who advocated the right of self-defense or as the famed Harlem Renaissance poet, Claude McKay, put it, "fighting back." Some Yorkers, particularly black and white moderates, sought to maintain a middle ground, as evidenced by calls for and ultimately the appearance of the Pennsylvania Human Relations Commission in the fall of 1968. Yet even the strongly worded recommendations of this body fell on deaf ears at City Hall making a bad situation worse. As a result, York experienced a series of mini riots in 1968 followed by a much more significant revolt in the summer of 1969.

"All You've Got Is Agitation"

In 1966, Lionell Bailey and Theodore Holmes formed a local branch of the Congress of Racial Equality (CORE), which had recently endorsed the call for black power. The local branch invited James Farmer to speak at a rally at the Alcazar ballroom in downtown York, where the longtime CORE leader described York's housing "as bad as I have ever seen." Visiting York was like rereading Ralph Ellison's *The Invisible Man*, Farmer observed, because the "Negro in York is invisible, swept under the rug." In addition to supporting the chapter's call for better housing, Farmer endorsed CORE's demand that the city create a police advisory board to address the numerous cases of police abuse.[1]

The rise of more militant black organizations produced some rifts in the larger black community, with better-off blacks advancing more moderate positions while working-class blacks advocated more militant one. Such rifts were not unique to the late 1960s. In a 1955 speech at York's Jewish Community Center, Mordecai Johnson, the president of Howard University, spoke nary a word about race relations in York, or even the *Brown* decision, focusing instead on the Cold War and the battle between the United States and Russia, and for the allegiance of non-whites around the world. Several years later, Edward Simmons, the Executive Director of the Crispus Attucks Center, preached the value of hard work and lifting oneself up by one's own bootstraps, as opposed to marching on Washington (most likely a reference to the 1957 Prayer Pilgrimage). Likewise, in the spring of 1960, as the sit-ins took place from Greensboro, North Carolina, to Nashville, Tennessee, Democritus, the pen name of a black author from York, called for "more patience" not civil disobedience, which could "incite riots," regardless of the righteousness of the cause.[2]

One place where this split reappeared in the latter half of the 1960s was over the future of the Crispus Attucks Center (CA). Faced with deteriorating buildings and diminishing financial resources, the longtime center abruptly closed its doors at the end of 1966, leaving local residents with the loss of a crucial recreational facility and forcing a nearby church to house its daycare program. For several years, some of York's most prominent citizens, including the leaders of the United Fund (the predecessor to the United Way) advocated merging CA into the YWCA (Young Women's Christian Association), claiming this would create a "truly integrated neighborhood center." But others resisted the loss of an institution identified with the black community, favoring, instead, greater

[1] "CORE Head Finds York Slum Typical of Northern Cities," *YGD*, January 17, 1966, p. 1; Philadelphia SAC to J. Edgar Hoover, January 18, 1966, Federal Bureau of Investigations (FBI) Philadelphia Office Case File 157-PH-1711-v. 1, National Archives, Record Group 65, Box 58. Theodore Holmes, "Letter to the Editor: White Racism Needs Treatment," *YGD*, June 25, 1968; "Militant Leader with a Past," *York Dispatch*, March 9, 2003, online edition [accessed January 10, 2014].
[2] "Mordecai Johnson – Poet and Educator," *Afro-American*, April 2, 1955, p. A10; Jim Kalish, *Civil Rights in York*, pp. 39–40; Democritus, "Two Views on Sitdown Protests in the South," *New Journal and Guide*, April 9, 1960, p. 9.

independence. Wade Bowers, for one, a longtime staff member of CA, delineated the advantages of having black-owned and run institutions. "What Negro doesn't take pride in Negro owned churches, lodges, etc.?" Bowers rhetorically inquired. With the future of the CA's physical space and place still up in the air (there were calls for relocating to a larger piece of land), a group of militants sought to take control of the center. One of their leaders, Ocania Chalk, the editor of York CORE chapter's newspaper, and a case worker at the local social service agency, termed CA too beholden to the white establishment. Rather than accommodate whites so as to procure more funding, Chalk exuded blacks to "agitate, agitate, agitate ... You don't have ... a representative ... or judges or people sitting on city council. All you've got is agitation." Along with Lionel Bailey and Theodore Holmes, the militants established their own slate of officers, presented a plan for CA that included performing economic and cultural functions, and instilling pride in the black community. In other words, they sought to transform CA into the living embodiment of black power as sketched out by various black radicals across the nation.[3]

While this challenge failed – Bowers turned down the offer to head up CA on the grounds that the militant slate lacked the authority to make the offer – it nudged some centrist black leaders to adopt a more militant tone. Reverend Leslie Lawson, who became the new pastor at Small AME Zion Church in July of 1969, identified himself as a "soul brother" and warned that the "city powers" were "writing the agenda for summer riots." Similarly, a number of black business persons established the Association for the Advancement of Black-Owned Businesses. Describing liberal white efforts as "bankrupt," it pledged to aid "black enterprises that will benefit the community in terms of jobs, housing, and care for the young, sick and elderly."[4]

[3] Jim Kalish, *Civil Rights in York*, pp. 60–72; "Crispus Attucks Post Offered Roy O. Borom," *Afro-American*, February 17, 1968, p. 17. Chalk quoted in, Olysa Townsley, "When the Bubble Burst: Understanding the York Race Riots Through the Lens of a Community Resistant to Change," Senior thesis, York College, May 2010, p. 8 (in author's possession); "Benefit Concert for Poor People's March," *YGD*, June 18, 1968, p. 4; "Yorkers Skeptical on March Results," *YGD*, June 20, 1968, p. 3. "Public Housing Grievances Voiced by Community Group," *YGD*, June 13, 1968, p. 42.

[4] York Negroes Form New Body For Economic, Political Growth," *YGD*, August 13, 1968, p. 1; "Yorker Named to Area Office Aiding Negroes," *YGD*, August 14, 1968, p. 35; "Small AME Zion Get New Pastor," *YGD*, August 15, 1969. For another example of a rift, see "Grundy Says CORE Boycott Won't Hurt Race Workshop," *YGD*, December 2, 1967, p. 3; "Heaven for K-9 Dogs, Hell for Blacks," *Philadelphia Tribune*, April 14, 1970, p. 4.

As York's blacks debated the future of Crispus Attucks and aired their grievances with their heretofore white allies, tensions arising out of additional acts of police misconduct precipitated three "mini riots." The first occurred in mid-July 1968 when police ordered fifty black youths to leave Penn Common Park and arrested two for refusing to obey their orders. After the arrests, the situation escalated, culminating with shots being fired by police. At first the police denied they had fired their guns; subsequently, Police Chief Landis explained that Patrolman Wayne Toomey fired into the air, as a warning, though he acknowledged that this too violated police procedures. Both the shooting, which witnesses claimed nearly struck a nearby resident, as well as police obfuscation, angered the community, with one black man accusing Landis of harboring "racists in your outfit." News that the incident was precipitated by the police decision to enforce a curfew ordinance which had recently been annulled, exasperated many residents even more, with one youth inquiring, "Why do they have to disperse a group of Blacks? What's wrong with congregating in the park?"[5] In the immediate aftermath of the shooting, some stores were trashed, gunshots were exchanged, and the police were put on high alert. Perhaps just as importantly, investigations into the shooting lingered for months, including hearings held by the city council which provided further proof of police misconduct.[6]

The second disturbance, which took place in early August 1968, proved more serious than the first. This "riot" was precipitated by a confrontation between Chester Roach – a middle-aged white man who lived above Hoffman's meat market, at 226 South Penn Street, a mere block from where Schaad would be shot the following year – and young

[5] "Cops Shoot While Chasing Teenagers, Residents Say," *YGD*, July 12, 1968, p. 1; "Police Chief Says Patrolman Fired Shot And It Was a Mistake," *YGD*, July 13, 1968, p. 1; "Series of Events Thursday Led to Firing by Police," *YGD*, July 13, 1968, p. 1; "Curfew Blamed in Disorders; Officials Say No Law Exists," and "Rock Throwing and Assaults and Fire Mar City Weekend," both in *YGD*, July 15, 1968, p. 1; "Buck-passing By City On Disorders Feared"; "York Police Put on 12-Hour Shifts"; "2 Firebombs Came in Midst of False Alarms"; and "Ghetto Leaders Form Committee to Avoid Crisis," all in *YGD*, July 16, 1968, p. 1; "Black Adults, Youths Hold Discussion of Recent Acts"; "2 Persons Swear they Saw Toomey Fire His Pistol"; "Police Harassment Is Blamed for Violence by Black Youth"; all in *YGD*, July 17, 1968, p. 1; "Black Council Plans to Repair Damages; Will Give City a "Last Chance to Act," *YGD*, July 19, 1968, p. 1; "Disorders Began With Teenagers Were Cleared From Park by Police," *YGD*, July 22, 1968, p. 2; "Warning Shots Out of Line, Police Say," *York Dispatch*, July 13, 1968, p. 32; "Rid 'Problem Police' Negroes Prod Hose," *York Dispatch*, July 15, 1968, p. 30.
[6] "Council Hearing Witnesses Say Up to Six Shots Fired," *YGD*, August 22, 1968, p. 1.

blacks. While accounts of the altercation varied, it appears that the trouble began at 11:30 p.m. when Roach yelled at youths for making too much noise outside his window. Apparently, when the youths yelled back, Roach began firing at them first with a pellet gun and then with a shotgun, striking ten, at least one seriously. When police arrived they ignored black complaints and did not place Roach under arrest. Instead, they deployed two recently acquired armored vehicles and upwards of two-thirds of the police force in full riot equipment. Black anger over the shooting and police response reached new heights. "This is open warfare," declared one youth. "Whitey made his statement last night. He said, 'I hate you niggers and I'm going to kill you.' So baby if whitey is going to start shooting, you better bet I'm firing back." Another teen stated that he had "never thought very much about the black power philosophy but that the Penn [Roach] street shooting changed his mind," adding, "If he had been Black do you think the cops would have left him there firing a gun? Man, if a Black man had been in that house the cops would have bombed him out…But it was a white man. And…they were probably glad that he was just shooting some niggers that the cops wouldn't have to shoot themselves."[7]

When the Chamber of Commerce sought to intervene, black citizens proved much less accommodating than in the past. Rather than hold one more hearing or wait for the results of another report, one black resident declared that blacks needed to "arm to protect themselves." A different black Yorker warned that if the city did not rectify existing conditions, "the entire city will explode." At the time, members of the Chamber of Commerce and newspaper publisher J. W. Gitt criticized the militants for their obstinacy, but this response suggested that white moderates failed to recognize the accumulated anger of the black community, which felt that the days of empty dialogue had passed.[8]

A third "mini-riot" took place in the fall of 1968 following a football game between York's William Penn Senior High and Cedar Cliff High,

[7] "Police in Riot Dress Patrol York After Shooting of 11 Persons," *YGD*, August 5, 1968, p. 1; "Black Youths Angry After What They Feel Was Attack," *YGD*, August 5, 1968, p. 3; "Policeman Ordered Suspended," *YGD*, August 6, 1968; "20 Hurt as New Violence Rakes West End Area," *York Dispatch*, August 5, 1968, p. 28; "Key Developments in York's Latest Disturbance," *York Dispatch*, August 6, 1968, p. 32; "News of the Week," *New York Amsterdam News*, August 17, 1968, p. 2.
[8] "City Officials Commandeered Armored Truck," *YGD*, August 2, 1968, p. 4. "Chamber of Commerce Listens to Negro Complaint," *York Dispatch*, August 7, 1968, p. 32; Hamilton, *Rising From the Wilderness.* "Beyond the Bio: Bobby Simpson," www.witf.org/news/beyond-the-bio/2012/09/beyond-the-bio-bobby-simpson.php [accessed June 22, 2016].

from Camp Hill, a predominantly white suburb of Harrisburg, about twenty miles north of York. After the game, fights broke out between some of the fans. Then, as the crowd spilled into York's downtown, more disorders erupted. York's city police exacerbated the situation by selectively "siccing" their police dogs on black youths, at least seven of whom had to be hospitalized by night's end. Police asserted that those bitten had refused to obey their orders to clear the area. Reverend Adam Kitrell countered that the dogs attacked "a number of the youths" who were "doing nothing." In support of this claim, the *York Gazette and Daily* reported that two police officers stopped one of the youths, Calvin Stokes, for jaywalking in front of a car. While being detained, the newspaper added, a third policeman, Nevin Barley, who had a notorious reputation in the black community, sicced his dog on Stokes. Afterwards, the police threw Stokes into their patrol car and called him "one of those smart niggers." The police also took umbrage at reporter Arthur Magida, who sought to take photographs of the action. He claimed that they sicced a police dog on him and broke his camera. The police incredulously countered that Magida had thrown the camera down on the ground and broken it himself.[9]

Even before this third mini-riot, the Pennsylvania Human Relations Commission had convened a series of hearings in the city. At the hearings, black leaders accused the mayor and city council of neglecting their "legal and moral" obligations, adding that the recent disturbances reflected the repeated "failure of the local government" to address the needs of the black community in a meaningful way. NAACP leader James Colston Jr. provided several detailed examples of police abuse, including harassment of interracial couples, the siccing of dogs on black youths, and the suspicious death of Carl Williams, a black man who had been arrested for drunk driving in 1965. "We talk about law and order," Colston testified, "but we've had a mayor in office four years who flagrantly refused to comply with the law to create a police review board." Similarly, Carlton Trotman, the former director of the Community Progress Council, the local Community Action Agency, described the city's commitment to combating the social and economic problems that beset the black community as "minimal." Trotman also accused York's leaders of

9 "10 Injured, 15 Held in Disorder After York Football Game"; "Leaders Describe Police Dog Actions Against Black Youth"; and "Reporter Bitten by Police Dog, Camera Smashed"; all in *YGD*, September 21, 1968, p. 1; "Black Youth Bitten By Dog Tells of Police Encounter"; and "Another Newsman In Police Court," *YGD*, September 23, 1968, p. 1; "10 Injured as Disorders Sweep Mid-city in Wake of Grid Game," *York Dispatch*, September 21, 1968, p. 32.

having failed to "gain the participation of white poor Yorkers," which in his mind undermined the program from the start.[10]

Rather than respond constructively to these accusations, many white officials reacted belligerently. When Nathan Agran, the general counsel for the PHRC began to question Mayor Snyder, Snyder bolted from his seat. When he did not return, the city solicitor defended his action and accused the commission of "harassing" the mayor.[11] The following day Corporal Peter Chantiles of York went out of his way to disrupt the PHRC's hearings, openly calling it "useless" and warning one of the witnesses that he "better get [his] goddamn facts straight...[or] I'll fix you." When reporters asked Director of Public Safety Jacob Hose if Chantiles would face discipline for his public outburst, Hose responded that Chantiles would not.[12]

The racial polarization of York, symbolized by the failure of the PHRC and city leaders to reach a common ground, continued through the fall and winter of 1968–1969. While local developments explain much of this polarization, York was not an island, immune to the forces stirring around it. Outside of the city of York, the nation was in the midst of its most tumultuous times since the Civil War, including a massive wave of urban revolts following Martin Luther King Jr.'s assassination, intense protests at colleges and universities over the Vietnam War and a variety of other campus issues, feminist demonstrations against sexism at the Miss America pageant in Atlantic City, violent confrontations between police and largely young activists in the streets of Chicago during the Democratic convention, and the blossoming of the counterculture. All of these developments played themselves out to one degree or another in York. For instance, in the spring and summer of 1969, an assortment of local antiwar activists established the "York Free School Collective,"

[10] "Mayor Snyder, Council Attacked Before Human Relations Hearing," *YGD*, August 28, 1968, p. 1; "Counsel of 'Harassing' Mayor Snyder," *YGD*, August 28, 1968, p. 1; "Superiority 'Attitude' Causes Race Tension State Hearing Is Told," *YGD*, August 29, 1968, p. 1; "Chantiles Berated for His Conduct at Racial Hearing," *YGD*, August 29, 1969, p. 1.
[11] "Mayor Snyder, Council Attacked Before Human Relations Hearing," *YGD*, August 28, 1968, p. 1; "Counsel of 'Harassing' Mayor Snyder," *YGD*, August 28, 1968, p. 1; "Superiority 'Attitude' Causes Race Tension State Hearing Is Told," *YGD*, August 29, 1968, p. 1; "Chantiles Berated for His Conduct at Racial Hearing," *YGD*, August 29, 1969, p. 1.
[12] "Chantiles Berated for His Conduct at Racial Hearing"; and "Superiority 'Attitude' Causes Race Tension State Hearing is Told," *YGD*, August 29, 1968, p. 1; "Disorders Here Laid to 'Small Minority,'" *York Dispatch*, September 18, 1968, p. 32.

which helped support the upcoming national moratorium against the war and raise awareness about sexism. Not surprisingly, many of the whites who resisted implementing racial reforms also squared off against local manifestations of these New Left causes too.[13] For instance, in the fall of 1968, the Young Republicans held their state convention in the city, where Spiro Agnew served as their keynote speaker. Whereas the national press was in the midst of painting Agnew as a liability to the GOP ticket, the Young Republicans in York received him enthusiastically. While we do not know if Agnew had been briefed about York's recent racial turmoil, he made clear his opposition to "permissive" policies, including those that he implied had led to the outrageous behavior of white youths in Chicago during the Democratic Party's presidential convention. Unlike Johnson and the Democrats, Agnew added, the Nixon administration would be able to "separate the good guys from the bad guys."[14]

Election results reflected the breadth of white retrenchment and anti-radical sentiment in York. In 1964, President Johnson had won 70 percent of York's city's vote but in 1968, his vice-president, Hubert Humphrey, won just 45 percent of the city's vote and did even worse in the county. While race was not the only issue, 9 percent of the city voted for George Wallace, a symbol of Jim Crow. In the ninth ward of the city, which was overwhelming white and Democratic, Wallace won nearly 17 percent of the vote. In 1972, the city again displayed its absolute rejection of the politics of the New Left, personified by the Democratic nominee George McGovern. Even though Democrats continued to outnumber Republicans in the city, the Nixon–Agnew ticket won 68.2 percent of their vote.[15] The career of Congressman George Goodling's similarly displayed the region's political sentiments. First elected to Congress in 1960 as a moderate "Eisenhower/Rockefeller" Republican – he voted for the Civil Rights Act of 1964 – Goodling lost to Nathaniel Craley, a Democrat, in 1964. In 1966, Goodling won back his seat by playing to the burgeoning spirit of white retrenchment that was spreading across the nation. In 1968, he described the Poor People's Campaign as "the most disgusting sight I had ever seen," and disputed the claim that "chronic poverty" existed in America.[16] Like Agnew, Goodling rejected the Kerner

[13] "York Free School Personnel States Background on Formation, Guidance," *YGD*, June 8, 1970, p. 3; "An Oblique Look at the York Free School," *YGD*, June 9, 1970, p. 32

[14] "Agnew Raps Youth Involved in 'Unconscious Anarchy,'" *YGD*, September 6, 1968, p. 1.

[15] Vote totals come from: *The Pennsylvania Manual, 1968–69*, vol. 99 (Harrisburg: Department of Property and Supplies, 1969).

[16] Levy, "Spiro Agnew"; "Yorkers Skeptical on March Results; Disappointed at Talk with Goodling," *YGD*, June 20, 1968, p. 3.

Commission's claims that white racism caused rioting, as well as calls to spend more money on poverty programs. Espousing these positions, he not only won re-election easily in 1968, 1970, and 1972, he was succeeded by his equally conservative son, William Goodling, who years later would serve as a character witness for Charlie Robertson in 2002, describing Charlie and his brother Wibie – who was also a police officer – as "life-long friends."[17]

To make matters worse, Mayor Snyder and other leaders in York reaffirmed their opposition to the Pennsylvania Human Relations Commission when it issued its report in December 1968. The report called for wide ranging reforms, including improving communication between the races and availing itself of opportunities to address the employment and housing needs of the black community.[18] Rather than implement any of these reforms, Mayor Snyder dedicated a monument to police dogs, claiming they had made the city safer and asserted that he would employ more dogs if necessary. About a month later, local courts acquitted Chester Roach of all charges stemming from his armed confrontation with black youths the previous summer. During the trial, Judge George Atkins sided with a defense motion to drop charges of assault with intent to kill but allowed the trial on lesser charges to proceed. The state's case against Roach was weakened by a lack of forensic evidence. More specifically, the police claimed they had failed to locate the gun that Roach had allegedly used. When Roach testified that Earl Smith, a black youth, had shot at him first, Smith's mother screamed from the back of the courtroom that her son had never owned nor carried a gun. The state's attorney did little to try to impeach Roach's claim. Nor did the state pursue several other indictments against Roach relating to his alleged assaults against other black youths on the same day.[19]

Moreover, at the grassroots level, evidence of white retrenchment abounded. When WPHS's principal Dr. O. Meredith Parry allowed black students to stage a walkout following Martin Luther King Jr.'s assassination, one teacher not only protested that the students should have been forced to attend class, disciplined, or both, but he also added that "the auditorium would have to be fumigated because of the all Black

---

[17] "Agnew Raps Youth Involved in 'Unconscious Anarchy,'" *YGD*, September 6, 1968, p. 1; Testimony of William Goodling, in *Commonwealth v. Robert Messersmith et al.*

[18] PHRC, "Report"; PHRC, "Press Release," n.d.

[19] "Mayor Says Dog Corps May Be Expanded," *YGD*, May 24, 1968, p. 1; "Roach Found Not Guilty in August Disorder Shooting," *YGD*, June 16, 1969, p. 1; DA Criminal Docket, Chester Roach 89, August 1968 and DA Criminal Docket 172, October 1968, both in the York County District Court Archives.

assembly." When the Pennsylvania Human Relations Council endorsed the black community's demand for reforming the police, the "Citizens' Council of York" echoed Richard Nixon's call for "law and order." "It's time to stop appeasing this small minority – it's time to stop coddling the lawbreakers!" Likewise, an anonymous letter writer called for returning Officer Chantiles to the streets. "We need more men like him," the writer exclaimed. "Do we want our police to carry lollipops instead of guns?" Residents of the Salem Square neighborhood, which abutted the predominantly black West End neighborhood, similarly demonstrated that they had no intention of kowtowing to black demands. "They're trying to take over this county and we're not going to let them," one resident of the Salem Square neighborhood informed a newspaper reporter. "White people are roaming about Salem Square with weapons waiting for any Negro to leave his cordoned off ghetto," explained another white man. "The police had better get in charge of this situation or we will." Whereas civil rights groups in York demanded the suspension of Officers Toomey and Chantiles, one white teenager applauded them for having fired at black youths. "I wish I'd [been] out there with Toomey," the white teen explained, "blasting away at them niggers with a 30–20. I'd have gotten about 20 of them." Seeing York as fertile territory, Roy Frankhouser and George Houser, leaders of the KKK in Pennsylvania, planned a "robed march" in York for November 12, 1968. An early freak snowstorm, however, prompted them to call off the protest. (Some assert that York County's Klan leader, Albert Lentz, helped organize the "white power" rally that took place in the midst of the July 1969 riots – see below. Others have suggested that John Messersmith, the father of two of the NSB members ultimately indicted for Allen's murder, was the Grand Marshall of the KKK in York County in the years following the revolt.)[20]

"We Are Going to Give this White Power Structure Their Last Chance"

Rather than appease the voices of white retrenchment, a cluster of about thirty-five black adults and youths met at Bobby Simpson's home and

---

[20] Margaret Hassler to Raymond Shafer, 2 September 1968, Raymond Shafer Papers, MG209, Carton 164; SAC, Philadelphia (157-3239) to FBI Director, November 12, 1968, and SA Norman Hendricks to SAC (15701646) both in Records of the Federal Bureau of Investigation, RG 65 National Archives – FOIA Request RD 42541; also, Philadelphia, PA Civil Unrest, Hooded Ku Klux Klan March, 11/12/1968, 1957–1968, Record Group 65, Records of the Federal Bureau of Investigation, National Archives, College Park, FOIA request 157-WFO-3; "Klan Robes Sought In Case," *York Dispatch*, September 30, 2001; "Mail Bag," *York Dispatch*, October 10, 1968, p. 5.

formed a new all-black organization, which they initially called York City Youth. The group employed militant rhetoric, with Simpson asserting: "We are going to give this white power structure their last chance, and if they think they have seen something this past week, they ain't seen nothing yet." Years later, Simpson, who rose to become the leader of the Crispus Attucks Center and a leader in the York community in general, acknowledged being a "foot soldier" for changes and he did not regret doing so because "things needed to change."[21]

In mid-May 1969 the Black Unity Movement (BUM), an outgrowth of CORE and the York City Youth organization, held its first meeting at the Crispus Attucks Center on the anniversary of Malcolm X's birthday. At its inaugural event, Bill Thompson, a Black Power spokesperson from Reading, Pennsylvania, discussed Malcolm X's emphasis on black unity, which Thompson insisted underlay the goal of "social, political, economic, but most important of all military power." At the same meeting, "The Black Players," an all-black theater group from William Penn Senior High, presented its rendition of African American history, including an emotional depiction of the near-lynching of Elizabeth Eckford, on the day that Central High School in Little Rock, Arkansas, was slated for desegregation in the fall of 1957. Over the course of the summer, BUM focused much of its attention on the "need to protect themselves and their families ... because they didn't think that the York City Police Department was doing its job ... but was actually encouraging ... white supremacists, like Newberry Street [Boys] and company ... to do some bad stuff to blacks." This concept of armed self-defense mirrored views promoted by the Black Panther Party and other black nationalists. At the same time, a number of the members of BUM, including Leon Wright and Carl Williams Jr., the son of the black man allegedly killed by police in 1965, continued to work for improved recreational opportunities for black youth, an effort which paid off with the opening of a new sports program in the old York Junior College gymnasium. Ironically, the new program was slated to begin operation on the evening of July 17, 1969, at about the same time that the revolt started (see below).[22]

[21] "Beyond the Bio: Bobby Simpson," www.witf.org/news/beyond-the-bio/2012/09/beyond-the-bio-bobby-simpson.php [accessed June 22, 2016].
[22] "New Black Group to Hold Program," *YGD*, May 15, 1969, p. 3; "Malcolm X Honored At Crispus Attucks," *YGD*, May 19, 1969, p. 2; "Gym Set to Open," *YGD*, July 8, 1969, p. 2; "Sports Program Opens in College Area Gym," *YGD*, July 17, 1969. Terrence McGowan, "Opening Statement," in *Commonwealth of Pennsylvania v. Stephen D. Freeland*, Common Court of Pleas of York County, Pennsylvania.

During the same time period, many of York's black women displayed an increasingly militant posture. In a letter to the editor, Ernestine Rankin championed calls for black unity and pride. "The Whites never needed an identity. When they came into the world – Whites knew they were Whites, they had no reasons to try themselves and identity," Rankin explained. Blacks, in contrast, "we're brought here in chains, sold into slavery, beaten, treated like animals, lived like animals, and we're taught they were animals." Not only did they want the "same opportunity and chances as their white masters," blacks were beginning to investigate their African backgrounds, use the term "Soul Brother," and letting their "hair have a natural look"; they were trying to "find ourselves after so many years of being what someone else wanted us to be," adding "if Blacks want to call themselves black that's their business. And if blacks want to say black is beautiful let them."[23]

In addition to weighing in on the push for black pride, many black women agitated on a variety of housing issues. A subcommittee of the Community Action Group (CAG), comprised of Mary Jackson, Panchita Tompson (Bethune), Joan West, and Jane Shaffer led Mayor Snyder and city council members on a tour of dilapidated homes which landlords had failed to maintain. In a series of meetings, CAG members and unaffiliated black women voiced their grievances about existing public housing and complained about the threats posed by plans to clear more slums. Myrtis McMillen emphasized that poor women had "good ideas" about how to improve living conditions in public housing projects and that governmental agencies should "give them a voice." At a meeting regarding a potential urban renewal plan, an unidentified black women warned that the city needed to determine where it was "going to put thirty-four families," before it implemented the plan. In the past, she and others noted, promises had been made that homes would be found for displaced men and women but such promises had never been fully kept. Others complained that long-term delays on renewal projects prompted landlords to allow their homes to fall into worse repair and it was time for the city to act, one way or the other. "For fifteen years you all been beating around and now you're back again," and in those fifteen years her home hadn't been repaired once.[24] Some of these same women also participated in the

[23] Ernestine Rankin, "Letter to the Editor: Black Identity and Pride," *YGD*, July 3, 1968, p. 21.
[24] "Mayor and Lewis Shown Violations on Housing Tour," *YGD*, June 15, 1968, p. 1; Myrtis McMillen, "Loopholes in Public Housing Philosophy," *YGD*, June 25, 1968;

Poor People's Campaign in Washington, DC. Queenie Sexton, for one, lambasted Congressman Goodling for worrying more "about the grass at Resurrection City than about ending poverty."[25]

In spite of the growing polarization of the nation and the city, many Yorkers remained convinced that the White Rose City remained immune to the turmoil that was sweeping the nation. The York Chamber of Commerce published a history of greater York that totally glossed over the community's racial divide. The book described York as a beautiful balance of the old and new, where citizens had deep ties to the region and were welcoming of newcomers. Photographs in the book displayed clean shaven working men laboring away in the community's factories, smartly dressed women shopping at newly opened malls, and smiling children studying at school. Although 1968–1969 was one of the most tumultuous times in American History, the history book suggested that the city remained untouched by the unrest. The first black person pictured was a Ugandan foreign exchange student. And the only other two images of people of color were of black youths frolicking at a summer camp and of blacks and whites bowling together.[26] To an extent, this boosterish view of York, common among small and midsize business leaders across the nation, provided cover for city officials, especially Mayor Snyder, who as noted above, refused to disband the canine corps and the city council's decision not to implement any of the Pennsylvania Human Relations Commission's strongly worded recommendations.[27] Perhaps Nixon's election and his pledge to usher in a renewed era of law and order allowed them to react this way; or perhaps they continued to associate urban riots with much bigger cities with large black populations, in absolute and relative terms; or perhaps, in the absence of a political force powerful enough to compel them to act differently, they determined they could afford to do nothing. But, as we shall see, they soon discovered that York was no more immune to the Great Uprising than hundreds of other cities which had failed to deliver on their promises to the black men and

"Residents of Hope Ave. Park Area Raise Relocation Issue," *YGD*, June 12, 1968, p. 42; "Public Housing Grievances Voice by Community Group," *YGD*, June 13, 1968, p. 42.
[25] "Yorkers Skeptical On March Results; Disappointed At Talk with Goodling," *YGD*, June 20, 1968, p. 3.
[26] Lynn Smolens Taub, *Greater York in Action* (York, PA: The York Area Chamber of Commerce, 1968).
[27] "No More Major Riots Expected," *York Dispatch*, September 16, 1968, p. 1; "Disorders Here Laid to 'Small Minority,'" *York Dispatch*, September 18, 1968, p. 32; PHCR, "Press Release," n.d.

women and their sons and daughters who had migrated "north" in search of the American dream.

"More People ... with Guns than I've Ever Seen"

At a bit after 7 p.m. on July 17, 1969, Clifford Green, a twelve-year-old black youth checked into the York hospital to be treated for facial burns. He informed hospital authorities that members of the Girarders, one of York's white gangs, had set him afire. Temperatures had been excessively high for days in South Central Pennsylvania, so oppressive that the local utility company had called on its customers to limit their use of electricity in order to avert a possible brownout. Booming thunderstorms and strong rains on the evening of the 17th broke the heat wave but not before Green's accusation, which he later recanted, set off a firestorm that consumed the city for nearly a week. By some accounts, upon hearing of Green's claims, a group of young blacks set out for the Girarders's turf looking for those who they thought were responsible for Green's burning. In turn, Gregory Neff, the leader of the Girarders notified other white gangs, including the Newberry Street Boys that blacks were "looking for blood." Not long afterwards, fights broke out between black and white youths at a swimming pool near Farquhar Park, a few blocks away from where Lillie Belle Allen would be murdered several days later. Among those involved was Arthur Messersmith, a member of the Newberry Street Boys, who in his own words "got beat up" and Taka Nii Sweeney, a black youth. Afterwards, a cluster of young blacks smashed the windows of a cigar shop that served as the Newberry Street Boys' clubhouse.[28]

---

[28] *Rhoda Barton and Lewis Johnstone v. Eli Eichelberger, Mayor of City of York, Pennsylvania, et al.*, United State Court of Appeals for the Third Circuit, Records of the US Circuit Court of Appeals, 3rd Circuit, Briefs & Appendixes, 3 18986, National Archives, Philadelphia, PA (henceforth *Barton v. Eichelberger*, case file); *Rhoda Barton and Lewis Johnstone v. Eli Eichelberger, Mayor, City of York et al.*, 311 F. Supp. 1132; 1970 US Dist. Lexis 12284. See especially Judge Nealon's Finding of Fact; "Policemen, 7 Others Wounded By Gunfire on York's Streets," *YGD*, July 19, 1969, p. 1; "Boy's Fabricated Story of Being Set Afire Touched Off Clashes of Gangs," *YGD*, July 19, 1969, p. 1; Debra Noel, "The Grapes of Wrath: Seeds of Violence Were Planted Long Before the Fury," *York Sunday News*, July 25, 1968, p. A8; "Fear and Fury: The Riots of 1969: Special Report," *York Sunday News*, pp. A8–A10; "State Police Report: Disorder, York, Pennsylvania," September 8, 1969, Governor Shafer Papers, MG209, 9-1136, Carton 98, Folder 1; "Operational Report: Civil Disturbances – York, Pennsylvania, July 22–28, 1969," Governor Shafer Papers, MG209-1136, Carton 98, Folder 3; *Commonwealth v. Stephen Freeland; Commonwealth v. Leon Wright*, Court of Common Pleas of York County (2003), especially testimony of Anthony Brown and Taka Nii Sweeney. See also

This wasn't the first or only time that blacks and white youths had clashed. For instance, the previous fall Robert Messersmith, Arthur Messersmith's older brother, had gotten in a fist fight with blacks at the York County Fair, and "gotten the worst of it." As we have seen, Randy Graham, one of Robert Messersmith's fellow Newberry Street Boys members, acknowledged that the fair was a place where white youths often went looking to beat up local blacks. Nonetheless, such confrontations had never led to a full scale "riot" and the vast majority of black anger had been directed at the police, not white youths, in the preceding year.[29]

Standard accounts of York's riot trace the unrest to Greene's lie.[30] Yet, a more careful examination of the evidence suggests that the rumor alone did not spark the revolt. The first act of physical violence, beyond some rock throwing and the aforementioned fistfights, took place at approximately 11:40 p.m. on the 17th when the aforementioned Robert Messersmith fired at least two rifle shots at John Washington and Sweeney, hitting them both. Amazingly, at the time, the two were talking with Detective Smith, one of the few black members of York's police force. While Smith took Washington and Sweeny to the hospital, his fellow officers made *no* attempt to question any of the members of the NSBs and no one was arrested for this near fatal assault until after the revolt had subsided. This police reaction, or lack thereof, revived black memories of Chester Roach's shooting of unarmed blacks the summer before and the partial treatment he received from the courts and many other examples of mistreatment by the police.[31]

Commonwealth v. Robert Messersmith et al., especially testimony of Taka Nii Sweeney, Michael Sipe, Arthur Messersmith, Stewart Aldinger, and Stipulations Read into record by District Attorney Thomas Kelly; "Witness Called to Explain Story," *York Dispatch*, December 13, 2001.

[29] "Assaulted at Fair York Youths Report," *YGD*, September 16, 1968.

[30] Costopoulos, *Murder is the Charge*; Keisling, *The Wrong Car*; Conway Stewart, *No Peace, No Justice*; Kalish, *Civil Rights in York*; "Boy's Fabricated Story of Being Set Afire Touched Off Clashes of Gangs," *YGD*, July 19, 1969, p. 1.

[31] *Rhoda Barton and Lewis Johnstone v. Eli Eichelberger, Mayor of City of York, Pennsylvania, et al.*, United State Court of Appeals for the Third Circuit, Case File, Records of the US Circuit Court of Appeals, 3rd Circuit, Briefs & Appendixes, 3 18986, National Archives, Philadelphia, PA., see especially "Findings of Fact Proposed by Plaintiffs," December 24, 1969; and "Testimony of Chief Landis." *Rhoda Barton and Lewis Johnstone, v. Eli Eichelberger, Mayor, City of York et al.*, 311 F. Supp. 1132; 1970 US Dist. Lexis 12284 (henceforth *Barton v. Eichelberger*). *Commonwealth of Pennsylvania v. Stephen D. Freeland*, especially testimony of John Smith, Dean Coffman, and Josephine Giuffrida; "Black Violence Recounted," *York Dispatch*, March 6, 2003. "Policemen, 7 Others Wounded By Gunfire on York's Streets," *YGD*, July 19, 1969, p. 1; "Boy's Fabricated Story of Being Set Afire Touched Off Clashes of Gangs," *YGD*, July 19, 1969,

Over the next couple of hours, cars that drove through the Penn and College area were assaulted by rocks and bricks but the next use of firearms consisted of shots fired by two unidentified white drivers on the 500 block of West Princess Street, where the largely all-black community and the largely white Salem Street community abutted. Not long after this, John Smith, white, reported he was shot at about the same spot. As he recalled over thirty years later, he was driving home from work at the time when a group of black youths pulled alongside him, "stuck a gun out the window and shot." The shotgun blast struck Smith under the chin. Fortunately, the shot was not fatal.[32]

While discrepancies exist regarding the exact order of events that followed, most agree that by dawn, at least eighteen other men and women, black and white, had been shot or assaulted by rocks or bricks, many of them seriously. Mrs. Madelyn Bowman, a white woman, was struck by a brick, fracturing her jaw. Dean Coffman, also white, was driving to work at National Biscuit, when he encountered a crowd of thirty at the corner of Penn and College, which shot out his front windshield. Dolores Sipe and Rodney Brown, both black, were injured by gunshots, the former while entering a taxi cab, the latter while heading to work. A smattering of firebombs was thrown into buildings owned by white businessmen as well.[33]

As the sun set on the evening of the 18th, larger crowds gathered in the heart of the black community, sometimes known as the West End, and attacks on passersby's resumed. At 10:30 p.m. "Big Al," one of York City Police's two armored vehicles, was dispatched to assist fireman not

p. 1; Debra Noel, "The Grapes of Wrath: Seeds of Violence Were Planted Long Before the Fury," *York Sunday News*, July 25, 1968, p. A8; "Fear and Fury: The Riots of 1969: Special Report," *York Sunday News*, pp. A8–A10; "State Police Report: Disorder, York, Pennsylvania," September 8, 1969, Governor Shafer Papers, MG209, 9-1136, Carton 98, Folder 1; "Operational Report: Civil Disturbances – York, Pennsylvania, 22–28 July 1969"; *Commonwealth v. Stephen Freeland; Commonwealth v. Leon Wright*, Court of Common Pleas of York County (2003), especially testimony of Anthony Brown and Taka Nii Sweeney. See also *Commonwealth v. Robert Messersmith et al.*, especially testimony of Taka Nii Sweeney, Michael Sipe, Arthur Messersmith, Stewart Aldinger, and Stipulations Read into record by District Attorney Thomas Kelly. "Witness Called to Explain Story," *York Dispatch*, December 13, 2001.

32 *Barton v. Eichelberger*, Case File, especially "Findings of Fact."
33 *Barton v. Eichelberger*, Case File, see especially "Findings of Fact" and "Testimony of Chief Landis"; *Barton v. Eichelberger, Commonwealth of Pennsylvania v. Stephen D. Freeland*, especially Josephine Giuffrida; "Operational Report: Civil Disturbances – York, Pennsylvania, 22–28 July 1969"; "Black Violence Recounted," *York Dispatch*, March 6, 2003.

far from Penn and College. While there, Stanford Gilbert, who was riding home from work on his 1956 Triumph Thunderbird motorcycle, was shot and nearly killed. As he testified years later, he had never had a problem in the neighborhood before and had consumed a drink or two at Sam's Café, a local hangout, with some of his black biker buddies. But on this occasion, he was shot in the back and knocked unconscious.[34] It is possible that blacks in the area mistook Gilbert for a member of the Pagan's biker gang, who had been known to terrorize the community. In response, "Big Al," which was occupied by three police officers, including Henry Schaad, drove by the Penn and College intersection. A number of blacks testified years later that the policemen in the armored vehicle yelled: "Niggers, get off the corners, go to your homes" and/or fired first upon the crowd of at least twenty to thirty blacks, many of them armed. Police denied these charges. Regardless, shots were fired from the crowd at Big Al. More than one witness recalled Stephan Freeland exclaiming, "I hit the mother fucker," though few if anyone knew or believed that his bullet had pierced its armor. Officer Ronald McCoy recalled hearing a loud noise, "like boom." Not until Office Henry Schaad stated that he had been shot did McCoy realize that the noise he had heard came from a gun – later identified as a 34–40 Krag rifle – and that its bullet had penetrated the plating of the armored vehicle and fatally wounded his fellow officer (Schaad did not die until nearly two weeks later on August 1st).[35]

Following Schaad's shooting the violence intensified, to a large part because police, hearing of the attack on their fellow officer, decided to take revenge. Bennie Carter recollected: "This armored truck pulled up to the corner of Greens Street and College Avenue and it [*sic*] said, 'All you Black bastards get back in the house!' And then they started shooting... And then they [the police] came up in front of the house, and they had rifles trained upon us." Among those struck was Carter's close friend Clarence Ausby. After refusing to call for an ambulance, Carter recalled, they threw Ausby into the armored vehicle and drove away. Rather than go to the hospital, however, they drove him to the outskirts of the city where they kicked him and declared "Nigger, I hope you die before we get you to the hospital." Other blacks in the area reported similar examples of police wantonly firing into black neighborhoods. One black

---

[34] *Commonwealth of Pennsylvania v. Stephen D. Freeland*, Testimony of Stanford Gilbert.

[35] *Commonwealth of Pennsylvania v. Stephen D. Freeland*, especially testimony of Richard Rasco, Donald McCoy, Michael Wright, and Sherman Spells; "Schaad Case's Faded Images," *York Dispatch*, March 2, 2003; "Officer: No One Was Shooting from 'Big Al,'" York Dispatch, March 7, 2003.

couple, which preferred to remain anonymous, informed a *Gazette and Daily* reporter that "police stationed themselves on the roof of a factory" near the "south side of Codorus creek" and "they opened fire in the direction of any noise or anything that moved."[36]

Not long after Schaad was shot, two young black children, Lynn and Jeannette Register, ages two and eight, respectively, were hit by gunshots outside of the Parkway homes where they lived, presumably by stray police gunfire. Around the same time Bobby Simpson recalled hearing armored vans rumble up the street and then the sound of gunshots entering his home. "The unrelenting beating of bullets," wrote journalist Kim Strong years later, brought their young son, Mark, "running into their parents' bedroom," where Simpson "pulled him to the floor" until the firing stopped five to ten minutes later. Simpson suspected he was targeted due to his political activism. White gang members firebombed the home of Mr. and Mrs. Frank Meyers, the only blacks to live in the Cottage Hill/North Newberry Street neighborhood. When the Meyers's neighbor Clifton Kohler, who was white, reported the incident to police, officers responded that they could not do anything about it. Only after Meyers reported that his wife had been injured did the police arrive at their home. Yet, while driving her to the hospital, they declared that "four blacks would be killed for every white killed," according to one report. Ernestine Rankin, a black woman, was shot at while driving her Cadillac at North Newberry and Gay, virtually the same spot where Allen would be shot and killed the following day. Alexis Key was similarly attached by a gang of whites near the intersection of Newberry and Market Streets. One of their bullets ricocheted off the interior of her car and nearly blinded her niece. Moreover, when she went to City Hall to report the incident, the police informed her that "she had no business being in that neighborhood"; it was her own fault; she was "lucky to be alive," and she should go home. Likewise, Louis Multry and Mitchell Edwards had to flee their car after it was peppered by gunshots fired by white youth. Meanwhile, authorities arrested Lionel Bailey, a longtime civil rights activist, on charges of curfew violation, in spite of the fact that a top city official had authorized him to walk the streets in order to try to cool things. While in custody, "racial slurs and threats" were directed at him by police.[37]

---

[36] Interview with Bennie Carter; "Mike Hoover, The York Riots of 1969," *York Dispatch*, December 4, 2001; *Barton, v. Eichelberger*; "Police Criticized As Over-Reacting," *YGD*, July 25, 1969, p. 3.

[37] "Fear and Fury: The Riots of 1969: Special Report," *York Sunday News*, pp. A8–A10; "State Police Report: Disorder, York, Pennsylvania," September 8, 1969, Governor Shafer

In the midst of the tumult, York's Mayor John Snyder declared a state of emergency, imposed a curfew, and requested support from the state police. Jacob Hose, the director of public safety for the city, blamed the lawlessness on "a few persons" and pleaded with residents to "remain calm" and to stay in their homes.[38] Over the course of the day, nearly half a dozen more whites were shot, many near the Penn and College intersection where Officer Schaad had been hit. Dale Witmyer was struck in the chest; Norman Lehr in the midsection; John Dixon in his mouth, Dennis Keefer in his back, and Nelson Luckman on his the hand; remarkably, all of these shots proved nonfatal. One interviewee recalled seeing "more people in those four days with guns than I've ever seen. There were guns in the trunks of everybody's cars."[39]

During the first two days of the uprising more than a handful of business establishments were firebombed, leading to the consumption of a number of homes in the West Hope Avenue and Penn Street area and of the Hoffman Meat Market, the site of the confrontation with Chester Roach the summer before. A number of properties near South Street, Queen, and Maple Streets were set afire as well, as were the offices of the *York Gazette and Daily*, presumably by a white gang member or sympathizer. On multiple occasions, local and state police had to protect firemen who sought to extinguish these blazes. Thomas Gibbs, a volunteer fireman, recalled that he had "been in combat situations in the military," but that he "heard more shooting in York," while fighting fires, than he did overseas. Yet, at the same time, Landis noted that firefighters received the assistance of close to seventy-five black residents while battling the

Papers, MG209, 9-1136, Carton 98, Folder 1; "Operational Report: Civil Disturbances – York, Pennsylvania, 22–28, July 1969," Governor Shafer Papers, MG209-1136, Carton 98, Folder 3; *Barton v. Eichelberger*; "Gunfire Renews as Cyclists Scatter People in York, PA," *NYT*, July 21, 1969, p. 23; Mark Scolforo, "148 Might Testify: DA calls 11 more for 6\'69 Riots Case," *York Dispatch*, September 12, 2002; *Commonwealth v. Robert Messersmith*, especially testimony of Alexis Kay, Sherman Spells and Louis Multry and Stipulations Read into the Record by District Attorney Thomas Kelley; Kim Strong, "1969: York Riots: As He Lay Dying," http://www.ydr.com/story/archives/2016/04/19/he-lay-dying-murder-henry-c-schaad/83216906/ [accessed January 4, 2013]; Lauri Lebo, "Spells Details '69 Run-in with Messersmith," *York Dispatch*, August 25, 2005; Interview with Bennie Carter; "Mike Hoover, The York Riots of 1969," *York Dispatch*, December 4, 2001.

[38] Jacob Hose, "Press Release," n.d., Governor Raymond Shafer Papers, MG 209, Carton 98.

[39] "Operations of Disorder: Civil Disturbances – York, Pennsylvania, 22–28 July 1969"; *Barton v. Eichelberger*; Anonymous interviewee quoted in Karen Rice, "Ten Days: The '69 Riots in York, PA," April 24, 1992 (paper in possession of author). "No-Gun Ordinance Passed by Council," *YGD*, July 23, 1969, p. 1.

aforementioned West Hope Avenue fire. Little if any looting was reported throughout the uprising.[40]

On Sunday June 20th, at least a hundred white youths, most members of York's various white gangs – the Newberry Street Boys, the Girarders, the Yorklyns, and the Swampers – gathered at Farquhar Park about four blocks north of NSB's headquarters to discuss, as one witness recalled, "how they were going to protect their neighborhood." Rather than chase them out of the park, a handful of York City Police, including Charlie Robertson, rallied their spirits with shouts of "white power" and "we have to stick together." Some of those assembled recalled that the police emboldened them by displaying Office Schaad's blood in "Big Al," and by telling them if they "had guns or ammunition to bring them down to Newberry Street." As Stewart Aldinger, one young member of the NSB put it, the police left the clear impression that they "were on our side," as did the police decision not to disarm any of them when they gathered in the Newberry Street neighborhood the following evening. (In a region where hunting was popular, guns were ubiquitous.)[41]

Thirty years later, when Allen's murder case was reopened, a dispute developed over whether white gang members fired upon her in self-defense. The conventional wisdom was that Jimmy and Sherman Spells, two young black youths, angered by the firebombing of their mother's home the night before, presumably by the Newberry Street Boys, drove to the Messersmith's home on North Newberry Street, prior to Allen's shooting, and warned Robert Messersmith they "would hold him personally responsible" for her safety. Witnesses testified that the white gang members who shot Allen mistook the car she was driving in for the car that had been driven by the Spells brothers, which, they thought, had returned to seek revenge.[42]

Tom Kelly, the state's lead attorney in the trial that took place over thirty years later, strongly disagreed. Laying out a timeline that contrasted

---

[40] Testimony of Thomas Landis Jr., *Commonwealth of Pennsylvania v. Robert Messersmith et al.*; Debbie Noel, "Worse than Combat: Firefighting During the Riots," *York Dispatch*, December 5, 2001. "Reward Offered for Information," *YGD*, July 21, 1969, p. 1.

[41] *Commonwealth v. Robert Messersmith*, especially: Testimonies of Robert Stoner, Stewart Aldinger, Frederick Flickinger, Theodore Halloran, Robert Traettino, Thomas Smith, Rick Lynn Knouse, and grand jury testimony of Gregory Neff, read into record by Rodney George.

[42] "Spells details '69 run-in with Messersmith," *York Dispatch*, August 25, 2005; "Testimony of Sherman Spells," *Commonwealth of Pennsylvania v. Stephan Freeland*. "Opening Statement of Peter Solymous," "Testimony of James Brown," "Opening Statement of Harry Ness," all in *Commonwealth of Pennsylvania v. Robert Messersmith et al.*

with conventional wisdom, he showed that Robert Messersmith shot Taki Nii Sweeney and that the Newberry Street Boys had reached out to the Girarders to help them "shoot some niggers," days before the alleged Spells incident. Especially once Schaad had been shot, Kelly added, "an uneasy alliance" of police and white youths emerged dedicated to "drawing the line at Newberry Street," which included shooting any black person who came into their neighborhood. To claims that the gang members were "defending themselves," Kelly retorted, "they [were] using the riots as an excuse to shoot blacks," including, as noted above, Ernestine Rankin, Louis Multry, and Mitchell Edwards, all of whom had fled gunfire in the same neighborhood prior to the Spells brothers' alleged appearance. As to the urban legend that Lillie Belle Allen had ulterior motives or might have been armed, as suggested by one of the defense attorneys, Kelly demanded that the jury ask itself the question: Would Lillie Belle Allen, who had "come up from the segregated south" and "left her children in the care of a 13-year-old," go out for a ride with essentially all of the adults in her family, "to go shoot white people?" Not only was there never any evidence that Allen had any ulterior motives, or a gun, or posed a real threat to the whites who assembled on Newberry Street, the possibility that she would do so and jeopardize her children's future, local lore to the contrary, strained credibility.[43]

Shortly after Allen was shot, Mayor Snyder requested support from Pennsylvania's Governor Raymond Shafer who mobilized the National Guard. They arrived over 600 strong, astride armored personnel carriers (see Figure 8.1). Prior to their arrival, Bobby Simpson recalled twenty years later, black residents had "beat the hell" out of the city and state police. Though tensions remained high, once the Guard arrived, the tide turned and the violence essentially subsided. By the time that the final guardsmen departed on July 28, police reported that at least twenty-eight persons had suffered gunshot wounds, including two fatalities; at least a dozen other men and women were seriously injured by objects that had been thrown at them. One hundred and eight individuals were arrested for curfew or firearm violations. Prior to their departure, guardsmen assisted in the raid of several homes and the confiscation of two arsenals of guns and ammunition. From the home of Jerome Jones and Charles Rice, both

[43] Tom Kelly, "Closing Statement," *Commonwealth v. Charles Robertson et al.*; "Prosecutors Say York Police Opened Door to Race Killing," *Philadelphia Inquirer*, October 2, 2002; "In Pennsylvania, Ex-Mayor Stands Trial in a 1969 Death," *NYT*, October 2, 2002, p. A18.

FIGURE 8.1 National Guard units arrive in York, PA. By permission of the York History Center.

black, in the Penn and College neighborhood, they seized ten guns, ranging from double barrel shotguns and a Winchester rifle to a .38 caliber Colt revolver. From the home of John Messersmith at 229 North Newberry Street, they uncovered fifteen guns, ranging from rifles with scopes to twelve gauge pump action shotguns. Several sources suggested that the delay in raiding the Messersmith's home allowed gang members to disperse a much larger arsenal, including the gun that shot Allen. All told, based on the most extensive and widely used quantitative data set, York experienced the twenty-sixth most severe riot or urban revolt out of over 500 that occurred in the nation between 1963 and 1972. Adjusted for population, York's revolt may have been the most severe of the era.[44]

---

[44] "Policemen, 7 Others Wounded By Gunfire on York's Streets," *YGD*, July 19, 1969, p. 1; "Boy's Fabricated Story of Being Set Afire Touched Off Clashes of Gangs," *YGD*, July 19, 1969, p. 1; Debra Noel, "The Grapes of Wrath: Seeds of Violence Were Planted Long Before the Fury," *York Sunday News*, July 25, 1968, p. A8; "Fear and Fury: The Riots of 1969: Special Report," *York Sunday News*, pp. A8–A10; "State Police Report: Disorder, York, Pennsylvania," September 8, 1969, Governor Shafer Papers, MG209-1136, Carton 98, Folder 1; "Operational Report: Civil Disturbances – York, Pennsylvania, 22–28, July 1969." See also *Barton v. Eichelberger*"; Interview with Robert Simpson by Michael Breeland, October 6, 1987, York College Oral History Center.

Ironically, one day before the uprising began, numerous chiefs of police had participated in a seminar at York Community College to consider the best methods for controlling civil disorders. This included using minimum force to quell disturbances and focusing on containing rather than confronting crowds.[45] (Recall that the restrained use of force by National Guardsmen and federal troops in Baltimore, in 1968, had saved lives.) While York's top officer attended this training session, it does not appear that such methods filtered their way down to the rank and file or if they did, that many (if any) of the street cops practiced these procedures. Officer Chip Woodyard, one of a handful of blacks on the force, certainly did not believe they did. As a result, less than week after the end of the revolt, he resigned from the force, accusing York's police of "racism, bigotry and a double-standard of justice for whites and blacks."[46]

As with revolts elsewhere, incidents in York did not occur all over the city. Rather, battles between blacks and whites, including between the police, who were overwhelming white, and blacks, were concentrated in four sections, foremost in the southwest quadrant of the city, sometimes referred to as the West End or as Penn-College, and secondarily in the Cottage Hill Road–North Newberry Street neighborhood, approximately six blocks north of the intersection of Penn and College. These were the locales where Schaad and Allen, respectively were killed, and in the immediate aftermath of the disturbances where large caches of arms were confiscated. Whole swaths of the city, particularly those where very few blacks resided, not to mention the surrounding suburban and rural areas of the county, remained completely untouched.[47]

As suggested in the previous chapter, York's revolt grew out of long-term racial inequities in housing, employment, education, and mistreatment by City Hall and the local police and out of the unwillingness of whites in power to redress peaceful calls for change. During the Lillie Belle Allen and Officer Schaad murder trials, which took place over thirty years later, defense and prosecuting attorneys agreed that the revolt was

---

[45] "Pennsylvania State Police, "Operations of the York Disorder, July 17–27, 1969," and "Emergencies and/or Civil Disorders: Operations Manual," Draft, n.d., both in Raymond Shafer Papers, MG209, cartons 96 and 98, respectively.

[46] Keisling, *The Wrong Car*; Kindle edition, location 1781-1793 and 3445-3446; Michael Donahoe (Director, Community Relations Division, Pennsylvania State Police) to Commander Area III, 4 August 1969, Raymond Shafer Papers, MG209, carton 98. *Commonwealth v. Robert M. Messersmith*, Criminal Docket, 108, August 1969.

[47] Brandon MacDonald, "White Flight: Examining Demographics and Deindustrialization in York, Pennsylvania," unpublished senior thesis, York College, May 14, 2014 (in author's possession).

a particularly violent affair, accepting, without objection, over a hundred "stipulations" that laid out countless acts of gunfire, assault, and arson. But since these trials took place in a court of law, which sought to determine the guilt or innocence of the defendants, little time was spent exploring their origin (and/or the testimony was deemed impertinent to the charges under review). Nonetheless, during the last trial, Michael Wright, the brother of one of the defendants, Leon "Smickel" Wright, landed a bombshell that shed light on why a significant number of blacks decided to "fight back." At least fifteen to twenty young black men shot at the armored vehicle, including himself, Wright testified, because they had grown tired of mistreatment by the police and determined that it was time to defend their homes and neighborhood. Michael Wright had nothing to gain and everything to lose by admitting that he had fired shots that might have killed Schaad; he had not been charged with the crime and neither prosecuting or defense attorneys expected him to make this claim. Moreover, his testimony, though valuable to historians interested in what motivated blacks to take up arms, helped seal the case against his own brother. In fact, defense attorneys tried to get Wright to retract this statement during cross-examination but he refused to do so because he sought to set the historical record straight.[48]

In a separate, though to my mind never before discussed interview with Michael Breeland, a black York College student, conducted in 1987, well after the revolt and well before Robertson was arrested, Bobby Simpson offered a similar explanation. The rioting did not start in 1968 and 1969, Simpson asserted. Rather it began when the city introduced police dogs. When we were kids, Simpson recalled, Vandergreen, Sweeny, and other "'racist police'...used to make you get off [your] front porch. Sweeny would declare, 'Niggers' [and] put [his] dogs on them [us]. He never gave you respect and [there was] nothing you could do and the anger just built up." Meanwhile, between 1964 and 1968, Simpson explained, "lots of guys went to Vietnam" and when they returned they felt they had fought and died "for nothing" but the "segregated society they were living in."

---

[48] *Commonwealth v. Messersmith et al.*, especially, Opening Statement by Peter Solymos; Closing Statement of William Costopoulos; Stipulations read into the record by Thomas Kelley. Since Mayor Robertson was not accused of actually firing shots, Costopoulos had an easier task of challenging those who claimed that his client had supplied either ammunition or the gun that had killed Allen. *Commonwealth v. Stephen D. Freeland* and *Commonwealth v. Leon F. Wright*, especially testimony of Michael Wright; "Brother: We All Shot at Car," *York Dispatch*, March 7, 2002. "Trial Testimony Colorful but Inconsistent," *York Dispatch*, March 9, 2003.

As a result, Simpson concluded, "we didn't mind dying" and determined to "fight the cops."[49]

Put somewhat differently, blacks who rebelled in York in 1969 did not do so because they were "seeking the thrill and excitement occasioned by looting and burning," conservative understandings of the riots notwithstanding.[50] Indeed, a number of the defendants in Officer Schaad's murder trial, including Stephan Freeland and Leon Wright, had been active in efforts to address the racial divide in York long before the uprising occurred. They did not shoot at Schaad's armored vehicle because they were opportunists but rather because following years of mistreatment by law enforcement authorities they had become converts to the philosophy of self-defense. Gender also shaped the uprising in York. Black men proved the most willing to attack whites who ventured into the Penn-College neighborhood and/or to engage in armed clashes with the police and white gang members, in part because they were more likely than woman to experience confrontations with the police and with white gangs. Men not women, both black and white, also took up arms, because of a desire to appear "manly," to protect, to appear strong, and perhaps just a traditional familiarity with guns. At the same time, there is no evidence that black or white men lost support or backing from women of their fellow race for doing so. On the contrary, in so far as a code of silence pervaded both communities after the revolts, effectively hindering attempts to apprehend the killers of Allen and Schaad, we have no reason to believe that women, on either side, disapproved of the developments of July 1969 anymore than men did.

Explaining the action of white youths who initiated the violence and then congregated on Newberry Street to shoot at cars driven by blacks demands a bit more conjecture. Perhaps Max Herman's theory, which makes use of geo-spatial analysis, offers some insight. "Rioting" most often took place in communities experiencing "ethnic succession," argues Herman. And York's Newberry Street Boys lived in a neighborhood that abutted a black community which had been growing in size for several decades. Fearing, what Herman called "succession," they became firmly committed to defending "their neighborhood." They were joined by other white gang members whose investment in identity politics prodded them to defend what they deemed as white turf, even if they did not live there themselves. Herman's analysis dovetails with the broader

---

[49] Interview with Robert Simpson by Michael Breeland, York College Oral History Center.
[50] Banfield, *The Unheavenly City*, pp. 185–209.

theories of Manuel Castells, who contends that battles over "definition of urban space," lay at the root of much urban unrest. This space included both physical spaces, such as parks and main streets, which had been the sites of police crackdowns on young blacks, and political or cultural spaces, where blacks sought to challenge the racial status quo. Blacks sought access to these spaces. In contrast, whites wanted to maintain their privileged place or space and to keep black in less privileged ones.[51]

But what made York's revolt such a violent one was the fact that white youths enjoyed the explicit support of the police. In this case, the closing statement of Harry Ness, the defense attorney of Gregory Neff, who like Robert Messersmith was charged with Allen's murder, proves instructive. Neff, according to his attorney, did not do anything after the Clifford Green incident or after the NSB's club quarter's windows were broken. Not until he had been invited by the police to go to a rally at Farqhar Park, not until he and other youths had been told that they "had to do something," in other words not until "they were incited to do what they ended up doing" by shouts of "white power" and calls to "protect your own neighborhood ... draw a line on Newberry Street ... and we'll protect you," by the police – and "I mean police in the plural," Ness contended, did his client, Gregory Neff, and by implication the other white youths, take up arms and shoot at Allen's car.[52]

---

[51] Herman, *Fighting in the Streets*; Manuel Castells, *The City and the Grassroots: A Cross-Cultural Theory of Urban Social Movements* (Berkeley: University of California Press, 1983).

[52] Harry Ness, "Closing Statement." While Robertson was not convicted, Ness and Messersmith were (see below).

9

An Uneasy Peace

If the riots hadn't taken place, nothing would have changed.
Robert Simpson, Oral History, 1987

Unlike the revolts in Cambridge and Baltimore, York's garnered little national attention and, not surprisingly, neither it nor the other uprisings that took place 1969 or the early 1970s convinced the Nixon Administration to jettison its call for law and order in favor of a domestic Marshall Plan. Still, York's revolt did not mark a rupture with the past, a destructive and unconstructive moment in the fight for racial equality. Rather, the uprising energized and unified York's black community, which in turn helped convince significant segments of the white community to engage in far more serious dialogues about the issues that underlay the revolt than had ever taken place in the past. More specifically, York's revolt was followed by the convening of a charrette, an unprecedented community dialogue. Particularly considering that blacks in York comprised only a small proportion of the population and thus had far less political leverage than they did in many big cities, this was no small accomplishment. Nonetheless, the charrette did not alter the structures of racial inequality and the disparities between blacks and whites in the region tended to increase due to broader social and economic trends and the ongoing politics of white retrenchment in the years that followed. As a result, when Mayor Charlie Robertson was arrested for aiding in the murder of Lillie Belle Allen in May 2001, the community was still divided along racial lines. Whether the trial could overcome or heal these divisions, as some hoped it could, remained to be seen.

"The Truth Would Have Involved the Arrest of Many Police"

In the immediate aftermath of York's revolt, state and local police and the Justice Department conducted investigations into Lillie Belle Allen's and Henry Schaad's deaths. Somewhat surprisingly, especially given that Schaad was the son of a popular policeman and the first York officer to be killed while on duty in the city's history, and that Allen was an innocent bystander, neither case resulted in *any* arrests, not to mention any trials or convictions for over thirty years. How come? William Costopoulos, Mayor Robertson's lead defense attorney in the 2002 Lillie Belle Allen murder trial, asserted that city officials knew right away who had killed Schaad. He added that the "'69 investigations were thorough and complete" and specifically complimented the work of the Pennsylvania State Police and the United States Attorney's office. They "could have made arrests for the death of Officer Schaad," Costopoulos insisted, but District Attorney John Rauhauser chose not to because he feared that if he got a conviction in the Schaad case but not in the Allen murder, the city "could have erupted again." Hence, to borrow Costopoulos's words, Rauhauser chose to "let it go," to kill the investigation "in the best interest of the community."[1]

William Keisling, whose book *The Wrong Car: The Death of Lillie Belle Allen* was published shortly before Charlie Robertson's trial began, strongly disagreed with Costopoulos's theory and the bulk of documentary evidence appears to support Keisling's views. Whereas Costopoulos praised the state's investigation, Keisling contends it was shoddy from the start. "Days would pass before anyone would bother to examine the crime scene, or take the names of many witnesses." Police allowed the Cadillac which Allen's family drove, to "leave the scene of the crime," did not examine the car for three days, and in the year's in between the shooting and the ultimate trial, allowed the car to be destroyed and lost the bullets that had been recovered from her body.[2]

Keisling contends that this shoddy or sloppy police work was not the by-product of the "craziness of the times," as some asserted, but rather the result of a "cover-up" that began almost immediately following Allen's death, aimed at protecting relatively widespread malfeasance if not criminal complicity by numerous police officers during the revolt. Moreover,

---

[1] *Commonwealth v. Messersmith et al.*; "Closing Statement by William Costopoulos"; Costopoulos, *Murder is the Charge*, pp. 78–79, 186–187.
[2] Keisling, *The Wrong Car* [Kindle edition], location 579–582.

Keisling argued that Robertson was scapegoated by his political enemies when the case was reopened because he had risen to political power. To prove this claim, Keisling spent chapters delineating the course of the investigations that followed. In contrast, Costopoulos devoted only a couple of paragraphs to explaining why no charges had initially been filed. Keisling also posted numerous documents, from copies of the original interviews by state police investigators to excerpts from grand jury hearings, on a public website. Costopoulos provided neither supportive documents nor references for his assertions.[3]

While this is not the place and time to review all of Keisling's argument a brief summary of his major points follows. First, local police or state troopers allowed Hattie Dickinson to drive her car down Newberry Street in the first place, even though they were stationed, with a barricade, on the corner of Philadelphia and Newberry and should have prevented her from entering an area they knew was unsafe. During the Lillie Belle Allen trial, Officer Ronald Zenger, who for years denied such claims, admitted under oath that even though "he had been instructed to keep cars out of North Newberry Street," he allowed Dickinson's car to pass.[4] Second, according to Keisling, other policemen were in the vicinity of 229 North Newberry Street when Allen was shot – some lived in the neighborhood as well – and expressed their approval of the decision of the gang members to shoot at her. Wayne Ruppert, writes Keisling, told the boys they "did the right thing." In addition to wanting to protect Zenger and Ruppert, and any other law enforcement officers who might have allowed Dickinson to drive down Newberry Street in the first place and/or were at the scene of the crime, the police, and by inference City Hall, wanted to cover up the complicity of other policemen who may have been involved in inciting the gang members to arm themselves – and their actual arming – in the first place. "To arrest the boys [white gang members] would mean to arrest some cops," Keisling reiterated. "No matter how they sliced and diced it, too many cops kept turning up at the murder scene as witnesses, cheerleaders, or passive bystanders."[5]

And Keisling was not the only one to see a cover-up or at least suspect that the city authorities feared implicating the police. In 2002, Robert

[3] Keisling, *The Wrong Car*; Costopoulos, *Murder is the Charge*, pp. 186–187; York County Detectives, Uniform Supplemental Report, www.yardbird.com/pdfs/wrong_car_documents.pdf [accessed July 21, 2016].
[4] "Ex-cop: I Let Car Through," *York Dispatch*, October 2, 2002, p. 1; Keisling, *The Wrong Car*, Location 579–582 and 3130–3139.
[5] Keisling, *The Wrong Car*.

Messersmith, who was accused and later convicted of Allen's murder, asserted that the city still did not "want to know the truth," because the truth "would have involved the arrest of many police officers."[6] Perhaps more tellingly, upon their return to South Carolina in late July 1969, in an interview with the Federal Bureau of Investigation, Allen's extended family suggested that it had doubts about the direction the investigation was taking (or not taking). They stated that there "may have been a 'trooper' or police in the community" where the shooting took place. They also declared that there were "approximately 15–20 police officers" at the corner of Philadelphia and Newberry Streets, who "did not stop the[ir] car" from proceeding into the ambush.[7]

Allen's family's concerns helped convince the Department of Justice to authorize a broader investigation into possible civil rights violations. Yet local and state policemen impeded this investigation. For instance, on December 1, 1969, the York Police Department and State Police informed Jerris Leonard, the Assistant Attorney in the Department of Justice, that they "would advise [the Department of Justice] of *any* [emphasis added] breaks in this matter," adding that they "still had *no* [emphasis added] suspects." In fact, by September 4, 1969 investigators already had identified multiple "suspects" but chose to withhold this information from federal authorities. Maybe they wanted, as Costopoulos asserted, to let things go. But such obfuscation, perhaps abetted by FBI agents, who, in the words of Keisling were the chums of local law enforcement officers, suggests that averting another "riot" was not their main concern.[8]

---

[6] Keisling, *The Wrong Car*.

[7] See Lillie Belle Allen File, Part 1 of I, FBI Records: The Vault, https://vault.fbi.gov/Lillie%20Belle%20Allen%20/Lillie%20Belle%20Allen%20Part%201%20of%201/view [accessed July 21, 2016], especially "Unknown Subjects: Lillie Belle Allen (Deceased) – Victims," August 6, 1969.

[8] See *The Wrong Car* Documents, www.yardbird.com/pdfs/wrong_car_documents.pdf, especially Pennsylvania State Police, "Supplemental Report," August 28, 1969; Gabriel Mark Barr, "Statement," September 3, 1969; Pennsylvania State Police, "Supplemental Report," September 4, 1969; Beatrice Mosley, "Statement," July 22, 1969; Federal Bureau of Investigation, "Memo: Unknown Subject," December 1, 1969; Federal Bureau of Investigation, "Memo: Unknown Subjects," May 5, 1970; and Lillie Belle Allen, FBI – The Vault, especially Director, FBI, to SAC, Philadelphia, February 4, 1970; SAC, Philadelphia to Director, FBI, February 2, 1970. See also: Keisling, *The Wrong Car*, Location 3130–3139 to 3297–3300. Joseph David Cress, *Murder & Mayhem in York County* (Charleston, SC: The History Press, 2011), pp 11–31; "FBI Stymied in Probe of Allen Death," *York Dispatch*, October 20, 2002.

"Writing the Agenda for [Another] Summer of Riots"

While black people in York could not have known all of these details, certainly the inability of authorities to present a list of suspects in Allen's murder, coupled with the slothful arrest of Robert Messersmith for the shooting of Taki Nii Sweeney, deepened their mistrust of the criminal justice system. Officer Woodyard's resignation from the police force because of its alleged "racism," "bigotry," and "double standards of justice for blacks and whites," did so as well. NAACP local chapter head Richard J. Manning's pronouncement that "York has one law for blacks and one for whites" was particularly telling, because prior to the revolt he had recommended that blacks should "let the law handle the situation." But the actions of law enforcement authorities during the revolt convinced him that he would have to change his tune.[9] Similarly, Irwin Kittrell, the president of the board of directors of Crispus Attucks and another long-time moderate, explained that blacks "feel they have to defend the home front," because all other efforts to address the community's grievances "have been ineffective." Citing a persistent lack of communication with City Hall and the police, Kittrell also announced the formation of a newly formed "Black coalition," which united York's black community around a fairly militant agenda.[10]

Most significantly, this coalition filed a lawsuit that called for the federal courts to place the city's police force under outside supervision on the grounds that the city had demonstrated that it could not or would not police itself. This suit nearly achieved landmark status and even though the courts ultimately ruled against the plaintiffs, prefigured an array of suits and federal actions against a variety of police departments, from Ferguson, Missouri, to Cleveland, Ohio, which resulted in significant outside intervention decades later.[11] Initially filed by two local lawyers, the suit quickly attracted the attention and help of several of the nation's

9 "'Racism, Bigotry' of Police Leads Patrolmen to Quit," *YGD*, July 24, 1969, p. 1; "NAACP Head Won't Tell Negroes to 'Let the Law Handle the Situation,'" *YGD*, July 28, 1969, p. 1.
10 "Police Relations, Housing Blamed for Violence Here," *YGD*, July 23, 1969, p. 3.
11 "State Dismisses Police Brutality Complaints," *YGD*, August 1, 1968, p. 1; "State Police File Dog Bite Report," *YGD*, June 13, 1968, p. 1; "Justice Department Probe of Complaints Into Police Brutality Still Secret," *YGD*, July 20, 1968, p. 1; "Suit IDs Abuses by K-9s; Record of Dismissed Cases Released by City Officials," *York Dispatch*, January 4, 2002. "Suit Asks City Be Enjoined From Press 'Interference,'" *YGD*, August 24, 1968, p. 1.

most famous civil rights attorneys, including Jack Greenberg and James Nabritt, of the NAACP's Legal Defense Fund, and Anthony Amsterdam, also a one-time NAACP attorney and one of the pioneers of clinical legal education. In their *amicus curiae* brief, they contended that the "ultimate issue" was "whether the judiciary can respond effectively to the abuses of the constitutional rights of black citizens by the police." This suit, they asserted, rivaled those that the NAACP and other organizations had filed to desegregate education, gain voting rights, and overcome employment and housing discrimination. In all of these instances, they observed, the federal courts had demonstrated a willingness to intervene. By inference, the plaintiffs' attorneys suggested that the government should do the same in this case. To bolster their claim, they cited a long list of precedents, including the *Mapp* (1961) and *Miranda* (1966) decisions, which had expanded the fourth amendment rights of criminal defendants. They also cited conclusions made by two recent presidential commissions, namely that police abuse stood as one of the primary causes of the nation's disorders. In sum, the plaintiff's attorneys asserted that the York case represented a "test" of the court's ability to develop "a workable judicial solution" to the problem of "police lawlessness and discrimination." The failure to do so would result in a further deterioration in the community's faith in the law and perhaps lead to more revolts.[12]

In support of their claims, the plaintiff's attorneys called a long list of witnesses, ranging from Bennie Carter and Clarence Ausby, who vividly described how police had shot at them "without provocation" to Chip Woodyard, the black policeman who had resigned from the force following the revolt because of, in his words, the "racist attitudes" of many of his co-workers.[13] Others who came forth included Rhoda Barton and Lewis Johnstone, the two named plaintiffs in the case. Jeannette Register, age eight, testified that she was shot by police while she and a small group of friends watched a different policeman beat a black man, and Robert Simpson and Lionel Bailey, who contended that police had threatened their lives during the revolt. Bailey also alluded to a pattern of police abuse, especially by the canine force, going back to the early 1960s. A

---

[12] Jack Greenberg, James M. Nabritt III, Michael Melsner, Melvyn Zarr, and Anthony G. Amsterdam, "Amici Curiae," in *Barton v. Eichelberger*, case file.

[13] See testimony in appendix of *Barton v. Eichelberger*, case file, especially "Testimony of Clarence Ausby"; "Blacks Tell Court Police Shot them Without Reason," *YGD*, August 7, 1969, p. 1; "U.S. Court Asked to Reopen Hearing on York Disorders," *YGD*, September 3, 1969, p. 1; "Court to Reopen Disorder Hearings," *YGD*, September 16, 1969, p. 1.

number of white witnesses corroborated these accusations. For instance, Fred Flickinger, a member of the Newberry Street Boys, testified that the police had advised white gang members to hold a "white power meeting," and that, when they did, police, including Charlie Robertson, "shouted White Power and we all cheered."[14]

Unrepentant, York's policemen and officials nearly unanimously defended their actions. York's Chief of Police, Leonard Landis, testified that there was minimal racism in the ranks and sought to deflect accusations against the police by focusing on the false accusation made by a black youth who, he alleged, had set off the "disorder" in the first place. Officers Charles McCaffery and Wasser blamed "black snipers" for the injuries incurred by Jeanette Register, adding that there was no proof that it was their bullets that had hit the black children. (The police presented no forensic evidence to support this claim.) York's District Attorney, John F. Rauhauser, testified that claims that policemen had abused black arrestees during the disorders "were all lies." In a separate testimony, Lieutenant Steven Gibbs, the head of York's canine corps, championed the use of dogs on the grounds that they served as a strong deterrent against illegal acts. Gibbs added that most men on the force "wanted *more* [emphasis added] dogs" so that they would not "have to put up with so much trouble." At the same time, various groups, ranging from the Fraternal Order of Police to community organizations rallied to the defense of the city police and in opposition to plans to establish a Citizen's Review Board and/or to enact procedures which might restrict the actions of the police on the beat.[15]

Somewhat along the same lines, the local Democratic slate for city offices in 1969 picked a page from Richard Nixon's presidential

[14] While the original case file has been "lost" by the National Archives, transcripts of the original testimony can be found in the Appendices of the Appeal of the case, *Barton v. Eichelberger*, case file. See also *Barton v. Eichelberger*, especially Judge Nealon's Finding of Fact. *Rhoda Barton and Lewis Johnstone v. John Snyder et al.*, Complaint, Filed July 24, 1969, Governor Raymond Shafer Papers, MG209, 9–1136, Box 98; "Court Told Policeman Saw Reporter Beaten," *YGD*, August 15, 1969, p. 1; "13 Give Testimony as Hearings End in York Disorders," *YGD*, August 15, 1969, p. 1; "Blacks Tell Court Police Shot them Without Reason," YGD, August 7, 1969, p. 1; "Police Shot Children, Child Testifies," YGD, August 8, 1969, p. 1; "Judge Hears 'Racial Disturbances' Arguments," *YGD*, December 20, 1969, p. 1 (includes Plaintiff's Brief).

[15] "City Brief," *YGD*, December 20, 1969, p. 1; "Statements Lies, Witness Asserts," *YGD*, October 9, 1969, p. 3; "Police Favor More Use of Dogs," *YGD*, October 9, 1969, p. 1; "FOP Asks Parley on Police Code," October 29, 1969, p. 1; "Police Deny Brutality," *YGD*, August 9, 1969, p. 1; "York Police Deny Racist Attitudes," *YGD*, August 9, 1969, p. 1.

playbook, emphasizing the issue of law and order. "Do you remember when you could feel safe on the streets and in your homes!" inquired Eli Eichelberger and Harold Fitzkee, the Democratic candidates for mayor and district attorney respectively. Given that Fitzkee had been the city's public defender and that Eichelberger was cast as a reformer in comparison to Snyder, this was a pretty strong statement. (Snyder died from a heart attack not long after the revolt.) In the face of such white sentiments, E. Nelson Reed, the Republican candidate for mayor, admitted that "as a practical and realistic politician" he could not afford to speak out against racism. "If I were to speak out on racism before the election," Reed informed an audience of potential black voters, "I might as well have stayed home and not run for mayor."[16]

As the lawsuit worked its way through the courts, acts of white racism and retribution proliferated. Black members of Local 786 of the UAW (United Automobile Workers), which represented workers at York's Caterpillar Tractor plant, walked out of their union meeting after their white coworkers refused to donate funds to the Lillie Belle Allen Fund. "I work with these people every day," stated one black worker, yet "I never really realized how deep the[ir] prejudices are and how strongly embedded their racism is." Notably, the union's black workers had supported a similar fund for the family of Officer Henry Schaad.[17] During the same time period, the Ku Klux Klan and some other white supremacist groups sought to recruit new members. For instance, they distributed membership applications outside a "Citizens' meeting" held at the First Church of the Brethren. During the same time period, white authorities arrested an array of black men and women suspected of participating in the revolt on unrelated charges. Leon Wright was charged with "corrupting the morals of a minor," Steven Freeland with burglary, Michael Wright for auto theft, Samuel Day for resisting arrest, Lionel Bailey for attempted arson, and Taka Nii Sweeney for resisting arrest. Subsequently, the two named plaintiffs in the suit against the city, Lewis Johnstone and Rhoda Barton, were also charged with selling marijuana and prostitution, respectively. The arrest of Michael Wright on auto theft, in particular, displayed the nefarious intentions of the police, with officers presenting perjured testimony in order to gain his conviction. (The conviction was later overturned when the person who had actually stolen the vehicle that Wright was accused

---

[16] "Read Claims He Can't Win If He Talks Against Racists," *YGD*, September 19, 1969, p. 1. "Democratic Party Advertisement," *YGD*, November 4, 1969.

[17] "Black Union Members Blame Racism for Meeting Walkout," *YGD*, September 25, 1969, p. 1.

of stealing confessed to the crime.)[18] Sympathetic whites were targeted as well. Most notably, reporter Michael Cronin was badly beaten by gang members while, as Cronin later recalled, "A York police car with officers watched but did not intercede."[19]

While Judge Nealon pondered his decision, York's black community demonstrated that it would not be cowed. Whereas prior to the revolt black militants and moderates had often disagreed, afterwards, they displayed a united front. Led by Reverend Leslie Lawson, the newly established York Black Coalition (YBC) pledged to bridge "all segments of the black community," including "the Black Unity Movement, Black Panthers, National Association for the Advancement of Colored People, Congress of Racial Equality, [and the] church." Echoing H. Rap Brown's tone, Lawson questioned the value of obeying laws "we have no voice in making." Along the same lines, the YBC increasingly trained its attacks on York's elite, rather than just the police and white gangs. "You cannot solve your problem merely by putting a few black cops in blue uniforms," Lawson explained. "It is not the man, it's what he represents." More to the point, Lawson made clear that black people could not expect the system to change until the city's industrial and merchant leaders exerted themselves "for the good of York."[20]

A series of articles in the *Philadelphia Tribune*, a black newspaper, captured the militant spirit that prevailed in York in the wake of the revolts. In "York Called Heaven for K-9 Dogs, Hell for Blacks," Pamela Haynes reported that "young people" were "tired of talking" and warned that

---

[18] "More Held After Drug Raids," *YGD*, March 24, 1970, p. 1; "Jury Convicts Johnstone After Informers Testify," *YGD*, August 27, 1970; "Attempted Arson Nets $500 Fine," *YGD*, January 10, 1970, p. 3. "Grand Jury Indicts Six, Frees Three," July 30, 1969, p. 3; "Probe Ordered In Shooting of Youth By Police," *YGD*, January 13, 1970, p. 1. "Youth Wounded By City Police," *YGD*, January 12, 1970, p. 1; "Lawyer Hits Probe Clearing Policemen," *YGD*, January 24, 1970, p. 1. On rumors regarding Freeland and Wright see "Federal Judge Hears Additional Testimony on Racial Disorders," *YGD*, September 18, 1969, p. 1; "York Blacks Claim They Have 'Plenty of Nothing,'" *Philadelphia Tribune*, April 18, 1970, p. 40; "York Called Heaven for K-9 Dogs, Hell for Blacks," *Philadelphia Tribune*, April 14, 1970, p. 4; "Grand Jury," *YGD*, April 14, 1971, p. 4; Interview with Mark Woodbury by Raul Uraanga (in author's possession). Woodbury recalls that two policeman claimed they could identify Wright and the color of both his shirt and the buttons of his shirt in the absolute dark, a claim Woodbury deems implausible.

[19] Kalish, *Civil Rights in York*, p. 80; Cronin quoted in Mary Hamilton, *Rising from the Wilderness*, p. 217.

[20] "New Group Seeks to Unite Blacks to Bring About Changes," *YGD*, September 10, 1969, p. 1; "Pastor Scores City Office on Police 'Review' Inaction," *YGD*, September 20, 1969, p. 1; "NAACP Head Won't Tell Negroes to 'Let the Law Handle the Situation,'" *YGD*, July 28, 1969, p. 1. "Street Shooting Trial Commences," *YGD*, October 29, 1969, p. 3.

they were "ready to use violence" if the "city administration refused to listen." Reverend Lawson added that city leaders were "writing the agenda for [another] summer of riots," if they did not act soon. In a follow-up article, Haynes presented gripping detail of one recent example of ongoing police abuse. Samuel Day, a local community activist, she wrote, was "beaten bloody by city police" who sought to send a message to him. In the same article, Haynes observed that the police were only part of the problem. "Political representation is nil"; there were few black businesses, and the "attitude of the city administration" is "white gentility struggling to keep the 'darkies' down."[21]

In addition to demanding reforms to the criminal justice system, York's black community pushed for other changes that echoed the broader national cry for black power. In a meeting with York's Rotarians, Joseph Douglas, a black assistant professor at Penn State York, defended James Forman's recent call for reparations, which Forman had posted on the door of Riverside Church in New York City. For the past 150 years, Douglas explained, America's churches and synagogues had failed to live up to their own doctrines. Instead, they had given "de facto approval" of discrimination. Hence, Forman, and by extension at least some blacks in York, sought to provide churches in York and elsewhere with the opportunity to rectify this error. Rev. Richard Click, the white pastor of St. Paul Lutheran Church, who accompanied Professor Douglas to the podium, suggested that this payment did not necessarily need to come in the form of specified funds of money, which amounted to only "$2 from each white man." Instead, Click asserted, it might be preferable for churches to "truly commit themselves" by "working directly within the ghettos" rather than "playing the game at a safe distance."[22]

On the cultural front, black Yorkers displayed an increasing sense of black pride and militancy. For instance, the Princess Players brought together a troop of primarily young black thespians to stage racially themed plays, including Martin Duberman's off-Broadway drama "In White America" and Loraine Hansberry's "A Raisin in the Sun." As late as July 17, 1969, the Players sought "white youths" to join the troop in their performances. But in the aftermath of the revolt, the Players were more concerned with raising black consciousness than in building cross-race alliances. The black community also used such

[21] "York Called Heaven for K-9 Dogs, Hell for Blacks," *Philadelphia Tribune*, April 14, 1970, p. 4; "York Blacks Claim They Have 'Plenty of Nothing'" *Philadelphia Tribune*, April 18, 1970, p. 40.

[22] "York Black Coalition Forms Groups To Work in Political, Housing Areas," *YGD*, October 1, 1969, p. 3.

performances to raise funds for the two surviving children of Lillie Belle Allen.[23]

York's black residents also partnered with newly created Hispanic rights groups to protest a wide array of inequities. In 1970, York's Hispanic population was relatively small but it was growing rapidly and the revolt galvanized many to become more involved in public protest. Like York's black citizens, Hispanics focused much of their attention on inadequate housing, employment discrimination, prejudiced teachers, an educational curriculum insufficient to their needs, and bias in the criminal justice system. For instance, Jose Hernandez, of the Progressive Spanish-American Council, joined Reverend Lawson in demanding the abolition of the city's "police court" and the appointment of interpreters for Spanish speaking defendants in court, something York's legal system did not provide. Following the lead of the local NAACP, the council also charged a large food chain with unfair labor practices.[24]

On March 31, 1970, Judge William Nealon issued his opinion in *Rhoda Barton and Lewis Johnstone v. the Mayor of York et al.* Nealon found much that disturbed him, including the "rash and excessive" actions that led to the shooting of Jeanette Register and her sister and mother, the antagonistic attitude of the police toward CORE leader Lionel Bailey, and the "'white power'" utterances of members of the York Police Department. Nonetheless, emphasizing the danger of the moment and questioning the credibility of some of the black witnesses, he ruled against the plaintiffs. Moreover, the remedy sought by the plaintiffs – outside receivership – Nealon explained, was too severe, especially since one of the primary defendants, Mayor Snyder, had died since the revolt. His successor, Eli Eichelberger, Nealon added, deserved the opportunity to enact reforms.[25] (Nealon's identification of police officer Charlie Robertson as

---

[23] "Princess Players Seek White Youths for Play," *YGD*, July 7, 1969, p. 4; "Princess Players Postpone Drama," *YGD*, August 15, 1969, p. 10; "$10,000 Goal Set for Fund," *YGD*, November 12, 1969, p. 1; "Victim's Children Aided," *YGD*, December 15, 1969, p. 3; "Photos," York's African-American Historical Preservation Society, www.facebook.com/yorksblackhistory/ [accessed December 2, 2016].

[24] For the initial announcement of the formation of the Progressive Spanish-American Council, see *YGD*, November 14, 1969, p. 4; "Abolish Police Court Now," *YGD*, January 3, 1970, p. 1; "Spanish-Speaking Yorkers Air Their Problems," *YGD*, October 3, 1969, p. 3: "Spanish Group Here Elects Officers," *YGD*, November 17, 1969, p. 3; "Officials Hold Spanish-Speaking Man 42 Hours Without an Interpreter," *YGD*, January 26, 1970, p. 3.

[25] *Barton v. Eichelberger*; *Rhoda Barton and Lewis Johnstone v. Eli Eichelberger*, US Court of Appeals for the Third Circuit, 451 F. 2d 263 (1971), http://law.justia.com/cases/federal/appellate-courts/F2/451/263/71555/ [accessed November 20, 2014]; "Court Hearing Oral Arguments in Riots," *York Dispatch*," December 19, 1969.

one of the offensive parties, served as one of the bases for reopening the case thirty years later.)

Contending that Nealon's ruling was "erroneous" both in terms of the law and the facts, the plaintiffs' lawyers immediately filed an appeal. In addition to arguing that the city had failed to rebut much of the testimony presented during the trial, they questioned whether recent pledges of reform, initiated, at least in part by the suit itself, would materialize and/or, if they did, whether they would last once the pressure to retain them diminished. While the United States Court of Appeals from the Third Circuit weighed these arguments, the situation in York remained tense and the city, as some had warned, experienced another mini rising.[26]

This one began in the hallways of William Penn High School with a fight between two males, one white, one black, with the former taking offense at the latter's "familiarity" with his white "girlfriend." The fact that this relationship was consensual apparently did not matter to the white student or to his fellow white classmates. Looked at more broadly, this high school clash grew out of the increasingly assertive posture of black students in York and across the nation and white student resentment and resistance to such assertiveness. In a sense, young blacks and whites faced off over physical and cultural spaces. In the case of York, this comprised including more material on African and African American history and culture in the curriculum, more non-white teachers, and fairer treatment by teachers, counselors, and fellow students. Clearly influenced by the Black Panther Party, the Black Student Union of York even issued a ten point program which demanded "education for our people," the exclusion of "racist teachers," "the immediate end to police brutality," and "an end to the robbery by the capitalist of our black community." On April 1st, following the initial hallway fight, the battle moved outside, with, according to one report, 200 whites "openly brandishing baseball bats, clubs, and chains," and perhaps guns. When the police arrived, they sided with the whites, selectively siccing their dogs and arresting several black youths. In response, Mayor Eli Eichelberger, declared a state of emergency, established a curfew and closed all schools.[27]

[26] Jack Greenberg, James M. Nabritt, et al., "Statement of Interest of the Amici"; "Peter Hearn and Edith G. Laver, "Brief of the Appellant"; and David Bupp and Jay Yost, "Brief of the Apelles"; Appeal from the Judgment of the United States District Court for the Middle District of Pennsylvania in Civil Action 69–286, all in *Barton v. Eli Eichelberger*, case file.

[27] "White Racism Has York 'On Brink' of Another Explosion, Blacks Say," *Philadelphia Tribune*, April 11, 1970, p. 1; "York High Incidents Spark Race Violence," *YGD*, April 4, 1970, p. 1; "York City Schools to Remain Closed," *YGD*, April 6, 1970, p. 1.

Over the course of the following week, this student-sparked clash spilled over into the broader community. Large delegations of black parents demonstrated their support for their children and demanded the firing of racist teachers. While male activists got most of the press, black women played a large role, with one black women lashing out at the council for its lack of empathy. You should be "jet black" for several minutes she declared. When white parents pushed for greater police presence in the schools, more than one black parent observed that the history of unfair treatment by the police made such calls problematic.[28]

A few days later when William Penn High School was opened, authorities detained three white students in the parking lot for possessing a gun. When the student who possessed the gun turned out to be the son of a city council member, police took him into their custody but did not charge him with a crime. (The same student had been detained a year earlier for possession of a tear gas gun.) When the city council called the Black Student Union's ten point platform unrepresentative of the views of the black community, Reverend Leslie Lawson despondently responded, "I don't know what the next step will be." Panchita Bethune added that the disparate treatment of black and white students had left the former with few choices. "They have been using the dogs since 1963 and will continue to do so until black people get up enough guts to deal with them." The black community, she warned, would shut the city down if these abuses did not stop.[29]

"The Medium Is the Message"

With the city on the precipice of another revolt, black activists joined hands with white moderates to organize the "Charrettes." Named after a French word which essentially means to work on or finish a product, the Charrettes aimed at promoting open and honest dialogues about a range of issues, from health care and housing to employment and education. Years later, York newspaper editor James McClure wondered if

[28] "York High Opens Peacefully, But 40 Pct. of Students Out," *YGD*, April 10, 1970, p. 1; "York High Will Open But Parents Worried Over Student Safety, *YGD*, April 9, 1970, p. 1; "KKK Circular Put on Cars Outside Citizens' Meeting," *YGD*, April 7, 1970, p. 1; "York Called Heaven for K-9 Dogs, Hell for Blacks," *Philadelphia Tribune*, April 14, 1970, p. 4.
[29] "Black Adults to Meet with Officials," *YGD*, April 7, 1970, p. 1; "Black Adults Request Support from Council of 10-Point Program," *YGD*, April 8, 1969, p. 1; "York High Will Open But Parents Worry Over Student Safety," *YGD*, April 9, 1970, p. 1; "York Called Heaven for K-9 Dogs," *Philadelphia Tribune*, April 14, 1968, p. 1.

they should be known as "charades or charrette." He concluded the latter. Likewise, in his history of civil rights in York, Jim Kalish called the Charrettes "the high point in York's relationship between whites and blacks." And in his Master's thesis, York City school teacher Raul Urrunaga concluded that the Charrettes demonstrated that "members of a diverse community who less than a year earlier had been at odds with each other got together and talked about common problems," adding that they paved the way for meaningful reforms. Even if the Charrettes "did not solve all the problems of inequality" and racism, Urrunaga insisted, they served as a "forum where people could confront root problems of violence and discrimination." Likewise, in his contemporary book on the Charrettes, George Shumway observed: "Just holding it was important."[30]

In other words, the post-revolt period in York culminated in a unique grassroots effort to honestly discuss the city's racial problems and to arrive at meaningful and practical solutions. These discussions went well beyond anything the community had done in the past and they demonstrated that blacks in York, though a numerical minority, could pressure key players in the city to take their concerns seriously. Or, as Robert Simpson put it, "If the riots hadn't taken place, nothing would have changed." One of the leading forces behind the Charrettes was Lionel Bailey, who less than a year earlier police had swept off the street because they feared him as a dangerous militant. Poverty worker and longtime activist Charles Trotter also helped organize the Charrettes. During the eight-day meeting, Bill Thompson, a black nationalist from Redding, Pennsylvania, played a key role and, with the support of the black community, refused to resign after white "moderates" objected to his promotion of the radical film "The Battle of Algiers," which in the view of most white people contradicted the spirit of the Charrettes. The Charrettes also enlisted the support of an impressive list of well-respected whites, including Reverend Franklin D. Fry of the Christ Lutheran Church, which could trace its origins back to 1733, four years after York was first settled, Sister Francis Sheridan, the head of the Catholic Social Services, and Chris Keslar, the president of the York Jaycees. Institutional support came from the Chamber of Commerce, the local Bar Association, the YMCA, and the city's Human Relations Commission. Key business and civic leaders, including managers at

---

[30] Raul Urrunaga, "The York Charrette, April 19–27, 1970," unpublished MA thesis, Millersville University, December 12, 2010; Raul Urrunaga, "The York Charrette, April 19–27, 1970," *Journal of the York County Heritage Trust* (September 2011), pp. 32–39; Kalish, *Civil Rights in York*, pp. 92–95; George Shumway, *Charrette at York, PA, April 1970* (York, PA: George Shumway Publisher, 1973).

Caterpillar, Bendix, and the Allis Chalmers corporations, raised money to run the Charrettes.[31]

To facilitate the Charrettes, York turned to Bill Riddick, a veteran community activist and educator. Lionel Bailey first encountered Riddick at a housing seminar in Durham, North Carolina, in the late fall of 1969. George Shumway described Riddick as "a large and dynamic black man who came up the hard way, beginning on a peanut farm in North Carolina." After earning his BA degree from North Carolina A&T State University (students from A&T were at the center of the historical 1960 Greensboro sit-ins) and an MS degree from North Carolina State, Riddick worked as a community activist before becoming the director of the University Extension at Shaw University, the birthplace of SNCC. One of Riddick's chief tasks was galvanizing grassroots support and participation. He did this by enlisting the help of local newspapers, radio and television stations, orchestrating a bus tour, and plastering the city with posters and billboards, establishing a "speakers bureau," and most importantly, reaching out to an extensive list of local associations and clubs, from Crispus Attucks and the NAACP to the American Legion and the Daughters of the American Revolution. The Charrette's organizers made a special effort to convince young Yorkers to participate by establishing a youth committee which held a series of "Youth Caucuses" in the weeks leading up to the official meetings.[32]

About 350 men and women attended the opening session on April 19, 1970. Afterwards, participants took part in thrice-a-day sessions organized around six themes: youth, education, employment, local government, housing, and health. Professional consultants helped moderate each session, which sought to arrive at concrete recommendations for reform. For instance, Dr. Ira Harrison, a local physician, ran the sessions on health, during which participants displayed their concerns on poster boards and construction paper. One poster, for example, displayed mortality rates by race; another suggested establishing community health centers and publishing public health pamphlets in Spanish. Likewise, the session on housing produced calls for the establishment of a York housing development

---

[31] Kalish, *Civil Rights in York*, pp. 91–95; Urrunaga, "The York Charrette, April 19–27, 1970," *Journal of the York County Heritage Trust*; Shumway, *Charrette at York, PA*; Urrunaga, "The York Charrette, April 19–27, 1970," MA thesis.

[32] Urrunaga, "The York Charrette, April 19–27, 1970," *Journal of the York County Heritage Trust*; Shumway, *Charrette at York, PA*; Urrunaga, "The York Charrette, April 19–27, 1970," MA thesis.

corporation, which would build and/or rehabilitate low-cost units, for sale and rent, and guard against housing discrimination.[33]

After a week of meetings, representatives from each one of the subgroups summarized their findings and delivered their recommendations to a "Reaction Panel," which included Mayor Eli Eichelberger, the chief of police, two city councilmen, and the heads of a number of government agencies. Much to their consternation, the mayor and the city's other top leaders responded in a "non-committal" way. The school board president, Ralph Runkle, for instance, who previously had suggested he was amenable to the recommendations of the Charrette's education subgroup, refused to commit the school system to implementing the Charrette's proposed reforms. Rather than accept this response, the Charrette's leaders caucused and asked the Reaction Panel to attend its closing session, where they hoped city's leaders would respond more favorably. At this session, business leaders agreed to an affirmative action plan, School Board Chief Runkle suggested he would adopt the education group's recommendations after all, and public and private officials committed themselves to creating a community health center and housing authority. (The latter did not actually get off the ground until after Hurricane Agnes devastated the city a couple of years later.) The mayor also agreed to provide resources to "carry out the Charrettes recommendations." Finally, in Bill Riddick's estimation, the primary accomplishment of the Charrettes was that they established a process for ongoing reform. Or as Mark Woodbury, who led the youth discussions recalled, the Charrettes established "communication" between blacks and whites whereas there "hadn't been communication up to then."[34]

This said, it would be imprecise to exaggerate the impact of the Charrettes. White gang members refused to participate in the meetings. Calls for reforming the police produced minimal and delayed results – the canine force was disbanded in 1973 – and to this date the force remains disproportionately white. And there is reason to believe that the reforms that were implemented were influenced as much by the city's desire to affect the Court of Appeals, which ultimately upheld Nealon's decision,

---

[33] Urrunaga, "The York Charrette, April 19–27, 1970," *Journal of the York County Heritage Trust*; George Shumway, *Charrette at York, PA*; Urrunaga, "The York Charrette, April 19–27, 1970," MA thesis.

[34] Urrunaga, "The York Charrette, April 19–27, 1970," *Journal of the York County Heritage Trust*; Shumway, *Charrette at York, PA*; Urrunaga, "The York Charrette, April 19–27, 1970," MA thesis; Interview of Mark Woodbury, by Raul Urrunaga, December 2010, York, Pennsylvania (in author's possession).

two to one, as they were by the spring 1970s dialogue. Furthermore, the Charrettes did little to counter long-term structural trends that divided blacks and whites, nearly all of which had begun before the uprising and which deepened in the years that followed.[35]

Like many other cities across the nation, York's black population increased in size and the city became poorer in the last third of the twentieth century. By 1990 the York metro area, according to one study, was "more racially segregated than any of its peer communities except Harrisburg." Such demographic and economic shifts, all of which began well before 1969, demanded regional solutions. Yet such approaches were not forthcoming. In York's case, the call for greater metropolitan reforms proved even more difficult to achieve due to the Balkanized municipal structure of government in Pennsylvania and the fierce attachment to localism. In the racialized spaces where they resided, blacks and whites proved less likely to discuss their common past and, in so far as they thought about the revolts, they spun a memory that argued that the riots had created white flight and residential segregation and the concentration of poverty, rather than recognizing that these conditions were as much if not more the cause rather than the effect of the uprisings.[36]

To make matters worse, the region, like much of America, experienced an economic transformation, namely a dramatic decline in manufacturing, which hit blacks disproportionately. During the 1950s and 1960s, just under 50 percent of all workers in York worked in factories. The prospect of such work, as noted above, helped explain the migration of thousands of blacks to York City. In contrast, by the end of the twentieth century, less than a quarter of all of York County's workers were employed in manufacturing, and many of these jobs were not in York City.[37] To prevent the city's death, urbanist David Rusk called for the greater York region to unite to devise regional solutions to the city's problems and to the delivery of public services in general. Both the editorial board of the *York*

---

[35] Urrunaga, "The York Charrette, April 19–27, 1970," *Journal of the York County Heritage Trust*; Shumway, *Charrette at York, PA*; Urrunaga, "The York Charrette, April 19–27, 1970," MA thesis.

[36] David Rusk, "The Rusk Report: The Future of Greater York," republished in *York Daily Record*, November 20, 1997; "City Schools and Race," *York Dispatch*, December 5, 2001; "Editorial: Ready Yet for Metro York?" *York Dispatch*, January 24, 2002; "York Officials Protest View of City as 'Past Point of No Return,'" The Associate Press State and Local Wire, August 11, 2002.

[37] "Rusk Report II: A Challenge to Change," *YDR*, February 27, 2013, www.ydr .com/story/archives/2013/02/27/rusk-report-ii-challenge-change/74264722/ [accessed May 21, 2015].

Dispatch and some other moderates endorsed this recommendation. As Tom Wolfe (who would be elected governor of Pennsylvania in 2014) declared, Rusk's warnings "shouldn't be dismissed." Or as the *York Dispatch* cautioned, "Suburbanite municipalities may be fat and happy now...but as they become built out, their tax base will stagnate, new development and investment will move outward...and so forth." The "solipsism" of the suburban towns "will eventually be their downfall. The same city problems are creeping their way, like a cancer."[38] Yet, such solutions were not forthcoming. For example, York's county commissioners favored low taxes and local control. In regards to the specific issue of race relations, the county commissioners rejected calls to establish a countywide human relations commission on the grounds, as one commissioner put it, that there was no "call from people in the surrounding boroughs and townships" for one.[39]

Indeed, even if the York region had rallied around a call for significant racial reforms, it is problematic that greater racial equality could have been achieved because the region itself was part and parcel of a larger political and economic system. This system, from the mid-1970s onward (if not before), was putting tremendous pressure on local industries to cut costs, by attacking union power, relocating plants abroad, or both. Many of York's largest employers, such as Caterpillar, closed their plants. At the same time, the federal government cut back on "discretionary" spending, such as job training and public housing, placed a heavier emphasis on "fighting crime," all of which disproportionately hurt the black community. Competition among states and localities for jobs, which resulted in "givebacks" to multinational corporations to relocate or stay in an area, further diminished tax revenues necessary to maintain, not to mention enhance public services, such as public education, which in turn reinforced racial inequality rather than reversing it. As a result, by the early 2000s, the City of York was on the road to insolvency, with a bond rating that plummeted to BBB– and a tax base that consisted of just over one-third of the city's properties.[40]

[38] "York Officials Protest"; "Editorial: Ready yet for Metro York"; "Editorial: Not Enough Has Changed," *York Dispatch*, December 1, 2001.
[39] "York County Still Won't Fund a Human Relations Commission," *York Sunday News*, February 24, 2002.
[40] Greg Bivona, "Wounded, Cornered, and Bound: Present and Possible Future Examination of the Fiscal Crisis in York, Pennsylvania," Senior thesis, York College, May 2013 (in author's possession).

"The Ghosts of Racism Past"

It was within this context of increasing concentrations of poverty and a growing demographic divide between the non-white city of York and the white county of York that the riot-related trials of Charlie Robertson occurred. Some hoped that the trials would show that the system, even if flawed, worked. The *New York Times* suggested that the city now had the opportunity to overcome, the "Ghost of Racism Past and Present." The *Philadelphia Inquirer* described the trial as "part of a new wave of civil-rights-era-cases," which would allow York, like Mississippi, to lay the ghosts of the past to rest. The *Christian Science Monitor* argued that the trial "put on display York's as well as the nation's unresolved racial hatreds and indignities…as well as tentative hope for healing."[41]

Yet, on the local level, the reopening of the case produced a mixed reaction. By publishing an extensive series on the revolts in the summer of 1999, the local newspapers helped precipitate the reopening of the investigation in the first case. Then they lent full support to the district attorney's decision to indict Robertson but most of the city's political and business elite did not. In December 2001, ninety-four of York County's business leaders signed a letter criticizing the newspapers for their coverage of the investigation, terming it "excessive and irresponsible." The newspapers coverage, the letter continued, "threatens to undo the selfless efforts of hundreds of citizens from all over the community who over the past 30 years have managed to heal the social wounds resulting from the riots." While the names of all of the signees were never revealed in public (the letter was sent as a private communique to the editors and publishers of the city's two newspapers), former congressman William Goodling, who admitted signing the piece, explained: "I didn't want to see the community…torn apart…I didn't want to see that happen again." Reopening the case, he continued, threatened "to undo all the wonderful things we have accomplished since that particular time in the city of

---

[41] Frances Clines, "The Ghosts of Racism Past and Present are Haunting a Pennsylvania Town," *NYT*, May 27, 2001, p. 14; Amy Worden, "In York, as in Mississippi," *Philadelphia Inquirer*, March 26, 2003, p. B7; Stephanie Romei, "Another 1960s Race Death Trial," *The Weekend Australian*, May 19, 2001, p. 17; Alexandra Marks, "A Pennsylvania Town Faces Up to Old Race Tensions," *Christian Science Monitor*, June 29, 2001, p. 1; "Pa. City Looks for Healing from Summer of '69," *USA Today*, July 26, 2001, p. 4. Elizabeth Evans, "Judge: The Race Riot Case Must Go On," *Hanover Evening Sun*, December 19, 2001. "York, Pa., Discusses Race and Politics," National Public Radio, September 10, 2008, www.npr.org/templates/story/story.php?storyId=94481275 [accessed November 19, 2014].

York." Robert Pullo, president of Waypoint Bank, complained that sensationalist newspaper coverage had attracted unnecessary and unfavorable national attention. But neither Goodling nor many others who opposed reopening the case elaborated on what they meant in terms of accomplishments since 1969. Moreover, there was a good deal of evidence that racial animosities continued to run deep.[42]

Even before the trial began, a Confederate flag was raised on a radio tower near where Allen was shot. (Ironically, in July 1863 Confederate troops, en route to nearby Gettysburg, had nearly burned York to the ground.) A few weeks later, stickers were placed around the town that read: "Earth's Most Endangered Species: The White Race. Help Preserve It." As the Allen trial grew nearer, a coalition of right-wing groups, including the World Church of the Creator, the KKK, the National Alliance and the Aryan Nation, scheduled a recruitment rally in the city's center.[43] The White Rose (York) Fraternal Order of Police distributed T-shirts to honor Schaad labeled "Gone but not Forgotten," and "Let Justice Be Done, Though the Heavens Fall." As the shirts were distributed, rumors spread that Schaad's case was not getting equal time and that the grand jury would not indict his murderers, or as one leaflets put it, "what about Schaad?" Such sentiments did not disappear after indictments were handed out against Stephan Freeland and Leon Wright for Schaad's murder, in part because their trials did not begin until March 2003, nearly two years after the first arrests in the Allen case.[44]

Seeking to allay these divisions a number of key community groups held special events where they emphasized unity and black progress, including the first annual Unity March and an African/African American "Love Feast." At the latter, black leaders presented members of the Schaad and Allen families with plaques and held a candlelight vigil to make clear that whites and blacks could come together to heal old wounds. Somewhat along the same lines, a "Freedom Museum" committee was established to help turn the William Goodridge House, a historic property in the center of the city, into a museum on the underground railroad, which

---

[42] "Goodling: Trial May Bring Violence," *York Dispatch*, October 13, 2002.

[43] "Charges in '69 Race Riots Fanning Flames in York," *Philadelphia Inquirer*, April 28, 2001; "York Is Divided Still, Some Say," *Philadelphia Inquirer*, May 22, 2001, p. B10; "York Officials Brace for Supremacists," *Philadelphia Inquirer*, January 11, 2002, p. B5; "25 Arrested At Meeting of Supremacists," *Philadelphia Inquirer*, January 13, 2002, p. B1; "Pastor Offers Christian Response Racism," *York Dispatch*, February 10, 2002.

[44] "Don't Hijack a Good Man," *York Dispatch*, October 18, 2001; "1969 York Riots: Timeline and Map," *York Daily Record*, August 20, 2013.

in the estimation of the local newspaper would help show that "York is not a fundamentally racist community."[45]

Yet it is not clear that these efforts worked. White supremacist red-baited the organizations that sponsored these initiatives. Rather than honoring Martin Luther King on his birthday, they blamed King for York's riots and contended that the city had a double standard when it came to granting protest permits.[46] The Goodridge house did not open for more than a dozen years, and even then it remained vastly understaffed and underfunded.[47] Moreover, continuities with the past, including concerns over who should preside over the trial, continued to haunt the city. Several of York's minority officials called for Judge Uhler to recuse himself from the case on the grounds that he had served as York's district attorney when several key pieces of evidence, including the bullets that killed Allen, had been lost. Muckraking author William Keisling argued that the failure to pursue the Allen case was tied to the desire to cover-up widespread corruption in York involving the police, DA's office, and the bench. Moving beyond words, Keisling circulated a petition and organized a rally at the state capitol demanding that Uhler step down or face impeachment. But Uhler refused to recuse himself. Along the same lines, three of five York City Council members requested that the federal government launch a probe into the actions of the York and Pennsylvania Police during and after the riots. "You have to bring the whole truth forward or questions will remain," declared Councilman Cameron Texter, who voted for the request.[48]

Statements by Mayor Robertson's attorney raised questions about the degree to which the reopening of the case symbolized racial progress too. The six defendants who pled guilty in the case, William Costopoulos contended, did so *not* because their conscious troubled them or because they sought community healing. On the contrary, they pled guilty so they could

---

[45] "March Seeks to Combat Racism," *York Dispatch*, July 14, 2001; They Want Officer's Killers Caught," *Philadelphia Inquirer*, May 27, 2001, p. B1; "A Pennsylvania Town Faces Up to Old Race Tensions," *Christian Science Monitor*, June 29, 2001, p. 1. The Unity movement did not disband with the trials. See "Stepping Out for Unity," *York Dispatch*, August 15, 2003. "Love Feast Celebrates Unity," York Dispatch, February 3, 2002; "Good Idea on Museum," *York Dispatch*, October 6, 2002.

[46] "Don't Hijack a Good Man," *York Dispatch*, October 18, 2001. See "Unity Movement a Communist Plot," *York Dispatch*, September 1, 2002.

[47] www.goodridgemuseum.weebly.com/ [accessed September 8, 2007].

[48] Larry Hicks, "Council Members Grandstand on Riot Issue," *York Dispatch*, October 6, 2002; "Federal Probe Sought in York," *York Dispatch*, September 20, 2002, p. 1.

avoid going to jail for twenty years to life.[49] To bolster his portrayal of
Robertson as an outstanding citizen, Costopoulos called to the stand several representatives of the York elite all of whom testified to Robertson's
"impeccable" character and dedication to the community, including former Congressman William Goodling, a Republican, and State Legislature
Steve Stetler, a Democrat.[50]

Whereas the reopening of the case generated claims that it would allow
the community to overcome its racial divisions, the conclusion of the
Allen trial suggested otherwise. When the jury returned a guilty verdict
on second-degree murder charges against Robert Messersmith and Gregory Neff, Messersmith's wife cried "I hope you all burn in hell." At the
same time, Charlie Robertson's not guilty verdict provoked Leo Cooper
of the NAACP to declare: "Thirty-three years ago, they gave him a pass,
and tonight they gave him another pass." Members of the Allen family
expressed ambivalence regarding the trial in general, with Hattie Dickson noting that at least "two [Messersmith and Neff] have got theirs."
But speaking on behalf of the Allens, Mrs. M. B. Whisler of the NAACP
stated: "The business powerhouses that came and testified for the mayor
let that jury know that they are the rulers of this county," adding that
the jury feared flouting their wishes lest they lose their jobs. Two months
later, the family filed a civil suit against the city. Their attorney, Harold
Goodman explained that Messersmith and Neff were mere "cogs in the
machine," who had been armed and inspired by the police to kill blacks, a
claim bolstered by Robert Messersmith's statement that he was a "scapegoat." Columnist Larry Hicks echoed Messersmith's point, declaring that
the York Police were the common denominator in both murders. "Some,
not all – were racist instigators, consistently fueling the fires of hatred on
both sides of this equation and fanning the flames as well."[51]

While Robertson did not say much after the verdict was reached,
except that he was tired and wanted to go home, over time he and his
supporters asserted that he was a changed man. While acknowledging

[49] William Costopoulos, "Closing Statement," *Commonwealth v. Messersmith et al.*
October 17, 2002, http://media.ydr.com/history/AllenClosingCostopoulos.pdf [accessed
December 3, 2015; website active at time of access].
[50] "Robertson Defense Opens; Costopoulos May Call Up to 50," *York Dispatch*, October
11, 2002. A tenth defendant, Ezra Slick, was charged separately. He later pled guilty.
"Plea Entered Over Role in Slaying," *The Gazette* (Montreal), April 3, 2003.
[51] "York Ex-Mayor Acquitted," *Philadelphia Inquirer*, October 20, 2002, p. A1; "Next in
Court: York's Police," *York Dispatch*, December 19, 2002; "Once Again, Police on Trial,
Too," *York Dispatch*, March 9, 2003; Whisler quoted in Conway Stewart, *No Peace, No
Justice*, location 7166–7176.

that Robertson had harbored racist attitudes in 1969, his supporters insisted that he no longer did and they maintained that the charges against Robertson had always been motivated by politics. Yet others questioned the validity of such claims. Leo Cooper, for one, stated that Robertson had "learned how to disguise" his racism, just like "Strom Thurmond and George Wallace learned how to coexist with people they supposedly hated," adding that he questioned how much sensitivity training could really achieve; the Allen family remained largely unconvinced that Robertson was truly repentant.[52]

The broader public's reaction to the verdict and post-trial developments were just as mixed. Accusing the "liberal press" of bias, David Abel, a suburban York resident, asserted that the whole affair came down to black "revenge."[53] Lee Shry, of York, termed the entire affair a "witch hunt," adding that the newspapers should have spent more time explaining how blacks started the riots. In her self-published book, Mary Conway Stewart, a middle-aged white native, asserted that all along the Allen family had been after money, adding that the cost of the potential settlement could bankrupt the city. Kenneth Thompson, a black man who lived adjacent to Penn Park, strongly disagreed, asserting that "Robertson should not have gotten off" and that others should have been tried.[54] Regional newspapers termed the verdict "justice of a sort," adding that the second-degree murder conviction of Messersmith and Neff represented a "compromise" and the very fact that people had voted for Robertson for mayor in the first place, when his "dirty little secret" was well known, remained inexplicable.[55]

With the verdict in the Allen trial having failed to bring racial healing, attention turned to the Schaad murder case. While the local press sought to portray the two trials as parallel, a closer examination suggests that there were significant dissimilarities, illustrative of the historical and

[52] "NAACP Chief Rips Robertson," *York Dispatch*, December 4, 2001.

[53] David G. Abel, "Letter to the Editor," *York Dispatch*, October 20, 2002.

[54] "Residents Grapple With Verdict," *Philadelphia Inquirer*, October 21, 2002, p. A1; Lee Shry, "Letter to Editor," *York Dispatch*, October 28, 2002; Conway Stewart, *No Peace, No Justice*.

[55] "Altering History," *Intelligencer Journal* (Lancaster, PA), October 22, 2002; Stewart, *No Peace, No Justice*; "Allen Lawsuit Delay Requested," *York Dispatch*, March 7, 2003; "Insurer Sues City Over Liability in Allen Murder," *York Dispatch*, December 19, 2002; "Allen Ruling Fought," *York Dispatch*, December 30, 2003. *Clarendon National Insurance v. City of York*, US District Court for the Middle District of Pennsylvania, Civil Action No. 1: CV-02-1500; *Clarendon National Insurance v. City of York*, United States Court of Appeals for the Third Circuit, No. 03-4680.

ongoing inequities that existed in American society. To begin, whereas Robertson had risen from beat cop to mayor and garnered the support of powerful business people and politicians, since 1969, Stephan Freeland and Leon Wright, the two defendants in the Schaad case, had experienced years of underemployment and time in jail. Indeed, by focusing on the latter, the press helped prejudice the community against them.[56] The inequities in the system became even clearer when the trial commenced. Whereas Mayor Robertson enjoyed a team of talented lawyers, Freeland and Wright did not. Freeland's attorney, Terry McGowan, for example, allowed his client to take the stand and did not conduct any redirect examination after the DA, Bill Graff, painted his client as a white-hating cop killer. Nor did Freeland's attorney call any other witnesses. In addition, the state used its power of prosecutorial discretion differently in the two trials, negotiating lesser sentences for white people who were accused of killing Allen while threatening black witnesses with jail time if they did not testify against Freeland and Wright. Moreover, the juries were not equally impartial because the pool of jurists was drawn from York County, which was overwhelmingly white. As a result, the jury that was seated in the Schaad murder case included only one black person – even though the city was approaching a non-white majority.[57] Finally, Judge John Chronister, who presided over the Schaad case, tended to issue rulings that favored prosecutors whereas Judge Uhler had done the exact opposite in the trial of Robertson et al.[58]

The biggest difference between the two cases, however, lay with the actions of the main defendants. Robertson, Messersmith, and Neff – as was their right – chose not to take the stand, allowing their attorneys to do their best to win an acquittal. In contrast, Stephen Freeland took the stand where he spoke directly to the causes of the 1969 uprising. To understand the events of 1969, Freeland described the fight that erupted after the football game in the fall of 1968, after which blacks were forced to run "a gauntlet" by York police. "And I never forget this," Freeland continued. "This white officer ran up in the middle of the street and he had a list...[and] he started calling out names off the list. And he said, get Freeland...[and] the officers behind...put the dog on me." On this

56 "Even as a Teen, Freeland Well Known to Cops," *York Dispatch*, October 31, 2001.
57 "Potential Witness Is Jailed to Make Sure He Show for Court," *York Dispatch*, February 27, 2003; Graff quoted in "Thieves, Scoundrels," *York Dispatch*, March 4, 2003.
58 "Trial Nears Finish," *York Dispatch*, March 11, 2003; "Potential Witness is Jailed to Make Sure He Shows for Court," *York Dispatch*, February 27, 2003; Testimony of Stephen Freeland, *Commonwealth v. Stephen Freeland*.

occasion, Freeland added, he was able to escape, so the police, according to Freeland, "turned the dogs on Smickel" (Freeland's co-defendant in the Schaad case). All the time, Freeland insisted, the police were using the "'N' word," and siccing their dogs on other blacks. And this was not the only occasion of police abuse, Freeland maintained. "There were many occasions when those incidents would happen, and it wasn't that we was doing things for them to do anything to us."[59]

Freeland also testified that blacks often clashed with members of white gangs, like the motorcycle gang "the Pagans," who were subsequently identified as one of the most violent white supremacist clubs or gangs in the nation, and the Newberry Street Boys, and according to Freeland the police routinely took the side of the gangs.[60] Additionally, Freeland sought to put the shooting at Penn and College in July 1969 in a broader context by claiming that white nightriders had raced through the community in the early days of the "riot," including a "white dude" in a pickup truck with "a .30 caliber machine gun mounted on the back." (Freeland's defense attorney produced no evidence to corroborate these claims although a recording of it had been made during the trial before Judge Nealon thirty years earlier.) Then Freeland admitted to shouldering a rifle at the time of Schaad's shooting but suggested that the jury needed to understand that many others were armed as well. "I seen 30.06's; I seen .300 Savages. I seen 7 millimeter Mags...I seen 30–40 Drags, I seen...Mossbergs."[61]

This testimony, while insightful in terms of understanding the underlying causes of the 1969 uprising and the widespread tension that existed on the streets on the night that Schaad was shot, certainly made it harder for Freeland to escape the charges leveled against him. Put somewhat differently, by taking the stand, Freeland strengthened the prosecutor's case. Why his defense attorney allowed him to testify and why he failed to give his client the opportunity to clarify his actions on redirect, or follow-up with witnesses who might have bolstered his testimony regarding the history of police abuse, remains unclear.[62]

District Attorney Bill Graff asserted that the jury's verdict in the Schaad case closed a chapter of York's history and allowed the city to "move

---

[59] Testimony of Stephan Freeland, *Commonwealth v. Stephen Freeland.*
[60] On the Pagans, see www.segag.org/mcgangs/pagan.html and www.fbi.gov/pittsburgh/press-releases/2009/pt100609.htm, [all accessed December 11, 2014].
[61] Testimony of Stephan Freeland, *Commonwealth v. Stephen Freeland.*
[62] Testimony of Stephan Freeland and Closing Statement of DA Bill Graff. See also: "Schaad Trial: Final Argument by Bill Graff," *York Dispatch*, March 12, 2003.

on" – Freeland and Wright were convicted – a view endorsed by Mayor Brenner and the local newspaper.[63] Likewise, the national media cast the cases in a favorable light. "In York, as in Mississippi," the *Philadelphia Inquirer* insisted, "ghosts [had] finally [been] laid to rest." Ignoring the warnings of naysayers, the *Inquirer* continued, York's prosecutors joined those of numerous southern cases in "battling the obstacles of time and succeeding in finding justice."[64] Many local black residents, however, disagreed. Making reference to blues' singer Billy Holiday's famous song, Lorita Freeland described the verdict as "strange fruit." Another one of Freeland's relatives avowed "it's still 1969." Jane Adams declared that she did not think that "no black man could ever get a fair trial in York," a view echoed by Mary Tribune a member of the York School Board. While neither M. B. Whisler of the NAACP, or William Smallwood, a black member of the town council went this far, both harbored reservations about the results.[65]

In sum, continuity, not change, stands out when one focuses on the underlying factors that produced York's revolt. The socioeconomic gap between white and black people, especially between black people who live in the urban core, is as great if not greater than it was in the 1960s. As suggested by David Rusk's study of York, the "gap in household income . . . hasn't narrowed," and the disparity in wealth between blacks and whites has actually grown wider. While school segregation declined from the 1960s through the 1970s, re-segregation has been the main trend since. Perhaps most startlingly, the "racial disparity in incarceration rates" has increased since the 1960s, so that black men, nationwide, are six times as likely as white men to end up in prison, a pattern replicated in York.[66] Moreover, unlike some of the nation's larger urban areas, like Washington, DC, and Baltimore, the vast majority of blacks in York County continue to reside within city limits – less than 3 percent of York County's blacks resided outside of York City in 2010 – making regional solutions to the

[63] "Like it or not; Race Riots Case Over," *York Dispatch*, March 16, 2003; "In the Aftermath," *York Dispatch*, April 27, 2003.

[64] "In York, as in Mississippi, Ghosts Finally Laid to Rest," *Philadelphia Inquirer*, March 16, 2002, p. B7.

[65] "Still, It's the Prism of Race," *York Dispatch*, March 14, 2003; "Family: Freeland Didn't Get Fair Trial," *York Dispatch*, March 14, 2003; "Like it or not; Race Riots Case Over," *York Dispatch*, March 16, 2003.

[66] Brad Plummer, "These Ten Charts Show the Black–White Economic Gap Hasn't Budged in 50 Years," *Washington Post*, August 28, 1963, www.washingtonpost.com/blogs/wonkblog/wp/2013/08/28/these-seven-charts-show-the-black-white-economic-gap-hasnt-budged-in-50-years/ [accessed December 5, 2014].

racial divide even more difficult to achieve. Whether York, like Baltimore, will experience another uprising remains to be seen. But, as the *York Daily Record* recently put it, all of the "ingredients" for one still exist.[67]

[67] "When Will We Pull Out the Roots of York's 1969 Riots," *York Daily Record*, May 1, 2015, www.ydr.com/story/opinion/2015/04/29/when-will-we-pull-out-roots-yorks-1969/31270519/ [accessed May 20, 2015]. In numerous instances in the past ten years York has garnered the attention of the national press due to ongoing racial concerns. See in particular: Keystone Crossroad, "Grappling with Racial Tension," https://grapplepodcast.atavist.com/grappling-with-racial-tension [accessed June 9, 2017]; National Public Radio, "The York Project: Race & the 2008 Vote," www.npr.org/series/95934562/the-york-project-race-the-08-vote [accessed June 9, 2017] and National Public Radio, "'York Project' Revisited: 2008 Voters Weigh In On 2016 Race," www.npr.org/2016/12/16/504988900/york-project-revisited-2008-voters-weigh-in-on-2016-race [accessed June 9, 2017].

Conclusion

I read [the] report ... of the 1919 riot in Chicago, and it is as if I were reading
the report of the investigating committee on the Harlem riot of '35, the
report of the investigating committee on the Harlem riot of '43, the report
of the McCone Commission on the Watts riot. I must again in candor say to
you members of this Commission – it is a kind of Alice in Wonderland – with
the same moving picture re-shown over and over again, the same analysis,
the same recommendations, and the same inaction.
    Kenneth Clark, "Testimony to the Kerner Commission," 1967

The central aim of this work has been to enrich our understanding of the
Great Uprising, beginning by demonstrating that one took place. I also
sought to stretch our conceptualization of the geography and chronology
of the urban revolts of the 1960s to examine why the Great Uprising took
place and to test much of the conventional wisdom regarding their nature
or typology. Additionally, I hoped to deepen our sense of the impact that
the revolts had on ordinary Americans and to assess their relationship to
the civil rights movement. Though Cambridge, Baltimore, and York are
regionally proximate, their demographic differences provided us with an
excellent opportunity for achieving these goals.

It is worth reiterating that the nation experienced over 750 racially
oriented uprisings in upwards of 525 cities, including nearly every one
with a black population over 50,000. Over 73 million people or about
one-third of the entire nation lived in communities that experienced uprisings and tens of millions more Americans knew people impacted by the
revolts. The riots also attracted considerable media attention, with the
New York Times and *Washington Post*, alone, publishing just short of

30,000 separate articles on the uprisings (riots, civil disorders, revolts) between January 1, 1963 and December 31, 1972.[1] In addition, the revolts became a dominant feature of political discourse. Some politicians, such as Spiro Agnew, rose from obscurity to national prominence by attacking alleged riot makers and their so-called liberal enablers. Others, most notably Richard Nixon, appealed for votes by emphasizing the call for law and order. The fact that the revolts took place across a span of nearly ten years in every region of the nation and in cities of virtually every size magnified their impact. Put somewhat differently, the sheer number of revolts, coupled with their geographic and chronological breadth and their impact on political life, compels us to view them collectively as a Great Uprising.

While all three case studies lend weight to the Kerner Commission's conclusions that the revolts grew out of the social and economic ills of the ghetto, they also suggest that this interpretation was insufficient. In each instance, the revolts were preceded by sustained protests against racial inequality and equally persistent white resistance to fundamentally altering the racial status quo. This view contrasts with the classic presentation of the urban race revolts of the 1960s as spontaneous explosions of anger which, even if understandable, failed to present constructive solutions and, to make matters worse, unleashed white backlash. This interpretive framework, as Jeanne Theoharis insightfully observes, allowed white people at the time and since to "demonize" black people "for the outpouring of anger during the uprising." It simultaneously made it easier for society to "avoid responsibility" for the perpetuation of racial injustices and inequalities, which blacks outside of Dixie had protested against for years.[2]

All three case studies challenge the conservative claim that radicals or riot makers caused the riots. The main reason Cambridge attracted contemporary national attention was because politicians and the media cast it as the poster boy of this interpretation. Yet, when asked if H. Rap Brown had caused the riots, General Gelston astutely responded, "if there were no problem, there would have been no invitation" in the first place. Moreover, as Gelston and others made clear, rioting did *not* break out immediately following Brown's address and the fire which devastated the

---

[1] This figure was calculated by running a search using the Proquest search engine with the terms "civil disorders," "riots," or "revolts" and limiting results to "articles." Half as many articles were written about the same subjects in the following decade, many if not most on revolts that took place outside the United States.

[2] Jeanne Theoharis, "'Alabama on Avalon.'"

all-black Second Ward spread because Police Chief Brice Kinnamon and the all-white fire force refused to put it out. To make matters worse, rather than help Brown challenge the criminal charges that had been filed against him, the Kerner Commission chose to omit its investigation of Cambridge from its report.

Similarly, Baltimore demonstrated that the revolts were not caused by radicals or spontaneous or inexplicable eruptions. For decades, local civil rights activists had demanded an end to racial discrimination in housing, employment, the schools, and the criminal justice system, but the best that "moderate" leaders could produce was token change. While neither Mayor McKeldin nor D'Alesandro resorted to the politics of resentment, or white backlash, a sizable chunk of the city's white working-class voters supported George Wallace and George Mahoney, two icons of white supremacy, before, not after, Baltimore experienced its Holy Week Uprising. As activist Walter Brooks put it when CORE targeted Baltimore in 1966, the city continued to combine "most of the worst features of the old-style Southern segregation with the complacency, indifference and de facto segregation prevalent in the North." Rather than blaming these militants or "radicals" for causing Baltimore's revolt, as I have suggested, their activism may have been the reason why the city did not "riot" prior to 1968.

Likewise, for years York's political leaders rebuffed nearly every demand of the local civil rights movement. Mayor Snyder expanded rather than disbanded the much-despised canine force, thwarted efforts to establish a civilian review board of the police, and along with other officials did little to combat discriminatory practices in education or employment, not to mention deplorable housing conditions in the disproportionately black sections of the city. When the Pennsylvania Human Relations Commission reacted to these circumstances by holding hearings, numerous local officials refused to cooperate and then ignored the commission's recommendations. Meanwhile, the business community feigned either ignorance or impotence, as evidenced by the publication of a history of York by the Chamber of Commerce that cast the community as an ideal blend of old and new, urban and suburban, without any reference to its racial inequities or the prevalence of racist white gangs.

Put somewhat differently, perhaps it is more accurate to see the revolts as an epilogue rather than as a prologue. None other than Martin Luther King Jr. suggested that it was incorrect to blame the riots for white backlash, because, as he observed, it was more precise to see things the other way around: the revolts were the consequences not the cause of white backlash. At the same time, as suggested in the body of the work, it is wrong to portray the revolts simply as calamities because for many black people the uprising proved an empowering moment. In spite of a spree of arrests and threats to form vigilante groups, militant black activists in Cambridge continued to protest in the streets and to demand equality at City Hall both after its 1963 and 1964 revolts and after the "Brown riot." Though they faced formidable obstacles, these black activists made some inroads, including winning increased funding for federal welfare programs, the removal of James Busick, who had hindered real school desegregation for years, and ultimately the election of additional blacks to political office, including Lemuel Chester, one of the leaders of the Black Activist Federation which had invited H. Rap Brown to town in July 1967.

The black power surge in Baltimore, which built upon the efforts of CORE's Target City project, grew in size and strength after the Holy Week Uprising, uniting much of the civil rights community around a variety of goals. Black women, often with the support of CORE and SNCC veterans, pushed for and won welfare and housing reforms from City Hall, union recognition from Johns Hopkins University Hospital, and helped elect an increasing number of blacks to political office. The rise of a local chapter of the Black Panther similarly illustrated that the revolts did not signal the end of the local black freedom struggle. And though the Panthers disintegrated in the face of local, state, and federal repression, their message of black pride spread to others, especially black youths and workers, who formed black student unions at their schools and staged strikes, respectively.

In York, the turn toward black power began before its 1969 uprising and continued afterwards. In the wake of the revolt, black residents filed a path-breaking civil suit, in which they demanded that an outside authority take command of the police, railed against abusive and unequal treatment in the schools, and exposed the hypocrisy of their white union brothers, who refused to raise funds for Lillie Belle Allen's family while simultaneously collecting money for Officer Henry Schaad's widow. York's revolt in combination with this surge of militancy also pressured white people into conducting charrettes, which planted the seeds for a number of significant reforms.

Regarding the more academic issues of the geography, chronology, and typology of the revolts, this study suggests that several revisions to the established cannon are in order. For years Americans mistakenly conceived of race as a "southern problem" and believed that Jim Crow only

resided south of the Mason–Dixon Line. The uprisings of the 1960s rudely
awakened the nation to the speciousness of this belief. Yet, ironically, we
have tended to replace it with an equally fallacious notion that race is
primarily a problem of our large cities and their inner city ghettos, when
in fact, race is a national problem that transcends simple geographic categories. In fact, as evidenced by the case studies of Cambridge and York,
blacks in many small and midsize cities, particularly those where they
comprise at best one-third of the population, may have faced even more
daunting barriers to achieving equality than in many larger places. Blacks
in these communities often did not have many of the same institutional
resources at their disposal that their brothers and sisters did in larger
cities. For instance, neither Cambridge nor York had a black newspaper
or college or university and their branches of the NAACP and CORE
were much smaller and less powerful than those in Baltimore, Detroit, or
Chicago. Without these institutions and with smaller numbers, absolutely
and relatively, blacks exercised little if any political power.

Regarding the chronology of the revolts, this study suggests that the
conventional wisdom is in need of revision as well. Rather than beginning our study in 1965 and ending in the spring of 1968, I intentionally
selected communities that had uprisings before and after these dates to
draw attention to the existence of a significant number of revolts outside this timeframe. Indeed, 243 other communities experienced revolts
between 1969 and 1971, nearly seven times as many as took place in
the summers of 1964, 1965, and 1966.[3] Beyond simply getting the years
of the Great Uprising wrong, this truncation of the chronology of the
Great Uprising leads to a major mis-conceptualization of the black freedom struggle by reinforcing the faulty notion that race revolts did not take
place until after the struggle for civil rights had been completed and that
the movement came to an end with King's death. In other words, rather
than separating the "civil rights years" into two distinct phases, a nonviolent, southern, and constructive phase, followed by a violent, northern,
destructive one, where the first phase is framed as one of progress and the
latter as one of decline, this work suggests that the revolts did not signal
a sharp break from the past or spell the demise of the movement. Rather,
they were part and parcel of the struggle for racial equality all along.

---

[3] Kerner Commission, *Report*; US Senate, Permanent Subcommittee on Investigations of the
Committee on Government Operations, *Hearings: Riots, Civil and Criminal Disorders*,
(Washington, DC: GPO, 1968); Riot Data Review, 2 (August 1968); Baskin et al., *The
Long Hot Summer?*

In terms of the nature of the revolts or as the Kerner Commission posed it, what took place, our case studies similarly indicate that much of the accepted wisdom is imprecise. Social scientists and historians too quickly differentiated the race revolts of the 1960s from those earlier in the century. Fixating on events in Watts, Newark, and Detroit, they contended that the nation had experienced a wave of commodity riots not interracial communal riots, like those of the red summer of 1919.[4] This is not to argue that the United States did not experience commodity riots during the 1960s. But our case studies reveal that "communal revolts" were not an aberration. In York, blacks and whites violently clashed for several days and barely any looting took place. Likewise, in Cambridge, the revolts of 1963 and 1964 as well as the "Brown riot" did not center on the looting of commodities. Rather blacks and whites, including white authorities, physically clashed, leaving more than one observer to marvel that no one was killed.

Assessing the qualitative impact of these revolts on ordinary men and women is a more difficult task, yet material presented in the body of the work suggests it was substantial. Forty years later, the Pats sisters could still vividly recall returning from Sunday school to discover that their neighborhood was on fire and that their parents would have to abandon their home and business forever. Louis Randall, one of the first blacks to graduate from the University of Maryland's Medical School, just as clearly recollected that he was delivering a baby at Provident hospital when the revolt began and rushing to his office to post a "Soul Brother" sign on his office door and standing guard, gun in hand, hoping he wouldn't have to shoot anyone to preserve what he had worked so hard to achieve. Joe DiBlasi nearly broke down in tears when he watched students from Baltimore's School for the Arts portray him in a play on Baltimore's revolt based upon his remembrances and those of others. And Robert Birt recounted the utter irony of the moment when Baltimore's uprising began – "Mayor D'Alesandro…said he thought it was commendable how black citizens of Baltimore in this trying time didn't resort to an explosion of mass anger," while simultaneously "I started to notice

---

[4] Janowitz, *Social Control of Escalated Riots*. Janowitz's views as summarized and quoted in, Hugh Davis Graham, "Violence, Social Theorists, and the Historians," in Violence in America, ed. by Ted Gurr, p. 334; Gilje, *Rioting in America*. For an interesting twist on the commodity riot concept, see Guy Debord, "The Decline and Fall of the Spectacle-Commodity Economy," *International situationniste*, 10 (March 1966), Translated by Ken Knabb.

some things were happening. It's almost as if the riot was beginning just as he was commending us for not doing it."[5]

For Hansel Green, James Lewis, Robert Bradby, Henry Schaad, Lillie Belle Allen, and many others, the revolts had a dramatic impact that went well beyond vivid memories. Henry Schaad, a rookie police officer, and Lillie Belle Allen, a young mother of two, never had the opportunity to recollect the uprisings. In part because York's policemen allowed her sister to drive down Newberry Street, in spite of days of shootings and assaults, Allen never even knew one was taking place. Green too lost his life, to his own hands, because, as his wife put it, "When you see a lifetime of work go up in flames, it gets to you." Green's tragic death easily could have been averted if only Police Chief Brice Kinnamon and the Rescue and Fire Company had not rebuffed his pleas to provide "one lousy truck" to put out the fire which had started at the nearby Pine Street Elementary School. James Lewis, also of Cambridge, spent years in prison for the shooting of Office Wrotten even though Lewis insisted for the rest of his life that he had not committed the crime. Likewise, after confessing to having thrown a Molotov cocktail into Gabriel's Spaghetti House, where unbeknownst to anyone Louis Albrecht had sought refuge, Robert Bradby found himself sentenced to life in prison, in spite of Judge Liss's acknowledgment that Bradby "would never have done [what he did] under normal circumstances."

Unfortunately, the nation adopted the wrong lessons from these tragedies. Rather than redoubling federal efforts to address the social and economic ills which underlay the revolts, the nation as a whole decided to construct what some have termed a new system of Jim Crow in the form of a carceral state. Indeed, Spiro Agnew and Richard Nixon were not alone in promoting law and order as the primary response to the revolts. As Kathryn Hinton has shown, Lyndon Johnson began constructing the carceral state in response to the earliest revolts of the decade. Kennedy, Johnson, and Nixon all participated in the repression of black activists, symbolized by the creation of COINTELPRO and the crusade to lock H. Rap Brown in jail. The refusal and/or inability of liberal Democrats to muster support for the recommendations of the Kerner Commission simply made it easier for conservatives such as Agnew and Nixon to garner

[5] See oral histories of Pats Sisters, Louis Randall, Robert Birt, and Joseph DiBlasi, all in http://archives.ubalt.edu/bsr/oral-histories/index.html. The play was entitled: "One Particular Saturday," and was performed by students from the Baltimore City College High School, on April 4, 2008.

support for what soon became a national "war on crime," and the burgeoning war on drugs. Agnew's assertion, that "an American citizen's first right is safety for himself and his family," dovetailed with Mayor Daley's call to shoot to kill arsonists and the rejection of approaches that emphasized enhancing community–police relations and minimizing the use of lethal forces, as promoted by Ramsey Clark and General Gelston.

Finally, I will end this work with a suggestion for future research, namely an analysis of the public's memory of the Great Uprising. Memory studies, ranging from those of the Civil War to those of the Holocaust, have proliferated in recent years, adding a new layer of complexity and richness to our understanding of the past. Let me suggest to those who undertake this task, that it will be helpful to imagine an alternative memory to the currently constructed one, which casts the riots as betrayals of the real civil rights movement and which has deflected blame away from those who caused the revolts onto American citizens who continue to have to endure inhuman conditions. Indeed, the intellectual jujitsu, which casts the riots as the cause of the decline of urban America and the break-up of the liberal coalition is as dishonest as the retelling of antebellum and Reconstruction eras, which presented slavery as a benign institution and slave owners as benevolent caretakers and the post-Civil War experiment with interracial equality as the darkest chapter in US history. Our distorted memory of the riots of the 1960s has also allowed us to downplay its geographical reach, to truncate its chronology, to depoliticize its participants and ultimately to diminish its overarching significance. Or put somewhat differently, it has allowed Americans to obscure the fact that the United States experienced a Great Uprising, a development as momentous and as central as the Great Depression, which in turn makes it easier to ignore the persistence of the racial divide and the failure of America to deliver on its promise.

Index

Girarders, 239–241, 266, 272–273
Gitt, J. W., 244, 248–251, 257
Glenn, David, 162
Glover, Ruby, 172
Goldberg, Louis, 90, 111, 146
Golden, William, 211
Goldman, Israel (Rabbi), 162
Goldwag, Arnold, 28
Goldwater, Barry, 127, 139
Goode, Alexander (Rabbi), 243
Goodling, George, 260, 265
Goodling, William, 261, 297–298, 300
Goodman, Harrold, 300
Goon Squad, 146, 212–214
Goucher, William, 191
Goucher College, 39
Graff, Bill, 302–303
Graham, Hugh Davis, 84
Graham, Randy, 2, 239, 267
Grant, Danny, 147, 159
Gray, Freddie, 119–120
Grayson, Charles, 243
Great Depression, 1, 135, 313
Great Migration, 11, 96, 145, 228,
    230–231, 243, 266, 295
Great Uprising. *See* riots
Green, Clifford, 266, 278
Green, Hansel, 73, 76–77, 100–101, 312
Green, Lena, 76
Green, Sampson, 142
Green, William, 75, 100
Greenberg, James, 284
Greensboro, NC, 121–122, 127, 254, 293
Gregory, Dick, 41–42, 103, 123
Griffin, James, 142, 157, 213
Grimshaw, Allen, 85
Grosklos, Phil, 240
Grubb, Enez, 49
Guthrie, Woody, 229
Guyot, Lawrence, 115
Gwynn Oak Amusement Park, 123

Halderon, Frieda, 175
Hamilton, Mary, 250
Hammer, Fannie Lou, 143
Hanna Penn Junior High School, 237
Hansberry, Loraine, 288
Hansen, William, 24–25, 28, 50, 61
Hardrick, Herbert, 165
Harlem, NY, 9, 43, 124, 141, 156, 251,
    253, 306

Harrington, Calvin, 62
Harris, William "Box," 160, 173
Harrisburg, PA, 258, 295
Harrison, Ira, 293
Harrisson, William, 166
Hartford County, MD, courthouse, 112,
    203
Harvard University, 242
Harvey, Alexander II (Judge), 63
Hay, John, 199
Hayes, Chester, 243
Haynes, Pamela, 287–288
Head Start, 57, 104
health care, 134, 141, 144, 212, 222,
    242–243, 291, 293
Heidelberg Reformed Church, 242
Hemphill, William, 25
Henry, W. Laird, Jr. (Judge), 28, 30
Herman, Max, 277
Hernandez, Jose, 289
Hersey, John, 111
Hicks, Helen, 123
Hicks, Larry, 300
high school student protests, 9, 162, 211,
    290–291
Highlander Folk School, 115
Hildebrand, Walter, 218
Hill, Robert, 185
Hines-Harris, Julia, 230, 237
Hinton, Kathryn, 312
Hirch, Arnold, 120
Hitler, Adolph, 105
Hoffman's Meat Market, 256, 271
Hofstadter, Richard, 198–199
Hogan, Frank, 114
Holiday, Billie, 304
Holmes, Theodore, 253, 255
Holocaust, 178, 313
Holt, Thomas, 46
Holy Week Uprising. *See* riots
homeownership, 51, 132, 231
Hoover, J. Edgar, 31, 114. *See also*
    FBI
Hopkins, Samuel, 150
Horton, Myles, 115
Hose, Jacob, 259, 271
Houser, George, 262
housing, 12, 24, 26, 36, 45, 51, 54, 57–59,
    77, 80, 95, 98, 120, 122–123, 131,
    141–142, 149, 213, 231, 236, 243,
    254–255, 261, 264, 275, 289, 291,

Pacha, Clement, 136
Pagans, 269, 303
Page, Wayne, 69
Palmieri, Victor, 108
Parker, William, 97
Parks, Henry J., 213
Parks, Nicky, 59–61
Parks, Rosa, 26, 236
Parkville, MD, 171
Parkway homes, 270
Parrish, William, 221
Parry, Meredith, 261
Pats, Betty, 177
Pats, Ida, 177
Pats, Sharon, 177
Pats sisters, 163, 176–177, 311
Patterson, William, 245
Patterson Park, 137, 170, 184
Payne, William, 112, 116
Peaceful Committee for Immediate Action
  (PCIA), 248, 250
Pelosi, Nancy, 159
Penn Common Park, 256
Penn State York, 288
Pennsylvania
  government structure in, 295
Pennsylvania Avenue, 144, 152, 157,
  171–173, 181–182
Pennsylvania Human Relations
  Commission (PHRC), 222, 235–239,
  253, 258–259, 261–262, 265, 308
Pennsylvania State Police, 280, 282
penny trials, 28
Perlstein, Richard, 197
Perry, Robert, 48
Peters, Maurice, 248, 250
Peters, Maurice, Jr., 248
Peterson, John, 165, 167
Philadelphia, PA, 36, 43, 115, 213, 230,
  248
  riot of 1964, 141
Philadelphia Inquirer, 297, 304
Philadelphia Plan, 213
Philadelphia Tribune, 287
Phillips, Wendell, 214
Phillips, Yvonee, 165
Phillips Packing Company, 23, 44, 55, 57
Pine Street Elementary School, 60, 63,
  66–67, 69, 73, 79, 87–88, 101, 103,
  312
Pittsburg Courier, 107
police advisory board, 251, 254

Police Advisory Committee on Community
  Relations (Baltimore), 125
police brutality, 35, 97, 102, 124, 142,
  290
Pomerleau, Donald, 158, 160, 162,
  166–167
Poor People's Campaign, 155, 215–219,
  260
Powell, Adam Clayton, 103
Prague, Czechoslovakia, 155
"Prairie Fires," 158
press. *See* media, mass
Pressman, Hyman, 125, 203
Prettyman, James "Dinno," 80
Price, Louis, 205
Prince George County, MD, 170
Princess Anne County, MD, 20, 65
Princess Players, 263, 288
Prison revolts, 9
Pritchett, Osvrey, 42, 46, 52, 54, 57, 80
Progressive Party, 244, 246
Progressive Spanish-American Council,
  289
property damage, 1, 17, 75–77, 97, 110,
  153, 179
Proposition, 2, 39
Provident Hospital, 172, 311
public accommodations. *See* Baltimore,
  MD: public accommodations;
  Cambridge, MD: public
  accommodations
public housing. *See* housing, public
public opinion, 83, 99, 102, 140, 155, 200,
  202–203, 217
Pullo, Robert, 298
Punch, Fred, 219

Quakers, 242
Quayle, Dan, 180

race revolts. *See* riots
Race Street, 20, 30–31, 48, 70–71
racial discrimination, 6, 9–11, 19, 24, 39,
  42, 47, 49, 51, 53–54, 57–59, 84, 97,
  100, 104, 122, 130, 136, 138–139,
  141, 145, 148, 150, 166, 196–197,
  202, 215, 227–240, 244–245, 251,
  260, 279, 286, 292, 295, 300,
  307–309, 312. *See also* criminal justice
  system and police; economy and
  employment discrimination; housing;
  recreation